DOUBLE TAXATION RELIEF
FOR SHIPPING

DOUBLE TAXATION RELIEF FOR SHIPPING

By

RALPH NEWNS

AND

SHEILA PARRINGTON, LL B

|L|L|P|

LONDON   NEW YORK   HAMBURG   HONG KONG

LLOYD'S OF LONDON PRESS LTD

1988

Lloyd's of London Press Ltd
Legal Publishing and Conferences Division
One Singer Street, London EC2A 4LQ
Great Britain

USA AND CANADA
Lloyd's of London Press Inc
Suite 523, 611 Broadway
New York, NY 10012 USA

GERMANY
Lloyd's of London Press GmbH
59 Ehrenbergstrasse
2000 Hamburg 50
West Germany

SOUTH-EAST ASIA
Lloyd's of London Press (Far East) Ltd
903 Chung Nam Building
1 Lockhart Road, Wanchai
Hong Kong

British Library Cataloguing in Publication Data
Newns, Ralph
Double taxation relief for shipping.
1. Shipping services. Double taxation—
Treaties
I. Title   II. Parrington, Sheila
341.7'5668

ISBN 1–85044–165–0

Text typeset in 9 on 10pt Linotron 202 Bembo by
Promenade Graphics, Cheltenham, Glos.
Printed in Great Britain by
WBC Print Ltd, Bristol

PREFACE

The importance of removing tax barriers from international shipping traffic has been accepted by Parliament for over 60 years. Section 18 of the Finance Act 1923 authorised the Sovereign to give statutory effect, by Order in Council, to double taxation agreements relating to "the business of shipping". Corresponding provisions relating to air transport were added in 1931. It was not until 1945, however, that the Sovereign's powers were extended to comprehensive double taxation agreements; the Irish comprehensive agreement of 1926 had had to be put into effect by Act of Parliament. The 1945 legislation made the existing specific powers relating to shipping and air transport agreements otiose, but in fact the original 1923 powers were preserved in both the 1952 and the 1970 consolidations of the Tax Acts; eventually they were repealed by the Finance Act 1987, in anticipation of the 1987 consolidation Bill.

The only agreement governed by the 1923 legislation which is still in force is that made with Iceland in 1928: the Relief from Double Income Tax on Shipping Profits (Iceland) Declaration 1928 (SR&O 1928/563) is expressly preserved by Part VII of Schedule 16 to the Finance Act 1987. The exemption from income tax, under this agreement, was extended to corporation tax by the Finance Act 1965.

Some countries, although not yet ready to conclude comprehensive double taxation agreements, have, since 1945, entered into limited agreements covering shipping (and air transport):

Double Taxation Relief (Shipping and Air Transport) Orders

Argentina	SI 1949/1435
Brazil	SI 1968/572
Jordan	SI 1979/300
Lebanon	SI 1964/278
Venezuela	SI 1979/301 (not yet in force)
Zaire	SI 1977/1298

Generally speaking, the provisions relating to shipping in comprehensive double taxation agreements follow the principles recommended by the Organisation for Economic Cooperation and Development in Articles 8 and 13(3) of the 1977 Model Convention:

Article 8—Shipping, inland waterways transport and air transport

(1) Profits from the operation of ships or aircraft in international traffic shall be taxable only in the Contracting State in which the place of effective management of the enterprise is situated.

(2) Profits from the operation of boats engaged in inland waterways transport shall be taxable only in the Contracting State in which the place of effective management of the enterprise is situated.

(3) If the place of effective management of a shipping enterprise or of an inland waterways transport enterprise is aboard a ship or boat, then it shall be deemed to be situated in the Contracting State in which the home harbour of the ship or boat is situated or, if there is no such home harbour, in the Contracting State of which the operator of the ship or boat is a resident.

(4) The provisions of paragraph (1) shall also apply to profits from the participation in a pool, a joint business or an international operating agency.

Article 13—Capital gains

(3) Gains from the alienation of ships or aircraft operated in international traffic, boats engaged in inland waterways transport, or movable property pertaining to the operation of such ships, aircraft or boats, shall be taxable only in the Contracting State in which the place of effective management of the enterprise is situated.

Article 3—General definitions

(1)(d) The term "international traffic" means any transport by a ship or aircraft operated by an enterprise which has its place of effective management in a Contracting State, except where the ship or aircraft is operated solely between places in the other Contracting State.

Where an agreement incorporates an article covering offshore activities, eg oilfield exploitation, that article generally includes rules for the taxation of shipping profits connected with such activities. There is no corresponding article in the OECD Model.

In relation to wealth taxes, comprehensive agreements generally follow the principles of the OECD Model:

Article 22—Capital

(3) Capital represented by ships and aircraft operated in international traffic and by boats engaged in inland waterways transport, and by movable property pertaining to the operation of such ships, aircraft and boats, shall be taxable only in the Contracting State in which the place of effective management of the enterprise is situated.

Notes

Words appearing in square brackets in headings have been added to assist the reader and are not part of the text of the original agreement.

We are grateful to the Controller of Her Majesty's Stationery Office for permission to reproduce Crown copyright material.

February 1988   RALPH NEWNS AND SHEILA PARRINGTON

CONTENTS

CONTENTS

CONTENTS

DOUBLE TAXATION AGREEMENTS

Agreements are printed in the form in which they have effect on 6 April 1988

(Developments between 6 April and 1 May 1988 have been noted as appropriate)

ANTIGUA AND BARBUDA

Arrangement of 19 December 1947 (SR & O 1947 No 2865)

Printed as amended by the Agreement of 5 March 1968 (SI 1968 No 1096).

Paragraph 1 [Taxes covered]

(1) The taxes which are the subject of this Arrangement are—
    (*a*) In the United Kingdom:
        The income tax (including surtax) and the profits tax (hereinafter referred to as "United Kingdom tax").
    (*b*) In Antigua:
        The income tax (hereinafter referred to as "Antigua tax").

(2) This Arrangement shall also apply to any other taxes of a substantially similar character imposed in the United Kingdom or Antigua after this Arrangement has come into force.

Corporation tax: This Arrangement covers United Kingdom corporation tax, by virtue of ICTA 1988, s 789(1).

Paragraph 2 [General definitions]

(1) In this Arrangement, unless the context otherwise requires—
    (*a*) The term "United Kingdom" means Great Britain and Northern Ireland, excluding the Channel Islands and the Isle of Man.
    (*b*) . . .
    (*c*) The terms "one of the territories" and "the other territory" mean the United Kingdom or Antigua, as the context requires.
    (*d*) The term "tax" means United Kingdom tax or Antigua tax, as the context requires.
    (*e*) The term "person" includes any body of persons, corporate or not corporate.
    (*f*) The term "company" includes any body corporate.
    (*g*) The terms "resident of the United Kingdom" and "resident of Antigua" mean respectively any person who is resident in the United Kingdom for the purposes of United Kingdom tax and not resident in Antigua for the purposes of Antigua tax and any person who is resident in Antigua for the purposes of Antigua tax and not resident in the United Kingdom for the purposes of United Kingdom tax; and a company shall be regarded as resident in the United Kingdom if its business is managed and controlled in the United Kingdom and as resident in Antigua if its business is managed and controlled in Antigua.
    (*h*) The terms "resident of one of the territories" and "resident of the other territory" mean a person who is a resident of the United Kingdom or a person who is a resident of Antigua, as the context requires.
    (*i*) –(*k*) . . .

(2) Where under this Arrangement any income is exempt from tax in one of the territories if (with or without other conditions) it is subject to tax in the other territory, and that income is subject to tax in that other territory by reference to the amount thereof which is remitted to

3

or received in that other territory, the exemption to be allowed under this Arrangement in the first-mentioned territory shall apply only to the amount so remitted or received.

(3) In the application of the provisions of this Arrangement by the United Kingdom or Antigua, any term not otherwise defined shall, unless the context otherwise requires, have the meaning which it has under the laws of the United Kingdom, or, as the case may be, Antigua, relating to the taxes which are the subject of this Arrangement.

Excluded companies: For companies excluded from this Arrangement see Article 13A.

Paragraph 5 [Shipping and air transport]

Notwithstanding the provisions of paragraphs 3 and 4, profits which a resident of one of the territories derives from operating ships or aircraft shall be exempt from tax in the other territory.

Paragraph 3: Taxation of industrial or commercial profits.
Paragraph 4: Taxation of profits of associated enterprises.

Paragraph 13A [Exclusion of certain companies]

This Arrangement shall not apply to companies entitled to any special tax benefit under the Antigua International Business Companies (Exemption from Income Tax) Ordinance 1967 as in effect on 1st January 1968, or any substantially similar law enacted by Antigua after that date.

Paragraph 14 [Exchange of information]

(1) The taxation authorities of the United Kingdom and Antigua shall exchange such information (being information available under their respective taxation laws) as is necessary for carrying out the provisions of this Arrangement or for the prevention of fraud or the administration of statutory provisions against legal avoidance in relation to the taxes which are the subject of this Arrangement. Any information so exchanged shall be treated as secret and shall not be disclosed to any persons other than those concerned with the assessment and collection of the taxes which are the subject of this Arrangement. No information shall be exchanged which would disclose any trade secret or trade process.

(2) As used in this paragraph, the term "taxation authorities" means the Commissioners of Inland Revenue or their authorised representative in the case of the United Kingdom and the Income Tax Commissioners or their authorised representative in the case of Antigua.

Paragraph 15 [Entry into force]

Note: Paragraph 15 provided for the entry into force of this Agreement. The Agreement takes effect in the UK in its amended form from the year of assessment 1968–69 (income tax) and from the financial year beginning on 1 April 1968 (corporation tax).

Official language: English.

ARGENTINA

Agreement of 28 July 1949 (SI 1949 No 1435)

Paragraph (1) [Exemption of UK undertakings]

The Argentine Government, in exercise of the powers conferred on them by Article 10 of Law 11,682 enacted in 1947, shall exempt all income derived from the business of sea or air transport between the Argentine Republic and other countries by United Kingdom undertakings engaged in such business from income tax and all other taxes on profits which are chargeable in the Argentine Republic.

Paragraph (2) [Exemption of Argentine undertakings]

The Government of the United Kingdom shall exempt all income derived from the business of sea or air transport between the United Kingdom and other countries by Argentine undertakings engaged in such business from income tax and all other taxes on profits which are chargeable in the United Kingdom and shall take the necessary action under Section 51 of the Act of Parliament of the United Kingdom known as the Finance No. 2 Act, 1945, with a view to giving the force of law to the exemption aforesaid.

Paragraph (3) [Definition of "the business of sea or air transport"]

The expression "the business of sea or air transport" means the business of transporting persons, goods or mail carried on by the owner or charterer of ships or aircraft.

Paragraph (4) [Definition of "United Kingdom undertakings"]

The expression "United Kingdom undertakings" means the Government of the United Kingdom, physical persons resident in the United Kingdom and not resident in the Argentine Republic, and corporations and partnerships constituted under the laws of the United Kingdom and managed and controlled in the United Kingdom.

Paragraph (5) [Definition of "Argentine undertakings"]

The expression "Argentine undertakings" means the Argentine Government, physical persons resident in the Argentine Republic and not resident in the United Kingdom, and corporations and partnerships constituted under the laws of the Argentine Republic and managed and controlled in the Argentine Republic.

Paragraph (6) [Entry into force]

The exemption provided for in paragraphs (1) and (2) above shall apply to all income earned as from the 1st January, 1946.

Official language: English.

ARUBA

Note: Aruba ceased to form part of the Netherlands Antilles with effect from 1 January 1986. It is understood, however, that both parties agree that this Convention remains in force in relation to Aruba as well as the Netherlands Antilles.

Convention of 31 October 1967 (SI 1968 No 577)

Extended to the Netherlands Antilles by the Extending Arrangement of 24 July 1970 (SI 1970 No 1949).

Article 1 Persons covered

This Convention shall apply to persons who are residents of one or both of the States.

Article 2 Taxes covered

(1) The taxes which are the subject of this Convention are:
  (*a*) In the United Kingdom of Great Britain and Northern Ireland:
     the income tax including surtax, the corporation tax and the capital gains tax (hereinafter referred to as "United Kingdom tax").
  (*b*) In the Netherlands Antilles:
     the income tax (*inkomstenbelasting*), the profits tax (*winstbelasting*) and the surtaxes on the income and profits taxes
     (hereinafter referred to as "Netherlands Antilles tax").

(2) This Convention shall also apply to any identical or substantially similar future taxes which are imposed in addition to, or in place of, the existing taxes by either State. The taxation authorities of the States shall notify to each other any substantial changes which have been made in their respective taxation laws.

Article 3 General definitions

(1) In this Convention, unless the context otherwise requires—
  (*a*) the term "United Kingdom" means Great Britain and Northern Ireland, including any area outside the territorial sea of the United Kingdom which in accordance with international law has been or may hereafter be designated, under the laws of the United Kingdom concerning the Continental Shelf, as an area within which the rights of the United Kingdom with respect to the sea-bed and sub-soil and their natural resources may be exercised;
  (*b*) the term "Netherlands Antilles" means the part of the Kingdom of the Netherlands that is situated in the Caribbean area and consisting of the islands Aruba, Bonaire, Curaçao, Saba, St. Eustatius and St. Martin (Dutch part) and the part of

the sea bed and its sub-soil under the Caribbean Sea over which the Kingdom of the Netherlands has sovereign rights in accordance with international law;

(c) the term "State" means the United Kingdom or the Netherlands Antilles, as the context requires; the term "States" means the United Kingdom and the Netherlands Antilles;

(d) the term "person" comprises an individual, a company and any other body of persons;

(e) the term "company" means any body corporate or any entity which is treated as a body corporate for tax purposes;

(f) the terms "enterprise of one of the States" and "enterprise of the other State" mean respectively an enterprise carried on by a resident of one of the States and an enterprise carried on by a resident of the other State;

(g) the term "taxation authorities" means, in the case of the United Kingdom, the Commissioners of Inland Revenue or their authorised representative; in the case of the Netherlands Antilles, the Minister of Finance (*de Minister von Financiën*) or his authorised representative;

(h) the term "tax" means United Kingdom tax or Netherlands Antilles tax as the context requires;

(i) the term "international traffic" includes any voyage of a ship or aircraft other than a voyage solely between places in the State which is not the State of which the person deriving the profits from the operation of the ship or aircraft is a resident.

(2) As regards the application of the Convention by one of the States any term not otherwise defined shall, unless the context otherwise requires, have the meaning which it has under the laws of that State relating to the taxes which are the subject of the Convention.

Article 4 Residence

(1) For the purposes of this Convention, the term "resident of one of the States" means any person who, under the law of that State, is liable to taxation therein by reason of his domicile, residence, place of management or any other criterion of a similar nature but the term does not include any person who is liable to tax in that State only if he derives income from sources therein. The terms "resident of the United Kingdom" and "resident of the Netherlands Antilles" shall be construed accordingly.

(2) Where by reason of the provisions of paragraph (1) an individual is a resident of both States, then his status shall be determined in accordance with the following rules:

(a) he shall be deemed to be a resident of the State in which he had a permanent home available to him. If he has a permanent home available to him in both States, he shall be deemed to be a resident of the State with which his personal and economic relations are closest (centre of vital interests);

(b) if the State in which he has his centre of vital interests cannot be determined, or if he has not a permanent home available to him in either State, he shall be deemed to be a resident of the State in which he has an habitual abode;

(c) if he has an habitual abode in both States or in neither of them, he shall be deemed to be a resident of the State of which he is a national;

(d) if he is a national of both States or of neither of them, the taxation authorities of the States shall settle the question by mutual agreement.

(3) Where by reason of the provisions of paragraph (1) a person other than an individual is a resident of both States, then it shall be deemed to be a resident of the State in which its place of effective management is situated.

Article 7 Immovable property

(1) (Taxation of income from immovable property.)

(2) (a) The term "immovable property" shall, subject to sub-paragraph (b) below, be defined in accordance with the law of the State in which the property in question is situated.

(b) The term "immovable property" shall in any case include property accessory to immovable property, livestock and equipment used in agriculture and forestry, rights to which the provisions of general law respecting landed property apply, usufruct of immovable property and rights to variable or fixed payments as consideration for the working of, or the right to work, mineral deposits, sources and other natural resources; ships, boats and aircraft shall not be regarded as immovable property.

(3) . . .

(4) . . .

Article 9 Shipping and air transport

Profits which a resident of one of the States derives from the operation of ships or aircraft in international traffic shall be taxable only in that State.

Article 15 Capital gains

(1) (Taxation of gains.)

(2) Notwithstanding paragraph (1) of this Article, gains derived by a resident of one of the States from the alienation of ships and aircraft operated in international traffic and movable property pertaining to the operation of such ships and aircraft shall be taxable only in that State.

(3) . . .

(4) . . .

Article 24 Capital

(1) . . .

(2) (Taxation of capital represented by movable business property.)

(3) Notwithstanding paragraph (2) of this Article, ships and aircraft operated in international traffic and movable property pertaining to the operation of such ships and aircraft shall be taxable only in the State of which the operator is a resident.

(4) . . .

Article 27 Non-discrimination

(1) The nationals of one of the States shall not be subjected in the other State to any taxation or any requirement connected therewith which is other or more burdensome than the taxation and connected requirements to which nationals of that other State in the same circumstances are or may be subjected.

(2) The term "national" means:

(a) in relation to the United Kingdom:
   (i) all British subjects deriving their status as such from connection with the United Kingdom and all British subjects and British protected persons residing in the United Kingdom;
   (ii) all legal persons, partnerships, associations and other entities deriving their status as such from the law of the United Kingdom;

(b) in relation to the Netherlands Antilles:
   (i) all individuals possessing the Netherlands nationality;
   (ii) all legal persons, partnerships, associations and other entities deriving their status as such from the law in force in the Netherlands Antilles.

(3) The taxation on a permanent establishment which an enterprise of one of the States has in the other State shall not be less favourably levied in that other State than the taxation levied on enterprises of that other State carrying on the same activities.

Nothing contained in this paragraph shall be construed as obliging either State to grant to individuals not resident in the State any of the personal allowances and reliefs for tax purposes which are granted to individuals so resident, nor as conferring any exemption from tax in a State in respect of dividends paid to a company which is a resident of the other State.

(4) Enterprises of one of the States, the capital of which is wholly or partly owned or controlled, directly or indirectly, by one or more residents of the other State, shall not be subjected in the first-mentioned State to any taxation or any requirement connected therewith which is other or more burdensome than the taxation and connected requirements to which other similar enterprises of that first-mentioned State are or may be subjected.

(5) In determining for the purpose of United Kingdom tax whether a company is a close company, the term "recognised stock exchange" shall include any stock exchange in the Netherlands Antilles which is a stock exchange within the meaning of the Netherlands Antilles law relating to stock exchanges.

(6) In this Article the term "taxation" means taxes of every kind and description.

Article 28 Mutual agreement

(1) Where a resident of one of the States considers that the actions of one or both of the States result or will result for him in taxation not in accordance with this Convention, he may, notwithstanding the remedies provided by the national laws of those States, present his case to the taxation authority of the State of which he is a resident or a national.

(2) The taxation authority shall endeavour, if the objection appears to it to be justified and if it is not itself able to arrive at an appropriate solution, to resolve the case by mutual agreement with the taxation authority of the other State, with a view to the avoidance of taxation not in accordance with the Convention.

(3) The taxation authorities of the States shall endeavour to resolve by mutual agreement any difficulties or doubts arising as to the interpretation or application of the Convention. . . .

Article 29 Exchange of information

(1) The taxation authorities of the States shall exchange such information (being information which such authorities have at their disposal) as is necessary for carrying out the provisions of this Convention or for the prevention of fraud or for the administration of statutory provisions against legal avoidance in relation to the taxes which are the subject of the Convention. Any information so exchanged shall be treated as secret and shall not be disclosed to any persons other than persons (including a Court or administrative body) concerned with the assessment or collection of, or prosecution in respect of, or the determination of appeals in relation to, the taxes which are the subject of the Convention.

(2) In no case shall the provisions of paragraph (1) be construed so as to impose on the taxation authority of either State the obligation:

(*a*) to carry out administrative measures at variance with the laws or administrative practice prevailing in that or the other State;

(*b*) to supply particulars which are not obtainable under the laws or in the normal course of the administration in that or the other State; or

(*c*) to supply information which would disclose any trade, business, industrial, commercial or professional secret or trade process, or information the disclosure of which would be contrary to public policy in that or the other State.

SI 1970 No 1949 Sch (3), (4) Entry into force

Note: Paragraph (3) provided for the entry into force of this Convention in relation to Aruba. The Convention takes effect in the UK from the year of assessment 1970–71 (income tax and capital gains tax) and from the financial year beginning on 1 April 1970 (corporation tax) under the provisions of para (4).

Official languages: The Netherlands language text and the English language text of this Convention are equally authoritative.

AUSTRALIA

Agreement of 7 December 1967 (SI 1968 No 305)

(The Protocol of 29 January 1980 (SI 1980 No 707) does not amend the Articles printed below.)

Article 1 [Taxes covered]

(1) The taxes which are the subject of this Agreement are—
    (a) in the United Kingdom of Great Britain and Northern Ireland:
    the income tax (including surtax), the corporation tax and the capital gains tax;
    (b) in Australia:
    the Commonwealth income tax, including the additional tax upon the undistributed amount of the distributable income of a private company.

(2) This Agreement shall also apply to any identical or substantially similar taxes which are imposed after the date of signature of this Agreement in addition to, or in place of, the existing taxes by either Government or by the Government of any territory to which the present Agreement is extended under Article 22.

Article 2 [General definitions]

(1) In this Agreement, unless the context otherwise requires—
    (a) the term "United Kingdom" means Great Britain and Northern Ireland, including any area outside the territorial sea of the United Kingdom which in accordance with international law has been or may hereafter be designated, under the laws of the United Kingdom concerning the Continental Shelf, as an area within which the rights of the United Kingdom with respect to the sea-bed and sub-soil and their natural resources may be exercised;
    (b) the term "the Commonwealth" means the Commonwealth of Australia;
    (c) the term "Australia" means the whole of the Commonwealth and includes—
        (i) the Territory of Norfolk Island;
        (ii) the Territory of Christmas Island;
        (iii) the Territory of Cocos (Keeling) Islands;
        (iv) the Territory of Ashmore and Cartier Islands; and
        (v) any area outside the territorial limits of the Commonwealth and the said Territories in respect of which there is for the time being in force a law of the Commonwealth or of a State or part of the Commonwealth or of a Territory aforesaid dealing with the exploitation of any of the natural resources of the sea-bed and sub-soil of the Continental Shelf;
    (d) the terms "territory", "one of the territories" and "the other territory" mean the United Kingdom or Australia as the context requires;
    (e) the term "taxation authority" means, in the case of the United Kingdom, the Commissioners of Inland Revenue or their authorised representative; in the case of Australia, the Commissioner of Taxation or his authorised representative;
    (f) the term "United Kingdom tax" means tax imposed by the United Kingdom being tax to which this Agreement applies by virtue of Article 1; the term "Australian tax" means tax imposed by the Commonwealth being tax to which this Agreement applies by virtue of Article 1;

(*g*) the term "tax" means United Kingdom tax or Australian tax as the context requires;

(*h*) the term "person" includes any body of persons corporate or not corporate;

(*i*) the term "company" means any body corporate;

(*j*) the term "resident in the United Kingdom" has the meaning which it has under the laws of the United Kingdom relating to United Kingdom tax;

(*k*) the term "resident of Australia" has the meaning which it has under the laws of Australia relating to Australian tax;

(*l*) words in the singular include the plural, and words in the plural include the singular.

(2) The terms "Australian tax" and "United Kingdom tax" do not include any amount which represents a penalty or interest imposed under the law of either territory relating to the taxes which are the subject of the present Agreement.

(3) Where under this Agreement income is relieved from tax in one of the territories and, under the law in force in the other territory an individual, in respect of the said income, is subject to tax by reference to the amount thereof which is remitted to or received in that other territory and not by reference to the full amount thereof, then the relief to be allowed under this Agreement in the first-mentioned territory shall apply only to so much of the income as is remitted to or received in the other territory.

(3A) . . .

(4) In the application of the provisions of this Agreement by one of the Contracting Governments any term not otherwise defined shall, unless the context otherwise requires, have the meaning which it has under the laws of that Government relating to the taxes which are the subject of this Agreement.

Article 3 [Residence]

(1) For the purposes of this Agreement—

(*a*) the term "Australian company" means any company which being a resident of Australia—

(i) is incorporated in Australia and has its centre of administrative or practical management in Australia whether or not any person outside Australia exercises or is capable of exercising any overriding control or direction of the company or of its policy or affairs in any way whatsoever; or

(ii) is managed and controlled in Australia;

(*b*) the term "United Kingdom company" means any company which is managed and controlled in the United Kingdom and which is not an Australian company;

(*c*) the term "United Kingdom resident" means any United Kingdom company and any person (other than a company) who is resident in the United Kingdom but the term does not include any individual, not being ordinarily resident in the United Kingdom, who is liable to tax in the United Kingdom only if he derives income from sources therein; and

(*d*) the term "Australian resident" means any Australian company and any other person (other than a United Kingdom company) who is a resident of Australia but the term does not include any individual, not being ordinarily resident in Australia, who is liable to tax in Australia only if he derives income from sources therein.

(2) Where by reason of the provisions of paragraph (1) of this Article an individual is both a United Kingdom resident and an Australian resident—

(*a*) he shall be treated solely as a United Kingdom resident—

(i) if he has a permanent home available to him in the United Kingdom and has not a permanent home available to him in Australia;

(ii) if sub-paragraph (*a*) (i) of this paragraph is not applicable but he has an habitual abode in the United Kingdom and has not an habitual abode in Australia;

(iii) if neither sub-paragraph (*a*) (i) nor sub-paragraph (*a*) (ii) of this paragraph is applicable but the territory with which his personal and economic relations are closest is the United Kingdom;

11

(b) he shall be treated solely as an Australian resident—

    (i) if he has a permanent home available to him in Australia and has not a permanent home available to him in the United Kingdom;

    (ii) if sub-paragraph (b) (i) of this paragraph is not applicable but he has an habitual abode in Australia and has not an habitual abode in the United Kingdom;

    (iii) if neither sub-paragraph (b) (i) nor sub-paragraph (b) (ii) of this paragraph is applicable but the territory with which his personal and economic relations are closest is Australia.

(3) Where by reason of the provisions of paragraph (1) of this Article a person other than an individual is both a United Kingdom resident and an Australian resident—

    (a) it shall be treated solely as a United Kingdom resident if it is managed and controlled in the United Kingdom;

    (b) it shall be treated solely as an Australian resident if it is managed and controlled in Australia.

(4) The terms "resident of one of the territories" and "resident of the other territory" mean a person who is a United Kingdom resident or a person who is an Australian resident as the context requires.

(5) The terms "United Kingdom enterprise" and "Australian enterprise" mean respectively an industrial or commercial enterprise or undertaking carried on by a United Kingdom resident and an industrial or commercial enterprise or undertaking carried on by an Australian resident, and the terms "enterprise of one of the territories" and "enterprise of the other territory" mean a United Kingdom enterprise or an Australian enterprise, as the context requires.

Article 6 [Shipping and air transport]

(1) A resident of one of the territories shall be exempt from tax in the other territory on profits from the operation of ships or aircraft, other than profits from voyages or operations of ships or aircraft confined solely to places in the other territory, voyages of ships or aircraft between a place in Australia and a place in the Territory of Papua or the Territory of New Guinea being treated as voyages between places within Australia.

(2) The amount which shall be charged to tax in one of the territories as profits from voyages of ships in respect of which a resident of the other territory is not exempt from tax in the first-mentioned territory under paragraph (1) of this Article shall not exceed 5 per cent. of the amounts paid or payable (net of rebates) in respect of such voyages for the carriage of passengers, livestock, mails or goods shipped in the first-mentioned territory.

(3) Paragraph (2) of this Article shall not apply to the profits derived from the operation of ships by a United Kingdom enterprise whose principal place of business is in Australia, but there shall be excluded from the profits on which any such enterprise is charged to Australia tax any amounts of profits taxed in the Territory of Papua or the Territory of New Guinea.

Papua New Guinea: Since this Agreement was signed, the Territories of Papua and New Guinea have attained independence as Papua New Guinea.

Article 20 [Mutual agreement procedure]

(1) Where a taxpayer considers that the action of the taxation authority of either territory has resulted or will result in taxation contrary to the provisions of this Agreement, he shall be entitled to present his case to either taxation authority. Should the taxpayer's claim be deemed worthy of consideration, the taxation authority to which the claim is made shall endeavour to come to an agreement with the other taxation authority with a view to a satisfactory adjustment.

(2) The taxation authorities may communicate with each other directly to implement the provisions of this Agreement and to assure its consistent interpretation and application. In particular, the taxation authorities may consult together to endeavour to resolve disputes aris-

ing out of the application of paragraph (3) of Article 5 or Article 7, or the determination of the source of particular items of income.

Article 5: Taxation of industrial or commercial profits.
Article 7: Taxation of profits of associated enterprises.

Article 21 [Exchange of information]

The taxation authorities shall exchange such information (being information which is at their disposal under their respective taxation laws in the normal course of administration) as is necessary for carrying out the provisions of this Agreement or for the prevention of fraud or for the administration of statutory provisions against legal avoidance in relation to the taxes which are the subject of this Agreement. Any information so exchanged shall be treated as secret but may be disclosed to persons (including a court or tribunal) concerned with the assessment, collection, enforcement or prosecution in respect of the taxes which are the subject of this Agreement. No information as aforesaid shall be exchanged which would disclose any trade, business, industrial or professional secret or trade process.

Article 23 [Entry into force]

Note: Article 23 provided for the entry into force of this Agreement. It takes effect in the UK from the year of assessment 1965–66 (capital gains tax), 1967–68 (income tax) and from the financial year beginning on 1 April 1964 (corporation tax), subject to transitional provisions where greater relief would have been afforded under the 1946 Agreement.

Official language: English.

AUSTRIA

Convention of 30 April 1969 (SI 1970 No 1947)

(The Protocol of 17 November 1977 (SI 1979 No 117) does not amend the Articles printed below.)

Article 1 Personal scope

This Convention shall apply to persons who are residents of one or both of the Contracting States.

Article 2 Taxes covered

(1) The taxes which are the subject of this Convention are:
    (*a*) in the United Kingdom of Great Britain and Northern Ireland:
        (i) the income tax (including surtax);

(ii) the corporation tax; and

(iii) the capital gains tax;

(b) in Austria:

(i) the income tax (*die Einkommensteuer*);

(ii) the corporation tax (*die Körperschaftsteuer*);

(iii) the contribution from income for the promotion of residential building and for the equalisation of family burdens (*der Beitrag vom Einkommen zur Förderung des Wohnbaues und für Zwecke des Familienlastenausgleiches*);

(iv) the contribution from income to the emergency fund (*der Katastrophenfondsbeitrag vom Einkommen*);

(v) the directors' tax (*die Aufsichtsratsabgabe*);

(vi) the tax on commercial and industrial enterprises, including the tax levied on the sum of wages (*die Gewerbesteuer einschliesslich der Lohnsummensteuer*);

(vii) the special tax on income (*die Sonderabgabe vom Einkommen*).

(2) This Convention shall also apply to any identical or substantially similar taxes which are imposed by either Contracting State after the date of signature of this Convention in addition to, or in place of, the existing taxes. The competent authorities of the Contracting States shall notify to each other any changes which are made in their respective taxation laws.

Article 3 General definitions

(1) In this Convention, unless the context otherwise requires:

(a) the term "United Kingdom" means Great Britain and Northern Ireland, including any area outside the territorial sea of the United Kingdom which in accordance with international law has been or may hereafter be designated, under the laws of the United Kingdom concerning the Continental Shelf, as an area within which the rights of the United Kingdom with respect to the sea-bed and sub-soil and their natural resources may be exercised;

(b) the term "Austria" means the Republic of Austria;

(c) the term "nationals" means:

(i) in relation to the United Kingdom, all citizens of the United Kingdom and Colonies who derive their status as such from their connection with the United Kingdom and all legal persons, partnerships and associations deriving their status as such from the law in force in the United Kingdom;

(ii) in relation to Austria, all Austrian nationals and all legal persons, partnerships, associations and other entities deriving their status as such from the law in force in Austria;

(d) the terms "a Contracting State" and "the other Contracting State" mean the United Kingdom or Austria, as the context requires;

(e) the term "person" comprises an individual, a company and any other body of persons;

(f) the term "company" means any body corporate or any entity which is treated as a body corporate for tax purposes;

(g) the terms "enterprise of a Contracting State" and "enterprise of the other Contracting State" mean respectively an enterprise carried on by a resident of a Contracting State and an enterprise carried on by a resident of the other Contracting State;

(h) the term "competent authority" means, in the case of the United Kingdom the Commissioners of Inland Revenue or their authorised representative, and in the case of Austria the Federal Ministry of Finance.

(2) Where under any provision of this Convention income is relieved from Austrian tax and, under the law in force in the United Kingdom, an individual, in respect of the said income, is subject to tax by reference to the amount thereof which is remitted to or received in the United Kingdom and not by reference to the full amount thereof, then the relief to be allowed under this Convention in Austria shall apply only to so much of the income as is remitted to or received in the United Kingdom.

(3) As regards the application of this Convention by a Contracting State any term not otherwise defined shall, unless the context otherwise requires, have the meaning which it has under the laws of that Contracting State relating to the taxes which are the subject of this Convention.

Article 4 Fiscal domicile

(1) For the purposes of this Convention, the term "resident of a Contracting State" means, subject to the provisions of paragraphs (2) and (3) of this Article, any person who, under the law of that State, is liable to taxation therein by reason of his domicile, residence, place of management or any other criterion of a similar nature; the term does not include any individual who is liable to tax in that Contracting State only if he derives income from sources therein. The terms " resident of the United Kingdom" and "resident of Austria" shall be construed accordingly.

(2) Where by reason of the provisions of paragraph (1) of this Article an individual is a resident of both Contracting States, then his status shall be determined in accordance with the following rules:

(a) he shall be deemed to be a resident of the Contracting State in which he has a permanent home available to him. If he has a permanent home available to him in both Contracting States, he shall be deemed to be a resident of the Contracting State with which his personal and economic relations are closest (centre of vital interests);

(b) if the Contracting State in which he has his centre of vital interests cannot be determined, or if he has not a permanent home available to him in either Contracting State, he shall be deemed to be a resident of the Contracting State in which he has an habitual abode;

(c) if he has an habitual abode in both Contracting States or in neither of them, he shall be deemed to be a resident of the Contracting State of which he is a national;

(d) if he is a national of both Contracting States or of neither of them, the competent authorities of the Contracting States shall endeavour to settle the question by mutual agreement.

(3) Where by reason of the provisions of paragraph (1) of this Article a person other than an individual is a resident of both Contracting States, then it shall be deemed to be a resident of the Contracting State in which its place of effective management is situated.

Article 8 Shipping and air transport

(1) A resident of a Contracting State shall be taxable only in that Contracting State on profits from the operation of ships or aircraft other than profits from voyages of ships or aircraft confined solely to places in the other Contracting State.

(2) In respect of the operation of ships or aircraft in international traffic a resident of the United Kingdom shall be exempt from any Austrian taxes on capital.

Article 26 Non-discrimination

(1) The nationals of a Contracting State shall not be subjected in the other Contracting State to any taxation or any requirement connected therewith which is other or more burdensome than the taxation and connected requirements to which nationals of that other State in the same circumstances are or may be subjected.

(2) The taxation on a permanent establishment which an enterprise of a Contracting State has in the other Contracting State shall not be less favourably levied in that other State than the taxation levied on enterprises of that other State carrying on the same activities.

(3) Enterprises of a Contracting State, the capital of which is wholly or partly owned or controlled, directly or indirectly, by one or more residents of the other Contracting State, shall not be subjected in the first-mentioned Contracting State to any taxation or any requirement connected therewith which is other or more burdensome than the taxation and con-

nected requirements to which other similar enterprises of that first-mentioned State are or may be subjected,

(4) In determining for the purpose of United Kingdom tax whether a company is a close company, the term "recognised stock exchange" shall include any stock exchange in Austria which is a stock exchange within the meaning of the Austrian law relating to stock exchanges.

(5) Nothing contained in this Article shall be construed as obliging either Contracting State to grant to individuals not resident in that State any of the personal allowances, reliefs and reductions for tax purposes on account of civil status or family responsibilities which are granted to individuals so resident, nor as conferring any exemption from tax in a Contracting State in respect of dividends paid to a company which is a resident of the other Contracting State.

Article 27 Mutual agreement procedure

(1) Where a resident of a Contracting State considers that the actions of one or both of the Contracting States result or will result for him in taxation not in accordance with this Convention, he may, notwithstanding the remedies provided by the national laws of those States, present his case to the competent authority of the Contracting State of which he is a resident.

(2) The competent authority shall endeavour, if the objection appears to it to be justified and if it is not itself able to arrive at an appropriate solution, to resolve the case by mutual agreement with the competent authority of the other Contracting State, with a view to the avoidance of taxation not in accordance with the Convention.

(3) The competent authorities of the Contracting States shall endeavour to resolve by mutual agreement any difficulties or doubts arising as to the interpretation or application of the Convention.

(4) The competent authorities of the Contracting States may communicate with each other directly for the purpose of reaching an agreement in the sense of the preceding paragraphs.

Article 28 Exchange of information

The competent authorities of the Contracting States shall exchange such information (being information which is at their disposal under their respective taxation laws in the normal course of administration) as is necessary for carrying out the provisions of this Convention or for the prevention of fraud or the administration of statutory provisions against legal avoidance in relation to the taxes which are the subject of this Convention. Any information so exchanged shall be treated as secret but may be disclosed to persons (including a court or administrative body) concerned with assessment and collection of taxes which are the subject of this Convention. No information shall be exchanged which would disclose any trade, business, industrial or professional secret or any trade process, or the disclosure of which would be contrary to public policy.

Article 30 Entry into force

Note: Article 30 provided for the entry into force of this Convention. It takes effect in the UK from the year of assessment 1969–70 (income tax and capital gains tax) and from the financial year beginning on 1 April 1969 (corporation tax).

Official languages: The German language text and the English language text of this Convention are equally authoritative.

BANGLADESH

Convention of 8 August 1979 (SI 1980 No 708)

Article 1 Personal scope

This Convention shall apply to persons who are residents of one or both of the Contracting States.

Article 2 Taxes covered

(1) The taxes which are the subject of this Convention are:
    (a) in the United Kingdom of Great Britain and Northern Ireland:
        (i) the income tax;
        (ii) the corporation tax; and
        (iii) the capital gains tax;
        (hereinafter referred to as "United Kingdom tax");
    (b) in the People's Republic of Bangladesh:
        (i) the income-tax; and
        (ii) the super-tax;
        (hereinafter referred to as "Bangladesh tax").

(2) This Convention shall also apply to any identical or substantially similar taxes which are imposed by either Contracting State after the date of signature of this Convention in addition to, or in place of, the existing taxes.

(3) The competent authorities of the Contracting States shall notify each other of any substantial changes which have been made in their respective taxation laws.

Article 3 General definitions

(1) In this Convention, unless the context otherwise requires:
    (a) the term "United Kingdom" means Great Britain and Northern Ireland, including any area outside the territorial sea of the United Kingdom which under the laws of the United Kingdom is an area within which the rights of the United Kingdom with respect to the sea-bed and sub-soil and their natural resources may be exercised;
    (b) the term "Bangladesh" means the territory of the People's Republic of Bangladesh, including any area outside the territorial waters of Bangladesh which under the laws of Bangladesh is an area within which the rights of Bangladesh with respect to the sea bed and subsoil and their natural resources may be exercised;
    (c) the term "national" means:
        (i) in relation to the United Kingdom, any citizen of the United Kingdom and Colonies, or any British subject not possessing that citizenship or the citizenship of any other commonwealth country or territory, provided that in either case he has the right of abode in the United Kingdom; and includes any legal

17

person, partnership, association or other entity deriving its status as such from the law in force in the United Kingdom;

(ii) in relation to Bangladesh, any individual possessing the nationality of Bangladesh and includes any legal person, partnership, association or other entity deriving its status as such from the law in force in Bangladesh;

(d) the terms "a Contracting State" and "the other Contracting State" mean the United Kingdom or Bangladesh, as the context requires;

(e) the term "person" comprises an individual, a company and any other body of persons;

(f) the term "company" means any body corporate or any entity which is treated as a body corporate for tax purposes;

(g) the terms "enterprise of a Contracting State" and "enterprise of the other Contracting State" mean respectively an enterprise carried on by a resident of a Contracting State and an enterprise carried on by a resident of the other Contracting State;

(h) the term "competent authority" means, in the case of the United Kingdom the Commissioners of Inland Revenue or their authorised representative, and in the case of Bangladesh the National Board of Revenue or its authorised representative;

(i) the term "international traffic" means any transport by a ship or aircraft operated by an enterprise which has its place of effective management in a Contracting State except when the ship or aircraft is operated wholly or mainly between places in the other Contracting State;

(j) the term "political subdivision", in relation to the United Kingdom, includes Northern Ireland.

(2) As regards the application of this Convention by a Contracting State any term not otherwise defined shall, unless the context otherwise requires, have the meaning which it has under the laws of that Contracting State relating to the taxes which are the subject of this Convention.

Article 4 Fiscal domicile

(1) For the purposes of this Convention, the term "resident of a Contracting State" means, subject to the provisions of paragraphs (2) and (3) of this Article, any person who, under the law of that State, is liable to taxation therein by reason of his domicile, residence, place of management or any other criterion of a similar nature; the term does not include any individual who is liable to tax in that Contracting State in respect only of income from sources therein.

(2) Where by reason of the provisions of paragraph (1) of this Article an individual is a resident of both Contracting States, then his status shall be determined in accordance with the following rules:

(a) he shall be deemed to be a resident of the Contracting State in which he has a permanent home available to him. If he has a permanent home available to him in both Contracting States, he shall be deemed to be a resident of the Contracting State with which his personal and economic relations are closer (centre of vital interests);

(b) if the Contracting State in which he has his centre of vital interests cannot be determined, or if he has not a permanent home available to him in either Contracting State, he shall be deemed to be a resident of the Contracting State in which he has an habitual abode;

(c) if he has an habitual abode in both Contracting States or in neither of them, he shall be deemed to be a resident of the Contracting State of which he is a national;

(d) if he is a national of both Contracting States or of neither of them, the competent authorities of the Contracting States shall settle the question by mutual agreement.

(3) Where by reason of the provisions of paragraph (1) of this Article a person other than an individual is a resident of both Contracting States, then it shall be deemed to be a resident of the Contracting State in which its place of effective management is situated.

18

Article 6 Income from immovable property

(1) (Taxation of income from immovable property.)

(2) (*a*) The term "immovable property" shall, subject to the provisions of sub-paragraph (*b*) below, be defined in accordance with the law of the Contracting State in which the property in question is situated.

(*b*) The term "immovable property" shall in any case include property accessory to immovable property, livestock and equipment used in agriculture, forestry and fisheries, rights to which the provisions of general law respecting landed property apply, usufruct of immovable property and rights to variable or fixed payments as consideration for the working of, or the right to work, mineral deposits, sources and other natural resources; ships, boats and aircraft shall not be regarded as immovable property.

(3) . . .

(4) . . .

Article 7 Business profits

(1)–(5) . . .

(6) For the purposes of this Article the term "profits" does not include income from the operation of ships.

Article 13 Capital gains

(1) . . .

(2) (Capital gains from the alienation of movable property.)

(3) Notwithstanding the provisions of paragraph (2) of this Article, capital gains derived by a resident of a Contracting State from the alienation of ships and aircraft operated in international traffic and movable property pertaining to the operation of such ships and aircraft shall be taxable only in that Contracting State.

(4) . . .

Article 23 Non-discrimination

(1) The nationals of a Contracting State shall not be subjected in the other Contracting State to any taxation or any requirement connected therewith which is other or more burdensome than the taxation and connected requirements to which nationals of that other State in the same circumstances are or may be subjected.

(2) The taxation on a permanent establishment which an enterprise of a Contracting State has in the other Contracting State shall not be less favourably levied in that other State than the taxation levied on enterprises of that other State carrying on the same activities.

(3) Enterprises of a Contracting State, the capital of which is wholly or partly owned or controlled, directly or indirectly, by one or more residents of the other Contracting State, shall not be subjected in the first-mentioned Contracting State to any taxation or any requirement connected therewith which is other or more burdensome than the taxation and connected requirements to which other similar enterprises of that first-mentioned State are or may be subjected.

(4) Nothing contained in this Article shall be construed as obliging either Contracting State to grant to individuals not resident in that State any of the personal allowances, reliefs and reductions for tax purposes which are granted to individuals so resident. For the purposes of this paragraph the term "individuals" includes, in the case of Bangladesh, unregistered firms, associations of persons and Hindu undivided families which are entitled to the same personal allowance, reliefs and reductions as individuals.

(5) In this Article the term "taxation" means taxes which are the subject of this Convention.

Article 24 Mutual agreement procedure

(1) Where a resident of a Contracting State considers that the actions of one or both of the Contracting States result or will result for him in taxation not in accordance with this Convention, he may, notwithstanding the remedies provided by the national laws of those States, present his case to the competent authority of the Contracting State of which he is a resident.

(2) The competent authority shall endeavour, if the objection appears to it to be justified and if it is not itself able to arrive at an appropriate solution, to resolve the case by mutual agreement with the competent authority of the other Contracting State, with a view to the avoidance of taxation not in accordance with the Convention.

(3) The competent authorities of the Contracting States shall endeavour to resolve by mutual agreement any difficulties or doubts arising as to the interpretation or application of the Convention.

(4) The competent authorities of the Contracting States may communicate with each other directly for the purpose of reaching an agreement in the sense of the preceding paragraphs of this Article.

Article 25 Exchange of information

(1) The competent authorities of the Contracting States shall exchange such information as is necessary for the carrying out of this Convention and of the domestic laws of the Contracting States concerning taxes covered by this Convention insofar as the taxation thereunder is in accordance with this Convention. Any information so exchanged shall be treated as secret and shall not be disclosed to any persons or authorities other than those concerned with the assessment or collection of the taxes which are the subject of the Convention.

(2) In no case shall the provisions of paragraph (1) of this Article be construed so as to impose on one of the Contracting States the obligation:

    (*a*) to carry out administrative measures at variance with the laws or the administrative practice of that or of the other Contracting State;

    (*b*) to supply particulars which are not obtainable under the laws or in the normal course of the administration of that or of the other Contracting State;

    (*c*) to supply information which would disclose any trade, business, industrial, commercial or professional secret or trade process, or information, the disclosure of which would be contrary to public policy.

Article 26 Entry into force

Note: Article 26 provides for the entry into force of this Convention. It takes effect in the UK from the year of assessment 1978–79 (income tax and capital gains tax) and from the financial year beginning on 1 April 1978 (corporation tax).

Official language: English.

BARBADOS

Agreement of 26 March 1970 (SI 1970 No 952)

(The Protocol of 18 September 1973 (SI 1973 No 2096) does not amend the Articles printed below.)

Article 1 Taxes covered

(1) The taxes which are the subject of this Agreement are:
    (*a*) in the United Kingdom of Great Britain and Northern Ireland:
        (i) the income tax (including surtax);
        (ii) the corporation tax; and
        (iii) the capital gains tax
        (hereinafter referred to as "United Kingdom tax");
    (*b*) in Barbados:
        (i) the income tax;
        (ii) the petroleum winning operations tax; and
        (iii) the trade tax
        (hereinafter referred to as "Barbados tax").

(2) This Agreement shall also apply to any identical or substantially similar taxes which are imposed by either Contracting State after the date of signature of this Agreement in addition to, or in place of, the existing taxes.

Article 2 General definitions

(1) In this Agreement, unless the context otherwise requires:
    (*a*) "United Kingdom" means Great Britain and Northern Ireland, including any area outside the territorial sea of the United Kingdom which in accordance with international law has been or may hereafter be designated, under the laws of the United Kingdom concerning the Continental Shelf, as an area within which the rights of the United Kingdom with respect to the sea-bed and sub-soil and their natural resources may be exercised;
    (*b*) "Barbados" means the island of Barbados and the territorial waters thereof including any area outside such territorial waters which in accordance with international law and the laws of Barbados is an area within which the rights of Barbados with respect to the sea bed and sub-soil and their natural resources may be exercised;
    (*c*) "company" means any body corporate or any entity which is treated as a body corporate for tax purposes;
    (*d*) "a Contracting State" and "the other Contracting State" mean the United Kingdom or Barbados, as the context requires;
    (*e*) "enterprise of a Contracting State" and "enterprise of the other Contracting State" mean respectively an enterprise carried on by a resident of a Contracting State and an enterprise carried on by a resident of the other Contracting State;
    (*f*) "international traffic" includes traffic between places in one country in the course of a voyage which extends over more than one country;
    (*g*) "national" means:
        (i) in relation to the United Kingdom:
            (*aa*) any citizen of the United Kingdom and Colonies who derives his status as such from connection with the United Kingdom;
            (*bb*) any legal person, association or other entity deriving its status as such from the law of the United Kingdom;
        (ii) in relation to Barbados:

(*aa*) any individual who is a citizen of Barbados;

(*bb*) any legal person, partnership or association deriving its status as such from the law of Barbados;

(*h*) "person" comprises an individual, a company and any other body of persons;

(*i*) "tax" means United Kingdom tax or Barbados tax, as the context requires;

(*j*) "taxation authorities" means, in the case of the United Kingdom, the Commissioners of Inland Revenue or their authorised representative; in the case of Barbados, the Commissioner of Inland Revenue or his authorised representative.

(2) In the application of the provisions of this Agreement by a Contracting State, any term not otherwise defined shall, unless the context otherwise requires, have the meaning which it has under the laws of that Contracting State relating to the taxes which are the subject of this Agreement.

Excluded companies: For companies excluded from this Agreement see Article 23.

Article 3 Fiscal domicile

(1) For the purposes of this Agreement, "resident of a Contracting State" means, subject to the provisions of paragraphs (2) and (3) of this Article, any person who, under the law of that State, is liable to taxation therein by reason of his domicile, residence, place of management or any other criterion of a similar nature; the term does not include any individual who is liable to tax in that Contracting State only if he derives income from sources therein. The terms "resident of the United Kingdom" and "resident of Barbados" shall be construed accordingly.

(2) Where by reason of the provisions of paragraph (1) of this Article an individual is a resident of both Contracting States, then his status shall be determined in accordance with the following rules:

(*a*) he shall be deemed to be a resident of the Contracting State in which he has a permanent home available to him. If he has a permanent home available to him in both Contracting States, he shall be deemed to be a resident of the Contracting State with which his personal and economic relations are closest (hereinafter referred to as his "centre of vital interests");

(*b*) if the Contracting State in which he has his centre of vital interests cannot be determined, or if he has not a permanent home available to him in either Contracting State, he shall be deemed to be a resident of the Contracting State in which he has an habitual abode;

(*c*) if he has an habitual abode in both Contracting States or in neither of them, he shall be deemed to be a resident of the Contracting State of which he is a national;

(*d*) if he is a national of both Contracting States or of neither of them, the taxation authorities of the Contracting States shall determine the question by mutual agreement.

(3) Where by reason of the provisions of paragraph (1) of this Article a person other than an individual is a resident of both Contracting States then it shall be deemed to be a resident of the Contracting State in which its place of effective management is situated.

Article 8 Shipping and air transport

A resident of a Contracting State shall be exempt from tax in the other Contracting State on profits from the operation of ships or aircraft other than profits from voyages of ships or aircraft confined solely to places in that other State.

Article 12 Immovable property

(1) (Taxation of income from immovable property.)

(2) The term "immovable property" shall be defined in accordance with the laws of the

Contracting State in which the property in question is situated. The term shall in any case include property accessory to immovable property, livestock and equipment of agricultural and forestry enterprises, rights to which the provisions of general law respecting landed property apply, usufruct of immovable property and rights to variable or fixed payments as consideration for the working of mineral deposits, sources and other natural resources; ships, boats and aircraft shall not be regarded as immovable property.

(3) . . .

(4) . . .

Article 13 Capital gains

(1) (Capital gains from the alienation of immovable property.)

(2) (Capital gains from the alienation of movable property.)

(3) Notwithstanding the provisions of paragraph (1) of this Article, capital gains derived by a resident of a Contracting State from the alienation of ships and aircraft operated in international traffic and of movable property pertaining to the operation of such ships and aircraft shall be taxable only in that State.

(4) . . .

(5) . . .

Article 23 Excluded companies

This Agreement shall not apply to companies entitled to any special tax benefit under the Barbados International Business Companies (Exemption from Income Tax) Act 1965–50 as in effect on 26th July 1965 or any substantially similar law enacted by Barbados after that date.

Article 24 Exchange of information

The taxation authorities of the Contracting States shall exchange such information (being information which is at their disposal under their respective taxation laws in the normal course of administration) as is necessary for carrying out the provisions of this Agreement or for the prevention of fraud or for the administration of statutory provisions against legal avoidance in relation to the taxes which are the subject of this Agreement. Any information so exchanged shall be treated as secret and shall not be disclosed to any persons other than those concerned with the assessment and collection of the taxes which are the subject of this Agreement. No information as aforesaid shall be exchanged which would disclose any trade, business, industrial or professional secret or trade process.

Article 25 Consultation

The taxation authorities of the Contracting States may communicate with each other directly for the purpose of giving effect to the provisions of this Agreement and for resolving any difficulty or doubt as to the application or interpretation of the Agreement.

Article 26 Non-discrimination

(1) The residents of a Contracting State shall not be subjected in the other Contracting State to any taxation or any requirement connected therewith which is other or more burdensome than the taxation and connected requirements to which the residents of that other State in the same circumstances are or may be subjected.

(2) Subject to the provisions of paragraph (5) of Article 6 of this Agreement, the taxation on a permanent establishment which an enterprise of a Contracting State has in the other Contracting State shall not be less favourably levied in that other State than the taxation levied on enterprises of that other State carrying on the same activities.

(3) Enterprises of a Contracting State, the capital of which is wholly or partly owned or controlled, directly or indirectly, by one or more residents of the other Contracting State,

shall not be subjected in the first-mentioned Contracting State to any taxation or any requirement connected therewith which is other or more burdensome than the taxation and connected requirements to which other similar enterprises of that first-mentioned State are or may be subjected.

(4) In this Article the term "taxation" means taxes of every kind and description.

(5) Nothing contained in this Article shall be construed as obliging either of the Contracting States to grant to persons not resident in that State those personal allowances and reliefs for tax purposes which are by law available only to persons who are so resident, nor as restricting the taxation of dividends paid to a company which is a resident of the other Contracting State.

Article 6(5): Taxation of a person who carries on a business of any form of insurance.

Article 28 Entry into force

Note: Article 28 provided for the entry into force of this Agreement. It takes effect in the UK from the year of assessment 1969–70 (income tax and capital gains tax) and from the financial year beginning on 1 April 1969 (corporation tax), subject to transitional provisions where greater relief would have been afforded under the 1949 Convention.

Official language: English.

BELGIUM

Convention of 1 June 1987 (SI 1987/Draft)

This Convention replaces the Convention of 29 August 1967 (SI 1970 No 636), see p 29.

Article 1 Personal scope

This Convention shall apply to persons who are residents of one or both of the Contracting States.

Article 2 Taxes covered

(1) The taxes which are the subject of this Convention are:

    (*a*) in the United Kingdom of Great Britain and Northern Ireland:

      (i) the income tax;
     (ii) the corporation tax;
   (iii) the petroleum revenue tax; and
   (iv) the capital gains tax;
   (hereinafter referred to as "United Kingdom tax");
  (b) in Belgium:
      (i) the individual income tax (*l'impôt des personnes physiques—de personenbelasting*);
     (ii) the corporate income tax (*l'impôt des sociétés—de vennootschapsbelasting*);
   (iii) the income tax on legal entities (*l'impôt des personnes morales—de rechtspersonenbelasting*);
   (iv) the income tax on non-residents (*l'impôt des non-residents—de belasting der niet-verblijfhouders*);
  including the prepayments, the surcharges on these taxes and prepayments, and the supplements to the individual income tax;
  (hereinafter referred to as "Belgian tax").

(2) The Convention shall also apply to any identical or substantially similar taxes which are imposed by a Contracting State or a political subdivision or a local authority thereof after the date of signature of the Convention in addition to, or in place of, the existing taxes. The competent authorities of the Contracting States shall notify each other of any substantial changes which have been made in their respective taxation laws.

Article 3 General definitions

(1) In this Convention, unless the context otherwise requires:
  (a) the term "United Kingdom", when used in a geographical sense, means Great Britain and Northern Ireland, including any area outside the territorial sea of the United Kingdom which in accordance with international law has been or may hereafter be designated, under the laws of the United Kingdom concerning the Continental Shelf, as an area within which the rights of the United Kingdom with respect to the sea-bed and sub-soil and their natural resources may be exercised;
  (b) the term "Belgium", when used in a geographical sense means the national territory, the territorial sea and any area adjacent to the territorial sea of Belgium within which in accordance with international law the sovereign rights of the Kingdom of Belgium with respect to the sea-bed and subsoil and their natural resources may be exercised;
  (c) the terms "a Contracting State" and "the other Contracting State" mean the United Kingdom or Belgium, as the context requires;
  (d) the term "tax" means United Kingdom tax or Belgian tax, as the context requires;
  (e) the term "person" comprises an individual, a company and any other body of persons;
  (f) the term "company" means any body corporate or any entity which is treated as a body corporate for tax purposes;
  (g) the terms "enterprise of a Contracting State" and "enterprise of the other Contracting State" mean respectively an enterprise carried on by a resident of a Contracting State and an enterprise carried on by a resident of the other Contracting State;
  (h) the term "national" means:
      (i) in relation to the United Kingdom, any British citizen or any British subject not possessing the citizenship of any other Commonwealth country or territory, provided he has the right of abode in the United Kingdom; and any legal person, partnership, association or other entity deriving its status as such from the law in force in the United Kingdom;
     (ii) in relation to Belgium, any individual possessing the nationality of Belgium and any legal person partnership or association deriving its status as such from the law in force in Belgium;
  (i) the term "international traffic" means any transport by a ship or aircraft operated

25

by an enterprise which has its place of effective management in a Contracting State, except when the ship or aircraft is operated solely between places in the other Contracting State;

(*j*) the term "competent authority" means:

(i) in the United Kingdom, the Commissioners of Inland Revenue or their authorised representative, and

(ii) in Belgium, the Director General of Direct Taxation or his authorised representative;

(*k*) the term "political subdivision", in relation to the United Kingdom, includes Northern Ireland.

(2) As regards the application of the Convention by a Contracting State any term not defined therein shall, unless the context otherwise requires, have the meaning which it has under the law of that State concerning the taxes to which the Convention applies.

Article 6 Income from immovable property

(1) (Taxation of income from immovable property.)

(2) The term "immovable property" shall have the meaning which it has under the law of the Contracting State in which the property in question is situated. The term shall in any case include property accessory to immovable property, livestock and equipment used in agriculture and forestry, rights to which the provisions of general law respecting landed property apply, usufruct of immovable property and rights to variable or fixed payments as consideration for the working of, or the right to work, mineral deposits, sources and other natural resources; ships, boats and aircraft shall not be regarded as immovable property.

(3) . . .

(4) . . .

Article 8 Shipping, inland waterways transport and air transport

(1) Profits from the operation of ships or aircraft in international traffic shall be taxable only in the Contracting State in which the place of effective management of the enterprise is situated.

(2) Profits from the operation of boats engaged in inland waterways transport shall be taxable only in the Contracting State in which the place of effective management of the enterprise is situated.

(3) If the place of effective management of a shipping enterprise or of an inland waterways transport enterprise is aboard a ship or boat, then it shall be deemed to be situated in the Contracting State in which the home harbour of the ship or boat is situated, or, if there is no such home harbour, in the Contracting State of which the operator of the ship or boat is a resident.

(4) Where profits within paragraph (1) of this Article are derived by an enterprise from participation in a pool, a joint business or an international operating agency, the profits attributable to that enterprise shall be taxable only in the State in which the place of effective management of that enterprise is situated.

Offshore activities: See also Article 21 (3) in relation to offshore activities.

Article 13 Capital gains

(1) . . .

(2) . . .

(3) Gains from the alienation of ships or aircraft operated in international traffic, boats engaged in inland waterways transport or movable property pertaining to the operation of such ships, aircraft or boats, shall be taxable only in the Contracting State in which the place of effective management of the enterprise is situated.

(4) . . .

Article 21 Offshore activities

(1) The provisions of this Article shall apply notwithstanding any other provision of this Convention where activities are carried on offshore in a Contracting State in connection with the exploration or exploitation of the sea-bed and subsoil and their natural resources situated in that State (in this Article referred to as "offshore activities").

(2) . . .

(3) Profits from the transportation of supplies or personnel by a ship or aircraft to a location where offshore activities are being carried on, or from the operation of tugboats or anchor handling vessels in connection with such activities, shall be taxable only in the Contracting State in which the place of effective management of the enterprise is situated.

(4) . . .

(5) . . .

Article 24 Non-discrimination

(1) Nationals of a Contracting State shall not be subjected in the other Contracting State to any taxation or any requirement connected therewith, which is other or more burdensome than the taxation and connected requirements to which nationals of that other State in the same circumstances are or may be subjected.

(2) The taxation on a permanent establishment which an enterprise of a Contracting State has in the other Contracting State shall not be less favourably levied in that other State than the taxation levied on enterprises of that other State carrying on the same activities.

(3) Nothing in this Article shall be construed as preventing Belgium:

  (a) from taxing the total amount of the profits attributable to a permanent establishment in Belgium of a company being a resident of the United Kingdom or of an association having its place of effective management in the United Kingdom at the rate of tax provided by the Belgian law, but this rate may not exceed the maximum rate applicable to the whole or a portion of the profits of companies which are residents of Belgium;

  (b) from imposing the movable property prepayment on dividends derived from a holding which is effectively connected with a permanent establishment or a fixed base maintained in Belgian by a company which is a resident of the United Kingdom or by an association which has its place of effective management in the United Kingdom and is taxable as a body corporate in Belgium.

(4) Nothing contained in this Article shall be construed as obliging a Contracting State to grant to residents of the other Contracting State any personal allowances, reliefs and reductions for taxation purposes, on account of civil status or family responsibilities or any other personal circumstances, which it grants to its own residents.

(5) Except where the provisions of paragraph (1) of Article 9, paragraph (6) of Article 11, or paragraph (4) of Article 12 of this Convention apply, interest, royalties and other disbursements paid by an enterprise of a Contracting State to a resident of the other Contracting State shall, for the purpose of determining the taxable profits of such enterprise, be deductible under the same conditions as if they had been paid to a resident of the first-mentioned State.

(6) Enterprises of a Contracting State, the capital of which is wholly or partly owned or controlled, directly or indirectly, by one or more residents of the other Contracting State, shall not be subjected in the first-mentioned State to any taxation or any requirement connected therewith which is other or more burdensome than the taxation and connected requirements to which other similar enterprises of the first-mentioned State are or may be subjected.

(7) The provisions of this Article shall apply to taxes of every kind and description.

Article 25 Mutual agreement procedure

(1) Where a person considers that the actions of one or both of the Contracting States result or will result for him in taxation not in accordance with the provisions of this Convention, he may, irrespective of the remedies provided by the domestic law of those States, pres-

ent his case to the competent authority of the Contracting State of which he is a resident. The case must be presented within three years from the first notification of the action resulting in taxation not in accordance with the provisions of the Convention.

(2) The competent authority shall endeavour, if the objection appears to it to be justified and if it is not itself able to arrive at a satisfactory solution, to resolve the case by mutual agreement with the competent authority of the other Contracting State, with a view to the avoidance of taxation which is not in accordance with the Convention.

(3) The competent authorities of the Contracting States shall endeavour to resolve by mutual agreement any difficulties or doubts arising as to the interpretation or application of the Convention. They may also consult together to consider measures to counteract improper use of the provisions of the Convention.

(4) The competent authorities of the Contracting States may communicate with each other directly for the purpose of reaching an agreement in the sense of the preceding paragraphs and for the purpose of giving effect to the provisions of the Convention.

Article 26 Exchange of information

(1) The competent authorities of the Contracting States shall exchange such information as is necessary for the carrying out of this Convention or of the domestic laws of the Contracting States concerning taxes covered by the Convention insofar as the taxation thereunder is not contrary to the Convention, as well as for the prevention of fiscal evasion. Any information received by a Contracting State shall be treated as secret in the same manner as information obtained under the domestic laws of that State and shall be disclosed only to persons or authorities (including courts and administrative bodies) involved in the assessment or collection of, the enforcement or prosecution in respect of, or the determination of appeals in relation to, the taxes covered by the Convention. Such persons or authorities shall use the information only for such purposes. These persons or authorities may disclose the information in public count proceedings or in judicial decisions.

(2) In no case shall the provisions of paragraph (1) of this Article be construed so as to impose on one of the Contracting States the obligation:

 (a) to carry out administrative measures at variance with the laws and administrative practice of that or of the other Contracting State;

 (b) to supply information which is not obtainable under the laws or in the normal course of the administration of that or of the other Contracting State;

 (c) to supply information which would disclose any trade, business, industrial, commercial or professional secret or trade process, or information, the disclosure of which would be contrary to public policy (*ordre public*).

Article 29 Entry into force

(1) Each of the Contracting States shall notify the other Contracting State of the completion of the procedures required by its law for the bringing into force of this Convention. The Convention shall enter into force on the fifteenth day after the date of the later of these notifications and shall have effect:

 (a) in the United Kingdom:

  (i) in respect of income tax and capital gains tax, for any year of assessment beginning on or after 6 April;

  (ii) in respect of corporation tax, for any financial year beginning on or after 1 April; and

  (iii) in respect of petroleum revenue tax, for any chargeable period beginning on or after 1 January;

 in the calendar year next following that in which the Convention enters into force;

 (b) in Belgium:

  (i) in respect of all tax due at source on income credited or payable on or after 1 January; and

  (ii) in respect of all tax other than tax due at source on income of any chargeable period ending on or after 31 December;

in the calendar year next following that in which the Convention enters into force.

(2) The Convention between Her Britannic Majesty in respect of the United Kingdom of Great Britain and Northern Ireland and His Majesty The King of the Belgians for the avoidance of double taxation and the prevention of fiscal evasion with respect to taxes on income signed at London on 29 August 1967 shall terminate and cease to be effective in relation to any tax for any period for which this Convention has effect in accordance with paragraph (1) of this Article as respects that tax.

Note: This Convention had not entered into force on 6 April 1988.

Official languages: The French language text, the Netherlands language text and the English language text of this Convention are equally authoritative.

Convention of 29 August 1967 (SI 1970 No 636)

This Convention has been replaced by the Convention of 1 June 1987 (SI 1987/Draft), see p 24.

Article I [Personal scope]

This Convention shall apply to persons who are residents of one or both of the territories.

Article II [Taxes covered]

(1) The taxes which are the subject of this Convention are:
 (a) in the United Kingdom of Great Britain and Northern Ireland:
  (i) the income tax (including surtax);
  (ii) the corporation tax;
  (iii) the capital gains tax
  (hereinafter referred to as "United Kingdom tax");
 (b) in Belgium:
  (i) the individual income tax (l'impôt des personnes physiques);
  (ii) the corporate income tax (l'impôt des sociétés);
  (iii) the income tax on legal entities (l'impôt des personnes morales);
  (iv) the income tax on non-residents (l'impôt des non-résidents);
  (v) the prepayments and additional prepayments (les précomptes et compléments de précomptes); and
  (vi) surcharges (centimes additionnels) on any of the taxes referred to in heads (i) to (v) including the communal supplement to the individual income tax (la taxe communale additionnelle à l'impôt des personnes physiques)
  (hereinafter referred to as "Belgian tax").

(2) The Convention shall also apply to any identical or substantially similar taxes which are subsequently imposed in addition to, or in place of, the existing taxes.

BELGIUM

Article III [General definitions]

(1) In this Convention, unless the context otherwise requires:

(a) the term "United Kingdom" means Great Britain and Northern Ireland including any area outside the territorial sea of the United Kingdom which has been or may hereafter be designated, under the laws of the United Kingdom concerning the Continental Shelf, as an area within which the rights of the United Kingdom with respect to the sea-bed and sub-soil and their natural resources may be exercised;

(b) the term "Belgium" means the territory of the Kingdom of Belgium; in the event of provision being made in Belgian law to that effect, it shall also include the sea bed and the subsoil of the North Sea outside the Belgian territorial sea with respect to which Belgium will exercise sovereign rights of exploration and exploitation; the delimitation of this area shall be, in this case, notified to the United Kingdom through diplomatic channels as soon as it has been established by agreements with the United Kingdom, France and the Netherlands;

(c) the terms "one of the territories" and "the other territory" mean the United Kingdom or Belgium as the context requires;

(d) the term "competent authority" means, in the case of Belgium the competent authority according to Belgian legislation; in the case of the United Kingdom the Commissioners of Inland Revenue or their authorised representative; and, in the case of any territory to which the Convention is extended under Article XXVIII, the competent authority for the administration in such territory of the taxes to which the Convention applies;

(e) the term "tax" means United Kingdom tax or Belgian tax, as the context requires;

(f) the term "person" comprises an individual, a company and any other body of persons;

(g) the term "company" means any body corporate or any entity which is treated as a body corporate for tax purposes;

(h) the terms "enterprise of one of the territories" and "enterprise of the other territory" mean respectively an enterprise carried on by a resident of one of the territories and an enterprise carried on by a resident of the other territory;

(i) the term "international traffic" includes traffic between places in any state in the course of a voyage which extends over two or more states.

(2) Where under the Convention a person is entitled to exemption or relief from tax in one of the territories on certain income if (with or without further conditions) he is subject to tax in the other territory in respect thereof and he is subject to tax there by reference to the amount of that income which is remitted to or received in, that other territory the amount of that income on which exemption or relief is to be allowed in the first-mentioned territory shall be limited to the amount so remitted or received.

(3) As regards the application of the Convention by either High Contracting Party any term not otherwise defined shall, unless the context otherwise requires, have the meaning which it has under the laws of that Party relating to the taxes which are the subject of the Convention.

Article VI [Income from immovable property]

(1) (Taxation of income from immovable property.)

(2) The term "immovable property" shall be defined in accordance with the law of the High Contracting Party of the territory in which the property in question is situated. The term shall in any case include property accessory to immovable property, livestock and equipment used in agriculture and forestry, rights to which the provisions of general law respecting landed property apply, usufruct of immovable property and rights to variable or fixed payments as consideration for the working of, or the right to work, mineral deposits, sources and other natural resources; ships, boats and aircraft shall not be regarded as immovable property.

(3) . . .

(4) . . .

Article VIII [Shipping and air transport]

(1) Profits from the operation of ships or aircraft in international traffic shall be taxable only in the territory in which the place of effective management of the enterprise is situated.

(2) If the place of effective management of a shipping enterprise is aboard a ship, then it shall be

deemed to be situated in the territory in which the home harbour of the ship is situated, or, if there is no such home harbour, in the territory of which the operator of the ship is a resident.

Article XIII [Capital gains]

(1) Gains from the alienation of property, whether movable or immovable, forming part of the business property of a permanent establishment which an enterprise of one of the territories has in the other territory or of property, whether movable or immovable, pertaining to a fixed base available to a resident of one of the territories in the other territory for the purpose of performing professional services, including such gains from the alienation of such a permanent establishment (alone or together with the whole enterprise) or of such a fixed base, may be taxed in the other territory. However, gains from the alienation of ships and aircraft operated in international traffic and movable property pertaining to the operation of such ships and aircraft shall be taxable only in the territory in which the place of effective management of the enterprise is situated.

(2) . . .

Article XXIV [Non-discrimination]

(1) The nationals of one High Contracting Party shall not be subjected in the territory of the other High Contracting Party to any taxation or any requirement connected therewith which is other or more burdensome than the taxation and connected requirements to which nationals of that latter Party in the same circumstances are or may be subjected.

(2) The term "nationals" means:

  (a) in relation to the United Kingdom, all British subjects and British protected persons

   (i) residing in the United Kingdom, or any territory to which this Convention is extended under Article XXVIII, or
   (ii) deriving their status as such from connection with the United Kingdom or any territory to which the Convention is extended under Article XXVIII,

  and all legal persons, partnerships and associations deriving their status as such from the law in force in the United Kingdom or in any territory to which the Convention is extended under Article XXVIII;

  (b) in relation to Belgium, all individuals possessing the nationality of Belgium and all legal persons, partnerships and associations deriving their status as such from the law in force in Belgium.

(3) The taxation on a permanent establishment which an enterprise of one of the territories has in the other territory shall not be less favourably levied in that other territory than the taxation levied on enterprises of that other territory carrying on the same activities.

This provision shall not be construed as preventing:

  (a) Belgium from charging the profits of a permanent establishment in Belgium of a company being a resident of the United Kingdom at a rate of tax which does not—before the application of surcharges mentioned in paragraph (1) (b) (vi) of Article II—exceed the basic rate (at present 30 per cent) charged on a company being a resident of Belgium by more than 5 percentage points; or

  (b) United Kingdom from charging the profits of a permanent establishment in the United Kingdom of a company being a resident of Belgium at a rate of tax which does not exceed the rate charged on a company being a resident of the United Kingdom by more than 5 percentage points.

(4) Enterprises of one of the territories, the capital of which is wholly or partly owned or controlled, directly or indirectly, by one or more residents of the other territory shall not be subjected in the first-mentioned territory to any taxation or any requirement connected therewith which is other or more burdensome than the taxation and connected requirements to which other similar enterprises of that first-mentioned territory are or may be subjected.

(5) This Article shall not be construed as entitling a resident of one of the territories to any personal allowances, reliefs and reductions for taxation purposes on account of civil status or family responsibilities which the laws of the other territory grant only to residents of that territory, or as restricting the taxation

of dividends paid by a company which is a resident of one of the territories to a company which is a resident of the other territory.

(6) In this Article the term "taxation" means taxes of every kind and description.

Article XXV [Mutual agreement procedure]

(1) Where a resident of one of the territories considers that the actions of one or both of the High Contracting Parties result or will result for him in double taxation not in accordance with this Convention, he may, independently of the remedies provided by the national laws of those Parties, address to the competent authority of the High Contracting Party of the territory of which he is a resident an application in writing stating the grounds for claiming revision of the incorrect taxation. The said application must be submitted before the expiry of a period of two years from the notification of liability to or the deduction at source of the second charge to tax.

(2) The competent authority shall endeavour, if the objection appears to it to be justified and if it is not itself able to arrive at an appropriate solution, to resolve the case by mutual agreement with the competent authority of the other High Contracting Party, with a view to the avoidance of double taxation not in accordance with the Convention.

(3) The competent authorities of the High Contracting Parties shall endeavour to resolve by mutual agreement any difficulties or doubts arising as to the interpretation or application of the Convention.

In case of differing interpretations of the same concept in the laws of both High Contracting Parties their competent authorities may, on a basis of reciprocity, reach a common interpretation for the purpose of applying the Convention.

(4) The competent authorities of the High Contracting Parties may communicate with each other directly for the purpose of reaching an agreement in the sense of the preceding paragraphs or for the purpose of giving effect to the provisions of the Convention.

Article XXVI [Exchange of information]

(1) The competent authorities of the High Contracting Parties shall exchange such information as is necessary for carrying out the provisions of this Convention or for the prevention of fraud or for the administration of statutory provisions against legal avoidance in relation to the taxes which are the subject of the Convention. Any information so exchanged shall be treated as secret and shall not be disclosed to any persons other than persons (including a Court) concerned with the assessment or collection of, or the determination of appeals in relation to, the taxes which are the subject of the Convention.

(2) In no case shall the provisions of paragraph (1) be construed so as to impose on the competent authority of either High Contracting Party the obligation:

(a) to carry out administrative measures at variance with the laws or administrative practice prevailing in either of the territories;

(b) to supply particulars which are not obtainable under the laws or in the normal course of the administration in that or the other territory; or

(c) to supply information which would disclose any trade, business, industrial, commercial or professional secret or trade process, or information the disclosure of which would be contrary to public policy (ordre public).

Article XXIX [Entry into force]

Note: Article XXIX provided for the entry into force of this Convention. It takes effect in the UK from the year of assessment 1965–66 (capital gains tax), 1966–67 (income tax) and from the financial year beginning on 1 April 1964 (corporation tax), subject to transitional provisions where greater relief would have been afforded under the 1953 Convention.

Article XXX [Termination]

This Convention shall remain in force until denounced by one of the High Contracting Parties. Either High Contracting Party may denounce the Convention, through diplomatic channels, by giving notice of termination at least six months before the end of any calendar year after the year 1970. In such event the Convention shall cease to have effect:

(a) in the United Kingdom:
  (i) as respects income tax (including surtax) and capital gains tax for any year of assessment beginning on or after the sixth day of April in the calendar year next following
  that in which the notice is given;
  (ii) as respects corporation tax for any financial year beginning on or after the first day in
  April in the calendar year next following that in which the notice is given;
(b) in Belgium:
  (i) as respects all tax due at source on income credited or payable on or after the first day of
  January in the calendar year next following that in which the notice is given;
  (ii) as respects all tax other than tax due at source on income taxable for any fiscal year
  (exercice d'imposition) beginning on or after the first day of January of the calendar
  year next following that in which the notice is given.

Note: This Convention is terminated by the Convention of 1 June 1987 (SI 1987/Draft) Article 29(2)
with effect from the date on which the 1987 Convention comes into effect (see p 24).

Official languages: The French language text, the Netherlands language text and the English
language text of this Convention are equally authoritative.

BELIZE

(formerly British Honduras)

Arrangement of 19 December 1947 (SR & O 1947 No 2866)

Printed as amended by the Arrangement of 12 December 1973 (SI 1973 No 2097). (The Arrangement of 8
April 1968 (SI 1968 No 573) does not amend the Articles printed below.)

Paragraph 1 [Taxes covered]

(1) The taxes which are the subject of this Arrangement are—
  (a) In the United Kingdom:
      The income tax (including surtax) and the profits tax (hereinafter referred to as
      "United Kingdom tax").
  (b) In Belize:
      The income tax (including surtax) (hereinafter referred to as "Belize tax").
(2) This Arrangement shall also apply to any other taxes of a substantially similar character imposed in the United Kingdom or Belize after this Arrangement has come into force.

Corporation tax: This Arrangement covers United Kingdom corporation tax, by virtue of ICTA
1988, s 789(1).

Paragraph 2 [General definitions]

(1) In this Arrangement, unless the context otherwise requires—
  (a) the term "United Kingdom" means Great Britain and Northern Ireland, exclud-
      ing the Channel Islands and the Isle of Man.
  (b) . . .
  (c) the terms "one of the territories" and "the other territory" mean the United King-
      dom or Belize, as the context requires.

(*d*) the term "tax" means United Kingdom tax or Belize tax, as the context requires.

(*e*) the term "person" includes any body of persons, corporate or not corporate.

(*f*) the term "company" includes any body corporate.

(*g*) the terms "resident of the United Kingdom" and "resident of Belize" mean respectively any person who is resident in the United Kingdom for the purposes of United Kingdom tax and not resident in Belize for the purposes of Belize tax and any person who is resident in Belize for the purposes of Belize tax and not resident in the United Kingdom for the purposes of United Kingdom tax; and a company shall be regarded as resident in the United Kingdom if its business is managed and controlled in the United Kingdom and as resident in Belize if its business is managed and controlled in Belize.

(*h*) the terms "resident of one of the territories" and "resident of the other territory" mean a person who is a resident of the United Kingdom or a person who is a resident of Belize, as the context requires.

(*i*) . . .

(*j*) . . .

(*k*) . . .

(2) Where under this Arrangement any income is exempt from tax in one of the territories if (with or without other conditions) it is subject to tax in the other territory, and that income is subject to tax in that other territory by reference to the amount thereof which is remitted to or received in that other territory, the exemption to be allowed under this Arrangement in the first-mentioned territory shall apply only to the amount so remitted or received.

(3) In the application of the provisions of this Arrangement by the United Kingdom or Belize, any term not otherwise defined shall, unless the context otherwise requires, have the meaning which it has under the laws of the United Kingdom, or, as the case may be, Belize, relating to the taxes which are the subject of this Arrangement.

Paragraph 5 [Shipping and air transport]

Notwithstanding the provisions of paragraphs 3 and 4, profits which a resident of one of the territories derives from operating ships or aircraft shall be exempt from tax in the other territory.

Paragraph 3: Taxation of industrial or commercial profits.
Paragraph 4: Taxation of profits of associated enterprises.

Paragraph 14 [Exchange of information]

(1) The taxation authorities of the United Kingdom and Belize shall exchange such information (being information available under their respective taxation laws) as is necessary for carrying out the provisions of this Arrangement or for the prevention of fraud or the administration of statutory provisions against legal avoidance in relation to the taxes which are the subject of this Arrangement. Any information so exchanged shall be treated as secret and shall not be disclosed to any persons other than those concerned with the assessment and collection of the taxes which are the subject of this Arrangement. No information shall be exchanged which would disclose any trade secret or trade process.

(2) As used in this paragraph, the term "taxation authorities" means the Commissioners of Inland Revenue or their authorised representative in the case of the United Kingdom and the Commissioners of Income Tax or their authorised representative in the case of Belize.

Paragraph 15 [Entry into force]

Note: Paragraph 15 provided for the entry into force of the 1947 Arrangement. It takes effect in the UK in its amended form from the year of assessment 1973–74 (income tax) and from the financial year beginning on 1 April 1973 (corporation tax).

Official language: English.

BOTSWANA

Agreement of 5 October 1977 (SI 1978 No 183)

Article 1 Taxes covered

(1) The taxes which are the subject of this Agreement are:
   (a) in the United Kingdom of Great Britain and Northern Ireland:
      (i) the income tax; and
      (ii) the corporation tax;
   (b) in Botswana:
      the income tax.

(2) This Agreement shall also apply to any identical or substantially similar taxes which are imposed by either Contracting State after the date of signature of this Agreement in addition to, or in place of, the existing taxes. The competent authorities of the Contracting States shall notify to each other any changes which are made in their respective taxation laws.

(3) . . .

Article 2 General definitions

(1) In this Agreement, unless the context otherwise requires:
   (a) the term "United Kingdom" means Great Britain and Northern Ireland, including any area outside the territorial sea of the United Kingdom which in accordance with international law has been or may hereafter be designated, under the laws of the United Kingdom concerning the Continental Shelf, as an area within which the rights of the United Kingdom with respect to the sea-bed and sub-soil and their natural resources may be exercised;
   (b) the term "Botswana" means the Republic of Botswana;
   (c) the term "national" means:
      (i) in relation to the United Kingdom, any citizen of the United Kingdom and Colonies, or any British subject not possessing that citizenship or the citizenship of any other Commonwealth country or territory, provided that in either case he has the right of abode in the United Kingdom; and any legal person, association or other entity deriving its status as such from the law in force in the United Kingdom;
      (ii) in relation to Botswana, any citizen of Botswana who derives his status as such from his connection with Botswana and any other person deriving its legal status as such from the law in force in Botswana;
   (d) the term "United Kingdom tax" means tax imposed by the United Kingdom being tax to which this Agreement applies by virtue of the provisions of Article 1; the term "Botswana tax" means tax imposed by Botswana being tax to which this Agreement applies by virtue of the provisions of Article 1;
   (e) the term "tax" means United Kingdom tax or Botswana tax, as the context requires;
   (f) the terms "a Contracting State" and "the other Contracting State" mean the United Kingdom or Botswana, as the context requires;

35

(g) the term "person" comprises an individual, a company and any other body of persons corporate or not corporate;

(h) the term "company" means any body corporate or any entity which is treated as a body corporate for tax purposes;

(i) the terms "enterprise of a Contracting State" and "enterprise of the other Contracting State" mean respectively an enterprise carried on by a resident of a Contracting State and an enterprise carried on by a resident of the other Contracting State;

(j) the term "competent authority" means, in the case of the United Kingdom the Commissioners of Inland Revenue or their authorised representative, and in the case of Botswana the Commissioners of Taxes or his authorised representative;

(k) . . .

(2) As regards the application of this Agreement by a Contracting State any term not otherwise defined shall, unless the context otherwise requires, have the meaning which it has under the laws of that Contracting State relating to the taxes which are the subject of this Agreement.

Article 3 Fiscal domicile

(1) For the purposes of this Agreement, the term "resident of a Contracting State" means, subject to the provisions of paragraphs (2) and (3) of this Article, any person who, under the law of that State, is liable to taxation therein by reason of his domicile, residence, place of management or any other criterion of a similar nature; the term does not include any individual who is liable to tax in that Contracting State only by reason of the fact that he derives income from sources therein. The terms "resident of the other Contracting State", "resident of both Contracting States", "resident of the United Kingdom" and "resident of Botswana" shall be construed accordingly.

(2) Where by reason of the provisions of paragraph (1) of this Article an individual is a resident of both Contracting States, then his status shall be determined in accordance with the following rules:

(a) he shall be deemed to be a resident of the Contracting State in which he has a permanent home available to him. If he has a permanent home available to him in both Contracting States, he shall be deemed to be a resident of the Contracting State with which his personal and economic relations are closer;

(b) if the Contracting State with which his personal and economic relations are closer cannot be determined, or if he has not a permanent home available to him in either Contracting State, he shall be deemed to be a resident of the Contracting State in which he has an habitual abode;

(c) if he has an habitual abode in both Contracting States or in neither of them, he shall be deemed to be a resident of the Contracting State of which he is a national;

(d) if he is a national of both Contracting States or of neither of them, the competent authorities of the Contracting States shall settle the question by mutual agreement.

(3) Where by reason of the provisions of paragraph (1) of this Article a person other than an individual is a resident of both Contracting States, then it shall be deemed to be a resident of the Contracting State in which its place of effective management is situated.

Article 6 Income from immovable property

(1) (Taxation of income from immovable property.)

(2) (a) the term "immovable property" shall, subject to the provisions of sub-paragraph (b) below, be defined in accordance with the law of the Contracting State in which the property in question is situated.

(b) the term "immovable property" shall in any case include property accessory to immovable property, livestock and equipment used in agriculture and forestry, rights to which the provisions of general law respecting landed property apply, usufruct of immovable property and rights to variable or fixed payments as consideration for the working of, or the right to work, or the right to prospect for, mineral deposits, sources and other natural resources, and mining and prospecting information; ships, boats and aircraft shall not be regarded as immovable property.

(3) . . .

(4) . . .

Article 8 Shipping and air transport

A resident of a Contracting State shall be exempt from tax in the other Contracting State on profits from the operation of ships or aircraft other than profits from voyages of ships or aircraft confined solely to places in the other Contracting State.

Article 21 Non-discrimination

(1) Nationals of a Contracting State shall not be subjected in the other Contracting State to any taxation or any requirement connected therewith which is other or more burdensome than the taxation and connected requirements to which nationals of that other State in the same circumstances are or may be subjected.

(2) The taxation on a permanent establishment which an enterprise of a Contracting State has in the other Contracting State shall not be less favourably levied in that other State than the taxation levied on enterprises of that other State carrying on the same activities.

(3) Enterprises of a Contracting State, the capital of which is wholly or partly owned or controlled, directly or indirectly, by one or more residents of the other Contracting State, shall not be subjected in the first-mentioned Contracting State to any taxation or any requirement connected therewith which is other or more burdensome than the taxation and connected requirements to which other similar enterprises of that first-mentioned State are or may be subjected.

(4) Nothing contained in this Article shall be construed as obliging either Contracting State to grant to individuals not resident in that State any of the personal allowances, reliefs and reductions for tax purposes which are granted to individuals so resident, nor as obliging the United Kingdom to grant to a company which is a resident of Botswana a greater relief from United Kingdom income tax chargeable on dividends received from a company which is a resident of the United Kingdom than the relief to which the first-mentioned company may be entitled under the provisions of Article 10 of this Agreement.

Article 22 Mutual agreement procedure

(1) Where a resident of a Contracting State considers that the actions of one or both of the Contracting States result or will result for him in taxation not in accordance with this Agreement, he may, notwithstanding the remedies provided by the national laws of those States, present his case to the competent authority of the Contracting State of which he is a resident.

(2) The competent authority shall endeavour, if the objection appears to it to be justified and if it is not itself able to arrive at an appropriate solution, to resolve the case by mutual agreement with the competent authority of the other Contracting State, with a view to the avoidance of taxation not in accordance with the Agreement.

(3) The competent authorities of the Contracting States shall endeavour to resolve by mutual agreement any difficulties or doubts arising as to the interpretation or application of the Agreement.

(4) The competent authorities of the Contracting States may communicate with each other directly for the purpose of reaching an agreement in the sense of the preceding paragraphs.

Article 23 Exchange of information

The competent authorities of the Contracting States shall exchange such information (being information which is at their disposal under their respective taxation laws in the normal course of administration) as is necessary for carrying out the provisions of this Agreement or for the prevention of fraud or the administration of statutory provisions against legal avoidance in relation to the taxes which are the subject of this Agreement. Any information so exchanged shall be treated as secret but may be disclosed to persons (including a court or administrative body) concerned with assessment, collection, enforcement or prosecution in respect of taxes which are the subject of this Agreement. No information shall be exchanged which would disclose any trade, business, industrial or professional secret or any trade process.

Article 24 Entry into force

Note: Article 24 provided for the entry into force of this Agreement. It takes effect in the UK from the year of assessment 1976–77 (income tax) and from the financial year beginning on 1 April 1976 (corporation tax).

Official language: English.

BRAZIL

Agreement of 29 December 1967 (SI 1968 No 572)

Paragraph (1) [Exemption of UK undertakings]

(1) The Government of Brazil shall in accordance with Article 22 of the Income Tax Regulations (Decree 58.400 of 10th May, 1965) exempt all income derived from the business of shipping and air transport in international traffic by United Kingdom undertakings engaged in such business from all taxes which are covered by the Federal income tax law and all similar Federal taxes on income or profits which are, or may become, chargeable in Brazil.

Paragraph (2) [Exemption of Brazilian undertakings]

(2) The Government of the United Kingdom shall exempt all income derived from the business of shipping and air transport in international traffic by Brazilian undertakings engaged in such business from income tax and corporation tax and all other taxes on income or profits which are, or may become, chargeable in the United Kingdom.

Paragraph (3) [Definitions]

(3) (*a*) The expression "United Kingdom undertakings" means the Government of the United Kingdom and companies managed and controlled in the United Kingdom, provided that they have their Head Offices in the United Kingdom.

(*b*) The expression "Brazilian undertakings" means the Government of Brazil and companies managed and controlled in Brazil, provided that they are established in accordance with Brazilian law and have their Head Offices in Brazil.

Paragraph (4) [Entry into force]

The exemptions provided for in paragraphs (1) and (2) above shall apply to all income earned from 1st January 1967.

Official language: English.

BRUNEI

Arrangement of 8 December 1950 (SI 1950 No 1977)

(The Arrangements of 4 March 1968 (SI 1968 No 306) and 12 December 1973 (SI 1973 No 2098) do not amend the Articles printed below.)

Paragraph 1 [Taxes covered]

(1) The taxes which are the subject of this Arrangement are—
    (*a*) In the United Kingdom:
        The income tax (including surtax) and the profits tax (hereinafter referred to as "United Kingdom tax").
    (*b*) In Brunei:
        The income tax (hereinafter referred to as "Brunei tax").
(2) This Arrangement shall also apply to any other taxes of a substantially similar character imposed in the United Kingdom or Brunei after this Arrangement has come into force.

Corporation tax: This Arrangement covers United Kingdom corporation tax, by virtue of ICTA 1988 s 789(1).

Paragraph 2 [General definitions]

(1) In this Arrangement, unless the context otherwise requires—
    (*a*) the term "United Kingdom " means Great Britain and Northern Ireland, excluding the Channel Islands and the Isle of Man.
    (*b*) the term "Brunei" means the State of Brunei.
    (*c*) the terms "one of the territories" and "the other territory" mean the United Kingdom or Brunei, as the context requires.
    (*d*) the term "tax" means United Kingdom tax or Brunei tax, as the context requires.
    (*e*) the term "person" includes any body of persons, corporate or not corporate.
    (*f*) the term "company" includes any body corporate.
    (*g*) the terms "resident of the United Kingdom" and "resident of Brunei" mean

respectively any person who is resident in the United Kingdom for the purposes of United Kingdom tax and not resident in Brunei for the purposes of Brunei tax and any person who is resident in Brunei for the purposes of Brunei tax and not resident in the United Kingdom for the purposes of United Kingdom tax; and a company shall be regarded as resident in the United Kingdom if its business is managed and controlled in the United Kingdom and as resident in Brunei if its business is managed and controlled in Brunei.

(h) the terms "resident of one of the territories" and "resident of the other territory" mean a person who is a resident of the United Kingdom or a person who is a resident of Brunei, as the context requires.

(i)–(k) . . .

(2) Where under this Arrangement any income is exempt from tax in one of the territories if (with or without other conditions) it is subject to tax in the other territory, and that income is subject to tax in that other territory by reference to the amount thereof which is remitted to or received in that other territory, the exemption to be allowed under this Arrangement in the first-mentioned territory shall apply only to the amount so remitted or received.

Paragraph 5 [Shipping and air transport]

Notwithstanding the provisions of paragraphs 3 and 4, profits which a resident of one of the territories derives from operating ships or aircraft shall be exempt from tax in the other territory.

Paragraph 3: Taxation of industrial or commercial profits.
Paragraph 4: Taxation of profits of associated enterprises.

Paragraph 13 [Exchange of information]

(1) The taxation authorities of the United Kingdom and Brunei shall exchange such information (being information available under their respective taxation laws) as is necessary for carrying out the provisions of this Arrangement or for the prevention of fraud or the administration of statutory provisions against legal avoidance in relation to the taxes which are the subject of this Arrangement. Any information so exchanged shall be treated as secret and shall not be disclosed to any persons other than those concerned with the assessment and collection of the taxes which are the subject of this Arrangement. No information shall be exchanged which would disclose any trade secret or trade process.

(2) As used in this paragraph, the term "taxation authorities" means the Commissioners of Inland Revenue or their authorised representative in the case of the United Kingdom and the Collector of Income Tax or his authorised representative in the case of Brunei.

Paragraph 14 [Entry into force]

· **Note:** Article 14 provided for the entry into force of this Arrangement. It takes effect, in general, from 1950–51.

Official language: English.

BULGARIA

Convention of 16 September 1987 (SI 1987 No 2054)

Article 1 Personal scope

This Convention shall apply to persons who are residents of one or both of the Contracting States.

Article 2 Taxes covered

(1) The taxes which are the subject of this Convention are:
(a) in the United Kingdom:
(i) the income tax;
(ii) the corporation tax; and
(iii) the capital gains tax;
(hereinafter referred to as "United Kingdom tax");
(b) in Bulgaria:
(i) tax on total income (*danak varhu obshtiya dohod*);
(ii) tax on income of single males and females, widows and widowers, divorced persons and families without children (*danak varhu dohoda na heozheneni, neomazheni, ovdoveli, razvedeni i semeyni bez detsa*);
(iii) tax on profits (*danak varhu pechalbi*);
(hereinafter referred to as "Bulgarian tax").

(2) This Convention shall also apply to any identical or substantially similar taxes which are imposed by either Contracting State after the date of signature of this Convention in addition to, or in place of, the taxes of that Contracting State referred to in paragraph (1) of this Article. The competent authorities of the Contracting States shall notify each other of any substantial changes which are made in their respective taxation laws.

Article 3 General definitions

(1) In this Convention, unless the context otherwise requires:
(a) the term "United Kingdom" means Great Britain and Northern Ireland, including any area outside the territorial sea of the United Kingdom which in accordance with international law has been or may hereafter be designated, under the laws of the United Kingdom concerning the Continental Shelf, as an area within which the rights of the United Kingdom with respect to the sea-bed and sub-soil and their natural resources may be exercised;
(b) the term "Bulgaria" means the People's Republic of Bulgaria and when used in a geographical sense the territory over which the People's Republic of Bulgaria

41

exercises its State sovereignty as well as the Continental Shelf and exclusive economic zone within which the People's Republic of Bulgaria exercises sovereign rights in accordance with international law;

(c) the term "national" means:

    (i) in relation to the United Kingdom, any British citizen or any British subject not possessing the citizenship of any other Commonwealth country or territory, provided he has the right of abode in the United Kingdom; and any legal person, partnership, association or other entity deriving its status as such from the law in force in the United Kingdom;

    (ii) in relation to Bulgaria, any individual who has under the law of Bulgaria the status of Bulgarian national and any legal person, partnership or other entity deriving its status as such from the law in force in Bulgaria;

(d) the terms "a Contracting State" and "the other Contracting State" mean the United Kingdom or Bulgaria as the context requires;

(e) the term "person" means an individual, and;

    (i) in the case of the United Kingdom, a body corporate (including companies or any other entity which is treated as a body corporate for tax purposes) and any other body of persons:

    (ii) in the case of Bulgaria, a legal person or any joint venture established in accordance with Bulgarian law, and any other body of persons;

but does not include a partnership which is not a legal person.

(f) the terms "enterprise of a Contracting State" and "enterprise of the other Contracting State" mean respectively an enterprise carried on by a resident of a Contracting State and an enterprise carried on by a resident of the other Contracting State;

(g) the term "international traffic" means any transport by a ship, aircraft or road vehicle operated by an enterprise which has its place of effective management in a Contracting State, except when the ship, aircraft or road vehicle is operated solely between places in the other Contracting State;

(h) the term "competent authority" means, in the case of the United Kingdom the Commissioners of Inland Revenue or their authorised representative, and in the case of Bulgaria the Minister of Finance or his authorised representative.

(2) As regards the application of this Convention by a Contracting State any term not otherwise defined shall, unless the context otherwise requires, have the meaning which it has under the laws of that Contracting State relating to the taxes which are the subject of this Convention.

Article 4 Residence

(1) For the purposes of this Convention, the term "resident of a Contracting State" means:

(a) in the case of the United Kingdom, any person who, under the law of the United Kingdom, is liable to tax therein by reason of his domicile, residence, place of management or any other criterion of a similar nature;

(b) in the case of Bulgaria, any individual who is a national of Bulgaria, as well as any legal person which has its head office in Bulgaria or is registered therein.

(2) (a) Where by reason of the provisions of paragraph (1) of this Article an individual is a resident of both Contracting States, then he shall be deemed to be a resident of the State with which his personal and economic relations are closer (centre of vital interests);

(b) if the Contracting State in which he has his centre of vital interests cannot be determined, the competent authorities of the Contracting States shall settle the question by mutual agreement.

(3) Where by reason of the provisions of paragraph (1) of this Article a person other than an individual is a resident of both Contracting States, then it shall be deemed to be a resident of the State in which its place of effective management is situated.

Article 6 Income from immovable property

(1) (Taxation of income from immovable property.)

(2) The term "immovable property" shall have the meaning which it has under the law of the Contracting State in which the property in question is situated. The term shall in any case include property accessory to immovable property, livestock and equipment used in agriculture and forestry, rights to which the provisions of general law respecting landed property apply, usufruct of immovable property and rights to variable or fixed payments as consideration for the working of, or the right to work, mineral deposits, sources and other natural resources; ships, aircraft and road vehicles shall not be regarded as immovable property.

(3) . . .

(4) . . .

Article 8 International traffic

(1) Profits from the operation of ships, aircraft or road vehicles in international traffic shall be taxable only in the Contracting State in which the place of effective management of the enterprise is situated.

(2) If the place of effective management of a shipping enterprise is aboard a ship, then it shall be deemed to be situated in the Contracting State in which the home harbour of the ship is situated, or, if there is no such home harbour, in the Contracting State of which the operator of the ship is resident.

(3) The provisions of paragraph (1) of this Article shall also apply to profits derived from participation in a pool, a joint business or an international operating agency.

Article 12 Capital gains

(1) . . .

(2) . . .

(3) Gains from the alienation of ships, aircraft or road vehicles operated in international traffic or movable property pertaining to the operation of such ships, aircraft or road vehicles shall be taxable only in the Contracting State in which the place of effective management of the enterprise is situated.

(4) . . .

Article 23 Non-discrimination

(1) Nationals of a Contracting State, as defined in Article 3 of this Convention, shall not be subjected in the other Contracting State to any taxation or any requirement connected therein which is other or more burdensome than the taxation and connected requirements to which nationals of that other State in the same circumstances are or may be subjected.

(2) The taxation on a permanent establishment which an enterprise of a Contracting State has in the other Contracting State shall not be less favourably levied in that other State than the taxation levied on enterprises of that other State carrying on the same activities.

(3) Except where the provisions of paragraph (4) of Article 10 or paragraph (4) of Article 11 of this Convention apply interest, royalties and other disbursements paid by an enterprise of a Contracting State to a resident of the other Contracting State shall, for the purpose of determining the taxable profits of such enterprise, be deductible under the same conditions as if they had been paid to a resident of the first-mentioned State.

(4) Enterprises of a Contracting State, the capital of which is wholly or partly owned, directly or indirectly, by one or more residents of the other Contracting State, shall not be subjected in the first-mentioned State to any taxation or any requirement connected therewith which is other or more burdensome than the taxation and connected requirements to which other similar enterprises of that first-mentioned State are or may be subjected.

(5) Nothing contained in this Article shall be construed as obliging either Contracting State to grant to individuals not resident in that State any of the personal allowances, reliefs and reductions for tax purposes which are granted to individuals so resident.

(6) In this Article the term "taxation" means the taxes covered by this Convention.

Article 24 Mutual agreement procedure

(1) Where a person considers that the actions of one or both of the Contracting States result or will result in taxation not in accordance with the provisions of this Convention, he may, irrespective of the remedies provided by the domestic law of those States, present his case to the competent authority of the Contracting State of which he is a resident or, if his case comes under paragraph (1) of Article 23 of this Convention, to that of the Contracting State of which he is a national. The case must be presented within three years from the first notification of the action resulting in taxation not in accordance with the provisions of the Convention.

(2) The competent authority shall endeavour, if the objection appears to it to be justified and if it is not itself able to arrive at a satisfactory solution, to resolve the case by mutual agreement with the competent authority of the other Contracting State, with a view to the avoidance of taxation not in accordance with the Convention.

(3) The competent authorities of the Contracting State shall endeavour to resolve by mutual agreement any difficulties or doubts arising as to the interpretation or application of the Convention.

(4) The competent authorities of the Contracting States may communicate with each other directly for the purpose of reaching an agreement in the sense of the preceding paragraphs.

Article 25 Exchange of information

(1) The competent authorities of the Contracting States shall exchange such information as is necessary for carrying out the provisions of this Convention or of the domestic laws of the Contracting States concerning taxes covered by the Convention insofar as the taxation thereunder is not contrary to the Convention. Any information received by a Contracting State shall be treated as secret and shall be disclosed only to persons or authorities (including courts and administrative bodies) involved in the assessment or collection of, the enforcement or prosecution in respect of, or the determination of appeals in relation to, the taxes covered by the Convention. Such persons or authorities shall use the information only for such purposes. They may disclose the information in public court proceedings or in judicial decisions.

(2) In no case shall the provisions of paragraph (1) of this Article be construed so as to impose on the competent authority of either Contracting State the obligation:

(a) to carry out administrative measures at variance with laws and administrative practice prevailing in either Contracting State;

(b) to supply information which is not obtainable under the laws or in the normal course of the administration of either Contracting State;

(c) to supply information which would disclose any trade, business, industrial, commercial or professional secret or trade process, or information the disclosure of which would be contrary to public policy (ordre public).

Article 27 Entry into force

Each of the Contracting States shall notify to the other the completion of the procedures required by its law for the bringing into force of this Convention. The Convention shall enter into force on the date of the later of these notifications:

(a) in the United Kingdom:

(i) in respect of income tax and capital gains tax, for any year of assessment beginning on or after 6 April in the calendar year next following that in which the Convention enters into force;

(ii) in respect of corporation tax, for any financial year beginning on or after 1 April in the calendar year next following that in which the Convention enters into force; and

(b) in Bulgaria:

in respect of income and capital gains arising for any tax year beginning on or after 1 January in the calendar year next following that in which the Convention enters into force.

Note: This Convention entered into force on 28 December 1987.

Official languages: The Bulgarian language text and the English language text of this Convention are equally authoritative.

BURMA

Agreement of 13 March 1950 (SI 1952 No 751)

Printed as amended by the Protocol of 4 April 1951 (SI 1952 No 751).

Article I [Taxes covered]

(1) The taxes which are the subject of the present Agreement are:—
  (a) In the United Kingdom of Great Britain and Northern Ireland:
      The income tax (including the surtax) and the profits tax (hereinafter referred to as "United Kingdom tax");
  (b) In Burma:
      The income tax, including the super tax and the business profits tax (hereinafter referred to as "Burma tax").

(2) The present Agreement shall also apply to any other taxes of a substantially similar character imposed in the United Kingdom or Burma subsequently to the date of signature of the present Agreement or in any territory to which the present Agreement is extended under Article XVII.

Corporation tax: This Agreement covers United Kingdom corporation tax, by virtue of ICTA 1988, s 789(1).

Article II [General definitions]

(1) In the present Agreement, unless the context otherwise requires:
  (a) The term "United Kingdom" means Great Britain and Northern Ireland, excluding the Channel Islands and the Isle of Man;
  (b) The term "Burma" means territories comprised within the Union of Burma;
  (c) The term "territory" means the United Kingdom or Burma, as the context requires;
  (d) The term "tax" means United Kingdom tax or Burma tax, as the context requires;
  (e) The term "person" includes any body of persons, corporate or not corporate;
  (f) The term "company" means any body corporate;
  (g) The terms "resident of the United Kingdom" and "resident of Burma" mean

45

respectively any person who is resident in the United Kingdom for the purposes of United Kingdom tax and not resident in Burma for the purposes of Burma tax, and any person who is resident in Burma for the purposes of Burma tax and not resident in the United Kingdom for the purposes of United Kingdom tax; a company shall be regarded as resident in the United Kingdom if its business is managed and controlled in the United Kingdom and as resident in Burma if its business is managed and controlled in Burma;

(*h*) The terms "resident of one of the territories" and "resident of the other territory" mean a person who is a resident of the United Kingdom or a person who is a resident of Burma, as the context requires;

(*i*) The terms "United Kingdom enterprise" and "Burma enterprise" mean respectively an industrial or commercial enterprise carried on by a resident of the United Kingdom and an industrial or commercial enterprise carried on by a resident of Burma, and the terms "enterprise of one of the territories" and "enterprise of the other territory" mean a United Kingdom enterprise or a Burma enterprise, as the context requires;

(*j*) . . .

(*k*) The term "permanent establishment", when used with respect to an enterprise of one of the territories, means a branch, management, factory, or other fixed place of business, but does not include an agency unless the agent has, and habitually exercises, a general authority to negotiate and conclude contracts on behalf of such enterprise or has a stock of merchandise from which he regularly fills orders on its behalf.

An enterprise of one of the territories shall not be deemed to have a permanent establishment in the other territory merely because it carries on business dealings in that other territory through a *bona fide* broker or general commission agent acting in the ordinary course of his business as such.

The fact than an enterprise of one of the territories maintains in the other territory a fixed place of business exclusively for the purchase of goods or merchandise shall not of itself constitute that fixed place of business a permanent establishment of the enterprise.

The fact that a company which is a resident of one of the territories has a subsidiary company which is a resident of the other territory or which is engaged in trade or business in that other territory (whether through a permanent establishment or otherwise) shall not of itself constitute that subsidiary company a permanent establishment of its parent company.

(2) In the application of the provisions of the present Agreement by one of the Contracting Governments any term not otherwise defined shall, unless the context otherwise requires, have the meaning which it has under the laws in force in the territory of that Contracting Government relating to the taxes which are the subject of the present Agreement.

Article V [Shipping and air transport]

Notwithstanding the provisions of Articles III and IV, profits which a resident of one of the territories derives from operating any ship or aircraft shall be exempt from tax in the other territory, unless the ship or aircraft is operated wholly or mainly between places within that other territory.

Article III: Taxation of industrial or commercial profits.
Article IV: Taxation of profits of associated enterprises.

Article XV [Exchange of information]

(1) The taxation authorities of the Contracting Governments shall exchange such information (being information available under the respective taxation laws of the Contracting Governments) as is necessary for carrying out the provisions of the present Agreement or for

the prevention of fraud or the administration of statutory provisions against legal avoidance in relation to the taxes which are the subject of the present Agreement. Any information so exchanged shall be treated as secret and shall not be disclosed to any persons other than those concerned with the assessment and collection of the taxes which are the subject of the present Agreement. No information shall be exchanged which would disclose any trade secret or trade process.

(2) As used in this Article, the term "taxation authorities" means, in the case of Burma, the Commissioner of Income Tax or his authorised representative; in the case of the United Kingdom, the Commissioners of Inland Revenue or their authorised representative; and, in the case of any territory to which the present Agreement is extended under Article XVII, the competent authority for the administration in such territory of the taxes to which the present Agreement applies.

Article XVI [Non-discrimination]

(1) The nationals of one of the Contracting Governments shall not be subjected in the territory of the other Contracting Government to any taxation or any requirement connected therewith which is other, higher or more burdensome than the taxation and connected requirements to which the nationals of the latter Contracting Government are or may be subjected.

(2) The enterprises of one of the territories shall not be subjected in the other territory, in respect of profits attributable to their permanent establishments in that other territory, to any taxation which is other, higher or more burdensome than the taxation to which the enterprises of that other territory are or may be subjected in respect of the like profits.

(3) Nothing in paragraph (1) or paragraph (2) of this Article shall be construed as obliging one of the Contracting Governments to grant to nationals of the other Contracting Government who are not resident in the territory of the former Government the same personal allowances, reliefs and reductions for tax purposes as are granted to its own nationals.

(4) In this Article the term "nationals" means—
  (a) in relation to Burma, persons who are under the law of the Union of Burma citizens thereof;
  (b) in relation to the United Kingdom, all British subjects and British-protected persons residing in or belonging to the United Kingdom or any territory to which the present Agreement applies by reason of extension made by the United Kingdom under Article XVII;

and includes all legal persons, partnerships and associations deriving their status as such from the law in force in any territory of the Contracting Governments to which the present Agreement applies.

Article XVIII [Entry into force]

Note: Article XVIII provided for the entry into force of the 1950 Agreement, which was amended before it entered into force by the 1951 Protocol. It takes effect in the UK from the year of assessment 1948–49 (income tax) and in general from the financial year beginning on 1 April 1948 (profits tax).

Official language: English.

CANADA

Convention of 8 September 1978 (SI 1980 No 709)

Printed as amended by the Protocol of 16 April 1985 (SI 1985 No 1996). (The Protocol of 15 April 1980 (SI 1980 No 1528) does not amend the Articles printed below.)

CANADA

Article 1 Personal scope

This Convention shall apply to persons who are residents of one or both of the Contracting States.

Article 2 Taxes covered

(1) The taxes which are the subject of this Convention are:
   (a) in Canada:
      the income taxes which are imposed by the Government of Canada (hereinafter referred to as "Canadian tax");
   (b) in the United Kingdom of Great Britain and Northern Ireland:
      the income tax, the corporation tax, the capital gains tax, the petroleum revenue tax and the development land tax (hereinafter referred to as "United Kingdom tax").

(2) The Convention shall apply also to any identical or substantially similar taxes which are imposed after the date of signature of this Convention in addition to, or in place of, the existing taxes by either Contracting State or by the Government of any territory to which the present Convention is extended under Article 26. The Contracting States shall notify each other of changes which have been made in their respective taxation laws.

Article 3 General definitions

(1) In this Convention, unless the context otherwise requires:
   (a) (i) the term "Canada" used in a geographical sense, means the territory of Canada, including any area beyond the territorial waters of Canada which is an area where Canada may, in accordance with its national legislation and international law, exercise sovereign rights with respect to the sea-bed and sub-soil and their natural resources;
      (ii) the term "United Kingdom" means Great Britain and Northern Ireland, including any area outside the territorial sea of the United Kingdom which in accordance with international law has been or may be hereafter designated, under the laws of the United Kingdom concerning the Continental Shelf, as an area within which the rights of the United Kingdom with respect to the sea-bed and sub-soil and their natural resources may be exercised;
   (b) the terms "a Contracting State" and "the other Contracting State" mean, as the context requires, the United Kingdom or Canada;
   (c) the term "person" comprises an individual, a company, any entity treated as a unit for tax purposes or any other body of persons;
   (d) the term "company" means any body corporate or any other entity which is treated as a body corporate for tax purposes; in French, the term "société" also means a "corporation" within the meaning of Canadian law;
   (e) the terms "enterprise of a Contracting State" and "enterprise of the other Contracting State" mean respectively an enterprise carried on by a resident of a Contracting State and an enterprise carried on by a resident of the other Contracting State;

(f) the term "competent authority" means:
  (i) in the case of Canada, the Minister of National Revenue or his authorised representative;
  (ii) in the case of the United Kingdom, the Commissioners of Inland Revenue or their authorised representative;
(g) the term "tax" means United Kingdom tax or Canadian tax, as the context requires;
(h) the term "national" means:
  (i) in relation to the United Kingdom all citizens of the United Kingdom and Colonies, British Subjects under Sections 2, 13(1) or 16 of the British Nationality Act 1948, and British Subjects by virtue of Section 1 of the British Nationality Act 1965, provided they are patrial within the meaning of the Immigration Act 1971, so far as these provisions are in force on the date of entry into force of this Convention or have been modified only in minor respects, so as not to affect their general character; and all legal persons, partnerships, and associations deriving their status as such from the law in force in the United Kingdom;
  (ii) in relation to Canada, all citizens of Canada and all legal persons, partnerships and associations deriving their status as such from the law in force in Canada.

(2) As regards the application of the Convention by a Contracting State any term not otherwise defined shall, unless the context otherwise requires, have the meaning which it has under the laws of that Contracting State relating to the taxes which are the subject of the Convention.

Article 4 Fiscal domicile

(1) For the purposes of this Convention, the term "resident of a Contracting State" means any person who, under the law of that State, is liable to taxation therein by reason of his domicile, residence, place of management or any other criterion of a similar nature. But this term does not include any person who is liable to tax in that Contracting State in respect only of income from sources therein.

(2) Where by reason of the provisions of paragraph (1) an individual is a resident of both Contracting States, then his status shall be determined as follows:
  (a) he shall be deemed to be a resident of the Contracting State in which he has a permanent home available to him. If he has a permanent home available to him in both Contracting States, he shall be deemed to be a resident of the Contracting State with which his personal and economic relations are closer (centre of vital interests);
  (b) if the Contracting State in which he has his centre of vital interests cannot be determined, or if he has not a permanent home available to him in either Contracting State, he shall be deemed to be a resident of the Contracting State in which he has an habitual abode;
  (c) if he has an habitual abode in both Contracting States or in neither of them, he shall be deemed to be a resident of the Contracting State of which he is a national;
  (d) if he is a national of both Contracting States or of neither of them, the competent authorities of the Contracting States shall settle the question by mutual agreement.

(3) Where by reason of the provisions of paragraph (1) a person other than an individual is a resident of both Contracting States, the competent authorities of the Contracting States shall by mutual agreement endeavour to settle the question and to determine the mode of application of the Convention to such person.

Article 6 Income from immovable property

(1) (Taxation of income from immovable property.)

(2) For the purposes of this Convention, the term "immovable property" shall be defined in accordance with the law of the Contracting State in which the property in question is situ-

ated. The term shall in any case include property accessory to immovable property, livestock and equipment used in agriculture and forestry, rights to which the provisions of general law respecting landed property apply, usufruct of immovable property and rights to variable or fixed payments as consideration for the working of, or the right to work, mineral deposits, sources and other natural resources; ships, boats and aircraft shall not be regarded as immovable property.

(3) . . .

(4) . . .

Article 8 Shipping and air transport

(1) Profits derived by an enterprise of a Contracting State from the operation of ships or aircraft in international traffic shall be taxable only in that State.

(2) Notwithstanding the provisions of paragraph (1) and Article 7, profits derived from the operation of ships used principally to transport passengers or goods exclusively between places in a Contracting State may be taxed in that State.

(3) Notwithstanding the provisions of Article 7, profits of an enterprise of a Contracting State from the use, maintenance or rental of containers (including trailers and related equipment for the transport of containers) used for the transport of goods or merchandise in international traffic shall be taxable only in that State.

(4) The provisions of this Article shall also apply to profits derived by an enterprise of a Contracting State from its participation in a pool, a joint business or an international operating agency.

Article 7: Taxation of business profits.

Offshore activities: See Article 27A in relation to offshore activities.

Article 13 Capital gains

(1) . . .

(2) . . .

(3) Gains derived by a resident of a Contracting State from the alienation of ships or aircraft operated in international traffic or movable property pertaining to the operation of such ships or aircraft, shall be taxable only in that Contracting State.

(4)–(9) . . .

Article 22 Non-discrimination

(1) The nationals of a Contracting State shall not be subjected in the other Contracting State to any taxation or any requirement connected therewith which is other or more burdensome than the taxation and connected requirements to which nationals of that other State in the same circumstances are or may be subjected.

(2) The taxation on a permanent establishment which an enterprise of a Contracting State has in the other Contracting State shall not be less favourably levied in that other State than the taxation levied on enterprises of that other State carrying on the same activities. This provision shall not be construed as obliging either Contracting State to grant to individuals not resident in its territory those personal allowances and reliefs for tax purposes which are by law available only to individuals who are so resident.

(3) Nothing in this Convention shall be construed as preventing a Contracting State from imposing on the earnings attributable to permanent establishments in that State of a company which is a resident of the other Contracting State, tax in addition to the tax which would be chargeable on the earnings of a company which is a resident of the first-mentioned State, provided that the rate of any additional tax so imposed shall not exceed 10 per cent of the amount of such earnings which have not been subjected to such additional tax in previous taxation years.

(4) For the purpose of paragraph 3 of this Article, the term "earnings" means the profits

attributable to permanent establishments in a Contracting State (including gains from the alienation of property forming part of the business property of such permanent establishments) in a year and previous year deducting therefrom:

(a) business losses attributable to such permanent establishments (including losses from the alienation of property forming part of the business property of such permanent establishments) in such year and previous years; and

(b) all taxes, other than the additional tax referred to in paragraph 3 of this Article, imposed on such profits in that State; and

(c) the profits reinvested in that State, provided that where that State is Canada, the amount of such deduction shall be determined in accordance with the existing provisions of the law of Canada regarding the computation of the allowance in respect of investment in property in Canada, and any subsequent modification of those provisions which shall not affect the general principle thereof; and

(d) five hundred thousand Canadian dollars ($500,000), or two hundred and fifty thousand pounds sterling (£250,000), whichever is the greater, less any amount deducted in that State under this sub-paragraph (d) a company associated therewith; for the purposes of this sub-paragraph (d) a company is associated with another company if one of them directly or indirectly has control of the other or both are directly or indirectly under the control of the same person, or if the two companies deal with each other not at arm's length.

(5) In this Article, the term "taxation" means taxes which are the subject of this Convention.

Article 23 Mutual agreement procedure

(1) Where a resident of a Contracting State considers that the actions of one or both of the Contracting States result or will result for him in taxation not in accordance with this Convention, he may, without prejudice to the remedies provided by the national laws of those States, address to the competent authority of the Contracting State of which he is a resident an application in writing stating the grounds for claiming the revision of such taxation.

(2) The competent authority referred to in paragraph (1) shall endeavour, if the objection appears to it to be justified and if it is not itself able to arrive at an appropriate solution, to resolve the case by mutual agreement with the competent authority of the other Contracting State, with a view to the avoidance of taxation not in accordance with the Convention.

(3) The competent authorities of the Contracting States shall endeavour to resolve by mutual agreement any difficulties or doubts arising as to the interpretation or application of the Convention. In particular, the competent authorities of the Contracting States may reach agreement on:

(a) the same attribution of profits to a resident of a Contracting State and its permanent establishment situated in the other Contracting State;

(b) the same allocation of income between a resident of a Contracting State and any associated person provided for in Article 9.

Article 24 Exchange of information

The competent authorities of the Contracting States shall exchange such information (being information which is at their disposal under their respective taxation laws in the normal course of administration) as is necessary for the carrying out of the provisions of this Convention or for the prevention of fraud or for the administration of statutory provisions against legal avoidance in relation to the taxes which are the subject of this Convention. Any information so exchanged shall be treated as secret and shall not be disclosed to persons other than persons (including a court or administrative tribunal) concerned with the assessment, collection or enforcement in respect of the taxes which are the subject of this Convention. No information as aforesaid shall be exchanged which would disclose any trade, business, industrial or professional secret or trade process.

Article 27A Miscellaneous rules applicable to certain overseas activities

(1) The provisions of this Article shall apply notwithstanding any other provision of this Convention.

(2) A person who is a resident of a Contracting State and carries on activities in the other Contracting State in connection with the exploration or exploitation of the sea-bed and sub-soil and their natural resources situated in that other Contracting State shall, subject to paragraph (3) of this Article, be deemed to be carrying on a business in that other Contracting State through a permanent establishment situated therein.

(3) The provisions of paragraph (2) of this Article shall not apply where the activities referred to therein are carried on for a period or periods not exceeding in the aggregate 30 days in any 12 month period. For the purposes of this paragraph:

(*a*) where a person carrying on activities referred to in paragraph (2) of this Article is associated with an enterprise carrying on substantially similar activities, that person shall be deemed to be carrying on those substantially similar activities of the enterprise with which he is associated, in addition to his own activities;

(*b*) two enterprises shall be deemed to be associated if one enterprise participates directly or indirectly in the management or control of the other enterprise or if the same persons participate directly or indirectly in the management or control of both enterprises.

(4) Salaries, wages and similar remuneration derived by a resident of a Contracting State in respect of an employment connected with the exploration or exploitation of the sea-bed and sub-soil and their natural resources situated in the other Contracting State may, to the extent that the duties are performed offshore in that other Contracting State, be taxed in that other Contracting State.

Article 28 Entry into force

Note: Article 28 provided for the entry into force of the 1978 Convention. It takes effect in the UK in its amended form for any year of assessment, financial year or chargeable period beginning after 31 March 1986.

Official language: The French language text and the English language text of this Convention are equally authoritative.

CHINA

Agreement of 26 July 1984 (SI 1984 No 1826)

Article 1 Personal scope

This Agreement shall apply to persons who are residents of one or both of the Contracting States.

Article 2 Taxes covered

(1) The existing taxes to which this Agreement applies are:
  (a) in the People's Republic of China:
    (i) the individual income tax;
    (ii) the income tax (including the additional local income tax) concerning joint ventures with Chinese and foreign investment; and
    (iii) the income tax (including the local income tax) concerning foreign enterprises;
    (hereinafter referred to as "Chinese tax");
  (b) in the United Kingdom of Great Britain and Northern Ireland:
    (i) the income tax;
    (ii) the corporation tax; and
    (iii) the capital gains tax;
    (hereinafter referred to as "United Kingdom tax").

(2) This Agreement shall also apply to any identical or substantially similar taxes which are imposed by either Contracting State after the date of signature of this Agreement in addition to, or in place of, the taxes referred to in paragraph (1) of this Article. The competent authorities of the Contracting States shall notify each other of any changes which are made in their respective taxation laws.

Article 3 General definitions

(1) In this Agreement, unless the context otherwise requires:
  (a) the term "China" means the People's Republic of China, including all the territory and the territorial sea of the People's Republic of China, in which the laws relating to Chinese tax are in force, and all the area beyond its territorial sea, and the sea-bed and sub-soil thereof, over which the People's Republic of China has jurisdiction in accordance with international law and in which the laws relating to Chinese tax are in force;
  (b) the term "United Kingdom" means Great Britain and Northern Ireland, including any area outside the territorial sea of the United Kingdom which in accordance with international law has been or may hereafter be designated, under the laws of the United Kingdom concerning the Continental Shelf, as an area within which the rights of the United Kingdom with respect to the sea bed and sub-soil and their natural resources may be exercised;
  (c) the terms "a Contracting State" and "the other Contracting State" mean China or the United Kingdom as the context requires;
  (d) the term "national" means:
    (i) in relation to China any individual who under the law in China possesses Chinese nationality; and any legal person, partnership or other body of persons deriving its status as such from the law in force in China;
    (ii) in relation to the United Kingdom, any individual who has under the law in the United Kingdom the status of United Kingdom national, provided he has the right of abode in the United Kingdom; and any legal person, partnership, association or other entity deriving its status as such from the law in force in the United Kingdom;
  (e) the term "person" means an individual, a company and any other body of persons;
  (f) the term "company" means any body corporate or any entity which is treated as a body corporate for tax purposes;
  (g) the terms "enterprise of a Contracting State" and "enterprise of the other Contracting State" mean respectively an enterprise carried on by a resident of a Contracting State and an enterprise carried on by a resident of the other Contracting State;
  (h) the term "international traffic" means any transport by a ship or aircraft operated by an enterprise which has its place of effective management of the business in a

Contracting State, except when the ship or aircraft is operated solely between places in the other Contracting State;

(i) the term "competent authority" means, in the case of China, the General Taxation Bureau of the Ministry of Finance or its authorised representatives, and in the case of the United Kingdom, the Board of Inland Revenue or their authorised representatives.

(2) As regards the application of this Agreement by a Contracting State any term not otherwise defined shall, unless the context otherwise requires, have the meaning which it has under the law of that Contracting State relating to the taxes to which this Agreement applies.

Article 4 Resident

(1) For the purposes of this Agreement, the term "resident of a Contracting State" means any person who, under the law of that State, is liable to tax therein by reason of his domicile, residence, place of head office, place of effective management or any other criterion of a similar nature.

(2) Where by reason of the provisions of paragraph (1) of this Article an individual is a resident of both Contracting States, then his status shall be determined in accordance with the following rules:

(a) he shall be deemed to be a resident of the State in which he has a permanent home available to him; if he has a permanent home available to him in both States, he shall be deemed to be a resident of the State with which his personal and economic relations are closer (centre of vital interests);

(b) if the State in which he has his centre of vital interests cannot be determined, or if he has not a permanent home available to him in either State, he shall be deemed to be a resident of the State in which he has an habitual abode;

(c) if he has an habitual abode in both States or in neither of them, he shall be deemed to be a resident of the State of which he is a national;

(d) if he is a national of both States or of neither of them, the competent authorities of the Contracting States shall settle the question by mutual agreement.

(3) Where by reason of the provisions of paragraph (1) of this Article a person other than an individual is a resident of both Contracting States, then it shall be deemed to be a resident of the State in which the place of effective management of its business is situated. However, where such a person has the place of effective management of its business in one of the Contracting States and the place of head office of its business in the other Contracting State, then the competent authorities of the Contracting States shall determine by mutual agreement the State of which the company shall be deemed to be a resident for the purposes of this Agreement.

Article 6 Income from immovable property

(1) (Taxation of income from immovable property.)

(2) The term "immovable property" shall have the meaning which it has under the law of the Contracting State in which the property in question is situated. The term shall in any case include property accessory to immovable property, livestock and equipment used in agriculture and forestry, rights to which the provisions of general law respecting landed property apply, usufruct of immovable property and rights to variable or fixed payments as consideration for the working of, or the right to work, mineral deposits, sources and other natural resources; ships and aircraft shall not be regarded as immovable property.

(3) . . .

(4) . . .

Article 8 Shipping and air transport

(1) Profits from the operation of ships or aircraft in international traffic shall be taxable only in the Contracting State in which the place of effective management of the business of the enterprise is situated.

(2) If the place of effective management of the business of a shipping enterprise is aboard a ship, then it shall be deemed to be situated in the Contracting State in which the home harbour of the ship is situated, or, if there is no such home harbour, in the Contracting State of which the operator of the ship is a resident.

(3) The provisions of this Article shall also apply to profits derived from participation in a pool, a joint business or an international operating agency.

Article 14 Capital gains

(1) (Taxation of capital gains.)

(2) Gains from the alienation of ships or aircraft operated in international traffic and any property, other than immovable property, pertaining to the operation of such ships or aircraft shall be taxable only in the Contracting State in which the place of effective management of the business of the enterprise is situated.

Article 24 Non-discrimination

(1) Nationals of a Contracting State shall not be subjected in the other Contracting State to any taxation or any requirement connected therewith which is other or more burdensome than the taxation and connected requirements to which nationals of that other State in the same circumstances are or may be subjected.

(2) The taxation on a permanent establishment which an enterprise of a Contracting State has in the other Contracting State shall not be less favourably levied in that other State than the taxation levied on enterprises of that other State carrying on the same activities.

(3) Enterprises of a Contracting State, the capital of which is wholly or partly owned or controlled, directly or indirectly, by one or more residents of the other Contracting State, shall not be subjected in the first-mentioned State to any taxation or any requirement connected therewith which is other or more burdensome than the taxation and connected requirements to which other similar enterprises of that first-mentioned State are or may be subjected.

(4) Except where the provisions of Article 9, paragraph (7) of Article 11, paragraph (6) of Article 12 or paragraph (6) of Article 13 apply, interest, royalties, technical fees and other disbursements paid by an enterprise of a Contracting State to a resident of the other Contracting State shall, for the purpose of determining the taxable profits of such enterprise, be deductible under the same conditions as if they had been paid to a resident of the first-mentioned State.

(5) Nothing contained in this Article shall be construed as obliging either Contracting State to grant to individuals not resident in that State any of the personal allowances, reliefs and reductions for tax purposes which are granted to individuals so resident.

Article 25 Mutual agreement procedure

(1) Where a resident of a Contracting State considers that the actions of one or both of the Contracting States result or will result for him in taxation not in accordance with the provisions of this Agreement, he may, irrespective of the remedies provided by the domestic laws of those States, present his case to the competent authority of the Contracting State of which he is a resident.

(2) The competent authority shall endeavour, if the objection appears to it to be justified and if it is not itself able to arrive at a satisfactory solution, to resolve the case by mutual agreement with the competent authority of the other Contracting State, with a view to the avoidance of taxation which is not in accordance with this Agreement.

(3) The competent authorities of the Contracting States shall endeavour to resolve by mutual agreement any difficulties or doubts arising as to the interpretation or application of this Agreement.

(4) The competent authorities of the Contracting States may communicate with each other directly for the purpose of reaching an agreement in the sense of paragraphs (2) and (3) of this Article.

Article 26 Exchange of information

(1) The competent authorities of the Contracting States shall exchange such information as is necessary for carrying out the provisions of this Agreement or of the domestic laws of the Contracting States concerning taxes covered by this Agreement insofar as the taxation thereunder is not contrary to the provisions of this Agreement, in particular for the prevention of fraud or fiscal evasion. The exchange of information shall not be restricted by Article 1. Any information so exchanged shall be treated as secret and shall be disclosed only to persons or authorities (including courts and administrative bodies) involved in the assessment or collection of, the enforcement or prosecution in respect of, or the determination of appeals in relation to, the taxes covered by the Agreement. Such persons or authorities shall use the information only for such purposes. They may disclose the information in public court proceedings or in judicial decisions.

(2) In no case shall the provisions of paragraph (1) of this Article be construed so as to impose on the competent authority of either Contracting State the obligation:

(*a*) to carry out administrative measures at variance with the law and administrative practice prevailing in either Contracting State;

(*b*) to supply information which is not obtainable under the law or in the normal course of the administration of either Contracting State; or

(*c*) to supply information which would disclose any trade, business, industrial, commercial or professional secret or trade process, or information the disclosure of which would be contrary to public policy.

Article 29 Entry into force

Note: Article 29 provided for the entry into force of this Agreement. It takes effect in the UK from the year of assessment 1985–86 (income tax and capital gains tax) and from the financial year beginning on 1 April 1985 (corporation tax).

Official language: The Chinese language text and the English language text of this Agreement are equally authoritative.

CYPRUS

Convention of 20 June 1974 (SI 1975 No 425)

Printed as amended by the Protocol of 2 April 1980 (SI 1980 No 1529).

Article 1 Personal scope

This Convention shall apply to persons who are residents of one or both of the Contracting States.

Article 2 Taxes covered

(1) The taxes which are the subject of this Convention are:
- (a) in the United Kingdom of Great Britain and Northern Ireland:
  - (i) the income tax; and
  - (ii) the corporation tax;
- (b) in Cyprus:
  the income tax.

(2) This Convention shall also apply to any identical or substantially similar taxes which are imposed by either Contracting State after the date of signature of this Convention in addition to, or in place of, the existing taxes. The competent authorities of the Contracting States shall notify to each other any changes which are made in their respective taxation laws.

Article 3 General definitions

(1) In this Convention, unless the context otherwise requires:
- (a) the term "Cyprus" means the Republic of Cyprus, and includes any area adjacent to the territorial waters of Cyprus which in accordance with international law has been or may hereafter be designated, under the laws of Cyprus concerning the Continental Shelf, as an area within which the rights of Cyprus with respect to the sea-bed and sub-soil and their natural resources may be exercised;
- (b) the term "United Kingdom" means Great Britain and Northern Ireland, including any area outside the territorial sea of the United Kingdom which in accordance with international law has been or may hereafter be designated, under the laws of the United Kingdom concerning the Continental Shelf, as an area within which the rights of the United Kingdom with respect to the sea bed and sub-soil and their natural resources may be exercised;
- (c) the terms "one of the Contracting States" and "the other Contracting State" mean the United Kingdom or Cyprus, as the context requires;
- (d) the term "United Kingdom tax" means tax imposed by the United Kingdom being tax to which this Convention applies by virtue of the provisions of Article 2; the term "Cyprus tax" means tax imposed by Cyprus, being tax to which this Convention applies by virtue of the provisions of Article 2;
- (e) the term "tax" means United Kingdom tax or Cyprus tax, as the context requires;
- (f) the term "company" means any body corporate or any entity which is treated as a body corporate for tax purposes;
- (g) the term "individual" means a natural person;
- (h) the term "person" includes an individual, a company and a body of persons, but does not include a partnership;
- (i) the terms "enterprise of one of the Contracting States" and "enterprise of the other Contracting State" mean respectively an enterprise carried on by a resident of one of the Contracting States and an enterprise carried on by a resident of the other Contracting State;
- (j) the term "national" means:
  - (i) in relation to Cyprus:
    - (aa) any individual possessing the citizenship of Cyprus;
    - (bb) any legal person, partnership, association or other entity deriving its status as such from the law in force in Cyprus;
  - (ii) in relation to the United Kingdom:
    - (aa) any citizen of the United Kingdom and Colonies who derives his status as such from his connection with the United Kingdom;
    - (bb) any legal person, partnership, association or other entity deriving its status as such from the law of the United Kingdom;
- (k) the term "competent authority" means, in the case of the United Kingdom, the Commissioners of Inland Revenue or their authorised representative; and in the case of Cyprus, the Commissioner of Income Tax or his authorised representative.

(2) In the application of this Convention by one of the Contracting States, any term not otherwise defined shall, unless the context otherwise requires, have the meaning which it has under the laws of that Contracting State relating to the taxes which are the subject of this Convention.

Excluded persons: For persons excluded from this Convention see Article 24A.

Article 4 Fiscal domicile

(1) For the purposes of this Convention, the term "resident of a Contracting State" means any person who, under the law of that State, is liable to taxation therein by reason of his domicile, residence, place of management or any other criterion of a similar nature.

(2) Where by reason of the provisions of paragraph (1) of this Article an individual is a resident of both Contracting States, then his status shall be determined in accordance with the following rules:

> (a) He shall be deemed to be a resident of the Contracting State in which he has a permanent home available to him. If he has a permanent home available to him in both Contracting States, he shall be deemed to be a resident of the Contracting State with which his personal economic relations are closer.

> (b) If the Contracting State with which his personal economic relations are closer cannot be determined, or if he has not a permanent home available to him in either Contracting State, he shall be deemed to be a resident of the Contracting State in which he has an habitual abode.

> (c) If he has an habitual abode in both Contracting States or in neither of them, he shall be deemed to be a resident of the Contracting State of which he is a national.

> (d) If he is a national of both Contracting States or of neither of them, the competent authorities of the Contracting States shall determine the question by mutual agreement.

(3) Where by reason of the provisions of paragraph (1) of this Article a person other than an individual is a resident of both Contracting States, then it shall be deemed to be a resident of the Contracting State in which its place of effective management is situated.

Article 7 Immovable property

(1) (Taxation of income from immovable property.)

> (2) (a) the term "immovable property" shall subject to the provisions of sub-paragraph (b) of this paragraph, be defined in accordance with the law of the Contracting State in which the property in question is situated.

> (b) The term shall in any case include property accessory to immovable property, livestock and equipment used in agriculture and forestry, rights to which the provisions of general law respecting landed property apply, usufruct of immovable property and rights to variable or fixed payments as consideration for the working of, or the right to work, mineral deposits, sources and other natural resources; ships, boats and aircraft shall not be regarded as immovable property.

(3) . . .

(4) . . .

Article 10 Shipping and air transport

(1) A resident of one of the Contracting States shall be exempt from tax in the other Contracting State on profits from the operation of ships or aircraft in international traffic.

(2) The provisions of paragraph (1) of this Article shall likewise apply in respect of participation in pools, in a joint business or in an international operations agency of any kind by enterprises engaged in the operation of ships or aircraft in international traffic.

Article 24A Excluded persons

(1) The provisions of paragraphs (1)(*b*) and (*c*) and (2) of Article 11, paragraph (1) of Article 12 and paragraphs (1) and (2) of Article 13 shall not apply to persons entitled to any special tax benefit under any of the Sections listed below of the Cyprus Income Tax Laws 1961 to 1977:

    (*a*) Section 5(2)(*c*)(i) in so far as the tax charged is at a rate less than the rate prescribed for individuals in paragraph 1 of the Second Schedule to the Cyprus Income Tax Laws 1961 to 1977 or which may hereafter otherwise be prescribed for individuals generally;

    (*b*) Section 8(*w*);

    (*c*) Section 28A:

Provided that where an individual is entitled to a special tax benefit under Section 5(2)(*c*)(i) of the Cyprus Income Tax Laws 1961 to 1977 this Article shall not apply in relation to the first £1,500 sterling of the income arising in the United Kingdom in a year of assessment, and otherwise subject to tax in accordance with United Kingdom law, in respect of which that benefit is enjoyed.

(2) This Article shall apply also to any provision of Cyprus law enacted after 1 January 1978 which is of an identical or substantially similar character to the provisions mentioned in paragraph (1) of this Article.

Article 25 Non-discrimination

(1) The nationals of one of the Contracting States shall not be subjected in the other Contracting State to any taxation or any requirement connected therewith which is other or more burdensome than the taxation and connected requirements to which nationals of that other Contracting State in the same circumstances are or may be subjected.

(2) The taxation of a permanent establishment which an enterprise of one of the Contracting States has in the other Contracting State shall not be less favourably levied in that other Contracting State than the taxation levied on an enterprise of that other Contracting State carrying on the same activities.

(3) Enterprises of one of the Contracting States, the capital of which is wholly or partly owned or controlled, directly or indirectly, by one or more residents of the other Contracting State, shall not be subjected in the first-mentioned Contracting State to any taxation or any requirement connected therewith which is other or more burdensome than the taxation and connected requirements to which other similar enterprises of that first-mentioned Contracting State are or may be subjected.

(4) Nothing contained in this Article shall be construed as obliging either Contracting State to grant to individuals not resident in that Contracting State any of the personal allowances, reliefs and reductions for tax purposes which are granted to individuals so resident.

(5) In this Article the term "taxation" means taxes which are the subject of this Convention.

Article 26 Exchange of information

(1) The competent authorities of the Contracting States shall exchange such information as is necessary for carrying out the provisions of this Convention or for the prevention of fiscal evasion or for the administration of statutory provisions against tax avoidance in relation to the taxes which are the subject of this Convention. Any information so exchanged shall be treated as secret and shall not be disclosed to any persons or authorities other than those, including a court or administrative body, concerned with assessment, collection, enforcement or prosecution in respect of those taxes or the determination of appeals in relation thereto.

(2) In no case shall the provisions of paragraph (1) of this Article be construed so as to impose on one of the Contracting States the obligation:

    (*a*) to carry out administrative measures at variance with the laws or the administrative practice of that or of the other Contracting State;

    (*b*) to supply particulars which are not obtainable under the laws or in the normal course of the administration of that or of the other Contracting State;

(c) to supply information which would disclose any trade, business, industrial, commercial or professional secret or trade process, or information the disclosure of which would be contrary to public policy.

Article 27 Mutual agreement procedure

(1) Where a resident of one of the Contracting States considers that the actions of one or both of the Contracting States result or will result for him in taxation not in accordance with this Convention, he may, notwithstanding the remedies provided by the taxation laws in force in the Contracting States, present his case to the competent authority of the Contracting State of which he is a resident.

(2) The competent authority of the first-mentioned Contracting State shall endeavour, if the objection appears to it to be justified and if it is not itself able to arrive at an appropriate solution, to resolve that case by mutual agreement with the competent authority of the other Contracting State with a view to the avoidance of taxation which is not in accordance with this Convention.

Article 29 Entry into force

Note: Article 29 provided for the entry into force of the 1975 Convention. It takes effect in the UK in its amended form from the year of assessment 1979–80 (income tax) and from financial years beginning on 1 April 1979 (corporation tax).

Official language: English.

DENMARK

Convention of 11 November 1980 (SI 1980 No 1960)

Article 1 Personal scope

This Convention shall apply to persons who are residents of one or both of the Contracting States.

Article 2 Taxes covered

(1) The taxes which are the subject of this Convention are:

    (a) in the United Kingdom of Great Britain and Northern Ireland:

        (i) the income tax;

    (ii) the corporation tax;

    (iii) the capital gains tax;

    (iv) the petroleum revenue tax; and

    (v) the development land tax

    (hereinafter referred to as "United Kingdom tax");

  (b) in the case of Denmark the income taxes to the state and to the municipalities (*indkomstskatterne til staten og til kommunerne*);

    (hereinafter referred to as "Danish tax").

(2) This Convention shall also apply to any identical or substantially similar taxes which are imposed by either Contracting State after the date of signature of this Convention in addition to, or in place of, the existing taxes. The competent authorities of the Contracting States shall notify each other of substantial changes which have been made in their respective taxation laws.

Article 3 General definitions

(1) In this Convention, unless the context otherwise requires:

  (a) the term "United Kingdom" means Great Britain and Northern Ireland, including any area outside the territorial sea of the United Kingdom which in accordance with international law has been or may hereafter be designated, under the laws of the United Kingdom concerning the Continental Shelf, as an area within which the rights of the United Kingdom with respect to the sea-bed and sub-soil and their natural resources may be exercised;

  (b) the term "Denmark" means the Kingdom of Denmark, including any area outside the territorial sea of Denmark which in accordance with international law has been or may hereafter be designated under Danish laws as an area within which Denmark may exercise sovereign rights with respect to the exploration and exploitation of the natural resources of the sea-bed or its sub-soil; the term does not comprise the Faroe Islands and Greenland.

  (c) the term "national" means:

    (i) in relation to the United Kingdom, any citizen of the United Kingdom and Colonies, or any British subject not possessing that citizenship or the citizenship of any other Commonwealth country or territory, provided in either case he has the right of abode in the United Kingdom, and any legal person, partnership or association deriving its status as such from the law in force in the United Kingdom;

    (ii) in relation to Denmark, any individual possessing the nationality of Denmark and any legal person, partnership or association deriving its status as such from the law in force in Denmark;

  (d) the term "tax" means United Kingdom tax or Danish tax, as the context requires;

  (e) the terms "a Contracting State" and "the other Contracting State" mean the United Kingdom or Denmark, as the context requires;

  (f) the term "person" comprises an individual, a company and any other body of persons;

  (g) the term "company" means any body corporate or any entity which is treated as a body corporate for tax purposes;

  (h) the terms "enterprise of a Contracting State" and "enterprise of the other Contracting State" mean respectively an enterprise carried on by a resident of a Contracting State and an enterprise carried on by a resident of the other Contracting State;

  (i) the term "international traffic" means any transport by a ship or aircraft operated by an enterprise which has its place of effective management in a Contracting State, except when the ship or aircraft is operated solely between places in the other Contracting State;

  (j) the term "competent authority" means in the case of the United Kingdom the Commissioners of Inland Revenue or their authorised representative, and in the case of Denmark the Minister for Inland Revenue, Customs and Excise or his authorised representative.

(2) As regards the application of the Convention by a Contracting State any term not defined therein shall, unless the context otherwise requires, have the meaning which it has under the law of that State concerning the taxes to which the Convention applies.

Article 4 Fiscal domicile

(1) For the purposes of this Convention, the term "resident of a Contracting State" means any person who, under the laws of that State, is liable to tax therein by reason of his domicile, residence, place of management or any other criterion of a similar nature. But this term does not include any person who is liable to tax in that State in respect only of income from sources in that State or capital situated therein.

(2) Where by reason of the provisions of paragraph (1) of this Article an individual is a resident of both Contracting States, then his status shall be determined as follows:

- (a) he shall be deemed to be a resident of the State in which he has a permanent home available to him; if he has a permanent home available to him in both States, he shall be deemed to be a resident of the State with which his personal and economic relations are closer (centre of vital interests);
- (b) if the State in which he has his centre of vital interests cannot be determined, or if he has not a permanent home available to him in either State, he shall be deemed to be a resident of the State in which he has an habitual abode;
- (c) if he has an habitual abode in both States or in neither of them, he shall be deemed to be a resident of the State of which he is a national;
- (d) if he is a national of both States or of neither of them, the competent authorities of the Contracting States shall settle the question by mutual agreement.

(3) Where by reason of the provisions of paragraph (1) of this Article a person other than an individual is a resident of both Contracting States, then it shall be deemed to be a resident of the State in which its place of effective management is situated.

Article 6 Income from immovable property

(1) (Taxation of income from immovable property.)

(2) The term "immovable property" shall have the meaning which it has under the law of the Contracting State in which the property in question is situated. The term shall in any case include property accessory to immovable property, livestock and equipment used in agriculture and forestry, rights to which the provisions of general law respecting landed property apply, usufruct of immovable property and rights to variable or fixed payments as consideration for the working of, or the right to work, mineral deposits, sources and other natural resources; ships, boats and aircraft shall not be regarded as immovable property.

(3) . . .

(4) . . .

Article 8 Shipping and air transport

(1) Profits from the operation of ships or aircraft in international traffic shall be taxable only in the Contracting State in which the place of effective management of the enterprise is situated.

(2) If the place of effective management of a shipping enterprise is aboard a ship then it shall be deemed to be situated in the Contracting State in which the home harbour of the ship is situated, or, if there is no such home harbour, in the State of which the operator of the ship is a resident.

(3) The provisions of paragraph (1) of this Article shall also apply to profits derived from the participation in a pool, a joint business or an international operating agency.

(4) With respect to profits derived by the Danish, Norwegian and Swedish air transport consortium, known as the Scandinavian Airlines System (SAS), the provisions of paragraphs

(1) and (3) of this Article shall only apply to such part of the profits as corresponds to the shareholding in the consortium held by Det Danske Luftfartsselskab (DDL), the Danish partner of Scandinavian Airlines System (SAS).

Article 13 Capital gains

(1) . . .

(2) . . .

(3) Gains from the alienation of ships or aircraft operated in international traffic, or movable property pertaining to the operation of such ships or aircraft shall be taxable only in the Contracting State in which the place of effective management of the enterprise is situated.

(4) . . .

Article 23 Non-discrimination

(1) Nationals of a Contracting State shall not be subjected in the other Contracting State to any taxation or any requirement connected therewith, which is other or more burdensome than the taxation and connected requirements to which nationals of that other State in the same circumstances are or may be subjected.

(2) The taxation on a permanent establishment which an enterprise of a Contracting State has in the other Contracting State shall not be less favourably levied in that other State than the taxation levied on enterprises of that other State carrying on the same activities.

(3) Nothing contained in this Article shall be construed as obliging either Contracting State to grant to individuals not resident in that State any of the personal allowances, reliefs and reductions for tax purposes which are granted to individuals so resident.

(4) Except where the provisions of paragraph (1) of Article 9, paragraph (4) of Article 11, or paragraph (4) of Article 12 apply, interest, royalties and other disbursements paid by an enterprise of a Contracting State to a resident of the other Contracting State shall, for the purpose of determining the taxable profits of such enterprise, be deductible under the same conditions as if they had been paid to a resident of the first-mentioned State.

(5) Enterprises of a Contracting State, the capital of which is wholly or partly owned or controlled, directly or indirectly, by one or more residents of the other Contracting State, shall not be subjected in the first-mentioned State to any taxation or any requirement connected therewith which is other or more burdensome than the taxation and connected requirements to which other similar enterprises of the first-mentioned State are or may be subjected.

(6) The provisions of this Article shall apply to taxes of every kind and description.

Article 24 Mutual agreement procedure

(1) Where a person considers that the actions of one or both of the Contracting States result or will result for him in taxation not in accordance with the provisions of this Convention, he may, irrespective of the remedies provided by the domestic law of those States, present his case to the competent authority of the Contracting State of which he is a resident.

(2) The competent authority shall endeavour, if the objection appears to it to be justified and if it is not itself able to arrive at a satisfactory solution, to resolve the case by mutual agreement with the competent authority of the other Contracting State, with a view to the avoidance of taxation which is not in accordance with the Convention.

(3) The competent authorities of the Contracting States shall endeavour to resolve by mutual agreement any difficulties or doubts arising as to the interpretation or application of the Convention. They may also consult together to consider measures to counteract improper use of the provisions of the Convention.

(4) The competent authorities of the Contracting States may communicate with each other directly for the purpose of reaching an agreement in the sense of the preceding paragraphs.

Article 25 Exchange of information

(1) The competent authorities of the Contracting States shall exchange such information as is necessary for carrying out the provisions of this Convention or of the domestic laws of the Contracting States concerning taxes covered by the Convention insofar as the taxation thereunder is not contrary to the Convention. Any information received by a Contracting State shall be treated as secret in the same manner as information obtained under the domestic laws of that State and shall be disclosed only to persons or authorities (including courts and administrative bodies) involved in the assessment or collection of, the enforcement or prosecution in respect of, or the determination of appeals in relation to, the taxes covered by the Convention. Such persons or authorities shall use the information only for such purposes. They may disclose the information in public court proceedings or in judicial decisions.

(2) In no case shall the provisions of paragraph (1) of this Article be construed so as to impose on a Contracting State the obligation:

(*a*) to carry out administrative measures at variance with the laws and administrative practice of that or of the other Contracting State;

(*b*) to supply information which is not obtainable under the laws or in the normal course of the administration of that or of the other Contracting State;

(*c*) to supply information which would disclose any trade, business, industrial, commercial or professional secret or trade process, or information, the disclosure of which would be contrary to public policy (*ordre public*).

Article 29 Entry into force

Note: Article 29 provided for the entry into force of this Convention. It takes effect in the UK from the year of assessment 1978–79 (income tax and capital gains tax) and from financial years beginning on 1 April 1978 (corporation tax).

Official languages: The Danish language text and the English language text of this Convention are equally authoritative.

EGYPT

Convention of 25 April 1977 (SI 1980 No 1091)

Article 1 Personal scope

This Convention shall apply to persons who are residents of one or both of the Contracting States.

Article 2 Taxes covered

(1) The taxes which are the subject of this Convention are:
  (*a*) in the United Kingdom of Great Britain and Northern Ireland:
    (i) the income tax;
    (ii) the corporation tax; and
    (iii) the capital gains tax
    (hereinafter referred to as "United Kingdom tax");
  (*b*) in the Arab Republic of Egypt:
    (i) the tax on income derived from immovable property (including the land tax, the building tax and the *ghaffir* tax);
    (ii) the tax on income from movable capital;
    (iii) the tax on commercial and industrial profits;
    (iv) the tax on wages, salaries, indemnities and pensions;
    (v) the tax on profits from liberal professions and all other non-commercial professions;
    (vi) the general income tax;
    (vii) the defence tax;
    (viii) the national security tax;
    (ix) the *jehad* tax; and
    (x) supplementary taxes imposed as a percentage of taxes which are the subject of this Convention
    (hereinafter referred to as "Egyptian tax").

(2) This Convention shall also apply to any identical or substantially similar taxes which are imposed by either Contracting State after the date of signature of this Convention in addition to, or in place of, the existing taxes. The competent authorities of the Contracting States shall notify each other of substantial changes which are made in their respective taxation laws.

Article 3 General definitions

(1) In this Convention, unless the context otherwise requires:
  (*a*) the term "United Kingdom" means Great Britain and Northern Ireland, including any area outside the territorial sea of the United Kingdom which in accordance with international law has been or may hereafter be designated, under the laws of the United Kingdom concerning the Continental Shelf, as an area within which the rights of the United Kingdom with respect to the sea-bed and sub-soil and their natural resources may be exercised:
  (*b*) (i) the term "Egypt" means the Arab Republic of Egypt; and
    (ii) when used in geographical sense the term "Egypt" includes:
      (*a*) the territorial sea thereof; and
      (*b*) the sea bed and subsoil of the submarine areas adjacent to the coast thereof, but beyond the territorial sea, over which Egypt exercises sovereign rights, in accordance with international law, for the purpose of exploration and exploitation of the natural resources of such area, but only to the extent that the person, property, or activity to which this Convention is being applied is connected with such exploration or exploitation;
  (*c*) the term "national" means:
    (i) in relation to the United Kingdom, any citizen of the United Kingdom and Colonies who derives his status as such from his connection with the United Kingdom and any legal person, partnership, association or other entity deriving its status as such from the law in force in the United Kingdom;
    (ii) in relation to Egypt, any individual possessing the nationality of the Arab Republic of Egypt; and any legal person, partnership and association deriving its status as such from the law in force in Egypt;

(*d*) the term "tax" means United Kingdom tax or Egyptian tax, as the context requires

(*e*) the terms "a Contracting State" and "the other Contracting State" mean the United Kingdom or Egypt, as the context requires;

(*f*) the term "person" comprises an individual, a company and any other body of persons;

(*g*) the term "company" means any body corporate or any entity which is treated as a body corporate for tax purposes;

(*h*) the terms "enterprise of a Contracting State" and "enterprise of the other Contracting State" mean respectively an enterprise carried on by a resident of a Contracting State and an enterprise carried on by a resident of the other Contracting State;

(*i*) the term "competent authority" means, in the case of the United Kingdom, the Commissioners of Inland Revenue or their authorised representative, and in the case of Egypt, the Minister of Finance or his authorised representative;

(*j*) the term "international traffic" includes traffic between places in one country in the course of a voyage which extends over more than one country.

(2) As regards the application of this Convention by a Contracting State any term not otherwise defined shall, unless the context otherwise requires, have the meaning which it has under the laws of that Contracting State relating to the taxes which are the subject of this Convention.

Article 4 Fiscal domicile

(1) For the purposes of this Convention, the term "resident of a Contracting State" means, subject to the provisions of paragraphs (2) and (3) of this Article, any person who, under the law of that State, is liable to taxation therein by reason of his domicile, residence, place of management or any other criterion of a similar nature.

(2) Where by reason of the provisions of paragraph (1) of this Article an individual is a resident of both Contracting States, then his status shall be determined in accordance with the following rules:

(*a*) he shall be deemed to be a resident of the Contracting State in which he has a permanent home available to him. If he has a permanent home available to him in both Contracting States, he shall be deemed to be a resident of the Contracting State with which his personal and economic relations are closer (centre of vital interests);

(*b*) if the Contracting State in which he has his centre of vital interests cannot be determined, or if he has not a permanent home available to him in either Contracting State, he shall be deemed to be a resident of the Contracting State in which he has an habitual abode;

(*c*) if he has an habitual abode in both Contracting States or in neither of them, he shall be deemed to be a resident of the Contracting State of which he is a national;

(*d*) if he is a national of both Contracting States or of neither of them, the competent authorities of the Contracting States shall settle the question by mutual agreement.

(3) Where by reason of the provisions of paragraph (1) of this Article a person other than an individual is a resident of both Contracting States, then it shall be deemed to be a resident of the Contracting State in which its place of effective management is situated.

Article 6 Income from immovable property

(1) (Taxation of income from immovable property.)

(2)(*a*) The term "immovable property" shall, subject to the provisions of sub-paragraph (*b*) of this paragraph, be defined in accordance with the law of the Contracting State in which the property in question is situated.

(*b*) The term "immovable property" shall in any case include property accessory to immovable property, livestock and equipment used in agriculture and forestry, rights to which the provisions of general law respecting landed property apply, usufruct of immovable property and rights to variable or fixed payments as consideration for the working of, or the right to work, mineral deposits, sources and other natural resources; ships, boats and aircraft shall not be regarded as immovable property.

(3) . . .

(4) . . .

Article 8 Shipping and air transport

(1) Profits from the operation of ships or aircraft in international traffic shall be taxable only in the Contracting State in which the place of effective management of the enterprise is situated.

(2) If the place of effective management of a shipping enterprise is aboard a ship or boat, it shall be deemed to be in the Contracting State in which the home harbour of the ship or boat is situated or, if there is no such home harbour, in the Contracting State of which the operator of the ship or boat is resident.

(3) The provisions of this Article shall likewise apply to the share in respect of participation in shipping or aircraft pools of any kind by such an enterprise engaged in shipping or air transport.

Article 13 Capital gains

(1) . . .

(2) (Capital gains from the alienation of movable property.)

(3) Notwithstanding the provisions of paragraph (2) of this Article, capital gains derived by a resident of a Contracting State from the alienation of ships and aircraft operated in international traffic and movable property pertaining to the operation of such ships and aircraft shall be taxable only in the Contracting State.

(4) . . .

(5) . . .

Article 23 Non-discrimination

(1) The nationals of a Contracting State shall not be subjected in the other Contracting State to any taxation or any requirement connected therewith which is other or more burdensome than the taxation and connected requirements to which nationals of that other State in the same circumstances are or may be subjected.

(2) The taxation on a permanent establishment which an enterprise of a Contracting State has in the other Contracting State shall not be less favourably levied in that other State than the taxation levied on enterprises of that other State carrying on the same activities.

(3) Enterprises of a Contracting State, the capital of which is wholly or partly owned or controlled, directly or indirectly, by one or more residents of the other Contracting State, shall not be subjected in the first-mentioned State to any taxation or any requirement connected therewith which is other or more burdensome than the taxation and connection requirements to which other similar enterprises of that first-mentioned State are or may be subjected.

(4) Nothing contained in this Article shall be construed as:

(a) obliging either Contracting State to grant to individuals not resident in that State any of the personal allowances, reliefs and reductions for tax purposes which are granted to individuals so resident;

(b) affecting the application in Egypt of Articles 5 and 6 of Law No 14 of 1939 (as they may be amended from time to time in minor respects without affecting the general principle thereof) provided that if the exemptions given by either of these Articles are made available to nationals of any State or territory other than a Contracting State such exemption shall likewise be made available to nationals of the United Kingdom;

(*c*) affecting the application in Egypt of Article 11 (paragraphs (1) and (2)) and Article 11 *bis* of law No 14 of 1939 (as they may be amended from time to time in minor respects without affecting the general principle thereof) provided that if any relief from the application of those provisions is given to nationals of any State or territory other than a Contracting State such relief shall likewise be given to nationals of the United Kingdom.

Article 24 Mutual agreement procedure

(1) Where a resident of a Contracting State considers that the actions of one or both of the Contracting States result or will result for him in taxation not in accordance with this Convention, he may, notwithstanding the remedies provided by the national laws of those States, present his case to the competent authority of the Contracting State of which he is a resident.

(2) The competent authority shall endeavour, if the objection appears to it to be justified and if it is not itself able to arrive at an appropriate solution, to resolve the case by mutual agreement with the competent authority of the Contracting State, with a view to the avoidance of taxation not in accordance with the Convention.

(3) The competent authorities of the Contracting States shall endeavour to resolve by mutual agreement any difficulties or doubts arising as to the interpretation or application of the Convention.

(4) The competent authorities of the Contracting States may communicate with each other for the purpose of reaching an agreement in the sense of the preceding paragraphs of this Article.

Article 25 Exchange of information

The competent authorities of the Contracting States shall exchange such information (being information which is at their disposal under their respective taxation laws in the normal course of administration) as is necessary for carrying out the provisions of this Convention or for the prevention of fraud or the administration of statutory provisions against legal avoidance in relation to the taxes which are the subject of this Convention. Any information so exchanged shall be treated as secret but may be disclosed to persons (including a court or administrative body) concerned with assessment, collection, enforcement or prosecution in respect of taxes which are the subject of this Convention. No information shall be exchanged which would disclose any trade, business, industrial or professional secret or any trade process.

Article 28 Entry into force

Note: Article 28 provided for the entry into force of this Convention. It takes effect in the UK from the year of assessment 1977–78 (income tax and capital gains tax) and from financial years beginning on 1 April 1977 (corporation tax).

Official language: English.

FALKLAND ISLANDS

Arrangement of 14 March 1984 (SI 1984 No 363)

Paragraph 1 Personal scope

This Arrangement shall apply to persons who are residents of one or both of the territories.

Paragraph 2 Taxes covered

(1) The taxes which are the subject of this Arrangement are:
    (a) in the United Kingdom of Great Britain and Northern Ireland:
        (i) the income tax;
        (ii) the corporation tax; and
        (iii) the capital gains tax:
        (hereinafter referred to as "United Kingdom tax");
    (b) in the Falkland Islands:
        (i) the income tax, including the tax on royalties and management fees; and
        (ii) the interest withholding tax;
        (hereinafter referred to as "Falkland Islands tax").
(2) This Arrangement shall also apply to any identical or substantially similar taxes which are imposed by either territory after the date upon which this Arrangement has effect in that territory in addition to, or in place of, the existing taxes. The competent authorities of the territories shall notify each other of the substantial changes which are made in their respective taxation laws.

Paragraph 3 General definitions

(1) In this Arrangement, unless the context otherwise requires:
    (a) the term "United Kingdom" means Great Britain and Northern Ireland, including any area outside the territorial sea of the United Kingdom which in accordance with international law has been or may hereafter be designated, under the laws of the United Kingdom concerning the Continental Shelf, as an area within which the rights of the United Kingdom with respect to the sea-bed and sub-soil and their natural resources may be exercised;
    (b) the term "Falkland Islands" means the Falkland Islands, including the Continental Shelf adjacent thereto;
    (c) the terms "a territory" and "the other territory" mean the United Kingdom or the Falkland Islands as the context requires;
    (d) the term "person" comprises an individual, a company and any other body of persons;
    (e) the term "company" means any body corporate or any entity which is treated as a body corporate for tax purposes;
    (f) the terms "enterprise of a territory" and "enterprise of the other territory" mean respectively an enterprise carried on by a resident of a territory and an enterprise carried on by a resident of the other territory;
    (g) the term "international traffic" means any transport by a ship or aircraft operated by an enterprise which has its place of effective management in a territory, except when the ship or aircraft is operated solely between places in the other territory;
    (h) the term "competent authority" means, in the case of the United Kingdom the

Commissioners of Inland Revenue or their authorised representative, and in the case of the Falkland Islands the Commissioner of Income Tax or his authorised representative.

(2) As regards the application of this Arrangement by a territory any term not otherwise defined shall, unless the context otherwise requires, have the meaning which it has under the laws of that territory concerning the taxes to which this Arrangement applies.

Paragraph 4 Fiscal domicile

(1) For the purposes of this Arrangement, the term "resident of a territory" means any person who, under the law of that territory, is liable to tax therein by reason of his domicile, residence, place of management or any other criterion of a similar nature. But this term does not include any person who is liable to tax in that territory in respect only of income from sources in that territory or capital situated therein.

(2) Where by reason of the provisions of sub-paragraph (1) of this Paragraph an individual is a resident of both territories, then his status shall be determined as follows:

    (a) he shall be deemed to be a resident of the territory in which he has a permanent home available to him; if he has a permanent home available to him in both territories, he shall be deemed to be a resident of the territory with which his personal and economic relations are closer (centre of vital interests):

    (b) if the territory in which he has his centre of vital interests cannot be determined, or if he has not a permanent home available to him in either territory, he shall be deemed to be a resident of the territory in which he has an habitual abode;

    (c) if he has an habitual abode in both territories or in neither of them, the competent authorities of the territories shall settle the question by mutual agreement.

(3) Where by reason of the provisions of sub-paragraph (1) of this Paragraph a person other than an individual is a resident of both territories, then it shall be deemed to be a resident of the territory in which its place of effective management is situated.

Paragraph 6 Income from immovable property

(1) (Taxation of income from immovable property.)

(2) The term "immovable property" shall have the meaning which it has under the law of the territory in which the property in question is situated. The term shall in any case include property accessory to immovable property, livestock and equipment used in agriculture and forestry, rights to which the provisions of general law respecting landed property apply, usufruct of immovable property and rights to variable or fixed payments consideration for the working of, or the right to work, mineral deposits, sources and other natural resources; ships, boats and aircraft shall not be regarded as immovable property.

(3) . . .

(4) . . .

Paragraph 8 Shipping and air transport

(1) Profits from the operation of ships or aircraft in international traffic shall be taxable only in the territory in which the place of effective management of the enterprise is situated.

(2) If the place of effective management of a shipping enterprise is aboard a ship then it shall be deemed to be situated in the territory in which the home harbour of the ship is situated, or, if there is no such home harbour, in the territory of which the operator of the ship is a resident.

(3) The provisions of sub-paragraph (1) of this Paragraph shall also apply to profits from the participation in a pool, a joint business or a joint operating agency.

Paragraph 15 Capital gains

(1) . . .

(2) . . .

(3) Gains from the alienation of ships or aircraft operated in international traffic or movable property pertaining to the operation of such ships or aircraft shall be taxable only in the territory in which the place of effective management of the enterprise is situated.

(4) . . .

(5) . . .

Paragraph 27 Non-discrimination

(1) A resident of a territory shall not be subjected in the other territory to any taxation or any requirement connected therewith which is other or more burdensome than the taxation and connected requirements to which any person not resident in that other territory in the same circumstances is or may be subjected.

(2) The taxation on a permanent establishment which an enterprise of a territory has in the other territory shall not be less favourably levied in that other territory than the taxation levied on enterprises of that other territory carrying on the same activities.

(3) Except where the provisions of sub-paragraph (1) of Paragraph 9, sub-paragraph (8) of Paragraph 11, sub-paragraph (5) of Paragraph 12 or sub-paragraph (7) of Paragraph 14 apply, interest, royalties, management fees or other disbursements paid by an enterprise of a territory to a resident of the other territory shall, for the purpose of determining the taxable profits of such enterprise, be deductible under the same conditions as if they had been paid to a resident of the first-mentioned territory.

(4) Enterprises of a territory, the capital of which is wholly or partly owned or controlled, directly or indirectly, by one or more residents of the other territory shall not be subjected in the first-mentioned territory to any taxation or any requirement connected therewith which is other or more burdensome that the taxation and connected requirements to which other similar enterprises of that first-mentioned territory are or may be subjected.

(5) Nothing contained in this Paragraph shall be construed as obliging either territory to grant to individuals not resident in that territory any of the personal allowances, reliefs and reductions for tax purposes, which are granted to individuals so resident.

(6) In this Paragraph the term "taxation" means taxes of every kind and description.

Paragraph 28 Mutual agreement procedure

(1) Where a resident of a territory considers that the actions of one or both of the territories result or will result for him in taxation not in accordance with this Arrangement, he may, irrespective of the remedies provided by the domestic law of those territories, present his case to the competent authority of the territory of which he is a resident.

(2) The competent authority shall endeavour, if the objection appears to it to be justified and if it is not itself able to arrive at a satisfactory solution, to resolve the case by mutual agreement with the competent authority of the other territory, with a view to the avoidance of taxation not in accordance with this Arrangement.

(3) The competent authorities of the territories shall endeavour to resolve by mutual agreement any difficulties or doubts arising as to the interpretation or application of this Arrangement.

(4) The competent authorities of the territories may communicate with each other directly for the purpose of reaching an agreement in the sense of the preceding sub-paragraphs.

Paragraph 29 Exchange of information

The competent authorities of the territories shall exchange such information (being information which is at their disposal under the respective taxation laws in the normal course of administration) as is necessary for carrying out the provisions of this Arrangement or for the prevention of fraud or the administration of statutory provisions against legal avoidance in relation to the taxes which are the subject of this Arrangement. Any information so exchanged shall be treated as secret and shall be disclosed only to persons (including a court or administrative body) concerned with the assessment, collection, enforcement or prosecution in respect of taxes which are the subject of this Arrangement. No information shall be exchanged which would disclose any trade, business, industrial or professional secret or any trade process or information, the disclosure of which would be contrary to public policy.

Paragraph 31 Entry into force

Note: Paragraph 31 provided for the entry into force of this Arrangement. It takes effect in the UK from the year of assessment 1982–83 (income tax and capital gains tax) and from financial years beginning on 1 April 1982 (corporation tax).

Official language: English.

FAROE ISLANDS

Danish Convention of 27 March 1950 (SI 1950 No 1195)

Extended to the Faroe Islands by the Extension of 31 October 1960 (SI 1961 No 579).

Printed as amended by the Supplementary Protocol of 18 September 1968 (SI 1969 No 1068), extended to the Faroe Islands by the Extension of 27 November 1970 (SI 1971 No 717).

(The Supplementary Protocol of 8 February 1973 (SI 1973 No 1326) does not amend the Articles printed below.)

Article I [Taxes covered]

(1) The taxes which are the subject of the present Convention are:
    (a) in the Faroe Islands:
        the provincial income tax (*skat til Landskassen*) and the communal income tax (*kommunal indkomstskat*)
        (hereinafter referred to as "Faroese tax");
    (b) in the United Kingdom of Great Britain and Northern Ireland:
        (i) the income tax (including surtax);
        (ii) the corporation tax; and
        (iii) the capital gains tax
        (hereinafter referred to as "United Kingdom tax").

(2) The present Convention shall also apply to any other taxes of a substantially similar character imposed in the Faroe Islands or the United Kingdom subsequently to the 31st day of October, 1960.

Article II [General definitions]

(1) In the present Convention, unless the context otherwise requires:
    (a) The term "United Kingdom" means Great Britain and Northern Ireland, excluding the Channel Islands and the Isle of Man;
    (b) . . .
    (c) The terms "one of the territories" and "the other territory" mean the United Kingdom or the Faroe Islands, as the context requires;
    (d) The term "tax" means United Kingdom tax or the Faroese Islands tax, as the context requires;

(e) The term "person" includes any body of persons, corporate or not corporate;

(f) The term "company" means any body corporate;

[(g) The terms "resident of the United Kingdom" and "resident of the Faroe Islands" mean respectively any person who is resident in the United Kingdom for the purposes of United Kingdom tax and not resident in the Faroe Islands for the purposes of Faroese tax, and any person who is resident in the Faroe Islands for the purposes of Faroese tax and not resident in the United Kingdom for the purposes of United Kingdom tax; a company shall be regarded as resident in the United Kingdom if its business is managed and controlled in the United Kingdom and as resident in the Faroe Islands if its business is managed and controlled in the Faroe Islands and it is resident in the Faroe Islands for the purposes of Faroese tax;]

(h) The terms "resident of one of the territories" and "resident of the other territory" mean a person who is a resident of the United Kingdom or a person who is a resident of the Faroe Islands, as the context requires;

(i) The terms "United Kingdom enterprise" and "Faroese enterprise" mean respectively an industrial or commercial enterprise or undertaking carried on by a resident of the United Kingdom and an industrial or commercial enterprise or undertaking carried on by a resident of the Faroe Islands, and the terms "enterprise of one of the territories" and "enterprise of the other territory" mean a United Kingdom enterprise or a Faroese enterprise, as the context requires;

(j) . . .

(k) The term "permanent establishment", when used with respect to an enterprise of one of the territories, means a branch, management, factory, or other fixed place of business, but does not include an agency unless the agent has, and habitually exercises, a general authority to negotiate and conclude contracts on behalf of such enterprise or has a stock of merchandise from which he regularly fills orders on its behalf. In this connexion—

   (i) An enterprise of one of the territories shall not be deemed to have a permanent establishment in the other territory merely because it carries on business dealings in that other territory through a *bona fide* broker or general commission agent acting in the ordinary course of his business as such;

   (ii) The fact that an enterprise of one of the territories maintains in the other territory a fixed place of business exclusively for the purchase of goods or merchandise shall not of itself constitute that fixed place of business a permanent establishment of the enterprise;

   (iii) The fact that a company which is a resident of one of the territories has a subsidiary company which is a resident of the other territory or which carries on a trade or business in that other territory (whether through a permanent establishment or otherwise) shall not of itself constitute that subsidiary company a permanent establishment of its parent company.

(2) Where under any provision of the present Convention income is relieved from Faroese tax and, under the law in force in the United Kingdom, an individual in respect of the said income is chargeable by reference to the amount thereof which is remitted to or received in the United Kingdom and not by reference to the full amount thereof, then the relief to be allowed under the present Convention in the Faroe Islands shall apply only to so much of the income as is remitted to or received in the United Kingdom.

(3) In the application of the provisions of the present Convention by one of the High Contracting Parties any term not otherwise defined shall, unless the context otherwise requires, have the meaning which it has under the laws in force in the territory of that Party relating to the taxes which are the subject of the present Convention.

Article VI [Shipping and air transport]

(1) Notwithstanding the provisions of Articles III, IV and V, profits which a resident of one of the territories derives from operating ships or aircraft shall be exempt from tax in the other territory.

(2) The Arrangement dated 18 December, 1924, between the United Kingdom and Denmark for the reciprocal exemption from Income Tax in certain cases of profits accruing from the business of shipping shall not have effect for any year or period for which the present Convention has effect.

Article III: Taxation of industrial or commercial profits.
Article IV: Taxation of profits of associated enterprises.
Article V: Deleted by the Protocol of 18 December 1968 (SI 1969 No 1068).

Article X [Capital gains]

A resident of one of the territories who does not carry on a trade or business in the other territory through a permanent establishment situated therein shall be exempt in that other territory from any tax on gains from the sale, transfer, or exchange of capital assets.

Article XVIII [Exchange of information]

(1) The taxation authorities of the High Contracting Parties shall exchange such information (being information which is at their disposal under their respective taxation laws in the normal course of administration) as is necessary for carrying out the provisions of the present Convention or for the prevention of fraud or for the administration of statutory provisions against legal avoidance in relation to the taxes which are the subject of the present Convention. Any information so exchanged shall be treated as secret and shall not be disclosed to any persons other than those concerned with the assessment and collection of the taxes which are the subject of the present Convention. No information as aforesaid shall be exchanged which would disclose any trade, business, industrial or professional secret or trade process.

(2) As used in this Article, the term "taxation authorities" means, in the case of the United Kingdom, the Commissioners of Inland Revenue or their authorised representatives; in the case of Denmark, the Director-General of Taxation or his authorised representative; and, in the case of any territory to which the present Convention is extended under Article XX, the competent authority for the administration in such territory of the taxes to which the present Convention applies.

Article XIX [Non-discrimination]

(1) The nationals of one of the High Contracting Parties shall not be subjected in the territory of the other High Contracting Party to any taxation or any requirement connected therewith which is other, higher, or more burdensome than the taxation and connected requirements to which the nationals of the latter Party are or may be subjected.

(2) The enterprises of one of the territories, whether carried on by a company, a body of persons or by individuals alone or in partnership, shall not be subjected in the other territory, in respect of profits or capital attributable to their permanent establishments in that other territory, to any taxation which is other, higher or more burdensome than the taxation to which the enterprises of that other territory similarly carried on are or may be subjected in respect of the like profits or capital.

(3) The income, profits and capital of an enterprise of one of the territories, the capital of which is wholly or partly owned or controlled, directly or indirectly, by a resident or residents of the other territory shall not be subjected in the first-mentioned territory to any taxation which is other, higher or more burdensome than the taxation to which other enterprises of that first-mentioned territory are or may be subjected in respect of the like income, profits and capital.

(4) Nothing contained in this Article shall be construed as obliging either territory to grant to individuals not resident in that territory any of the personal allowances, reliefs and reductions for tax purposes which are granted to individuals so resident, nor as conferring any exemption from tax in one of the territories in respect of dividends paid to a company which is a resident of the other territory.

(5) In this Article the term "nationals" means—

    (*a*) in relation to the Faroe Islands, all Danish citizens and all legal persons, partnerships, associations and other entities deriving their status as such from the law in force in Denmark or in any Danish territory to which the present Convention applies by reason of extension made under Article XX;

    (*b*) in relation to the United Kingdom, all British subjects and British-protected persons residing in the United Kingdom or any British territory to which the present Convention applies by reason of extension made under Article XX, and all legal persons, partnerships, associations and other entities deriving their status as such from the law in force in any British territory to which the present Convention applies.

SI 1960 No 579 para (2) Entry into force

Note: Paragraph (2) provided for the entry into force of the 1950 Convention as extended by the 1960 Protocol. It takes effect in the UK in its amended form from the year of assessment 1968–69 (income tax and capital gains tax) and from the financial year beginning on 1 April 1968 (corporation tax).

Official languages: The Danish language text and the English language text of this Convention are equally authoritative.

FIJI

Convention of 21 November 1975 (SI 1976 No 1342)

Article 1 Personal scope

This Convention shall apply to persons who are residents of one or both of the Contracting States.

Article 2 Taxes covered

(1) The taxes which are the subject of this Convention are:

    (*a*) in the United Kingdom of Great Britain and Northern Ireland:

        (i) the income tax;

        (ii) the corporation tax; and

        (iii) the capital gains tax;

    (*b*) in Fiji:

        (i) the income tax (including basic tax and normal tax);

        (ii) the non-resident dividend withholding tax, the interest withholding tax and the dividend tax; and

        (iii) the land sales tax.

(2) This Convention shall also apply to any identical or substantially similar taxes which are imposed by either Contracting State after the date of signature of this Convention in addition to, or in place of, the existing taxes. The competent authorities of the Contracting States shall notify to each other any changes which are made in their respective taxation laws.

Article 3 General definitions

(1) In this Convention, unless the context otherwise requires:

(a) the term "United Kingdom" means Great Britain and Northern Ireland, including any area outside the territorial sea of the United Kingdom which in accordance with international law has been or may hereafter be designated, under the laws of the United Kingdom concerning the Continental Shelf, as an area within which the rights of the United Kingdom with respect to the sea-bed and sub-soil and their natural resources may be exercised;

(b) the term "Fiji" means the islands of Fiji, including the island of Rotuma and its dependencies, and includes all areas of water which in accordance with international law have been or may hereafter be designated under the laws of Fiji as areas over which the sovereignty of Fiji may be exercised with respect to the sea, the sea bed and sub-soil and the natural resources thereof;

(c) the term "nationals" means:

(i) in relation to the United Kingdom, all citizens of the United Kingdom and Colonies who derive their status as such from their connection with the United Kingdom and all legal persons, partnerships and associations deriving their status as such from the law in force in the United Kingdom;

(ii) in relation to Fiji:

(a) all citizens of Fiji; and

(b) all legal persons, partnerships and associations deriving their status as such from the law of Fiji;

(d) the term "United Kingdom tax" means tax imposed by the United Kingdom being tax to which this Convention applies by virtue of the provisions of Article 2; the term "Fiji tax" means tax imposed by Fiji being tax to which this Convention applies by virtue of the provisions of Article 2;

(e) the term "tax" means United Kingdom tax or Fiji tax, as the context requires;

(f) the terms "a Contracting State" and "the other Contracting State" mean the United Kingdom or Fiji, as the context requires;

(g) the term "person" comprises an individual, a company and any other body of persons;

(h) the term "company" means any body corporate or any entity which is treated as a body corporate for tax purposes;

(i) the terms "enterprise of a Contracting State" and "enterprise of the other Contracting State" mean respectively an enterprise carried on by a resident of a Contracting State and an enterprise carried on by a resident of the other Contracting State;

(j) the term "competent authority" means, in the case of the United Kingdom the Commissioners of Inland Revenue or their authorised representative, and in the case of Fiji the Commissioner of Inland Revenue or his authorised representative;

(k) the term "international traffic" includes traffic between places in one country in the course of a voyage which extends over more than one country.

(2) As regards the application of this Convention by a Contracting State any term not otherwise defined shall, unless the context otherwise requires, have the meaning which it has under the laws of that Contracting State relating to the taxes which are the subject of this Convention.

Article 4 Fiscal domicile

(1) For the purposes of this Convention, the term "resident of a Contracting State" means, subject to paragraphs (2) and (3) of this Article, any person who, under the law of that

Contracting State, is liable to taxation therein by reason of his domicile, residence, place of management or any other criterion of a similar nature; the term does not include any individual who is liable to tax in that Contracting State only if he derives income from sources therein. The terms "resident of the United Kingdom" and "resident of Fiji" shall be construed accordingly.

(2) Where by reason of the provisions of paragraph (1) of this Article an individual is a resident of both Contracting States, then his status shall be determined in accordance with the following rules:

(a) he shall be deemed to be a resident of the Contracting State in which he has a permanent home available to him. If he has a permanent home available to him in both Contracting States, he shall be deemed to be a resident of the Contracting State with which his potential and economic relations are closer (centre of vital interests);

(b) if the Contracting State in which he has his centre of vital interests cannot be determined, or if he has not a permanent home available to him in either Contracting State, he shall be deemed to be a resident of the Contracting State in which he has an habitual abode;

(c) if he has an habitual abode in both Contracting States or in neither of them, he shall be deemed to be a resident of the Contracting State of which he is a national;

(d) if he is a national of both Contracting States or of neither of them, the competent authorities of the Contracting States shall settle the question by mutual agreement.

(3) Where by reason of the provisions of paragraph (1) of this Article a person other than an individual is a resident of both Contracting States, then it shall be deemed to be a resident of the Contracting State in which its place of effective management is situated.

Article 7 Income from immovable property

(1) (Taxation of income from immovable property.)

(2) (a) The term "immovable property" shall, subject to sub-paragraph (b) below, be defined in accordance with the law of the Contracting State in which the property in question is situated.

(b) The term "immovable property" shall in any case include property accessory to immovable property, livestock and equipment used in agriculture and forestry, rights to which the provisions of general law respecting landed property apply, usufruct of immovable property and rights to variable or fixed payments as consideration for the working of, or the right to work, mineral deposits, sources and other natural resources; ships, boats and aircraft shall not be regarded as immovable property.

(3) . . .

(4) . . .

Article 9 Shipping and air transport

A resident of a Contracting State shall be exempt from tax in the other Contracting State on profits from the operation of ships or aircraft other than profits from voyages of ships or aircraft confined wholly or mainly to places in the other Contracting State.

Article 14 Capital gains

(1) . . .

(2) . . .

(3) (Taxation of capital gains represented by movable property.)

(4) Notwithstanding the provisions of paragraph (3) of this Article capital gains derived by a resident of a Contracting State from the alienation of ships and aircraft operated in international traffic and movable property pertaining to the operation of such ships and aircraft shall be taxable only in the Contracting State.

77

(5) . . .

(6) . . .

Article 24 Non-discrimination

(1) The nationals of a Contracting State shall not be subjected in the other Contracting State to any taxation or any requirement connected therewith which is other or more burdensome than the taxation and connected requirements to which nationals of that other State in the same circumstances are or may be subjected.

(2) The taxation on a permanent establishment which an enterprise of a Contracting State has in the other Contracting State shall not be less favourably levied in that other State than the taxation levied on enterprises of that other State carrying on the same activities:

Provided that this paragraph shall not prevent the Government of a Contracting State from imposing on the profits attributable to a permanent establishment in that Contracting State of a company which is a resident of the other Contracting State an additional tax not exceeding 15 per cent of two-thirds of the profits of the permanent establishment after payment of the company or corporation tax on those profits.

(3) Enterprises of a Contracting State, the capital of which is wholly or partly owned or controlled, directly or indirectly, by one or more residents of the other Contracting State, shall not be subjected in the first-mentioned State to any taxation or any requirement connected therewith which is other or more burdensome than the taxation and connected requirements to which other similar enterprises of the first-mentioned State are or may be subjected.

(4) Nothing contained in this Article shall be construed as obliging either Contracting State to grant to individuals not resident in that State any of the personal allowances, reliefs and reductions for tax purposes which are granted to individuals so resident, nor as conferring any exemption from tax in a Contracting State in respect of dividends paid to a company which is a resident of the other Contracting State.

(5) In this Article the term "taxation" means taxes which are the subject of this Convention.

Article 25 Mutual agreement procedure

(1) Where a resident of a Contracting State considers that the actions of one or both of the Contracting States result or will result for him in taxation not in accordance with this Convention, he may, notwithstanding the remedies provided by the national laws of those States, present his case to the competent authority of the Contracting State of which he is a resident.

(2) The competent authority shall endeavour, if the objection appears to it to be justified and if it is not itself able to arrive at an appropriate solution, to resolve the case by mutual agreement with the competent authority of the other Contracting State, with a view to the avoidance of taxation not in accordance with the Convention.

(3) The competent authorities of the Contracting States shall endeavour to resolve by mutual agreement any difficulties or doubts arising as to the interpretation or application of the Convention.

(4) The competent authorities of the Contracting States may communicate with each other directly for the purpose of reaching an agreement in the sense of the preceding paragraphs.

Article 26 Exchange of information

The competent authorities of the Contracting States shall exchange such information (being information which is at their disposal under their respective taxation laws in the normal course of administration) as is necessary for carrying out the provisions of this Convention or for the prevention of fraud or the administration of statutory provisions against legal avoidance in relation to the taxes which are the subject of this Convention. Any information so exchanged shall be treated as secret but may be disclosed to persons (including a court or administrative body) concerned with assessment, collection, enforcement or prosecution in respect of taxes which are the subject of this Convention. No information shall be exchanged which would disclose any trade, business, industrial or professional secret or any trade process.

Article 27 Entry into force

Note: Article 27 provided for the entry into force of this Convention. It takes effect in the UK from the year of assessment 1975–76 (income tax and capital gains tax) and from the financial year beginning on 1 April 1975 (corporation tax).

Official language: English.

FINLAND

Convention of 17 July 1969 (SI 1970 No 153)

Printed as amended by the Protocols of 16 November 1979 (SI 1980 No 710) and 1 October 1985 (SI 1985 No 1997).

Article 1 Personal scope

This Convention shall apply to persons who are residents of one or both of the Contracting States.

Article 2 Taxes covered

(1) The taxes which are the subject of this Convention are:
    (*a*) in the United Kingdom of Great Britain and Northern Ireland:
        (i) the income tax;
        (ii) the corporation tax;
        (iii) the petroleum revenue tax;
        (iv) the development land tax; and
        (v) the capital gains tax;
    (*b*) in Finland:
        (i) the state income and capital tax;
        (ii) the communal tax;

  (iii) the church tax;
  (iv) the sailor's tax; and
  (v) the tax withheld at source from non-residents' income.

Article 3 General definitions

(1) In this Convention, unless the context otherwise requires:
  (a) the term "United Kingdom" means Great Britain and Northern Ireland, including any area outside the territorial sea of the United Kingdom which in accordance with international law has been or may hereafter be designated, under the laws of the United Kingdom concerning the Continental Shelf, as an area within which the rights of the United Kingdom with respect to the sea-bed and sub-soil and their natural resources may be exercised;
  (b) the term "Finland" means the Republic of Finland, including any area outside the territorial sea of Finland within which in accordance with international law and under the laws of Finland concerning the Continental Shelf the rights of Finland with respect to the sea bed and sub-soil and their natural resources may be exercised;
  (c) the term "nationals" means:
    (i) in relation to the United Kingdom, all citizens of the United Kingdom and Colonies who derive their status as such from their connection with the United Kingdom and all legal persons, partnerships and associations deriving their status as such from the law in force in the United Kingdom;
    (ii) in relation to Finland, all individuals possessing the nationality of Finland and all legal persons, partnerships, associations and other entities deriving their status as such from the law in force in Finland;
  (d) the term "United Kingdom tax" means tax imposed in the United Kingdom being tax to which this Convention applies by virtue of the provisions of Article 2; the term "Finnish tax" means tax imposed in Finland being tax to which this Convention applies by virtue of the provisions of Article 2;
  (e) the term "tax" means United Kingdom tax or Finnish tax, as the context requires;
  (f) the terms "a Contracting State" and "the other Contracting State" mean the United Kingdom or Finland, as the context requires;
  (g) the term "person" comprises an individual, a company and any other body of persons;
  (h) the term "company" means any body corporate or any entity which is treated as a body corporate for tax purposes;
  (i) the terms "enterprise of a Contracting State" and "enterprise of the other Contracting State" mean respectively an enterprise carried on by a resident of a Contracting State and an enterprise carried on by a resident of the other Contracting State;
  (j) the term "competent authority" means, in the case of the United Kingdom, the Commissioners of Inland Revenue or their authorised representative, and in the case of Finland, the Ministry of Finance or its authorised representative.

(2) As regards the application of this Convention by a Contracting State any term not otherwise defined shall, unless the context otherwise requires, have the meaning which it has under the laws of that Contracting State relating to the taxes which are the subject of this Convention.

Article 4 Fiscal domicile

(1) For the purposes of this Convention, the term "resident of a Contracting State" means, subject to the provisions of paragraphs (2) and (3) of this Article, any person who, under the law of that State, is liable to taxation therein by reason of his domicile, residence, place of management or any other criterion of a similar nature; the term does not include any individual who is liable to tax in that Contracting State only if he derives income from sources

therein. The terms "resident of the United Kingdom" and "resident of Finland" shall be construed accordingly.

(2) Where by reason of the provisions of paragraph (1) of this Article an individual is a resident of both Contracting States, then his status shall be determined in accordance with the following rules:

(a) he shall be deemed to be a resident of the Contracting State in which he has a permanent home available to him. If he has a permanent home available to him in both Contracting States, he shall be deemed to be a resident of the Contracting State with which his personal and economic relations are closest (centre of vital interests);

(b) if the Contracting State in which he has his centre of vital interests cannot be determined, or if he has not a permanent home available to him in either Contracting State, he shall be deemed to be a resident of the Contracting State in which he has an habitual abode;

(c) if he has an habitual abode in both Contracting States or in neither of them, he shall be deemed to be a resident of the Contracting State of which he is a national;

(d) if he is a national of both Contracting States or of neither of them, the competent authorities of the Contracting States shall settle the question by mutual agreement.

(3) Where by reason of the provisions of paragraph (1) of this Article a person other than an individual is a resident of both Contracting States, then it shall be deemed to be a resident of the Contracting State in which its place of effective management is situated.

Article 7 Income from immovable property

(1) (Taxation of income from immovable property.)

(2) (a) . . .

    (b) . . .

    (c) Ships, boats and aircraft shall not be regarded as immovable property.

(3)–(6) . . .

Article 9 Shipping and air transport

A resident of a Contracting State shall be taxable only in that Contracting State on profits from the operation of ships or aircraft other than profits from voyages of ships or aircraft confined solely to places in the other Contracting State.

Offshore activities: See Article 30A(5) in relation to offshore activities.

Article 14 Capital gains

(1) . . .

(2) . . .

(3) (Capital gains from the alienation of movable business property.)

(4) Notwithstanding the provisions of paragraph (3) of this Article, gains derived by a resident of a Contracting State from the alienation of ships or aircraft operated in international traffic and movable property pertaining to the operation of such ships or aircraft shall be taxable only in that State.

(5)–(7) . . .

Article 24 Capital

(1) . . .

(2) . . .

(3) (Capital represented by movable business property.)

(4) Notwithstanding the provisions of paragraph (3) of this Article, capital represented by

ships or aircraft operated in international traffic and by movable property pertaining to the operation of such ships or aircraft shall be taxable only in the Contracting State of which the operator is a resident.

(5) . . .

Article 27 Non-discrimination

(1) The nationals of a Contracting State shall not be subjected in the other Contracting State to any taxation or any requirement connected therewith which is other or more burdensome than the taxation and connected requirements to which nationals of that other State in the same circumstances are or may be subjected.

(2) The taxation on a permanent establishment which an enterprise of a Contracting State has in the other Contracting State shall not be less favourably levied in that other State than the taxation levied on enterprises of that other State carrying on the same activities.

(3) Enterprises of a Contracting State, the capital of which is wholly or partly owned or controlled, directly or indirectly by one or more residents of the other Contracting State, shall not be subjected in the first-mentioned Contracting State to any taxation or any requirement connected therewith which is other or more burdensome than the taxation and connected requirements to which other similar enterprises of that first-mentioned State are or may be subjected.

(4) In determining for the purpose of United Kingdom tax whether a company is a close company, the term "recognised stock exchange" shall include the Helsinki Stock Exchange.

(5) Nothing contained in this Article shall be construed as obliging either Contracting State to grant to individuals not resident in that State any of the personal allowances, reliefs and reductions for tax purposes which are granted to individuals so resident, nor as obliging the United Kingdom to grant to a company which is a resident of Finland a greater relief from United Kingdom income tax chargeable upon dividends received from a company which is a resident of the United Kingdom than the relief to which the first-mentioned company may be entitled under the provisions of Article 11 of this Convention.

(6) In this Article the term "taxation" means taxes of every kind and description.

Article 28 Mutual agreement procedure

(1) Where a resident of a Contracting State considers that the actions of one or both of the Contracting States result or will result for him in taxation not in accordance with this Convention, he may, notwithstanding the remedies provided by the national laws of those States, present his case to the competent authority of the Contracting State of which he is a resident.

(2) The competent authority shall endeavour, if the objection appears to it to be justified and if it is not itself able to arrive at an appropriate solution, to resolve the case by mutual agreement with the competent authority of the other Contracting State, with a view to the avoidance of taxation not in accordance with the Convention.

(3) The competent authorities of the Contracting States shall endeavour to resolve by mutual agreement any difficulties or doubts arising as to the interpretation or application of the Convention. They may also consult together to consider measures to counteract improper use of the provisions of the Convention.

(4) The competent authorities of the Contracting States may communicate with each other directly for the purpose of reaching an agreement in the sense of the preceding paragraphs.

Article 29 Exchange of information

The competent authorities of the Contracting States shall exchange such information (being information which is at their disposal under their respective taxation laws in the normal course of administration) as is necessary for carrying out the provisions of this Convention or for the prevention of fraud or the administration of statutory provisions against legal avoidance in relation to the taxes which are the subject of this Convention. Any information so exchanged shall be treated as secret but may be disclosed to persons (including a court or administrative body) concerned with assessment, collection, enforcement or prosecution in respect of taxes which are the subject of this Convention. No information shall be exchanged which would disclose any trade, business, industrial or professional secret or any trade process.

Article 30A Miscellaneous rules applicable to certain offshore activities

(1) The provisions of this Article shall apply notwithstanding any other provision of this Convention where activities are carried on offshore (in this Article called "offshore activities") in connection with the exploration or exploitation of the sea bed and sub-soil and their natural resources situated in a Contracting State.

(2)–(4) . . .

(5) Profits derived by a resident of a Contracting State from the transportation of supplies or personnel by a ship or aircraft to a location where offshore activities are being carried on, or from the operation of tugboats or anchor handling vessels in connection with such activities, shall be taxable only in the Contracting State of which he is a resident.

(6) . . .

Article 31 Entry into force

Note: Article 30 provided for the entry into force of the 1969 Convention. It takes effect in the UK in its amended form from the year of assessment 1988–89 (income tax and capital gains tax) and from the financial year beginning on 1 April 1988 (corporation tax).

Official language: The Finnish language text and the English language text of this Convention are equally authoritative.

FRANCE

Convention of 22 May 1968 (SI 1968 No 1869)

Printed as amended by the Protocols of 12 June 1986 (SI 1987 No 466) and 15 October 1987 (SI 1987 No 2055).
(The amending Supplementary Protocol of 14 May 1973 (SI 1973 No 1328) does not amend the Articles printed below.)

FRANCE

Article 1 [Taxes covered]

(1) The taxes which are the subject of this Convention are:
  (*a*) in the United Kingdom of Great Britain and Northern Ireland:
      the income tax including surtax, the corporation tax and the capital gains tax (hereinafter referred to as "United Kingdom tax");
  (*b*) in France:
      the income tax, the corporation tax, including any withholding tax, prepayment (*précompte*) or advance payment with respect to the aforesaid taxes (hereinafter referred to as "French tax").

(2) This Convention shall also apply to any identical or substantially similar future taxes which are imposed in addition to, or in place of, the existing taxes by either Contracting State or by the Government of any territory to which this Convention is extended under Article 29. The competent authorities of the Contracting States shall notify to each other any changes which have been made in their respective taxation laws.

Article 2 [General definitions]

(1) In this Convention:
  (*a*) the term "United Kingdom" means Great Britain and Northern Ireland, including any area outside the territorial sea of the United Kingdom which is, in accordance with international law, an area within which the United Kingdom may exercise rights with respect to the sea-bed and sub-soil and their natural resources;
  (*b*) the term "France" means the European and Overseas Departments (Guadeloupe, Guyane, Martinique and Réunion) of the French Republic, including any area outside the territorial sea of France which is, in accordance with international law, an area within which France may exercise rights with respect to the sea bed and sub-soil and their natural resources;
  (*c*) the terms "a Contracting State" and "the other Contracting State" mean the United Kingdom or France as the context requires;
  (*d*) the term "competent authorities" means, in the case of the United Kingdom, the Commissioners of Inland Revenue or their authorised representative; in the case of France, the Minister of Economy and Finance (*le Ministre de l'Economie et des Finances*) or his authorised representative; and, in the case of any territory to which this Convention is extended under Article 29, the competent authority for the administration in such territory of the taxes to which this Convention applies;
  (*e*) the term "tax" means United Kingdom tax or French tax as the context requires;
  (*f*) the term "person" comprises an individual, a company and any other body of persons;
  (*g*) the term "company" means any body corporate or any entity which is treated as a body corporate for tax purposes;
  (*h*) the terms "enterprise of a Contracting State" "enterprise of the other Contracting State" mean respectively an enterprise carried on by a resident of a Contracting State and an enterprise carried on by a resident of the other Contracting State;
  (*i*) the term "international traffic" includes any voyage of a ship or aircraft other than a voyage solely between places in the Contracting State which is not the Contracting State of which a person deriving the profits of the operation of a ship or aircraft is a resident.

(2) In the application of the provisions of this Convention by a Contracting State any term not otherwise defined shall, unless the context otherwise requires, have the meaning which it has under the laws of that Contracting State relating to the taxes which are the subject of this Convention.

Article 3 [Fiscal domicile]

(1) For the purposes of this Convention, the term "resident of a Contracting State" means any person who, under the laws of that State, is liable to tax therein by reason of his domicile,

residence, place of management or any other criterion of a similar nature. But this term does not include any person who is liable to tax in that State in respect only of income from sources in that State.

(2) Where by reason of the provisions of paragraph (1) an individual is a resident of both Contracting States, then this case shall be determined in accordance with the following rules:

    (a) He shall be deemed to be a resident of the Contracting State in which he has a permanent home available to him. If he has a permanent home available to him in both Contracting States, he shall be deemed to be a resident of the Contracting State with which his personal and economic relations are closest (centre of vital interests).

    (b) If the Contracting State in which he has his centre of vital interests cannot be determined, or if he has not a permanent home available to him in either Contracting State, he shall be deemed to be a resident of the Contracting State in which he has an habitual abode.

    (c) If he has an habitual abode in both Contracting States or in neither of them, he shall be deemed to be a resident of the Contracting State of which he is a national.

    (d) If he is a national of both Contracting States or of neither of them, the competent authorities of the Contracting States shall settle the question by mutual agreement.

(3) Where by reason of the provisions of paragraph (1) a person other than an individual is a resident of both Contracting States, then it shall be deemed to be a resident of the Contracting State in which its place of effective management is situated.

(4) The term "resident of a Contracting State" and "resident of the other Contracting State" means a person who is a resident of the United Kingdom, or a person who is a resident of France, as the context requires.

Article 5 [Income from immovable property]

(1) (Taxation of income from immovable property.)

(2) (a) The term "immovable property" shall, subject to the provisions of sub-paragraphs (b), (c) and (d) below, have the meaning which it has under the law of the Contracting State in which the property in question is situated.

    (b) . . .

    (c) . . .

    (d) ships and aircraft shall not be regarded as immovable property.

(3) . . .

(4) . . .

Article 7 [Shipping and air transport]

(1) Profits which a resident of one of the Contracting States derives from the operation of ships or aircraft in international traffic shall be taxable only in that State.

(2) Where profits within paragraph (1) of this Article are derived by a resident of a Contracting State from participation in a pool, a joint business or an international operating agency, the profits attributable to that resident shall be taxable only in the Contracting State of which he is a resident.

Offshore activities: See Article 29A(4) in relation to offshore activities.

Article 13 [Capital gains]

(1) . . .

(2) Gains from the alienation of movable property forming part of the business property of a permanent establishment which an enterprise of a Contracting State has in the other Contracting State or of movable property pertaining to a fixed base available to a resident of a Contracting State in the other Contracting State for the purposes of performing professional

services, including such gains from the alienation of such a permanent establishment (alone or together with the whole enterprise) or of such a fixed base, may be taxed in the other State. However, gains derived by a resident of a Contracting State from the alienation of ships and aircraft operated in international traffic and notable property pertaining to the operation of such ships and aircraft shall be taxable only in that Contracting State.

(3) . . .

(4) . . .

Article 25 [Non-discrimination]

(1) The nationals of a Contracting State shall not be subjected in the other Contracting State to any taxation or any requirement connected therewith which is other or more burdensome than the taxation and connected requirements to which nationals of that other State in the same circumstances are or may be subjected.

(2) The term "national" means:

    (a) in relation to the United Kingdom, any British citizen or any British subject not possessing the citizenship of any other Commonwealth country or territory, provided he has the right of abode in the United Kingdom; and any legal person, partnership, association or other entity deriving its status as such from the law in force in the United Kingdom;

    (b) in relation to France:

        (i) all individuals who have French nationality;

        (ii) all legal persons, associations and other entities deriving their status as such from the law in force in France.

(3) The taxation on a permanent establishment which an enterprise of a Contracting State has in the other Contracting State shall not be less favourably levied in that other State than the taxation levied on enterprises of that other State carrying on the same activities; provided that this paragraph shall not prevent a Contracting State from imposing the tax referred to in Article 10.

(4) Enterprises of a Contracting State, the capital of which is wholly or partly owned or controlled, directly or indirectly, by one or more residents of the other Contracting State, shall not be subjected in the first-mentioned Contracting State to any taxation or any requirement connected therewith which is other or more burdensome than the taxation and connected requirements to which other similar enterprises of that first-mentioned State are or may be subjected.

(5) In determining for the purpose of United Kingdom tax whether a company is a close company the term "recognised stock exchange" shall include any stock exchange set up in France in accordance with the French legislation.

(6) Nothing contained in this Article shall be construed as obliging either Contracting State to grant to individuals not resident in that State any of the personal allowances and reliefs for tax purposes which are granted to individuals so resident.

(7) In this Article the term "taxation" means taxes of every kind and description.

(8) Payments made by an individual who is a resident of a Contracting State to a pension scheme established in the other Contracting State may be relieved from tax in the first-mentioned Contracting State provided that:

    (a) the individual was contributing to the pension scheme before he became a resident of the first-mentioned State; and

    (b) the pension scheme is accepted by the competent authority of that State as corresponding to a pension scheme recognised as such for tax purposes by that State.

In such case relief from tax shall be given in the same way as if the pension scheme was recognised as such by that State and payments to the pension scheme by the enterprise paying his remuneration shall not be deemed to be taxable income of the individual.

Article 26 [Mutual agreement procedure]

(1) Where a resident of a Contracting State considers that the actions of one or both of the Contracting States result or will result for him in taxation not in accordance with this Con-

vention, he may, notwithstanding the remedies provided by the national laws of those States, present his case to the competent authorities of either Contracting State.

(2) The competent authorities shall endeavour, if the objection appears to them to be justified and if they are not themselves able to arrive at an appropriate solution, to resolve the case by mutual agreement with the competent authorities of the other Contracting State, with a view to the avoidance of taxation not in accordance with the Convention.

(3) The competent authorities of the Contracting States shall endeavour to resolve by mutual agreement any difficulties arising as to the application of the Convention. In particular the competent authorities may consult together to endeavour to resolve disputes arising out of the application of paragraph (2) of Article 6 or Article 8, or the determination of the source of particular items of income.

(4) The competent authorities of the Contracting States may communicate with each other directly for the purpose of reaching an agreement in the sense of the preceding paragraphs or for the purpose of giving effect to the provisions of the Convention and for resolving any difficulty as to the application of the Convention.

(5) In France where the income or profits of an enterprise are adjusted pursuant to Article 8, taxes shall be imposed on such income or profits, or refund of taxes shall be allowed, in accordance with the agreement reached by the competent authorities respecting such adjustments.

(6) In the United Kingdom where profits on which an enterprise of the United Kingdom has been charged to United Kingdom tax are also included in the profits of an enterprise of France in accordance with Article 8, the amount included in the profits of both enterprises shall be treated for the purposes of Article 24 as income from a source in France of an enterprise of the United Kingdom and credit shall be given accordingly in respect of the extra French tax chargeable as a result of the inclusion of the said amount.

Article 27 [Exchange of information]

(1) The competent authorities of the Contracting States shall exchange such information as is necessary for carrying out the provisions of this Convention or for the prevention of fraud or for the administration of statutory provisions against legal avoidance in relation to the taxes which are the subject of the Convention. Any information so exchanged shall be treated as secret and shall not be disclosed to any persons other than persons (including a Court or administrative body) concerned with the assessment or collection of, or prosecution in respect of, or the determination of appeals in relation to, the taxes which are the subject of the Convention.

(2) In no case shall the provisions of paragraph (1) be construed so as to impose on the competent authorities of either Contracting State the obligation:

    (a) to carry out administrative measures at variance with the laws or administrative practice prevailing in either Contracting State;

    (b) to supply particulars which are not obtainable under the laws or in the normal course of the administration in that or the other Contracting State; or

    (c) to supply information which would disclose any trade, business, industrial, commercial or professional secret or trade process, or information the disclosure of which would be contrary to public policy (*ordre public*).

Article 28 [Application of the Convention]

The competent authorities of the Contracting States shall settle the mode of application of this Convention. . . .

Article 29A [Miscellaneous rules applicable to certain offshore activities]

(1)–(3) . . .

(4) Profits derived by a resident of a Contracting State from the transportation of supplies or personnel to a location where activities in connection with the exploration or exploitation

of the sea bed and sub-soil and their natural resources are being carried on in areas which are under the jurisdiction of a Contracting State or from the operation of tugboats and similar vessels in connection with such activities, shall be taxable only in the Contracting State of which he is a resident.

(5) . . .

(6) . . .

Article 30 [Entry into force]

Note: Article 30 provided for the entry into force of the 1968 Convention. It takes effect in the UK in its amended form from the year of assessment 1988–89 (income tax and capital gains tax), from the financial year beginning on 1 April 1988 (corporation tax), and in France from 1 January 1988.

Official languages: The French language text and the English language text of this Convention are equally authoritative.

Capital taxes

Convention of 21 June 1963 (SI 1963 No 1319)

Article I [Duties covered]

(1) The present Convention shall apply:
    (*a*) in France, to the duty imposed on successions by death;
    (*b*) in the United Kingdom of Great Britain and Northern Ireland, to the estate duty imposed in Great Britain.

(2) The present Convention shall also apply to any other duties of a similar character imposed in France or Great Britain after the date of its signature or in any territory to which it may be extended under Article IX or applies under Article X.

Inheritance tax: This Convention covers United Kingdom capital transfer tax (now inheritance tax), by virtue of IHTA 1984, s 158(6), FA 1986, s 100.

Article II [General definitions]

(1) In the present Convention:
    (*a*) the term "France" means metropolitan France and the overseas départements;
    (*b*) the term "United Kingdom" means Great Britain and Northern Ireland;
    (*c*) the term "Great Britain" means England, Wales and Scotland, and does not include the Channel Islands and the Isle of Man;
    (*d*) the term "territory" when used in relation to one or the other Contracting Party, means France or Great Britain, as the context requires;

(*e*) the term "duty" means, as the context requires, the duty imposed in France on successions by death, or the estate duty imposed in Great Britain.

(2) In the application of the provisions of the present Convention by either Contracting Party any term not otherwise defined shall, unless the context otherwise requires, have the meaning which it has under the law of that Party relating to the duties which are the subject of the present Convention.

(3) (*a*) for the purposes of the present Convention, the question whether a deceased person was domiciled at the time of his death in any part of the territory of one of the Contracting Parties shall be determined in accordance with the law in force in that territory.

(*b*) Where by reason of the preceding sub-paragraph a deceased person is deemed to be domiciled in the territory of each of the Contracting Parties, then this case shall be solved in accordance with the following rules:—

(i) he shall be deemed to be domiciled in the territory of the Contracting Party in which he had a permanent home available to him at the time of his death; if he had a permanent home available to him in the territory of each of the Contracting Parties he shall be deemed to be domiciled in the territory of the Contracting Party with which his personal and economic relations were closest (centre of vital interests);

(ii) if the Contracting Party in whose territory he had his centre of vital interests cannot be determined, or if he had not a permanent home available to him in the territory of either Contracting Party, he shall be deemed to be domiciled in the territory of the Contracting Party in which he had an habitual abode;

(iii) if he had an habitual abode in the territory of each of the Contracting Parties or in the territory of neither, he shall be deemed to be domiciled in that of which he was a national;

(iv) if he was a national of both territories or of neither of them, the taxation authorities of the Contracting Parties shall determine the question by mutual agreement.

Article III [Situs]

(1) Where a person was at the time of his death domiciled in any part of the territory of one of the Contracting Parties, the situs of any property shall for the purposes of the imposition of duty and of any credit to be allowed under Article VI be determined exclusively in accordance with the rules in Article IV.

(2) Paragraph (1) of this Article shall apply only if, apart from the said Article IV:—

(*a*) duty would be imposed on the property under the law of each Contracting Party; or

(*b*) duty would be imposed on the property under the law of one of the Contracting Parties and would, but for some specific exemption, be imposed thereon under the law of the other Contracting Party.

Article IV [Deemed location of property]

The rules referred to in paragraph (1) of Article III are:

(*a*)–(*h*) . . .

(*i*) ships and aircraft and shares thereof shall be deemed to be situated at the place of registration of the ship or aircraft;

(*j*)–(*m*) . . .

Article V [Elimination of double taxation]

(1) Where a person was at the time of his death domiciled in some part of France duty shall not be imposed in Great Britain on any property which neither is situated in Great Britain, nor passes under a disposition or devolution regulated by the law of some part of Great Britain; and, in determining the amount or rate of duty payable in Great Britain, such property shall be disregarded.

(2) Where a person was at the time of his death domiciled in some part of Great Britain duty shall not be imposed in France on any property not situated in France; and in determining the amount or rate of duty payable on any property which is chargeable in France, any property not situated in France shall be disregarded.

(3) Where a Contracting Party imposes duty on the death of a person who at the time of his death was domiciled in the territory of the other Contracting Party, the former Party shall allow any exemption, allowance or relief, or any remission or reduction of duty (other than in respect of duty imposed by the other Party or by any other country) which would have been applicable under its law if the deceased had been domiciled in its territory.

Article VI [Tax credits]

Where one Contracting Party imposes duty on the death of a person who was domiciled in its territory at the time of his death on any property which, under the present Convention, is situated in the territory of the other Contracting Party, the former Party shall allow against so much of its duty, ascertained in accordance with its law, as is attributable to that property a credit (not exceeding the amount of the duty so attributable) equal to so much of the duty imposed by the other Contracting Party as is attributable to such property.

Article VII [Time limit]

(1) Any claim for a credit or for a refund of duty founded on the provisions of the present Convention shall be made within five years from the date of the death of the deceased person in respect of whose estate the claim is made, or, where the event causing duty to be payable occurs at some later date, within five years from that date.

(2) Any such refund shall be made without payment of interest on the amount so refunded.

Article VIII [Exchange of information]

(1) The taxation authorities of the Contracting Parties shall exchange such information (being information which is available under their respective taxation laws in the normal course of administration) as is necessary for ensuring the proper assessment and collection of the duty imposed by the Contracting Party in whose territory the deceased person was domiciled at the time of his death.

Any information so exchanged shall be treated as secret and shall not be disclosed to any person other than those concerned with the assessment and collection of the duties. No information as aforesaid shall be exchanged which would disclose any trade, business, industrial or professional secret or trade process.

(2) The taxation authorities of the Contracting Parties may consult together, as may be necessary, for the purpose of carrying out the provisions of the present Convention.

(3) In the present Convention, the term "taxation authorities" means:
  (a) in the case of Great Britain, the Commissioners of Inland Revenue;
  (b) in the case of France, the *Directeur Général des Impôts*;
  (c) in the case of Northern Ireland, to which the present Convention applies under Article X, the Minister of Finance; or
    in each case, the authorised representative; and
  (d) in the case of any territory to which the present Convention is extended under Article IX, the competent authority for the administration in such territory of the duties to which the present Convention applies.

Article XI [Entry into force]

Note: This Convention applies to estates or inheritances in relation to persons dying after 20 June 1963.

Official languages: The French language text and the English language text of this Convention are equally authoritative.

GAMBIA

Convention of 20 May 1980 (SI 1980 No 1963)

Article 1 Personal scope

This Convention shall apply to persons who are residents of one or both of the territories.

Article 2 Taxes covered

(1) The taxes which are the subject of this Convention are:
    (*a*) in the United Kingdom of Great Britain and Northern Ireland:
        (i) the income tax:
        (ii) the corporation tax; and
        (iii) the capital gains tax;
        (hereinafter referred to as "United Kingdom tax");
    (*b*) in The Gambia:
        the income tax;
        (hereinafter referred to as "Gambian tax");

(2) This Convention shall also apply to any other taxes of a substantially similar character to those referred to in the preceding paragraph imposed in either territory after the date of signature of this Convention.

Article 3 General definitions

(1) In this Convention, unless the context otherwise requires:
    (*a*) the term "United Kingdom" means Great Britain and Northern Ireland, including any area outside the territorial sea of the United Kingdom which under international law and the laws of the United Kingdom is an area within which the rights of the United Kingdom with respect to the sea-bed and sub-soil and their natural resources may be exercised;
    (*b*) the term "The Gambia" means the territory of The Gambia including any area outside the territorial waters of The Gambia which under international law and the laws of The Gambia is an area within which the rights of The Gambia with respect to the sea-bed and sub-soil and their natural resources may be exercised;
    (*c*) the term "nationals" means:
        (i) in relation to the United Kingdom, any citizen of the United Kingdom and Colonies, or any British subject not possessing that citizenship or the citizenship of any other Commonwealth country or territory, providing in either case he has the right of abode in the United Kingdom; and any legal person, partnership, association or other entity deriving its status as such from the law in force in the United Kingdom;
        (ii) in relation to The Gambia, all citizens of The Gambia as defined in the Constitution and other laws of The Gambia and all legal persons, partnerships and associations deriving their status from the law in force in The Gambia;

(*d*) the terms "one of the territories" and "the other territory" mean the United Kingdom or The Gambia as the context requires;

(*e*) the term "tax" means United Kingdom tax or Gambian tax, as the context requires;

(*f*) the term "United Kingdom tax" means tax imposed by the United Kingdom being tax to which this Convention applies by virtue of the provisions of Article 2; the term "Gambian tax" means tax imposed by The Gambia being tax to which this Convention applies by virtue of the provisions of Article 2;

(*g*) the term "person" comprises an individual, a company and any other body of persons;

(*h*) the term "company" means any body corporate or any entity which is treated as a body corporate for tax purposes;

(*i*) the terms "United Kingdom enterprise" and "Gambian enterprise" mean respectively an industrial or commercial enterprise or undertaking carried on by a resident of the United Kingdom and an industrial or commercial enterprise or undertaking carried on by a resident of The Gambia and the terms "enterprise of one of the territories" and "enterprise of the other territory" mean a United Kingdom enterprise or a Gambian enterprise as the context requires;

(*j*) the term "competent authority" means, in the case of the United Kingdom the Commissioners of Inland Revenue or their authorised representative, and in the case of The Gambia the Central Government in the Ministry of Finance or its authorised representative.

(2) As regards the application of this Convention by one of the territories any term not otherwise defined shall, unless the context otherwise requires, have the meaning which it has under the laws of that territory relating to the taxes which are the subject of this Convention.

Article 4 Fiscal domicile

(1) For the purposes of this Convention, the term "resident of a territory" means, subject to the provisions of paragraph (2) of this Article, any person who, under the law of that territory, is liable to taxation therein by reason of his domicile, residence, place of management or any other criterion of a similar nature. The terms "resident of the United Kingdom" and "resident of The Gambia" shall be construed accordingly.

(2) Where by reason of the provisions of paragraph (1) of this Article a person other than an individual is a resident of both territories, then it shall be deemed to be a resident of the territory where its business is managed and controlled.

Article 8 Income from immovable property

(1) (Taxation of income from immovable property.)

(2) (*a*) The term "immovable property" shall, subject to the provisions of sub-paragraph (*b*) of this paragraph, be defined in accordance with the law of the territory in which the property in question is situated.

(*b*) The term "immovable property" shall in any case include property accessory to immovable property, livestock and equipment used in agriculture and forestry, rights to which the provisions of general law respecting landed property apply, usufruct of immovable property and rights to variable or fixed payments as consideration for the working of, or the right to work, mineral deposits, sources and other natural resources; ships, boats and aircraft shall not be regarded as immovable property.

(3) . . .

(4) . . .

Article 10 Shipping and air transport

A resident of one of the territories shall be exempt from tax in the other territory on profits from the operation of ships or aircraft other than profits from voyages of ships or aircraft confined solely to places in the other territory.

Article 15 Capital gains

(1) . . .

(2) (Taxation of gains from alienation of movable business property.)

(3) Notwithstanding the provisions of paragraph (2) of this Article, capital gains derived by a resident of one of the territories from the alienation of ships and aircraft operated in international traffic and movable property pertaining to the operation of such ships and aircraft shall be taxable only in that territory.

Article 21 Non-discrimination

(1) The nationals of one of the territories shall not be subjected in the other territory to any taxation or any requirement connected therewith which is other or more burdensome than the taxation and connected requirements to which nationals of that other territory in the same circumstances are or may be subjected.

(2) The taxation on a permanent establishment which an enterprise of one of the territories has in the other territory shall not be less favourably levied in that other territory than the taxation levied on similar enterprises of that other territory carrying on the same or similar activities.

(3) Enterprises of one of the territories, the capital of which is wholly or partly owned or controlled, directly or indirectly, by one or more residents of the other territory, shall not be subjected in the first-mentioned territory to any taxation or any requirement connected therewith which is other or more burdensome than the taxation and connected requirements to which other similar enterprises of that first-mentioned territory are or may be subjected.

(4) Nothing contained in this Article shall be construed as obliging either territory to grant to individuals not resident in that territory any of the personal allowances, reliefs and reductions for tax purposes which are granted to individuals so resident, or to grant to individuals so resident any higher personal allowances for tax purposes which may be granted to citizens of that territory in respect of the education of their children outside the territory.

(5) In this Article the term "taxation" means taxes which are the subject of this Convention.

Article 22 Mutual agreement procedure

(1) Where a resident of one of the territories considers that the actions of one or both of the territories result or will result for him in taxation not in accordance with this Convention, he may, notwithstanding the remedies provided by the national laws of those territories, present his case to the competent authority of the territory of which he is a resident.

(2) The competent authority shall endeavour, if the objection appears to it to be justified and if it is not itself able to arrive at an appropriate solution, to resolve the case by mutual agreement with the competent authority of the other territory, with a view to the avoidance of taxation not in accordance with the Convention.

(3) The competent authorities of the territories shall endeavour to resolve by mutual agreement any difficulties or doubts arising as to the interpretation or application of the Convention.

(4) The competent authorities of the territories may communicate with each other directly for the purpose of reaching an agreement in the sense of the preceding paragraphs.

Article 23 Exchange of information

The competent authorities of the Contracting Governments shall exchange such information (being information which is at their disposal under their respective taxation laws in the normal course of administration) as is necessary for carrying out the provisions of this Convention or for the prevention of fraud or the administration of statutory provisions against legal avoidance in relation to the taxes which are the subject of this Convention. Any information so exchanged shall be treated as secret but may be disclosed to persons (including a court or administrative body) concerned with assessment, collection, enforcement or prosecution in respect of taxes which are the subject of this Convention. No information shall be exchanged which would disclose any trade, business, industrial or professional secret or any trade process.

Article 25 Entry into force

Note: Article 25 provided for the entry into force of this Convention. It takes effect from the year of assessment 1980–81 (income tax and capital gains tax) and from the financial year beginning on 1 April 1980 (corporation tax).

Official language: English.

GERMAN FEDERAL REPUBLIC

Convention of 26 November 1964 (SI 1967 No 25)

Printed as amended by the Protocol of 23 March 1970 (SI 1971 No 874).

Article I [Taxes covered]

(1) The taxes which are the subject of the present Convention are:
    (*a*) in the Federal Republic of Germany:
        the *Einkommensteuer* (income tax) including the *Ergänzungsabgabe* (surcharge) thereon,
        the *Körperschaftsteuer* (corporation tax) including the *Ergänzungsabgabe* (surcharge) thereon,
        the *Vermögensteuer* (capital tax), and
        the *Gewerbesteuer* (trade tax)
        (hereinafter referred to as "Federal Republic tax");
    (*b*) in the United Kingdom of Great Britain and Northern Ireland:
        the income tax (including surtax),
        the corporation tax, and
        the capital gains tax
        (hereinafter referred to as "United Kingdom tax").

(2) The present Convention shall also apply to any identical or substantially similar taxes which are imposed by either Contracting Party after the date of signature of the present Convention in addition to, or in place of, the existing taxes.

Article II [General definitions]

(1) In the present Convention, unless the context otherwise requires:
    (*a*) the term "United Kingdom" means Great Britain and Northern Ireland, including any area outside the territorial sea of the United Kingdom which in accordance

with international law has been or may hereafter be designated, under the laws of the United Kingdom concerning the Continental Shelf, as an area within which the rights of the United Kingdom with respect to the sea-bed and sub-soil and their natural resources may be exercised;

(b) the term "the Federal Republic", when used in a geographical sense, means the territory in which the Basic Law for the Federal Republic of Germany is in force, as well as any area adjacent to the territorial waters of the Federal Republic of Germany designated, in accordance with international law as related to the rights which the Federal Republic of Germany may exercise with respect to the sea bed and sub-soil and their natural resources, as domestic area for tax purposes;

(c) the terms "one of the territories" and "the other territory" mean the United Kingdom or the Federal Republic, as the context requires;

(d) the term "taxation authorities" means, in the case of the United Kingdom, the Commissioners of Inland Revenue or their authorised representatives, in the case of the Federal Republic, the Federal Minister of Finance, and, in the case of any territory to which the present Convention is extended under Article XXI, the competent authority for the administration in such territory of the taxes to which the present Convention applies;

(e) the term "tax" means United Kingdom tax or Federal Republic tax, as the context requires;

(f) the term "person" includes any body of persons, corporate or not corporate;

(g) the term "company" means any body corporate and any entity which is treated as a body corporate for tax purposes;

(h) (i) the terms "resident of the United Kingdom" and "resident of the Federal Republic" mean respectively any person who is resident in the United Kingdom for the purposes of United Kingdom tax and any person who is resident in the Federal Republic (subject to unlimited tax liability) for the purposes of Federal Republic tax; but

    (ii) where by reason of the provisions of sub-paragraph (h) (i) above an individual is a resident of both territories, then this case shall be solved in accordance with the following rules:

        (aa) he shall be deemed to be a resident of the territory in which he has a permanent home available to him. If he has a permanent home available to him in both territories, he shall be deemed to be a resident of the territory with which his personal and economic relations are closest (hereinafter referred to as his centre of vital interests);

        (bb) if the territory in which he has his centre of vital interests cannot be determined, or if he has not a permanent home available to him in either territory, he shall be deemed to be a resident of the territory in which he has an habitual abode;

        (cc) if he has an habitual abode in both territories or in neither of them, he shall be deemed to be a resident of the territory of the Contracting State of which he is a national;

        (dd) if he is a national of both Contracting States or of neither of them, the taxation authorities of the Contracting States shall determine the question by mutual agreement;

    (iii) where by reason of the provisions of sub-paragraph (h) (i) above a legal person is a resident of both territories, then it shall be deemed to be a resident of the territory in which its place of effective management is situated. The same provision shall apply to partnerships and associations which under the national laws by which they are governed are not legal persons;

(i) the terms "resident of one of the territories" and "resident of the other territory" mean a person who is a resident of the United Kingdom or a person who is resident of the Federal Republic, as the context requires;

(j) the terms "United Kingdom enterprise" and "Federal Republic enterprise" mean respectively an industrial or commercial enterprise or undertaking carried on by a resident of the United Kingdom and an industrial or commercial enterprise or undertaking carried on by a resident of the Federal Republic, and the terms "enterprise of one of the territories" and "enterprise of the other territory" mean a United Kingdom enterprise or a Federal Republic enterprise, as the context requires;

(k) . . .

(l)   (i) the term "permanent establishment" means a fixed place of business in which the business of the enterprise is wholly or partly carried on;

   (ii) a permanent establishment shall include especially:
   (aa) a place of management;
   (bb) a branch;
   (cc) an office;
   (dd) a factory;
   (ee) a workshop;
   (ff) a mine, quarry or other place of extraction of natural resources;
   (gg) a building site or construction or assembly project which exists for more than twelve months;

   (iii) the term "permanent establishment" shall not be deemed to include:
   (aa) the use of facilities solely for the purpose of storage, display or delivery of goods or merchandise belonging to the enterprise;
   (bb) the maintenance of a stock of goods or merchandise belonging to the enterprise solely for the purpose of storage, display or delivery;
   (cc) the maintenance of a stock of goods or merchandise belonging to the enterprise solely for the purpose of processing by another enterprise;
   (dd) the maintenance of a fixed place of business solely for the purpose of purchasing goods or merchandise, or for collecting information, for the enterprise;
   (ee) the maintenance of a fixed place of business solely for the purpose of advertising, for the supply of information, for scientific research or for similar activities which have a preparatory or auxiliary character, for the enterprise;

   (iv) a person acting in a territory on behalf of an enterprise of the other territory—other than an agent of an independent status to whom sub-paragraph (l) (v) below applies—shall be deemed to be a permanent establishment in the first-mentioned territory if he has, and habitually exercises in that territory, an authority to conclude contracts in the name of the enterprise, unless his activities are limited to the purchase of goods or merchandise for the enterprise;

   (v) an enterprise of one of the territories shall not be deemed to have a permanent establishment in the other territory merely because it carries on business in that other territory through a broker, general commission agent or any other agent of an independent status, where such persons are acting in the ordinary course of their business;

   (vi) the fact that a company which is a resident of one of the territories controls or is controlled by a company which is a resident of the other territory, or which carries on business in that other territory (whether through a permanent establishment or otherwise), shall not of itself constitute either company a permanent establishment of the other;

(m) the term "international traffic" includes traffic between places in any territory in the course of a voyage which extends over two or more territories.

(2) Where under any provision of this Convention income from a source in one of the territories is relieved from tax in that territory if it is subject to tax in the other territory, and, under the law in force in that other territory, the said income is subject to tax by reference to the amount thereof which is remitted to or received in that other territory and not by reference to the full amount thereof, then the relief to be allowed under this Convention in the first-mentioned territory shall apply only to so much of the income as is remitted to or received in the other territory.

(3) In the application of the provisions of the present Convention by one of the Contracting Parties any term not otherwise defined in the present Convention shall, unless the contract otherwise requires, have the meaning which it has under the laws in force in the territory of that Party relating to the taxes which are the subject of the present Convention.

Article V [Shipping and air transport]

(1) Profits from the operation of ships or aircraft in international traffic shall be subjected to tax only in the territory in which the place of effective management of the enterprise is situated.

(2) Paragraph (1) of this Article shall likewise apply in respect of the Gewerbesteuer (trade tax) computed on a basis other than profits.

Article VIII [Capital gains]

(1) . . .

(2) Capital gains from the alienation of movable property forming part of the business property of a permanent establishment which an enterprise of one of the territories has in the other territory or of movable property pertaining to a fixed base available to a resident of one of the territories in the other territory for the purpose of performing professional services, including such gains from the alienation of such a permanent establishment (alone or together with the whole enterprise) or of such a fixed base, may be taxed in the other territory. However, gains from the alienation of movable property of the kind referred to in paragraph (3) of Article XVI shall be taxable only in the territory in which such movable property is taxable according to the said Article.

(3) . . .

Article XII [Income from immovable property]

(1) (Taxation of income from immovable property.)

(2) The term "immovable property" shall be defined in accordance with the laws of the territory in which the property in question is situated. The term shall in any case include property accessory to immovable property, livestock and equipment of agricultural and forestry enterprises, rights to which the provisions of general law respecting landed property apply, usufruct of immovable property and rights to variable or fixed payments as consideration for the working of mineral deposits, sources and other natural resources; ships, boats and aircraft shall not be regarded as immovable property.

(3) . . .

(4) . . .

Article XVI [Capital]

(1) . . .

(2) . . .

(3) Ships and aircraft operated in international traffic and assets, other than immovable property, pertaining to the operation of such ships and aircraft may be subjected to tax only in the territory in which the place of effective management of the enterprise is situated.

(4) . . .

Article XVIIIA [Mutual agreement procedure]

(1) Where a resident of one of the territories considers that the actions of one or both of the Contracting Parties result or will result for him in taxation not in accordance with this Convention, he may, notwithstanding the remedies provided by the national laws of those territories, present his case to the taxation authority of the territory of which he is a resident.

(2) The taxation authority shall endeavour, if the objection appears to it to be justified and

if it is not itself able to arrive at an appropriate solution, to resolve the case by mutual agreement with the taxation authority of the other territory, with a view to the avoidance of taxation not in accordance with the Convention.

(3) The taxation authorities of the territories shall endeavour to resolve by mutual agreement any difficulties or doubts arising as to the application of the Convention.

(4) Nothing in this Convention shall prevent tax in one of the territories from being deducted at source at the rates which would apply if this Convention were not in force. Where the income concerned is exempt from tax in such territory under the provisions of this Convention or where the amount of tax so deducted exceeds the amount of tax chargeable under the provisions of this Convention, the tax so deducted or the excess amount of tax shall be refunded upon application to be made by the recipient of such income to the tax office concerned. The refund shall be made if it is applied for within a period of three years from the day on which the income has been received or within such longer period as is permitted under the law in force in the territory concerned.

(5) The taxation authorities of the territories may communicate with each other directly for the purpose of reaching an agreement in the sense of the preceding paragraphs or for the purpose of applying the provisions of the Convention.

Article XIX [Exchange of information]

(1) The taxation authorities of the Contracting Parties shall exchange such information (being information which is at their disposal under their respective taxation laws in the normal course of administration) as is necessary for carrying out the provisions of the present Convention or for the prevention of fraud or for the administration of statutory provisions against legal avoidance in relation to the taxes which are the subject of the present Convention. Any information so exchanged shall be treated as secret and shall not be disclosed to any persons other than those concerned with the assessment and collection of the taxes which are the subject of the present Convention. No information as aforesaid shall be exchanged which would disclose any trade, business, industrial or professional secret or trade process.

(2) The taxation authorities of the Contracting Parties shall consult each other at the earliest time possible in cases where this is necessary for the interpretation of the present Convention or the implementation of its provisions, in particular those contained in Articles III and IV.

Article XX [Non-discrimination]

(1) The nationals of one of the Contracting States shall not be subjected in the other State to any taxation or any requirement connected therewith which is other or more burdensome than the taxation and connected requirements to which nationals of that other State in the same circumstances are or may be subjected.

(2) The term "nationals" means—

(a) in relation to the Federal Republic, all Germans within the meaning of Article 116(1) of the Basic Law for the Federal Republic of Germany, and all legal persons, partnerships and associations deriving their status as such from the law in force in the Federal Republic;

(b) in relation to the United Kingdom, all British subjects and British protected persons—

(i) residing in the United Kingdom or any territory to which the present Convention is extended under Article XXI or—

(ii) deriving their status as such from connection with the United Kingdom or any territory to which the present Convention is extended under Article XXI, and all legal persons, partnerships and associations deriving their status as such from the law in force in the United Kingdom or in any territory to which the Convention is extended under Article XXI.

(3) The taxation on a permanent establishment which an enterprise of one of the territories has in the other territory shall not be less favourably levied in that other territory than

the taxation levied on enterprises of that other territory carrying on the same activities. This provision shall not be construed as obliging one Contracting State to grant to residents of the territory of the other Contracting State any personal allowances, reliefs and reductions for taxation purposes on account of civil status or family responsibilities which it grants to its own residents.

(4) Enterprises of one of the territories, the capital of which is wholly or partly owned or controlled, directly or indirectly, by one or more residents of the other territory, shall not be subjected in the first-mentioned territory to any taxation or any requirement connected therewith which is other or more burdensome than the taxation and connected requirements to which other similar enterprises of that first-mentioned territory are or may be subjected.

(5) In this Article the term "taxation" means taxes of every kind and description.

Article XXIII [Entry into force]

Note: Article XXIII provided for the entry into force of the 1964 Convention. It takes effect in the UK in its amended form from the year of assessment 1969–70 (income tax and capital gains tax) and from the financial year beginning on 1 April 1969 (corporation tax).

Official languages: The German language text and the English language text of this Convention are equally authoritative.

GHANA

Convention of 29 November 1977 (SI 1978 No 785)

Article 1 Personal scope

This Convention shall apply to persons who are residents of one or both of the Contracting States.

Article 2 Taxes covered

(1) The taxes which are the subject of this Convention are:
    (*a*) in the United Kingdom of Great Britain and Northern Ireland:
        (i) the income tax;
        (ii) the corporation tax;
        (iii) the capital gains tax; and
        (iv) the development land tax;
        (hereinafter referred to as "United Kingdom tax");
    (*b*) in Ghana:

(i) the income tax;
(ii) the mineral oil tax;
(iii) the tax on rents; and
(iv) the capital gains tax;
(hereinafter referred to as "Ghana tax").

(2) This Convention shall also apply to any identical or substantially similar taxes which are imposed by either Contracting State after the date of signature of this Convention in addition to, or in place of, the existing taxes. The competent authorities of the Contracting States shall notify to each other any changes which are made in their respective taxation laws.

Article 3 General definitions

(1) In this Convention, unless the context otherwise requires:

(a) the term "United Kingdom" means Great Britain and Northern Ireland, including any area outside the territorial sea of the United Kingdom which in accordance with international law has been designated, under the laws of the United Kingdom concerning the Continental Shelf, as an area within which the rights of the United Kingdom with respect to the sea-bed and sub-soil and their natural resources may be exercised;

(b) the term "Ghana" means the Republic of Ghana including any area outside the territorial sea of Ghana which in accordance with international law has been or may hereafter be designated, under the laws of Ghana concerning the Continental Shelf, as an area within which the rights of Ghana with respect to the sea-bed and sub-soil and their natural resources may be exercised;

(c) the term "national" means:

(i) in relation to the United Kingdom, any citizen of the United Kingdom and Colonies, or any British subject not possessing that citizenship or the citizenship of any other Commonwealth country or territory, providing in either case he has the right of abode in the United Kingdom; and any legal person, partnership association, or other entity deriving its status as such from the law in force in the United Kingdom;

(ii) in relation to Ghana, any citizen of Ghana and any legal person, partnership, association or other entity deriving its status as such from the law in force in Ghana;

(d) the term "United Kingdom tax" means tax imposed by the United Kingdom being tax to which this Convention applies by virtue of the provisions of Article 2; the term "Ghana tax" means tax imposed by Ghana being tax to which this Convention applies by virtue of the provisions of Article 2;

(e) the term "tax" means United Kingdom tax or Ghana tax, as the context requires;

(f) the terms "a Contracting State" and "the other Contracting State" mean the United Kingdom or Ghana, as the context requires;

(g) the term "person" comprises an individual, a company and any other body of persons;

(h) the term "company" means any body corporate or any entity which is treated as a body corporate for tax purposes;

(i) the terms "enterprise of a Contracting State" and "enterprise of the other Contracting State" mean respectively an enterprise carried on by a resident of a Contracting State and an enterprise carried on by a resident of the other Contracting State;

(j) the term "competent authority" means, in the case of the United Kingdom the Commissioners of Inland Revenue or their authorised representative, and in the case of Ghana the Commissioner of Income Tax or his authorised representative.

(2) As regards the application of this Convention by a Contracting State any term not otherwise defined shall, unless the context otherwise requires, have the meaning which it has under the laws of that Contracting State relating to the taxes which are the subject of this Convention.

Article 4 Residence

(1) For the purposes of this Convention, the term "resident of a Contracting State" means, subject to the provisions of paragraphs (2) and (3) of this Article, any person who, under the law of that State, is liable to taxation therein by reason of his residence. The terms "resident of the United Kingdom" and "resident of Ghana" shall be construed accordingly.

(2) Where by reason of the provisions of paragraph (1) of this Article an individual is a resident of both Contracting States, then his status shall be determined in accordance with the following rules:

(a) he shall be deemed to be a resident of the Contracting State in which he has a permanent home available to him. If he has a permanent home available to him in both Contracting States, he shall be deemed to be a resident of the Contracting State with which his personal and economic relations are closer (centre of vital interests);

(b) if the Contracting State in which he has his centre of vital interests cannot be determined, or if he has not a permanent home available to him in either Contracting State, he shall be deemed to be a resident of the Contracting State in which he has an habitual abode;

(c) if he has an habitual abode in both Contracting States or in neither of them, he shall be deemed to be a resident of the Contracting State of which he is a national;

(d) if he is a national of both Contracting States or of neither of them, the competent authorities of the Contracting States shall settle the question by mutual agreement.

(3) Where by reason of the provisions of paragraph (1) of this Article a person other than an individual is a resident of both Contracting States, then it shall be deemed to be a resident of the Contracting State in which its place of effective management is situated.

Article 7 Immovable property

(1) (Taxation of income from immovable property.)

(2) (a) The term "immovable property" shall, subject to the provisions of sub–paragraph (b) below, be defined in accordance with the law of the Contracting State in which the property in question is situated.

(b) The term "immovable property" shall in any case include property accessory to immovable property, livestock and equipment used in agriculture and forestry, rights to which the provisions of general law respecting landed property apply, usufruct of immovable property and rights to variable or fixed payments as consideration for the working of or the right to work, mineral deposits, sources and other natural resources. Ships, boats and aircraft shall not be regarded as immovable property.

(3) . . .

(4) . . .

Article 9 Shipping and air transport

A resident of a Contracting State shall be exempt from tax in the other Contracting State on profits from the operation of ships or aircraft other than profits from voyages of ships or aircraft confined solely to places in the other Contracting State.

Article 14 Capital gains

(1) (Taxation of gains from alienation of business property.)

(2) Notwithstanding the provisions of paragraph (1) of this Article, capital gains derived by a resident of a Contracting State from the alienation of ships and aircraft operated in international traffic and movable property pertaining to the operation of such ships and aircraft shall be taxable only in that Contracting State.

(3) . . .

(4) . . .

Article 23 Non-discrimination

(1) The nationals of a Contracting State shall not be subjected in the other Contracting State to any taxation or any requirement connected therewith which is other or more burdensome than the taxation and connected requirements to which nationals of that other State in the same circumstances are or may be subjected.

(2) The taxation on a permanent establishment which an enterprise of a Contracting State has in the other Contracting State shall not be less favourably levied in that other State than the taxation levied on enterprises of that other State carrying on the same activities.

(3) Enterprises of a Contracting State, the capital of which is wholly or partly owned or controlled, directly or indirectly, by one or more residents of the other Contracting State, shall not be subjected in the first-mentioned Contracting State to any taxation or any requirement connected therewith which is other or more burdensome than the taxation and connected requirements to which other similar enterprises of that first-mentioned State are or may be subjected.

(4) In this Article the term "taxation" means taxes which are the subject of this Convention.

(5) Nothing contained in this Article shall be construed as obliging either Contracting State to grant to individuals not resident in that State any of the personal allowances, reliefs and reductions for tax purposes which are granted to individuals so resident, nor as conferring any exemption from tax in a Contracting State in respect of dividends paid to a company which is a resident of the other Contracting State, nor as obliging one Contracting State to grant to a company which is a resident of the other Contracting State such lower rates of tax as may be levied on a company which is a resident of the first-mentioned Contracting State in consequence of its being wholly owned by nationals of that Contracting State.

Article 24 Mutual agreement procedure

(1) Where a resident of a Contracting State considers that the actions of one or both of the Contracting States result or will result for him in taxation not in accordance with this Convention, he may, notwithstanding the remedies provided by the national laws of those States, present his case to the competent authority of the Contracting State of which he is a resident.

(2) The competent authority shall endeavour, if the objection appears to it to be justified and if it is not itself able to arrive at an appropriate solution, to resolve the case by mutual agreement with the competent authority of the other Contracting State, with a view to the avoidance of taxation not in accordance with the Convention.

(3) The competent authorities of the Contracting States shall endeavour to resolve by mutual agreement any difficulties or doubts arising as to the interpretation or application of the Convention.

(4) The competent authorities of the Contracting States may communicate with each other directly for the purpose of reaching an agreement in the sense of the preceding paragraphs.

Article 25 Exchange of information

The competent authorities of the Contracting States shall exchange such information (being information which is at their disposal under their respective taxation laws in the normal course of administration) as is necessary for carrying out the provisions of this Convention or for the prevention of fraud or evasion or the administration of statutory provisions against legal avoidance in relation to the taxes which are the subject of this Convention. Any information so exchanged shall be treated as secret but may be disclosed to persons (including a court or administrative body) concerned with assessment, collection, enforcement or prosecution in respect of taxes which are the subject of this Convention. No information shall be exchanged which would disclose any trade, business, industrial or professional secret or any trade process.

Article 27 Entry into force

Note: Article 27 provided for the entry into force of this Convention. It takes effect in the UK from the year of assessment 1977–78 (income tax and capital gains tax) and from the financial year beginning on 1 April 1977 (corporation tax).

Official language: English.

GREECE

Convention of 25 June 1953 (SI 1954 No 142)

Article I [Taxes covered]

(1) The taxes which are the subject of the present Convention are:

    (*a*) in Greece:

        the income tax, including the schedular or analytical tax and the complementary tax (hereinafter referred to as "Greek tax");

    (*b*) in the United Kingdom of Great Britain and Northern Ireland:

        the income tax (including surtax), the profits tax and the excess profits levy (hereinafter referred to as "United Kingdom tax").

(2) The present Convention shall also apply to any other taxes of a substantially similar character imposed in Greece or the United Kingdom subsequently to the date of signature of the Convention.

Corporation tax: This Convention covers United Kingdom corporation tax, by virtue of ICTA 1988, s 789(1).

Article II [General definitions]

(1) In the present Convention, unless the context otherwise requires:

    (*a*) The term "United Kingdom" means Great Britain and Northern Ireland, excluding the Channel Islands and the Isle of Man;

    (*b*) The term "Greece" means the territories of the Kingdom of Greece;

    (*c*) The terms "one of the territories" and "the other territory" mean the United Kingdom or Greece, as the context requires;

    (*d*) The term "tax" means United Kingdom tax or Greek tax, as the context requires;

    (*e*) The term "person" includes any body of persons, corporate or not corporate;

    (*f*) The term "company" means any body corporate;

    (*g*) The terms "resident of the United Kingdom" and "resident of Greece" mean respectively any person who is resident in the United Kingdom for the purposes of United Kingdom tax and not domiciled or resident in Greece for the purposes of Greek tax, and any person who is domiciled or resident in Greece for the purposes of Greek tax and not resident in the United Kingdom for the purposes of

United Kingdom tax; and a company shall be regarded as resident in the United Kingdom if its business is managed and controlled in the United Kingdom and as resident in Greece if its business is managed and controlled in Greece;

(*h*) The terms "resident of one of the territories" and "resident of the other territory" mean a person who is a resident of the United Kingdom or a person who is a resident of Greece as the context requires;

(*i*) The terms "United Kingdom enterprise" and "Greek enterprise" mean respectively an industrial or commercial enterprise or undertaking carried on by a resident of the United Kingdom and an industrial or commercial enterprise or undertaking carried on by a resident of Greece, and the terms "enterprise of one of the territories" and "enterprise of the other territory" mean a United Kingdom enterprise or a Greek enterprise, as the context requires;

(*j*) The term "industrial or commercial profits" includes profits from mining and farming and rents or royalties in respect of cinematography films;

(*k*) The term "permanent establishment", when used with respect to an enterprise of one of the territories, means a branch, management, factory or other fixed place of business, and a farm, mine, quarry or other place of natural resources subject to exploitation, but does not include an agency unless the agent has, and habitually exercises, a general authority to negotiate and conclude contracts on behalf of such enterprise or has a stock of merchandise from which he regularly fills orders on its behalf.

In this connexion—

(i) An enterprise of one of the territories shall not be deemed to have a permanent establishment in the other territory merely because it carries on business dealings in that other territory through a *bona fide* broker or general commission agent acting in the ordinary course of his business as such;

(ii) The fact that an enterprise of one of the territories maintains in the other territory a fixed place of business exclusively for the purchase of goods or merchandise shall not of itself constitute that fixed place of business a permanent establishment of the enterprise;

(iii) The fact that a company which is a resident of one of the territories has a subsidiary company which is a resident of the other territory or which carries on a trade or business in that other territory (whether through a permanent establishment or otherwise) shall not of itself constitute that subsidiary company a permanent establishment of its parent company.

(2) Where the present Convention provides that income from a source in one of the territories shall be exempt from tax in that territory if (with or without other conditions) it is subject to tax in the other territory, and under the law in force in that other territory the said income is subject to tax by reference to the amount thereof which is remitted to or received in that other territory and not by reference to the full amount thereof, then the exemption to be allowed under the Convention in the first territory shall apply only to so much of the income as is remitted to or received in that other territory.

(3) In the application of the provisions of the present Convention by either Contracting Party any term not otherwise defined shall, unless the context otherwise requires, have the meaning which it has under the laws in force in the territory of that Party relating to the taxes which are the subject of the Convention.

Article V [Shipping and air transport]

(1) Notwithstanding the provisions of Articles III and IV, profits which a resident of the United Kingdom derives from operating ships whose port of registry is in the United Kingdom, or from operating aircraft, shall be exempt from Greek tax.

(2) Notwithstanding the provisions of Articles III and IV, profits which a resident of Greece derives from operating ships whose port of registry is in Greece, or from operating aircraft, shall be exempt from United Kingdom tax.

Article VII [Capital gains]

A resident of one of the territories who does not carry on a trade or business in the other territory through a permanent establishment situated therein shall be exempt in that other territory from any tax on gains from the sale, transfer or exchange of capital assets.

Article XV [Exchange of information]

(1) The taxation authorities of the Contracting Parties shall exchange such information (being information which is at their disposal under their respective taxation laws in the normal course of administration) as is necessary for carrying out the provisions of the present Convention or for the prevention of fraud or for the administration of statutory provisions against legal avoidance in relation to the taxes which are the subject of the Convention. Any information so exchanged shall be treated as secret and shall not be disclosed to any persons other than those concerned with the assessment and collection of the taxes which are the subject of the Convention. No information as aforesaid shall be exchanged which would disclose any trade, business, industrial or professional secret or trade process.

(2) As used in this Article, the term "taxation authorities" means, in the case of the United Kingdom, the Commissioners of Inland Revenue or their authorised representative; in the case of Greece, the Director-General of Taxes or his authorised representative; and, in the case of any territory to which the present Convention is extended under Article XVII, the competent authority for the administration in such territory of the taxes to which the Convention applies.

Article XVI [Non-discrimination]

(1) The nationals of one Contracting Party shall not be subjected in the territory of the other Contracting Party to any taxation or any requirement connected therewith which is other, higher or more burdensome than the taxation and connected requirements to which the nationals of the latter Party are or may be subjected.

(2) The enterprises of one of the territories, whether carried on by a company, a body of persons or by individuals alone or in partnership, shall not be subjected in the other territory, in respect of profits or capital attributable to their permanent establishments in that other territory, to any taxation which is other, higher or more burdensome than the taxation to which the enterprises of that other territory similarly carried on are or may be subjected in respect of the like profits or capital.

(3) The income, profits and capital of an enterprise of one of the territories, the capital of which is wholly or partly owned or controlled, directly or indirectly, by a resident or residents of the other territory, shall not be subjected in the first territory to any taxation which is other, higher or more burdensome than the taxation to which other enterprises of that first territory are or may be subjected in respect of the like income, profits and capital.

(4) Nothing in paragraph (1) or paragraph (2) of this Article shall be construed as obliging one Contracting Party to grant to nationals of the other Contracting Party who are not resident in the territory of the former Party the same personal allowances, reliefs and reductions for tax purposes as are granted to its own nationals.

(5) In this Article the term "nationals" means—
> (a) in relation to Greece, all individuals having Greek nationality in accordance with Greek law and all legal persons established under the laws of Greece;
> (b) in relation to the United Kingdom, all British subjects and British protected persons—
> > (i) residing in the United Kingdom or any British territory to which the present Convention is extended under Article XVII, or
> > (ii) deriving their status as such from connexion with the United Kingdom or any

British territory to which the present Convention is extended under Article XVII,

and all legal persons, partnerships, associations and other entities deriving their status as such from the law in force in any British territory to which the Convention applies.

(6) In this Article the term "taxation" means taxes of every kind and description levied on behalf of any authority whatsoever.

Article XX [Entry into force]

Note: Article XX provides for the entry into force of this Convention. It takes effect, in the UK, in general from April 1952.

Official languages: The Greek language text and the English language text of this Convention are equally authoritative.

GRENADA

Arrangement of 4 March 1949 (SI 1949 No 361)

Printed as amended by the Arrangement of 25 July 1968 (SI 1968 No 1867).

Paragraph 1 [Taxes covered]

(1) The taxes which are the subject of this Arrangement are—
   (a) In the United Kingdom:
       The income tax (including surtax) and the profits tax (hereinafter referred to as "United Kingdom tax").
   (b) In Grenada:
       The income tax (including surtax) (hereinafter referred to as "Grenada tax").

(2) This Arrangement shall also apply to any other taxes of a substantially similar character imposed in the United Kingdom or Grenada after this Arrangement has come into force.

Corporation tax: This Arrangement covers United Kingdom corporation tax, by virtue of ICTA 1988, s 789(1).

Paragraph 2 [General definitions]

(1) In this Arrangement, unless the context otherwise requires—
   (a) The term "United Kingdom" means Great Britain and Northern Ireland, excluding the Channel Islands and the Isle of Man.
   (b) . . .
   (c) The terms "one of the territories" and "the other territory" mean the United Kingdom or Grenada, as the context requires.
   (d) The term "tax" means United Kingdom tax or Grenada tax, as the context requires.
   (e) The term "person" includes any body of persons, corporate or not corporate.
   (f) The term "company" includes any body corporate.

(g) The terms "resident of the United Kingdom" and "resident of Grenada" mean respectively any person who is resident in the United Kingdom for the purposes of United Kingdom tax and not resident in Grenada for the purposes of Grenada tax and any person who is resident in Grenada for the purposes of Grenada tax and not resident in the United Kingdom for the purposes of United Kingdom tax; and a company shall be regarded as resident in the United Kingdom if its business is managed and controlled in the United Kingdom and as resident in Grenada if its business is managed and controlled in Grenada.

(h) The terms "resident of one of the territories" and "resident of the other territory" mean a person who is a resident of the United Kingdom or a person who is a resident of Grenada, as the context requires.

(i) The term "United Kingdom enterprise" and "Grenada enterprise" mean respectively an industrial or commercial enterprise or undertaking carried on by a resident of the United Kingdom and an industrial or commercial enterprise or undertaking carried on by a resident of Grenada; and the terms "enterprise of one of the territories" and "enterprise of the other territory" mean a United Kingdom enterprise or a Grenada enterprise, as the context requires.

(j) . . .

(k) . . .

(2) Where under this Arrangement any income is exempt from tax in one of the territories if (with or without other conditions) it is subject to tax in the other territory, and that income is subject to tax in that other territory by reference to the amount thereof which is remitted to or received in that other territory, the exemption to be allowed under this Arrangement in the first-mentioned territory shall apply only to the amount so remitted or received.

(3) In the application of the provisions of this Arrangement by the United Kingdom or Grenada, any term not otherwise defined shall, unless the context otherwise requires, have the meaning which it has under the laws of the United Kingdom, or, as the case may be, Grenada, relating to the taxes which are the subject of this Arrangement.

Paragraph 5 [Shipping and air transport]

Notwithstanding the provisions of paragraphs 3 and 4, profits which a resident of one of the territories derives from operating ships or aircraft shall be exempt from tax in the other territory.

Paragraph 3: Taxation of industrial or commercial profits.
Paragraph 4: Taxation of profits of associated enterprises.

Paragraph 14 [Exchange of information]

(1) The taxation authorities of the United Kingdom and Grenada shall exchange such information (being information available under their respective taxation laws) as is necessary for carrying out the provisions of this Arrangement or for the prevention of fraud or the administration of statutory provisions against legal avoidance in relation to the taxes which are the subject of this Arrangement. Any information so exchanged shall be treated as secret and shall not be disclosed to any persons other than those concerned with the assessment and collection of the taxes which are the subject of this Arrangement. No information shall be exchanged which would disclose any trade secret or trade process.

(2) As used in this paragraph, the term "taxation authorities" means the Commissioners of Inland Revenue or their authorised representative in the case of the United Kingdom and the Commissioner of Income Tax or his authorised representative in the case of Grenada.

Paragraph 15 [Entry into force]

Note: Paragraph 15 provided for the entry into force of the 1949 Convention. It takes effect in the UK in its amended form (in general) from 1968.

Official language: English.

GUERNSEY

Arrangement of 24 June 1952 (SI 1952 No 1215)

Paragraph 1 [Taxes covered]

(1) The taxes which are the subject of this Arrangement are:—
  (a) In the United Kingdom:
      The income tax (including surtax) and the profits tax (hereinafter referred to as "United Kingdom tax");
  (b) In Guernsey:
      The income tax (including super tax)
  (hereinafter referred to as "Guernsey tax").

(2) This Arrangement shall also apply to any other taxes of a substantially similar character imposed in the United Kingdom or Guernsey after this Arrangement has come into force.

Corporation tax: This Arrangement covers United Kingdom corporation tax, by virtue of ICTA 1988, s 789(1).

Paragraph 2 [General definitions]

(1) In this Arrangement, unless the context otherwise requires:
  (a) The term "United Kingdom" means Great Britain and Northern Ireland;
  (b) The term "Guernsey" means any island in which the Income Tax (Guernsey) Law, 1950, is in force;
  (c) The terms "one of the territories" and "the other territory" mean the United Kingdom or Guernsey, as the context requires;
  (d) The term "tax" means United Kingdom tax or Guernsey tax, as the context requires;
  (e) The term "person" includes any body of persons, corporate or not corporate;
  (f) The term "company" includes any body corporate;
  (g) The terms "resident of the United Kingdom" and "resident of Guernsey" mean respectively any person who is resident in the United Kingdom for the purposes of United Kingdom tax and not resident in Guernsey for the purposes of Guernsey tax and any person who is resident in Guernsey for the purposes of Guernsey tax and not resident in the United Kingdom for the purposes of United Kingdom tax; and a company shall be regarded as resident in the United Kingdom if its business is managed and controlled in the United Kingdom and as resident in Guernsey if its business is managed and controlled in Guernsey;
  (h) The terms "resident of one of the territories" and "resident of the other territory" mean a person who is a resident of the United Kingdom or a person who is a resident of Guernsey, as the context requires;
  (i)–(k) . . .

(2) Where under this Arrangement any income is exempt from tax in one of the territories if (with or without other conditions) it is subject to tax in the other territory, and the income is subject to tax in that other territory by reference to the amount thereof which is remitted to or received in that other territory, the exemption to be allowed under this Arrangement in the first-mentioned territory shall apply only to the amount so remitted or received.

(3) In the application of the provisions of this Arrangement by the United Kingdom or Guernsey any term not otherwise defined shall, unless the context otherwise requires, have the meaning which it has under the laws of the United Kingdom, or, as the case may be, Guernsey, relating to the taxes which are the subject of this Arrangement.

Paragraph 5 [Shipping and air transport]

Notwithstanding the provisions of paragraphs 3 and 4, profits which a resident of one of the territories derives from operating ships or aircraft shall be exempt from tax in the other territory.

Paragraph 3: Taxation of industrial or commercial profits.
Paragraph 4: Taxation of profits of associated enterprises.

Paragraph 10 [Exchange of information]

(1) The taxation authorities of the United Kingdom and Guernsey shall exchange such information (being information available under their respective taxation laws) as is necessary for carrying out the provisions of this Arrangement or for the prevention of fraud or the administration of statutory provisions against legal avoidance in relation to the taxes which are the subject of this Arrangement. Any information so exchanged shall be treated as secret and shall not be disclosed to any persons other than those concerned with the assessment and collection of the taxes which are the subject of this Arrangement. No information shall be exchanged which would disclose any trade secret or trade process.

(2) As used in this paragraph, the term "taxation authorities" means the Commissioners of Inland Revenue or their authorised representative in the case of the United Kingdom and the Administrator of Income Tax or his authorised representative in the case of Guernsey.

Paragraph 11 [Entry into force]

Note: Article 11 provided for the entry into force of this Arrangement. It takes effect in the UK from the year of assessment 1951–52 (income tax) and from April 1951 (profits tax).

Official language: English.

HUNGARY

Convention of 28 November 1977 (SI 1978 No 1056)

HUNGARY

Article 1 Personal scope

This Convention shall apply to persons who are residents of one or both of the Contracting States.

Article 2 Taxes covered

(1) The taxes which are the subject of this Convention are:
  (a) in the United Kingdom of Great Britain and Northern Ireland:
    (i) the income tax;
    (ii) the corporation tax;
    (iii) the capital gains tax;
    (iv) the development land tax;
    (hereinafter referred to as "United Kingdom tax");
  (b) in the Hungarian People's Republic:
    (i) the income taxes (*a jövedelemadók*);
    (ii) the profit taxes (*a nyereségadók*);
    (iii) the enterprises' special tax (*a vállalati különadó*);
    (iv) the contribution to communal development (*a községfejlesztési hozzájárulás*);
    (v) the levy on dividends and profit distributions of commercial companies (*a kereskedelmi társaságok osztalék és nyereség kifizetései utáni illeték*);
    (hereinafter referred to as "Hungarian tax").

(2) This Convention shall also apply to any identical or substantially similar taxes which are imposed by either Contracting State after the date of signature of this Convention in addition to, or in place of, the existing taxes.

Article 3 General definitions

(1) In this Convention, unless the context otherwise requires:
  (a) the term "United Kingdom" means Great Britain and Northern Ireland, including any area outside the territorial sea of the United Kingdom which in accordance with international law and the laws of the United Kingdom is an area within which the rights of the United Kingdom with respect to the sea-bed and sub-soil and their natural resources may be exercised;
  (b) the term "Hungarian People's Republic" means the territory of the Hungarian People's Republic;
  (c) the term "national" means:
    (i) in relation to the United Kingdom, any individual who has under the law in the United Kingdom the status of British subject, otherwise than by virtue of possessing the citizenship of an independent commonwealth country other than the United Kingdom, provided he has the right of abode in the United Kingdom; and any legal person, partnership, association or other entity deriving its status as such from the law in force in the United Kingdom;
    (ii) in relation to the Hungarian People's Republic, any individual having the citizenship of the Hungarian People's Republic and any legal person, partnership, association or other entity deriving its status as such from the law in force in the Hungarian People's Republic;
  (d) the terms "a Contracting State" and "the other Contracting State" mean the United Kingdom or the Hungarian People's Republic, as the context requires;
  (e) the term "person" comprises an individual, a company and any other body of persons;
  (f) the term "company" means any body corporate or any entity which is treated as a body corporate for tax purposes;
  (g) the terms "enterprise of a Contracting State" and "enterprise of the other Contracting State" mean respectively an enterprise carried on by a resident of a Contracting State and an enterprise carried on by a resident of the other Contracting State;

(h) the term "competent authority" means, in the case of the United Kingdom the Board of Inland Revenue or its authorised representative, and in the case of the Hungarian People's Republic the Minister of Finance or his authorised representative.

(2) As regards the application of this Convention by a Contracting State any term not otherwise defined shall, unless the context otherwise requires, have the meaning which it has under the laws of that Contracting State relating to the taxes which are the subject of this Convention.

Article 4 Fiscal domicile

(1) For the purposes of this Convention, the term "resident of a Contracting State" means, subject to the provisions of paragraphs (2) and (3) of this Article, any person who, under the law of that State, is liable to taxation therein by reason of his domicile, residence, place of management or any other criterion of a similar nature.

(2) Where by reason of the provisions of paragraph (1) of this Article an individual is a resident of both Contracting States, then his status shall be determined in accordance with the following rules:

(a) he shall be deemed to be a resident of the Contracting State in which he has a permanent home available to him. If he has a permanent home available to him in both Contracting States, he shall be deemed to be a resident of the Contracting State in which the centre of his vital interests is located;

(b) if the Contracting State in which he has his centre of vital interests cannot be determined, or if he has not a permanent home available to him in either Contracting State, he shall be deemed to be a resident of the Contracting State in which he has an habitual abode;

(c) if he has an habitual abode in both Contracting States or in neither of them, he shall be deemed to be a resident of the Contracting State of which he is a national;

(d) if he is a national of both Contracting States or of neither of them, the competent authorities of the Contracting States shall settle the question by mutual agreement in accordance with Article 25.

(3) Where by reason of the provisions of paragraph (1) of this Article a person other than an individual is a resident of both Contracting States, then it shall be deemed to be a resident of the Contracting State in which its place of effective management is situated.

Article 6 Income from immovable property

(1) (Taxation of income from immovable property.)

(2) (a) The term "immovable property" shall, subject to the provisions of sub-paragraph (b) of this paragraph , be defined in accordance with the law of the Contracting State in which the property in question is situated.

(b) The term "immovable property" shall in any case include property, accessory to immovable property, livestock and equipment used in agriculture and forestry, rights to which the provisions of general law respecting landed property apply usufruct or immovable property and rights to variable or fixed payments as consideration for the working of, or the right to work, mineral deposits sources and other natural resources; ships and aircraft shall not be regarded as immovable property.

(3) . . .

(4) . . .

Article 8 Shipping and air transport

(1) A resident of a Contracting State shall be exempt from tax in the other Contracting State on profits from the operation of ships or aircraft (including activities incidental thereto) whether owned or chartered by him other than profits from voyages of ships or aircraft confined solely to places in the other Contracting State.

(2) The provisions of paragraph (1) shall apply to an enterprise of a Contracting State which operates in the other State through an agency.

(3) The provisions of this Article shall also apply to profits derived from participation in a pool, a joint venture or an international operating agency.

Article 13 Capital gains

(1) . . .

(2) (Taxation of gains from alienation of movable business property.)

(3) Notwithstanding the provisions of paragraph (2) of this Article, capital gains derived by a resident of a Contracting State from the alienation of ships and aircraft operated in international traffic and movable property pertaining to the operation of such ships and aircraft shall be taxable only in that Contracting State.

(4) . . .

Article 24 Non-discrimination

(1) The nationals of a Contracting State shall not be subjected in the other Contracting State to any taxation or any requirement connected therewith which is other or more burdensome than the taxation and connected requirements to which nationals of that other State in the same circumstances are or may be subjected.

(2) The taxation on a permanent establishment which an enterprise of a Contracting State has in the other Contracting State shall not be less favourably levied in that other State than the taxation levied on enterprises of that other State carrying on the same activities.

This provision shall not be construed as obliging a Contracting State to grant to residents of the other Contracting State any personal allowances, reliefs and reductions for taxation purposes on account of civil status or family responsibilities which it grants to its own residents.

(3) Enterprises of a Contracting State, the capital of which is wholly or partly owned or controlled, directly or indirectly, by one or more residents of the other Contracting State, shall not be subjected in the first-mentioned State to any taxation or any requirement connected therewith which is more burdensome than the taxation and connected requirements to which other similar enterprises of that first-mentioned State are or may be subjected.

(4) In this Article the term "taxation" means taxes of every kind and description.

Article 25 Mutual agreement procedure

(1) Where a resident of a Contracting State considers that the actions of one or both of the Contracting States result or will result for him in taxation not in accordance with this Convention, he may, notwithstanding the remedies provided by the national laws of those States, present his case to the competent authority of the Contracting State of which he is a resident.

(2) The competent authority shall endeavour, if the objection appears to it to be justified and if it is not itself able to arrive at an appropriate solution, to resolve the case by mutual agreement with the competent authority of the other Contracting State, with a view to the avoidance of taxation not in accordance with the Convention.

(3) The competent authorities of the Contracting States shall endeavour to resolve by mutual agreement any difficulties or doubts arising as to the interpretation or application of the Convention.

(4) The competent authorities of the Contracting States may communicate with each other directly for the purpose of reaching an agreement in the sense of the preceding paragraphs.

Article 26 Exchange of information

(1) The competent authorities of the Contracting States shall exchange such information as is necessary for the carrying out of this Convention and of the domestic laws of the Con-

tracting States concerning taxes covered by this Convention. Any information so exchanged shall be treated as secret and shall not be disclosed to any persons other than persons (including a court or administrative body) concerned with the assessment or collection of, or prosecution in respect of, or the determination of appeals in relation to, the taxes which are the subject of this Convention.

(2) In no case shall the provisions of paragraph (1) be construed so as to impose on the competent authority of either Contracting State the obligation:

(*a*) to carry out administrative measures at variance with the laws or administrative practice prevailing in either Contracting State;

(*b*) to supply particulars which are not obtainable under the laws or in the normal course of the administration of that or of the other Contracting State;

(*c*) to supply information which would disclose any trade, business, industrial, commercial or professional secret or trade process, or information, the disclosure of which would be contrary to public policy (*ordre public*).

Article 28 Entry into force

Note: Article 28 provided for the entry into force of this Convention. It takes effect in the UK from the year of assessment 1975–76 (income tax and capital gains tax) and from the financial year beginning on 1 April 1975 (corporation tax).

Official languages: The Hungarian language text and the English language text of this Convention are equally authoritative.

ICELAND

(Discussions have been held at official level about the text of a new comprehensive double taxation Convention. The text of the new Convention had not been agreed at the time of going to press.)

Agreement of 27 April 1928 (SR & O 1928 No 563)

Article 1 [Shipping profits exempt in the UK]

His Britannic Majesty's Government in Great Britain agree to take the necessary steps under Section 18 of the Act of Parliament of the United Kingdom known as the Finance Act, 1923, for exempting from income tax (including super-tax) chargeable in Great Britain and Northern Ireland for the year of assessment 1923–24 commencing on the 6th day of April, 1923, and for every subsequent year of assessment, any profits which accrue from the business of shipping carried on by an individual resident in Iceland or by a company managing and controlling such business in Iceland. The arrangements made in accordance with this Article shall cease to have effect if and so soon as the laws of Iceland cease to give the relief indicated in Article 2.

Corporation tax: This Agreement covers United Kingdom corporation tax, by virtue of ICTA 1970, s 514(4), which was expressly preserved by FA 1987, Sch 16, Pt VII.

Article 2 [Shipping profits exempt in Iceland]

The Royal Icelandic Government have declared that under the laws of the Kingdom of Iceland regarding income tax and property tax, tax is not chargeable in respect of profits which accrue from the business of shipping carried on by an individual resident in Great Britain or Northern Ireland or by a company managing and controlling such business in Great Britain or Northern Ireland.

Article 3 [General definitions]

The expression "the business of shipping" means the business carried on by an owner of ships, and for the purposes of this definition the expression "owner" includes any charterer.

Official language: English.

INDIA

Convention of 16 April 1981 (SI 1981 No 1120)

Article 1 Personal scope

This Convention shall apply to persons who are residents of one or both of the Contracting States.

Article 2 Taxes covered

(1) The taxes which are the subject of this Convention are:
    (*a*) in the United Kingdom of Great Britain and Northern Ireland:
        (i) the income tax;
        (ii) the corporation tax;
        (iii) the capital gains tax;
        (iv) the petroleum revenue tax; and
        (v) the development land tax;
        (hereinafter referred to as "United Kingdom tax");
    (*b*) in India:
        (i) the income-tax and any surcharge thereon imposed under the Income-tax Act, 1961 (43 of 1961); and
        (ii) the surtax imposed under the Companies (Profits) Surtax Act, 1964 (7 of 1964);

(hereinafter referred to as "Indian tax").

(2) This Convention shall also apply to any identical or substantially similar taxes which are imposed by either Contracting State after the date of signature of this Convention in addition to, or in place of, the existing taxes. The competent authorities of the Contracting States shall notify each other of any substantial changes which are made in their respective taxation laws.

Article 3 General definitions

(1) In this Convention, unless the context otherwise requires:

    (a) the term "United Kingdom" means Great Britain and Northern Ireland, including any area outside the territorial sea of the United Kingdom which in accordance with international law has been or may hereafter be designated, under the laws of the United Kingdom concerning the Continental Shelf, as an area within which the rights of the United Kingdom with respect to the sea-bed and sub-soil and their natural resources may be exercised;

    (b) the term "tax" means United Kingdom tax or Indian tax, as the context requires;

    (c) the term "fiscal year" in relation to Indian tax means "previous year" as defined in the Income-tax Act, 1961 (43 of 1961);

    (d) the terms "a Contracting State" and "the other Contracting State" mean the United Kingdom or India, as the context requires;

    (e) the term "person" includes an individual, a company and any other body of persons;

    (f) the term "company" means any body corporate or any entity which is treated as a company or body corporate for tax purposes;

    (g) the terms "enterprise of a Contracting State" and "enterprise of the other Contracting State" mean respectively an enterprise carried on by a resident of a Contracting State and an enterprise carried on by a resident of the other Contracting State;

    (h) the term "competent authority" means, in the case of the United Kingdom the Commissioners of Inland Revenue or their authorised representative, and in the case of India the Central Government in the Department of Revenue;

    (i) the term "international traffic" means any transport by a ship or aircraft operated by an enterprise which has its place of effective management in a Contracting State except when the ship or aircraft is operated solely between places in the other Contracting State;

    (j) the term "Government" means the Government of a Contracting State or a political subdivision or local authority thereof. In relation to the United Kingdom, the term "political subdivision" shall include Northern Ireland.

(2) As regards the application of this Convention by a Contracting State any term not otherwise defined shall, unless the context otherwise requires, have the meaning which it has under the laws of that Contracting State relating to the taxes which are the subject of this Convention.

Article 4 Fiscal domicile

(1) For the purposes of this Convention, the term "resident of a Contracting State" means any person who, under the law of that State, is liable to taxation therein by reason of his domicile, residence, place of management or any other criterion of a similar nature.

(2) Where by reason of the provisions of paragraph (1) of this Article an individual is a resident of both Contracting States, then his status shall be determined in accordance with the following rules:

    (a) he shall be deemed to be a resident of the Contracting State in which he has a permanent home available to him. If he has a permanent home available to him in both Contracting States, he shall be deemed to be a resident of the Contracting State with which his personal and economic relations are closer (centre of vital interests);

115

(b) if the Contracting State in which he has his centre of vital interests cannot be determined, or if he has not a permanent home available to him in either Contracting State, he shall be deemed to be a resident of the Contracting State in which he has an habitual abode;

(c) if he has an habitual abode in both Contracting States or in neither of them, he shall be deemed to be a resident of the Contracting State of which he is a national;

(d) if he is a national of both Contracting States or of neither of them, the competent authorities of the Contracting States shall settle the question by mutual agreement.

(3) Where by reason of the provisions of paragraph (1) of this Article a person other than an individual is a resident of both Contracting States, then it shall be deemed to be a resident of the Contracting State in which its place of effective management is situated.

Article 6 Income from immovable property

(1) (Taxation of income from immovable property.)

(2)(a) The term "immovable property" shall, subject to the provisions of sub-paragraph (b) of this paragraph, be defined in accordance with the law of the Contracting State in which the property in question is situated.

(b) The term "immovable property" shall in any case include property accessory to immovable property, livestock and equipment used in agriculture and forestry, rights to which the provisions of general law respecting landed property apply, usufruct of immovable property and rights to variable or fixed payments as consideration for the working of, or the right to work, mineral deposits, sources and other natural resources. Ships and aircraft shall not be regarded as immovable property.

(3) . . .

(4) . . .

Article 9 Shipping

(1) Income of an enterprise of a Contracting State from the operation of ships in international traffic shall be taxable only in that State.

(2) Notwithstanding the provisions of paragraph (1) of this Article such income may be taxed in the other Contracting State from which it is derived provided that:

(a) the income is in respect of any one or more of the first ten fiscal years for which this Convention has effect;

(b) the tax chargeable on that income shall be 50 per cent of the tax which would have been chargeable in the absence of this Convention in respect of the income for the first five fiscal years for which this Convention has effect and 25 per cent of such tax for the next following five years.

(3) The provisions of paragraphs (1) and (2) of this Article shall not apply to income from journeys between places which are situated in a Contracting State.

(4) For the purposes of this Article, income from the operation of ships includes income derived from the rental on a bareboat basis of ships if such rental income is incidental to the income described in paragraph (1) of this Article.

(5) Notwithstanding the provisions of Article 7 (Business profits), the provisions of paragraphs (1), (2) and (3) of this Article shall likewise apply to income of an enterprise of a Contracting State from the use, maintenance or rental of containers (including trailers and related equipment for the transport of containers) used for the transport of goods or merchandise.

(6) The provisions of this Article shall apply also to income derived from participation in a pool, a joint business or an international operating agency.

(7) Gains derived by an enterprise of a Contracting State from the alienation of ships or containers owned and operated by the enterprise shall be taxed only in that State if either the income from the operation of the alienated ships or containers was taxed only in that State, or the ships or containers are situated outside the other Contracting State at the time of the alienation.

Article 14 Capital gains

Except as provided in Articles 8 (Air transport) and 9 (Shipping) of this Convention, each Contracting State may tax capital gains in accordance with the provisions of its domestic law.

Article 23 Non-discrimination

(1) The nationals of a Contracting State shall not be subjected in the other Contracting State to any taxation or any requirement connected therewith which is other or more burdensome than the taxation and connected requirements to which nationals of that other State in the same circumstances are or may be subjected.

(2) The taxation on a permanent establishment which an enterprise of a Contracting State has in the other Contracting State shall not be less favourably levied in that other State than the taxation levied on enterprises of that other State carrying on the same activities in the same circumstances or under the same conditions. This provision shall not be construed as preventing a Contracting State from charging the profits of a permanent establishment which an enterprise of the other Contracting State has in the first-mentioned State at a rate of tax which is higher than that imposed on the profits of a similar enterprise of the first-mentioned Contracting State, nor as being in conflict with the provisions of paragraph (4) of Article 7 of this Convention.

(3) Nothing contained in this Article shall be construed as obliging a Contracting State to grant to individuals not resident in that State any personal allowances, reliefs and reductions for taxation purposes which are by law available only to individuals who are so resident.

(4) Enterprises of a Contracting State, the capital of which is wholly or partly owned or controlled, directly or indirectly, by one or more residents of the other Contracting State, shall not be subjected in the first-mentioned Contracting State to any taxation or any requirement connected therewith which is other or more burdensome than the taxation and connected requirements to which other similar enterprises of that first-mentioned State are or may be subjected.

(5) In this Article, the term "taxation" means taxes which are the subject of this Convention.

Article 24 Mutual agreement procedure

(1) Where a resident of a Contracting State considers that the actions of one or both of the Contracting States result or will result for him in taxation not in accordance with this Convention, he may, notwithstanding the remedies provided by the national laws of those States, present his case to the competent authority of the Contracting State of which he is a resident.

(2) The competent authority shall endeavour, if the objection appears to it to be justified and if it is not itself able to arrive at an appropriate solution, to resolve the case by mutual agreement with the competent authority of the other Contracting State, with a view to the avoidance of taxation not in accordance with the Convention.

(3) The competent authorities of the Contracting States shall endeavour to resolve by mutual agreement any difficulties or doubts arising as to the interpretation or application of the Convention.

(4) The competent authorities of the Contracting States may communicate with each other directly for the purpose of reaching an agreement in the sense of the preceding paragraphs.

Article 25 Exchange of information

The competent authorities of the Contracting States shall exchange such information (being information and documents which are at their disposal under their respective taxation laws and obtained in the normal course of administration) as is necessary for carrying out the provisions of this Convention or for the prevention of fraud or the administration of statutory provisions against legal avoidance in relation to the taxes which are the subject of this Convention. Any information or documents so exchanged shall be treated as secret but may be disclosed to persons (including a court or administrative body) concerned with assessment, collection, enforcement or prosecution in respect of taxes which are the subject of this Convention. No information or documents shall be exchanged which would disclose any trade, business, industrial or professional secret or any trade process.

Article 27 Entry into force

Note: Article 27 provided for the entry into force of this Convention. It takes effect in the UK from the year of assessment 1982–83 (income tax and capital gains tax) and from the financial year beginning on 1 April 1982 (corporation tax).

Official language: The Hindi language text and the English language text of this Convention are equally authoritative.

Capital taxes

Agreement of 3 April 1956 (SI 1956 No 998)

Article I [Duties covered]

The duties which are the subject of the present Agreement are:—
(a) In India, the estate duty imposed under the Estate Duty Act, 1953 (No. 34 of 1953) and
(b) In the United Kingdom, the estate duty imposed in Great Britain.

Inheritance tax: This Agreement covers United Kingdom capital transfer tax (now inheritance tax), by virtue of IHTA 1984, s 158(6), FA 1986, s 100.

Article II [General definitions]

(1) In the present Agreement, unless the context otherwise requires:—
(a) The term "India" means all the States and territories comprised in the Union of India;
(b) The term "United Kingdom" means Great Britain and Northern Ireland;
(c) The term "Great Britain" means England, Wales and Scotland and does not include the Channel Islands and the Isle of Man;
(d) The term "territory" when used in relation to one or the other Contracting Government means India or Great Britain, as the context requires;
(e) The term "duty" means the estate duty imposed in India or the estate duty imposed in Great Britain, as the context requires.
(2) For the purposes of the present Agreement, the question whether a deceased person was at the time of his death domiciled in any part of the territory of one of the Contracting Governments shall be determined in accordance with the law in force in that territory.

(3) In the application of the provisions of the present Agreement by either Contracting Government, any term not otherwise defined shall, unless the context otherwise requires, have the meaning which it has under the law of that Contracting Government relating to duty.

Article III [Imposition of duty]

(1) Subject to paragraph (2) of this Article, duty shall not be imposed in India on the death of a person who was not domiciled at the time of his death in any part of India but was domiciled in some part of Great Britain on any property situate outside India:

Provided that nothing in this paragraph shall prevent the imposition of duty in India on—
  (a) any settled property of which the deceased was life tenant where the settlor was domiciled in India at the time the settlement took effect; or
  (b) property that passes under a disposition or devolution regulated by the law of some part of India.

(2) Nothing in the present Agreement shall affect any provision of the law of India imposing duty on shares in or debentures of a company incorporated outside India which carries on business in India and which has been treated for the purposes of the Indian Income Tax Act, 1922 (XI of 1922), as resident in India for two out of the three completed assessments immediately preceding the death; nor shall anything in the present Agreement be considered to confer a right to a credit against duty so imposed for any duty imposed in Great Britain on any such shares or debentures.

(3) Duty shall not be imposed in Great Britain on the death of a person who was not domiciled at the time of his death in any part of Great Britain but was domiciled in some part of India on any property situate outside Great Britain:

Provided that nothing in this paragraph shall prevent the imposition of duty in Great Britain on any property which passes under a disposition or devolution regulated by the law of some part of Great Britain.

Article IV [Situs]

(1) Subject to paragraph (2) of this Article, where a person was at the time of his death domiciled in any part of the territory of one of the Contracting Governments, the situs of any property which for the purposes of duty passes or is deemed to pass on his death shall, for the purposes of the imposition of duty and of the credit to be allowed under Article VI, be determined exclusively in accordance with the rules in Article V of the present Agreement.

(2) Paragraph (1) of this Article shall apply if, and only if, apart from the said Article V—
  (a) duty would be imposed on the property under the law of each of the Contracting Governments; or
  (b) duty would be imposed on the property under the law of one of the Contracting Governments and would, but for some specific exemption, also be imposed thereon under the law of the other Contracting Government.

Article V [Deemed situation of rights etc]

The rules referred to in paragraph (1) of Article IV are:—
  (a)–(i) . . .
  (j) Ships and aircraft and shares thereof shall be deemed to be situated at the place of registration of the ship or aircraft;
  (k)–(o) . . .

Article VI [Elimination of double taxation]

(1) Where one Contracting Government imposes duty on any property which is not situated in its territory but is situated in the territory of the other Contracting Government, the former Government shall allow against so much of its duty (as otherwise computed) as is

119

attributable to that property a credit (not exceeding the amount of the duty so attributable) equal to so much of the duty imposed in the territory of the other Contracting Government as is attributable to such property.

(2) Where each Contracting Government imposes duty on any property which is situated—

    (*a*) in the territory of both Governments, or

    (*b*) outside both territories,

each Government shall allow against so much of its duty (as otherwise computed) as is attributable to that property a credit which bears the same proportion to the amount of its duty so attributable or to the amount of the other Contracting Government's duty attributable to the same property, whichever is the less, as the former amount bears to the sum of both amounts.

(3) For the purpose of this Article, the amount of the duty of a Contracting Government attributable to any property shall be ascertained after taking into account any credit, allowance or relief, or any remission or reduction of duty, otherwise than in respect of duty payable in the territory of the other Contracting Government.

Article VII [Time limit]

(1) Any claim for a credit or for a refund of duty founded on the provisions of the present Agreement shall be made within six years from the date of the death of the deceased person in respect of whose estate the claim is made, or, in the case of a reversionary interest where payment of duty is deferred until the date on which the interest falls into possession, within six years from that date.

(2) Any such credit allowed or refund made shall be allowed or made without payment of interest on the amount credited or refunded.

Article VIII [Exchange of information]

(1) The taxation authorities of the Contracting Governments shall exchange such information (being information available under the respective taxation laws of the Contracting Governments) as is necessary for carrying out the provisions of the present Agreement or for the prevention of fraud or the administration of statutory provisions against legal avoidance in relation to the duties which are the subject of the present Agreement. Any information so exchanged shall be treated as secret and shall not be disclosed to any person other than those concerned with the administration, assessment and collection of the duties which are the subject of the present Agreement. No information shall be exchanged which might disclose any trade secret or trade process.

(2) As used in this Article, the term "taxation authorities" means—

    (*a*) in the case of India, the Central Board of Revenue or their authorised representative;

    (*b*) in the case of Great Britain, the Commissioners of Inland Revenue or their authorised representative;

    (*c*) in the case of Northern Ireland (to which the present Agreement applies under Article X), the Minister of Finance or his authorised representative;

    (*d*) in the case of any territory to which the present Agreement is extended under Article IX, the competent authority for the administration in such territory of the duties to which the present Agreement applies.

Article XI [Entry into force]

Note: This Agreement applies to the estates of persons dying after 29 June 1956 or, if the personal representatives so elect, to the estates of persons dying after 15 October 1953.

Official language: English.

INDONESIA

Agreement of 13 March 1974 (SI 1975 No 2191)

Article 1 Personal scope

This Agreement shall apply to persons who are residents of one or both of the Contracting States.

Article 2 Taxes covered

(1) The taxes which are the subject of this Agreement are:
    (*a*) in the case of Indonesia:
        (i) *pajak pendapatan* (income tax);
        (ii) *pajak perseroan* (company tax);
        (iii) *pajak kekayaan* (capital tax); and
        (iv) *pajak atas bunga, dividen dan royalty* (tax on interest, dividend and royalty);
        (hereinafter referred to as "Indonesian tax);
    (*b*) in the case of the United Kingdom of Great Britain and Northern Ireland:
        (i) the income tax;
        (ii) the corporation tax; and
        (iii) the capital gains tax;
        (hereinafter referred to as "United Kingdom tax").

(2) The Agreement shall also apply to any identical or substantially similar taxes which are imposed by either Contracting State after the date of signature of this Agreement in addition to, or in place of, the existing taxes. The competent authorities of the Contracting States shall notify each other of any substantial changes which have been made in their respective taxation laws.

Article 3 General definitions

(1) In this Agreement, unless the context otherwise requires:
    (*a*) the terms "a Contracting State" and "the other Contracting State" mean the United Kingdom or Indonesia, as the context requires;
    (*b*) the term "Indonesia" means the territory of the Republic of Indonesia and the parts of the sea-bed and sub-soil under the adjacent seas, over which the Republic of Indonesia has sovereign rights in accordance with international law;
    (*c*) the term "United Kingdom" means Great Britain and Northern Ireland, including any area outside the territorial sea of the United Kingdom which in accordance with international law has been or may hereafter be designated, under the laws of

121

the United Kingdom concerning the Continental Shelf, as an area within which the rights of the United Kingdom with respect to the seabed and subsoil and their natural resources may be exercised;

(d) the term "nationals" means:

(i) in relation to Indonesia, any national of Indonesia and any legal person, partnership, association and entity deriving their status as such from the laws in force in the Republic of Indonesia;

(ii) in relation to the United Kingdom, all citizens of the United Kingdom and Colonies who derive their status as such from their connection with the United Kingdom and all legal persons, partnerships and associations deriving their status as such from the law in force in the United Kingdom;

(e) the term "person" comprises an individual, a company and any other body of persons;

(f) the term "company" means any body corporate or any entity which is treated as a body corporate for tax purposes;

(g) the terms "enterprise of a Contracting State" and "enterprise of the other Contracting State" mean respectively an enterprise carried on by a resident of a Contracting State and an enterprise carried on by a resident of the other Contracting State;

(h) the term "competent authority" means:

(i) in Indonesia, the Minister of Finance or his duly authorised representative;

(ii) in the United Kingdom, the Commissioners of Inland Revenue or their duly authorised representative;

(i) the term "tax" means Indonesian tax or United Kingdom tax as the context requires.

(2) As regards the application of this Agreement by a Contracting State any term not otherwise defined shall, unless the context otherwise requires, have the meaning which it has under the laws of that State relating to the taxes which are the subject of this Agreement.

Article 4 Fiscal domicile

(1) For the purposes of this Agreement, the term "resident of a Contracting State" means, subject to the provisions of paragraphs (2) and (3) of this Article, any person who, under the law of that State, is liable to taxation therein by reason of his domicile, residence, place of management or any other criterion of a similar nature; the term does not include any individual who is liable to tax in that Contracting State only if he derives income from sources therein. The terms "resident of the United Kingdom" and "resident of Indonesia" shall be construed accordingly.

(2) Where by reason of the provisions of paragraph (1) of this Article an individual is a resident of both Contracting States, then his status shall be determined in accordance with the following rules:

(a) he shall be deemed to be a resident of the Contracting State in which he has a permanent home available to him. If he has a permanent home available to him in both Contracting States, he shall be deemed to be a resident of the Contracting State with which his personal and economic relations are closest (centre of vital interests);

(b) if the Contracting State in which he has his centre of vital interests cannot be determined, or if he has not a permanent home available to him in either Contracting State, he shall be deemed to be a resident of the Contracting State in which he has an habitual abode;

(c) if he has an habitual abode in both Contracting States or in neither of them the competent authorities of the Contracting States shall settle the question by mutual agreement.

(3) Where by reason of the provisions of paragraph (1) of this Article a person other than an individual is a resident of both Contracting States, then it shall be deemed to be a resident of the Contracting State in which its place of effective management is situated.

Article 7 Income from immovable property

(1) (Taxation of income from immovable property.)

(2)(*a*) The term "immovable property" shall, subject to the provisions of sub-paragraph (*b*) below, be defined in accordance with the law of the Contracting State in which the property in question is situated.

(*b*) The term "immovable property" shall in any case include property accessory to immovable property, livestock and equipment used in agriculture and forestry, rights to which the provisions of general law respecting landed property apply, usufruct of immovable property and rights to variable or fixed payments as consideration for the working of, or the right to work, mineral deposits, sources and other natural resources; ships, boats and aircraft shall not be regarded as immovable property.

(3) . . .

(4) . . .

Article 9 Shipping and air transport

(1) Subject to the provisions of paragraph (3) of this Article, a resident of a Contracting State shall be exempt from tax in the other Contracting State on profits from the operation of ships which are registered in the first-mentioned Contracting State or are operated under the Indonesia-Europe Freight Conference arrangements.

(2) Subject to the provisions of paragraph (3) of this Article, a resident of a Contracting State shall be exempt from tax in the other Contracting State on profits from the operation of aircraft.

(3) Profits from voyages of ships or aircraft confined solely to places in a Contracting State may be taxed in that State.

Article 14 Capital gains

(1) . . .

(2) (Taxation of gains from alienation of movable property.)

(3) Notwithstanding the provisions of paragraph (2) of this Article, capital gains derived by a resident of a Contracting State from the alienation of ships and aircraft operated in international traffic and movable property pertaining to the operation of such ships and aircraft shall be taxable only in that Contracting State.

(4) . . .

(5) . . .

Article 24 Capital

(1) (Taxation of business property of permanent establishment, etc.)

(2) Notwithstanding the provisions of paragraph (1) of this Article, ships and aircraft operated in international traffic and movable property pertaining to the operation of such ships and aircraft shall be taxable only in the Contracting State of which the operator is a resident.

(3) . . .

Article 27 Non-discrimination

(1) The nationals of a Contracting State shall not be subjected in the other Contracting State to any taxation or any requirement connected therewith which is other or more burdensome than the taxation and connected requirements to which nationals of that other State in the same circumstances are or may be subjected.

(2) The taxation on a permanent establishment which an enterprise of a Contracting State has in the other Contracting State shall not be less favourably levied in that other State than the taxation levied on enterprises of that other State carrying on the same activities.

(3) Enterprises of a Contracting State, the capital of which is wholly or partly owned or controlled, directly or indirectly, by one or more residents of the other Contracting State,

shall not be subjected in the first-mentioned Contracting State to any taxation or any requirement connected therewith which is other or more burdensome than the taxation and connected requirements to which other similar enterprises of that first-mentioned State are or may be subjected.

(4) Nothing contained in this Article shall be construed:

    (*a*) as obliging either Contracting State to grant to individuals not resident in that State any of the personal allowances, reliefs and reductions for tax purposes which are granted to individuals so resident; or

    (*b*) as being applicable to any tax of a preferential nature which a Contracting State may impose in pursuance of its programme of economic development and which the competent authorities of the Contracting States agree should be excluded from the provisions of this Article.

(5) In this Article the term "taxation" means taxes which are the subject of this Agreement.

Article 28 Mutual agreement procedure

(1) Where a resident of a Contracting State considers that the actions of one or both of the Contracting States result or will result for him in taxation not in accordance with this Agreement, he may, notwithstanding the remedies provided by the national laws of those States, present his case to the competent authority of the Contracting State of which he is a resident.

(2) The competent authority shall endeavour, if the objection appears to it to be justified and if it is not itself able to arrive at an appropriate solution, to resolve the case by mutual agreement with the competent authority of the other Contracting State, with a view to the avoidance of taxation not in accordance with the Agreement.

(3) The competent authorities of the Contracting States shall endeavour to resolve by mutual agreement any difficulties or doubts arising as to the interpretation or application of the Agreement.

(4) The competent authorities of the Contracting States may communicate with each other directly for the purpose of reaching an agreement in the sense of the preceding paragraphs.

Article 29 Exchange of information

The competent authorities of the Contracting States shall exchange such information (being information which is at their disposal under their respective taxation laws in the normal course of administration) as is necessary for carrying out the provisions of this Agreement or for the prevention of fraud or the administration of statutory provisions against legal avoidance in relation to the taxes which are the subject of this Agreement. Any information so exchanged shall be treated as secret but may be disclosed to persons (including a court or administrative body) concerned with assessment, collection, enforcement or prosecution in respect of taxes which are the subject of this Agreement. No information shall be exchanged which would disclose any trade, business, industrial or professional secret or any trade process.

Article 31 Entry into force

Note: Article 31 provided for the entry into force of this Agreement. It takes effect in the UK from the year of assessment 1974–75 (income tax and capital gains tax) and from the financial year beginning on 1 April 1974 (corporation tax).

Article 32 Termination

Note: This Agreement was terminated by notice given by the Indonesian government in June 1983. Pending agreement on the text of and entry into force of a new Agreement, however, the 1974 Agreement continues in force.

Official language: English.

IRISH REPUBLIC

Convention of 2 June 1976 (SI 1976 No 2151)

Printed as amended by the Protocol of 28 October 1976 (SI 1976 No 2152).

Article 1 Personal scope

This Convention shall apply to persons who are residents of one or both of the Contracting States.

Article 2 Taxes covered

(1) The taxes which are the subject of this Convention are:
    (a) in the Republic of Ireland:
        (i) the income tax;
        (ii) the corporation profits tax;
        (iii) the corporation tax; and
        (iv) the capital gains tax;
    (b) in the United Kingdom of Great Britain and Northern Ireland:
        (i) the income tax;
        (ii) the corporation tax;
        (iii) the petroleum revenue tax; and
        (iv) the capital gains tax.

(2) This Convention shall also apply to any identical or substantially similar taxes which are imposed by either Contracting State after the date of signature of this Convention in addition to, or in place of, the existing taxes.

Article 3 General definitions

(1) In this Convention, unless the context otherwise requires:
    (a) the term "Republic of Ireland" includes any area outside the territorial waters of the Republic of Ireland which in accordance with international law has been or may hereafter be designated, under the laws of the Republic of Ireland concerning the Continental Shelf, as an area within which the rights of the Republic of Ireland with respect to the sea-bed and sub-soil and their natural resources may be exercised;
    (b) the term "United Kingdom" includes any area outside the territorial sea of the United Kingdom which in accordance with international law has been or may hereafter be designated, under the laws of the United Kingdom concerning the

Continental Shelf, as an area within which the rights of the United Kingdom with respect to the sea bed and subsoil and their natural resources may be exercised;

(c) the term "nationals" means:

    (i) in relation to the Republic of Ireland, all citizens of Ireland and all legal persons, associations or other entities deriving their status as such from the laws in force in the Republic of Ireland;

    (ii) in relation to the United Kingdom, citizens of the United Kingdom and Colonies, British subjects under Section 2 of the British Nationality Act 1948 whose notices given under that Section have been acknowledged before the date of signature of this Convention, British subjects by virtue of Section 13(1) or Section 16 of the British Nationality Act 1948 or Section 1 of the British Nationality Act 1965, and British protected persons within the meaning of the British Nationality Act 1948; and all legal persons, associations or other entities deriving their status as such from the law in force in the United Kingdom;

(d) the term "United Kingdom tax" means tax imposed by the United Kingdom being tax to which this Convention applies by virtue of the provisions of Article 2; the term "Irish tax" means tax imposed by the Republic of Ireland being tax to which this Convention applies by virtue of the provisions of Article 2;

(e) the term "tax" means United Kingdom tax or Irish tax, as the context requires;

(f) the terms "a Contracting State" and "the other Contracting State" mean the United Kingdom or the Republic of Ireland, as the context requires;

(g) the term "person" comprises an individual, a company and any other body of persons;

(h) the term "company" means any body corporate or any entity which is treated as a body corporate for tax purposes;

(i) the terms "enterprise of a Contracting State" and "enterprise of the other Contracting State" mean respectively an enterprise carried on by a resident of a Contracting State and an enterprise carried on by a resident of the other Contracting State;

(j) the term "competent authority" means, in the case of the United Kingdom, the Commissioners of Inland Revenue or their authorised representative, and in the case of the Republic of Ireland, the Revenue Commissioners or their authorised representative.

(2) As regards the application of this Convention by a Contracting State any term not otherwise defined shall, unless the context otherwise requires, have the meaning which it has under the laws of that Contracting State relating to the taxes which are the subject of this Convention.

Article 4 Fiscal domicile

(1) For the purposes of this Convention, the term "resident of a Contracting State" means, subject to the provisions of paragraphs (2) and (3) of this Article, any person who, under the law of that State, is liable to taxation therein by reason of his domicile, residence, place of management or any other criterion of a similar nature; the term does not include any individual who is liable to tax in that Contracting State only if he derives income from sources therein. The terms "resident of the United Kingdom" and "resident of the Republic of Ireland" shall be construed accordingly.

(2) Where by reason of the provisions of paragraph (1) of this Article an individual is a resident of both Contracting States, then his status shall be determined in accordance with the following rules:

    (a) he shall be deemed to be a resident of the Contracting State in which he has a permanent home available to him. If he has a permanent home available to him in both Contracting States, he shall be deemed to be a resident of the Contracting State with which his personal and economic relations are closer (centre of vital interests);

(b) if the Contracting State in which he has his centre of vital interests cannot be determined, or if he has not a permanent home available to him in either Contracting State, he shall be deemed to be a resident of the Contracting State in which he has an habitual abode;

(c) if he has an habitual abode in both Contracting States or in neither of them, he shall be deemed to be a resident of the Contracting State of which he is a national;

(d) if he is a national of both Contracting States or of neither of them, the competent authorities of the Contracting States shall settle the question by mutual agreement.

(3) Where by reason of the provisions of paragraph (1) of this Article a person other than an individual is a resident of both Contracting States, then it shall be deemed to be a resident of the Contracting State in which its place of effective management is situated.

Article 7 Income from immovable property

(1) (Taxation of income from immovable property.)

(2) (a) The term "immovable property" shall, subject to the provisions of sub-paragraph (b) of this paragraph, be defined in accordance with the law of the Contracting State in which the property in question is situated.

(b) The term "immovable property" shall in any case include property accessory to immovable property, livestock and equipment used in agriculture and forestry, rights to which the provisions of general law respecting landed property apply, usufruct of immovable property and rights to variable or fixed payments as consideration for the working of, or the right to work, mineral deposits, sources and other natural resources; ships, boats and aircraft shall not be regarded as immovable property.

(3) . . .

(4) . . .

Article 9 Shipping and air transport

A resident of a Contracting State shall be exempt from tax in the other Contracting State on profits from the operation of ships or aircraft other than profits from voyages of ships or aircraft confined solely to places in the other Contracting State.

Article 14 Capital gains

(1) . . .

(2) Capital gains from the alienation of shares deriving their value or the greater part of their value directly or indirectly from immovable property, other than shares quoted on a stock exchange, may be taxed in the Contracting State in which such immovable property is situated.

(3) (Taxation of gains from alienation of movable business property.)

(4) Except as provided in paragraph (2) of this Article and notwithstanding the provisions of paragraph (3) of this Article, capital gains derived by a resident of a Contracting State from the alienation of ships and aircraft operated in international traffic and movable property pertaining to the operation of such ships and aircraft shall be taxable only in that Contracting State.

(5) . . .

(6) . . .

Article 23 Non-discrimination

(1) The nationals of a Contracting State shall not be subjected in the other Contracting State to any taxation or any requirement connected therewith which is other or more burdensome than the taxation and connected requirements to which nationals of that other State in the same circumstances are or may be subjected.

(2) The taxation on a permanent establishment which an enterprise of a Contracting State has in the other Contracting State shall not be less favourably levied in that other State than the taxation levied on enterprises of that other State carrying on the same activities.

(3) Enterprises of a Contracting State, the capital of which is wholly or partly owned or controlled, directly or indirectly, by one or more residents of the other Contracting State, shall not be subjected in the first-mentioned Contracting State to any taxation or any requirement connected therewith which is other or more burdensome than the taxation and connected requirements to which other similar enterprises of that first-mentioned State are or may be subjected.

(4) Nothing contained in this Article shall be construed as obliging either Contracting State to grant to individuals not resident in that State any of the personal allowances, reliefs and reductions for tax purposes which are granted to individuals so resident.

(5) Nothing contained in this Article shall be construed as obliging a Contracting State to grant to a company which is a resident of the other Contracting State a greater relief from income tax chargeable on dividends received from a company which is a resident of the first-mentioned Contracting State than the relief to which the first-mentioned company may be entitled under the provisions of Article 11 of this Convention.

(6) In this Article the term taxation means taxes of every kind and description.

Article 24 Mutual agreement procedure

(1) Where a resident of a Contracting State considers that the actions of one or both of the Contracting States result or will result for him in taxation not in accordance with this Convention, he may, notwithstanding the remedies provided by the national laws of those States, present his case to the competent authority of the Contracting State of which he is a resident.

(2) The competent authority shall endeavour, if the objection appears to it to be justified and if it is not itself able to arrive at an appropriate solution, to resolve the case by mutual agreement with the competent authority of the other Contracting State, with a view to the avoidance of taxation not in accordance with the Convention.

(3) The competent authorities of the Contracting States shall endeavour to resolve by mutual agreement any difficulties or doubts arising as to the interpretation or application of the Convention.

(4) The competent authorities of the Contracting States may communicate with each other directly for the purpose of reaching an agreement in the sense of the preceding paragraphs.

Article 25 Exchange of information

(1) The competent authorities of the Contracting States shall exchange such information as is necessary for the carrying out of this Convention and of the domestic laws of the Contracting States concerning taxes covered by this Convention insofar as the taxation thereunder is in accordance with this Convention. Any information so exchanged shall be treated as secret and shall not be disclosed to any persons other than persons (including a Court or administrative body) concerned with the assessment or collection of, or prosecution in respect of, or the determination of appeals in relation to, the taxes which are the subject of the Convention.

(2) In no case shall the provisions of paragraph (1) be construed so as to impose on the competent authority of either Contracting State the obligation:

    (a) to carry out administrative measures at variance with the laws or administrative practice prevailing in either Contracting State;

    (b) to supply particulars which are not obtainable under the laws or in the normal course of the administration of that or of the other Contracting State;

    (c) to supply information which would disclose any trade, business, industrial, commercial or professional secret or trade process, or information, the disclosure of which would be contrary to public policy.

Article 28 Entry into force

Note: Article 28 provided for the entry into force of this Convention, which was amended by the Protocol of 28 October 1976 before it entered into force. It takes effect in the UK from the year of assessment 1976–77 (income tax and capital gains tax) and from the financial year beginning on 1 April 1976 (corporation tax).

Official language: English.

Capital taxes

Convention of 7 December 1977 (SI 1978 No 1107)

Article 1 Scope

This Convention shall apply to any person who is within the scope of a tax which is the subject of this Convention, and to any property by reference to which there is a charge to such a tax.

Article 2 Taxes covered

(1) The taxes which are the subject of this Convention are:
    (*a*) in the Republic of Ireland:
        (i) the gift tax; and
        (ii) the inheritance tax;
    (*b*) in the United Kingdom of Great Britain and Northern Ireland, the capital transfer tax.

(2) This Convention shall also apply to any identical or substantially similar taxes which are imposed by either Contracting State after the date of signature of this Convention in addition to, or in place of, the existing taxes.

Inheritance tax: United Kingdom capital transfer tax is known as inheritance tax by virtue of FA 1986, s 100.

Article 3 General definitions

(1) In this Convention, unless the context otherwise requires:
    (*a*) the term "nationals" means:

(i) in relation to the Republic of Ireland, all citizens of Ireland and all legal persons, associations or other entities deriving their status as such from the law in force in the Republic of Ireland;

(ii) in relation to the United Kingdom, citizens of the United Kingdom and Colonies, British subjects under Section 2 of the British Nationality Act 1948 whose notices given under that Section have been acknowledged before the date of signature of this Convention, British subjects by virtue of Section 13(1) or Section 16 of the British Nationality Act 1948 or Section 1 of the British Nationality Act 1965, and British protected persons within the meaning of the British Nationality Act 1948; and all legal persons, associations or other entities deriving their status as such from the law in force in the United Kingdom;

(b) the term "tax" means the gift tax or the inheritance tax imposed in the Republic of Ireland or the capital transfer tax imposed in the United Kingdom, as the context requires;

(c) the terms "a Contracting State" and "the other Contracting State" mean the United Kingdom or the Republic of Ireland, as the context requires;

(d) the term "person" includes an individual, a company and any other body of persons;

(e) the term "company" means any body corporate or any entity which is treated as a body corporate for tax purposes;

(f) the term "competent authority" means, in the case of the United Kingdom, the Commissioners of Inland Revenue or their authorised representative, and in the case of the Republic of Ireland, the Revenue Commissioners or their authorised representative;

(g) the term "event" includes a death.

(2) As regards the application of this Convention by a Contracting State any term not otherwise defined shall, unless the context otherwise requires, have the meaning which it has under the law of that Contracting State relating to the taxes which are the subject of this Convention.

Article 4 Fiscal domicile

(1) For the purposes of this Convention, the question whether a person is, or was at any material time, domiciled in a Contracting State shall be determined by whether he is, or was at that time, domiciled in that Contracting State in accordance with the law of that Contracting State or is or was treated as so domiciled for the purposes of a tax which is the subject of this Convention.

(2) Where by reason of the provisions of paragraph (1) a person is, or was at any material time, domiciled in both Contracting States, then this question shall be determined in accordance with the following rules:

(a) he shall be deemed to be domiciled in the Contracting State in which he has, or had at the material time, a permanent home available to him. If he has or had a permanent home available to him in both Contracting States, the domicile shall be deemed to be in the Contracting State with which his personal and economic relations are, or were at the material time, closer (centre of vital interests);

(b) if the Contracting State in which he has or had his centre of vital interests cannot be determined, or if he has not or had not a permanent home available to him in either Contracting State, the domicile shall be deemed to be in the Contracting State in which he has, or had at the material time, an habitual abode;

(e) if he has or had an habitual abode in both Contracting States or in neither of them, the domicile shall be deemed to be in the Contracting State of which he is, or was at the material time, a national;

(d) if he is or was a national of both Contracting States or of neither of them, the competent authorities of the Contracting States shall settle the question by mutual agreement.

Article 5 Taxing rights

(1) Subject to the following provisions of this Convention, each Contracting State shall retain the right to tax which it would have under its own law apart from this Convention.

(2) For the purposes of paragraph (2) of Article 6 and paragraph (2) of Article 8, the Contracting State with subsidiary taxing rights shall be determined as follows:

(a) in relation to property other than property comprised in a settlement, where a person's domicile has been determined under paragraph (2) of Article 4, that Contracting State shall be the Contracting State in which the person is or was, by virtue of that paragraph, not domiciled;

(b) in relation to property comprised in a settlement:

(i) where the proper law of the settlement as regards that property at the time when the settlement was made was the law of the Republic of Ireland and the settlor's domicile at the time when the settlement was made has been determined under paragraph (1) of Article 4 as being in the United Kingdom, then that Contracting State shall be the United Kingdom;

(ii) where the proper law of the settlement as regards that property at the time when the settlement was made was not the law of the Republic of Ireland and the settlor's domicile at that time has been determined under paragraph (1) of Article 4 as being in the United Kingdom but under its own law the Republic of Ireland would impose tax on property outside its territory because at some later time either the proper law of the settlement as regards that property was the law of the Republic of Ireland or the settlor's domicile has been determined under the said paragraph as being in the Republic of Ireland, then that Contracting State shall be the Republic of Ireland;

(iii) subject to paragraph (ii) of this sub-paragraph, where the proper law of the settlement as regards that property at the time when the settlement was made was not the law of the Republic of Ireland and the settlor's domicile at that time has been determined under paragraph (2) of Article 4, then that Contracting State shall be the Contracting State in which the settlor was, by virtue of that paragraph, not domiciled at that time.

(3) In sub-paragraph (a) of paragraph (2) of this Article, the term "person" means, in the Republic of Ireland the disponer, and in the United Kingdom the transferor.

(4) In paragraph (2) of this Article, "settlement" has the meaning which it has under the law of the United Kingdom relating to capital transfer tax and for the purposes of that paragraph a settlement is made when property first becomes comprised in it.

Article 6 Situs

(1) For the purposes of this Convention, the situs of any property shall be determined by each Contracting State under its own law, except that, where part of the value by reference to which tax is imposed in the United Kingdom is represented by a liability to tax which is satisfied out of property situated outside the United Kingdom, then that part of the value shall be deemed to be attributable to that property.

(2) If the situs of any property as determined by one Contracting State under paragraph (1) of this Article is not the same as that so determined by the other Contracting State, and the credit to be allowed under Article 8 is thereby affected, then the question shall be determined exclusively under the law of the Contracting State which, by virtue of paragraph (2) of Article 5, has subsidiary taxing rights or, if there is no such Contracting State, it shall be determined by mutual agreement.

Article 7 Deduction of debts

In determining the amount on which tax is to be computed, permitted deductions shall be allowed under the law in force in the Contracting State in which the tax is imposed.

131

Article 8 Elimination of double taxation

(1) Where a Contracting State imposes tax on an event by reference to any property which is not situated in that Contracting State but is situated in the other Contracting State, the former Contracting State shall allow against so much of its tax (as otherwise computed) as is attributable to that property a credit (not exceeding the amount of tax so attributable) equal to so much of the tax imposed in the other Contracting State on the same event as is attributable to such property.

(2) Where both Contracting States impose tax on an event by reference to any property which is not situated in either Contracting State but is situated in a third territory, the Contracting State which, by virtue of paragraph (2) of Article 5, has subsidiary taxing rights shall allow against so much of its tax (as otherwise computed) as is attributable to that property a credit (not exceeding the amount of tax so attributable) equal to so much of the tax imposed in the other Contracting State on the same event as is attributable to such property.

(3) Any credit to be allowed in the Republic of Ireland under this Article in relation to gifts or inheritances shall be allowed only so as to relieve the tax imposed in the Republic of Ireland on the gift or inheritance which is reduced by the payment of the tax in respect of which that credit is to be allowed; and a gift which in the United Kingdom is a chargeable transfer shall be treated as reduced by the amount of tax imposed in the United Kingdom on that gift and borne by the transferor.

(4) For the purposes of this Article:

(a) the tax attributable to any property imposed in a Contracting State is tax as reduced by the amount of any credit allowed by that Contracting State in respect of tax attributable to that property imposed in a territory other than a Contracting State;

(b) tax is imposed in a Contracting State or a territory if it is chargeable under the law of that Contracting State or territory and duly paid;

(c) property includes property representing property.

Article 9 Time limit

Any claim for a credit or for a repayment of tax founded on the provisions of this Convention shall be made within six years from the date of the event in respect of which the claim is made.

Article 10 Non-discrimination

(1) The nationals of a Contracting State shall not be subjected in the other Contracting State to any taxation or any requirement connected therewith which is other or more burdensome than the taxation and connected requirements to which nationals of that other Contracting State in the same circumstances are or may be subjected.

(2) The taxation on a permanent establishment which an enterprise of a Contracting State has in the other Contracting State shall not be less favourably levied in that other Contracting State than the taxation levied on enterprises of that other Contracting State carrying on the same activities.

(3) Enterprises of a Contracting State, the capital of which is wholly or partly owned or controlled, directly or indirectly, by one or more residents of the other Contracting State, shall not be subjected in the first-mentioned Contracting State to any taxation or any requirement connected therewith which is other or more burdensome than the taxation and connected requirements to which other similar enterprises of that first-mentioned Contracting State are or may be subjected.

(4) Nothing contained in this Article shall be construed as obliging either Contracting State to grant to individuals not domiciled in that Contracting State, any of the personal allowances, reliefs, and reductions for tax purposes which are granted to individuals so domiciled.

(5) In this article the term "taxation" means taxes covered by this Convention.

Article 11 Mutual agreement procedure

(1) Where a person considers that the actions of one or both of the Contracting States result or will result for him in taxation not in accordance with the provisions of this Convention, he may, irrespective of the remedies provided by the domestic laws of those Contracting States, present his case to the competent authority of either Contracting State.

(2) The competent authority shall endeavour, if the objection appears to it to be justified and if it is not itself able to arrive at a satisfactory solution, to resolve the case by mutual agreement with the competent authority of the other Contracting State, with a view to the avoidance of taxation which is not in accordance with the provisions of this Convention.

(3) The competent authorities of the Contracting States shall endeavour to resolve by mutual agreement any difficulties or doubts arising as to the interpretation or application of this Convention.

(4) The competent authorities of the Contracting States may communicate with each other directly for the purpose of reaching an agreement in the sense of the preceding paragraphs.

Article 12 Exchange of information

(1) The competent authorities of the Contracting States shall exchange such information as is necessary for carrying out the provisions of this Convention and the domestic laws of the Contracting States concerning taxes covered by this Convention insofar as the taxation thereunder is in accordance with this Convention. Any information so exchanged shall be treated as secret and shall not be disclosed to any persons other than persons (including a Court or administrative body) concerned with the assessment or collection of, or prosecution in respect of, or the determination of appeals in relation to, the taxes which are the subject of this Convention.

(2) In no case shall the provisions of paragraph (1) be construed so as to impose on the competent authority of either Contracting State the obligation:

(a) to carry out administrative measures at variance with the laws or administrative practice prevailing in either Contracting State;

(b) to supply particulars which are not obtainable under the laws or in the normal course of the administration of that or of the other Contracting State;

(c) to supply information which would disclose any trade, business, industrial, commercial or professional secret or trade process, or information, the disclosure of which would be contrary to public policy.

Article 14 Entry into force

Note: This Convention applies in the UK in respect of capital transfer tax other than on death, from 27 March 1974, and in the case of capital transfer tax on death, from 13 March 1975.

Official language: English.

ISLE OF MAN

Arrangement of 29 July 1955 (SI 1955 No 1205)

ISLE OF MAN

Paragraph 1 [Taxes covered]

(1) The taxes which are the subject of this Arrangement are:—

    (*a*) In the United Kingdom:

        The income tax (including surtax), the profits tax and the excess profits levy (hereinafter referred to as "United Kingdom tax");

    (*b*) In the Isle of Man:

        The income tax (including surtax) (hereinafter referred to as "Manx tax").

(2) This Arrangement shall also supply to any other taxes of a substantially similar character imposed in the United Kingdom or the Isle of Man after this Arrangement has come into force.

Corporation tax: This Arrangement covers United Kingdom corporation tax, by virtue of ICTA 1988, s 789(1).

Paragraph 2 [General definitions]

(1) In this Arrangement, unless the context otherwise requires:

    (*a*) the term "United Kingdom" means Great Britain and Northern Ireland;

    (*b*) the term "The Island" means the Isle of Man;

    (*c*) the terms "one of the territories" and "the other territory" mean the United Kingdom or the Island, as the context requires;

    (*d*) the term "tax" means United Kingdom tax or Manx tax, as the context requires;

    (*e*) the term "person" includes any body of persons, corporate or not corporate;

    (*f*) the term "company" includes any body corporate;

    (*g*) the terms "resident of the United Kingdom" and "resident of the Island" mean respectively any person who is resident in the United Kingdom for the purposes of United Kingdom tax and not resident in the Island for the purposes of Manx tax and any person who is resident in the Island for the purposes of Manx tax and not resident in the United Kingdom for the purposes of United Kingdom tax; and a company shall be regarded as resident in the United Kingdom if its business is managed and controlled in the United Kingdom and as resident in the Island if its business is managed and controlled in the Island;

    (*h*) the terms "resident of one of the territories" and "resident of the other territory" mean a person who is a resident of the United Kingdom or a person who is a resident of the Island, as the context requires;

    (*i*)–(*k*) . . .

(2) Where under this Arrangement any income is exempt from tax in one of the territories if (with or without other conditions) it is subject to tax in the other territory, and that income is subject to tax in that other territory by reference to the amount thereof which is remitted to or received in that other territory, the exemption to be allowed under this Arrangement in the first-mentioned territory shall apply only to the amount so remitted or received.

(3) In the application of the provisions of this Arrangement by the United Kingdom or the Island, any term not otherwise defined shall, unless the context otherwise requires, have the meaning which it has under the law of the United Kingdom, or, as the case may be, the Island, relating to the taxes which are the subject of this Arrangement.

Paragraph 5 [Shipping and air transport]

Notwithstanding the provisions of paragraphs 3 and 4, profits which a resident of one of the territories derives from operating ships or aircraft shall be exempt from tax in the other territory.

Paragraph 3: Taxation of industrial or commercial profits.
Paragraph 4: Taxation of profits of associated enterprises.

Paragraph 10 [Exchange of information]

(1) The taxation authorities of the United Kingdom and the Island shall exchange such information (being information available under their respective taxation laws) as is necessary for carrying out the provisions of this Arrangement or for the prevention of fraud or the administration of statutory provisions against legal avoidance in relation to the taxes which are the subject of this Arrangement. Any information so exchanged shall be treated as secret and shall not be disclosed to any persons other than those concerned with the assessment and collection of the taxes which are the subject of this Arrangement. No information shall be exchanged which would disclose any trade secret or trade process.

(2) As used in this paragraph, the term "taxation authorities" means the Commissioners of Inland Revenue or their authorised representative in the case of the United Kingdom and the Assessor of Income Tax or his authorised representative in the case of the Island.

Paragraph 11 [Entry into force]

Note: Paragraph 11 provided for the entry into force of this Arrangement. It takes effect in the UK from the year of assessment 1955–56 (income tax) and from April 1955 (profits tax).

Official language: English.

ISRAEL

Convention of 26 September 1962 (SI 1963 No 616)

Printed as amended by the Protocol of 20 April 1970 (SI 1971 No 391).

Article I [Taxes covered]

(1) The taxes which are the subject of the present Convention are:
    (*a*) in the United Kingdom of Great Britain and Northern Ireland:
        (i) the income tax (including surtax);
        (ii) the corporation tax; and
        (iii) the capital gains tax
        (hereinafter referred to as "United Kingdom tax");
    (*b*) in Israel:
        (i) the income tax (including capital gains tax);

    (ii) the company tax;

    (iii) the security charge; and

    (iv) the tax on gains from the sale of land under the Land Appreciation Tax Law (hereinafter referred to as "Israel tax").

Article II [General definitions]

(1) In the present Convention, unless the context otherwise requires—

    (a) the term "United Kingdom" means Great Britain and Northern Ireland;

    (b) the term "Israel" means the territory in which the Government of Israel levy taxation;

    (c) the terms "one of the territories" and "the other territory" mean the United Kingdom or Israel, as the context requires;

    (d) the term "taxation authorities" means, in the case of the United Kingdom, the Commissioners of Inland Revenue or their authorised representative; in the case of Israel, the Minister of Finance or his authorised representative; and, in the case of any territory to which this Convention is extended under Article XXII, the competent authority for the administration in such territory of the taxes to which this Convention applies;

    (e) the term "tax" means the United Kingdom tax or Israel tax, as the context requires;

    (f) the term "person" includes any body of persons, corporate or not corporate;

    (g) the term "company" means any body corporate;

    (h) (i) the terms "resident of the United Kingdom" and "resident of Israel" mean respectively any person who is resident in the United Kingdom for the purposes of United Kingdom tax and any person who is resident in Israel for the purposes of Israel tax, but

        (ii) where by reason of the provisions of sub-paragraph (i) above an individual is a resident of both territories, then this case shall be solved in accordance with the following rules;

            (aa) he shall be deemed to be a resident of the territory in which he has a permanent home available to him. If he has a permanent home available to him in both territories, he shall be deemed to be a resident of the territory with which his personal and economic relations are closest (hereinafter referred to as his "centre of vital interests");

            (bb) if the territory in which he has his centre of vital interests cannot be determined, or if he has not a permanent home available to him in either territory, he shall be deemed to be a resident of the territory in which he has an habitual abode;

            (cc) if he has an habitual abode in both territories or in neither of them, he shall be deemed to be a resident of the territory of which he is a national;

            (dd) if he is a national of both territories or of neither of them, the taxation authorities of the territories shall determine the question by mutual agreement;

        (iii) where by reason of the provisions of sub-paragraph (i) above a legal person is a resident of both territories, then it shall be deemed to be a resident of the territory in which its place of effective management is situated; the same provision shall apply to partnerships and associations which under the national laws by which they are governed are not legal persons;

    (i) the terms "resident of one of the territories" and "resident of the other territory" mean a person who is a resident of the United Kingdom or a person who is a resident of Israel, as the context requires;

    (j) the terms "United Kingdom enterprise" and "Israel enterprise" mean respectively an industrial or commercial enterprise or undertaking carried on by a resident of the United Kingdom and an industrial or commercial enterprise or undertaking carried on by a resident of Israel, and the terms "enterprise of one of the territories" and "enterprise of the other territory" mean a United Kingdom enterprise or an Israel enterprise, as the context requires;

(k) (i) the term "permanent establishment" means a fixed place of business in which the business of the enterprise is wholly or partly carried on;

(ii) a permanent establishment shall include especially:

(aa) a place of management;

(bb) a branch;

(cc) an office;

(dd) a factory;

(ee) a workshop;

(ff) a mine, quarry or other place of extraction of natural resources;

(gg) a building site or construction or assembly project which exists for more than twelve months;

(iii) the term "permanent establishment" shall not be deemed to include:

(aa) the use of facilities solely for the purpose of storage, display or delivery of goods or merchandise belonging to the enterprise;

(bb) the maintenance of a stock of goods or merchandise belonging to the enterprise solely for the purpose of storage, display or delivery;

(cc) the maintenance of a stock of goods or merchandise belonging to the enterprise solely for the purpose of processing by another enterprise;

(dd) the maintenance of a fixed place of business solely for the purpose of purchasing goods or merchandise, or for collecting information, for the enterprise;

(ee) the maintenance of a fixed place of business solely for the purpose of advertising, for the supply of information, for scientific research or for similar activities which have a preparatory or auxiliary character, for the enterprise;

(iv) a person acting in one of the territories on behalf of an enterprise of the other territory—other than an agent of an independent status to whom subparagraph (v) applies—shall be deemed to be a permanent establishment in the first-named territory if he has, and habitually exercises in that territory, an authority to conclude contracts in the name of the enterprise, unless his activities are limited to the purchase of goods or merchandise for the enterprise;

(v) an enterprise of one of the territories shall not be deemed to have a permanent establishment in the other territory merely because it carries on business in that other territory through a broker, a general commission agent or any other agent of an independent status, where such persons are acting in the ordinary course of their business;

(vi) the fact that a company which is a resident of one of the territories controls or is controlled by a company which is a resident of the other territory, or which carries on business in that other territory (whether through a permanent establishment or otherwise), shall not of itself constitute either company a permanent establishment of the other;

(vii) an enterprise of one of the territories shall be deemed to have a permanent establishment in the other territory if it carries on a business which consists of providing the services within that other territory of public entertainers referred to in Article XIV.

(l) the term "international traffic" includes traffic between places in one country in the course of a voyage which extends over more than one country.

(2) Where under this Convention any income is exempt from tax or taxed at a reduced rate in one of the territories if (with or without other conditions) it is subject to tax in the other territory and that income is subject to tax in that other territory by reference to the amount thereof which is remitted to or received in that other territory, the exemption or reduction of tax to be allowed under this Convention in the first-mentioned territory shall apply only to the amount so remitted or received.

(3) In the application of the provisions of the present Convention by one of the Contract-

ing Parties any term not otherwise defined shall, unless the context otherwise requires, have the meaning which it has under the laws in force in the territory of that Party relating to the taxes which are the subject of the present Convention.

Article V [Shipping and air transport]

Notwithstanding the provisions of Articles III and IV income from the operation of ships or aircraft in international traffic shall be taxable only in the territory in which the place of effective management of the enterprise is situated.

Article III: Taxation of industrial or commercial profits.
Article IV: Taxation of profits of associated enterprises.

Article VIIIA [Capital gains]

(1) . . .
(2) (Taxation of gains from alienation of movable property.)
(3) Notwithstanding the provisions of paragraph (2) of this Article, capital gains derived by a resident of one of the territories from the alienation of ships and aircraft operated in international traffic and movable property pertaining to the operation of such ships and aircraft shall be taxable only in that territory.
(4) . . .

Article IX [Income from immovable property]

(1) (Taxation of income from immovable property.)
(2) The term "immovable property" shall be defined in accordance with the laws of the territory in which the property in question is situated. The term shall in any case include property accessory to immovable property, livestock and equipment of agricultural and forestry enterprises, rights to which the provisions of general law respecting landed property apply, usufruct of immovable property and rights to variable or fixed payments as consideration for the working of mineral deposits, sources and other natural resources; ships, boats and aircraft shall not be regarded as immovable property.
(3) . . .
(4) . . .

Article XIX [Exchange of information]

The taxation authorities of the Contracting Parties shall exchange such information (being information which is at their disposal under their respective taxation laws in the normal course of administration) as is necessary for carrying out the provisions of the present Convention or for the prevention of fraud or for the administration of statutory provisions against legal avoidance in relation to the taxes which are the subject of the present Convention. Any information so exchanged shall be treated as secret and shall not be disclosed to any persons other than those concerned with the assessment and collection of the taxes which are the subject of the present Convention. No information as aforesaid shall be exchanged which would disclose any trade, business, industrial or professional secret or trade process.

Article XX [Communication]

The taxation authorities of the Contracting Parties may communicate with each other directly for the purpose of giving effect to the provisions of this Convention and for resolving any difficulty or doubt as to the application or interpretation of the Convention.

Article XXI [Non-discrimination]

(1) The nationals of one of the Contracting Parties shall not be subjected in the territory of the other Contracting Party to any taxation or any requirement connected therewith which is

other or more burdensome than the taxation and connected requirements to which the nationals of the latter Party in the same circumstances are or may be subjected.

(2) The term "nationals" means—

  (a) in relation to the United Kingdom, all British subjects and British-protected persons

  (i) residing in the United Kingdom or any territory to which the present Convention is extended under Article XXII, or

  (ii) deriving their status as such from connexion with the United Kingdom or any territory to which the Convention is extended under Article XXII,

  and all legal persons, partnerships and associations deriving their status as such from the law in force in the United Kingdom or in any territory to which the Convention is extended under Article XXII;

  (b) in relation to Israel, all Israel subjects and all legal persons, partnerships and associations deriving their status as such from the law in force in Israel.

(3) The taxation on a permanent establishment which an enterprise of one of the territories has in the other territory shall not be less favourably levied in that other territory than the taxation levied on enterprises of that other territory carrying on the same activities.

(3A) Nothing contained in this Article shall be construed as obliging either Contracting Party to grant to individuals not resident in its territory any of the personal allowances, reliefs and reductions for tax purposes which are granted to individuals so resident, nor as conferring any exemption from tax in one of the territories in respect of dividends paid to a company which is a resident of the other territory.

(4) Enterprises of one of the territories, the capital of which is wholly or partly owned or controlled, directly or indirectly, by one or more residents of the other territory, shall not be subjected in the first-mentioned territory to any taxation or any requirement connected therewith which is other or more burdensome than the taxation and connected requirements to which other similar enterprises of that first-mentioned territory are or may be subjected.

In this Article the term "taxation" means taxes of every kind and description.

Article XXIII [Entry into force]

Note: Article XXIII provided for the entry into force of the 1962 Convention. It took effect in the UK in its amended form from the year of assessment 1968–69 (income tax and capital gains tax) and from the financial year beginning on 1 April 1968 (corporation tax).

Official languages: The Hebrew language text and the English language text of this Convention are equally authoritative.

ITALY

(Agreement has been reached on the text of a new comprehensive double taxation Convention and a Convention on the estates of deceased persons and on gifts. The text of these Conventions was not available at the time of going to press.)

Convention of 4 July 1960 (SI 1962 No 2787)

Printed as amended by the Exchange of Notes of 4 July 1960 (SI 1962 No 2787) and the Protocol of 28 April 1969 (SI 1973 No 1763).

ITALY

Article I [Taxes covered]

(1) The taxes which are the subject of the present Convention are:

    (*a*) in Italy (and hereinafter referred to as "Italian Tax"):

        (i) tax on land (*imposta sul reddito dei terreni*);

        (ii) tax on buildings (*imposta sul reddito dei fabbricati*);

        (iii) tax on income from movable wealth (*imposta sui redditi di ricchezza mobile*);

        (iv) tax on agricultural income (*imposta sui redditi agrari*);

        (v) complementary tax (*imposta complementare progressiva sul reddito*);

        (vi) tax on companies (*imposta sulle società*) in so far as the tax is charged on income and not on capital; and

        (vii) tax on profits distributed by companies (*imposta sugli utili distribuiti dalle società*);

    (*b*) in the United Kingdom of Great Britain and Northern Ireland (and hereinafter referred to as "United Kingdom tax"):

        the income tax (including surtax), the corporation tax, and the capital gains tax.

(2) The present Convention shall also apply to any other taxes of a substantially similar character imposed in Italy or the United Kingdom subsequently to the date of signature of the present Convention.

Article II [General definitions]

(1) In the present Convention, unless the context otherwise requires:

    (*a*) The term "United Kingdom" means Great Britain and Northern Ireland;

    (*b*) The term "Italy" shall be understood to mean all the territories for whose international relations the Italian Republic is now responsible;

    (*c*) The terms "one of the territories" and "the other territory" mean the United Kingdom or Italy, as the context requires;

    (*d*) The term "tax" means United Kingdom tax or Italian tax, as the context requires;

    (*e*) The term "person" includes any body of persons, corporate or not corporate;

    (*f*) The term "company" means any body corporate;

    (*g*) For the purposes of this Convention the term "resident of one of the territories" means any person who, under the law of that territory, is liable to taxation therein by reason of his domicile, residence, place of management or any other criterion of a similar nature. The terms "resident of the United Kingdom", "resident of Italy" and "resident of the other territory" shall be construed accordingly;

    (*h*) Where by reason of the provisions of sub-paragraph (*g*) an individual is a resident of both territories, then his status shall be determined in accordance with the following rules:

        (i) he shall be deemed to be a resident of the territory in which he has a permanent home available to him. If he has a permanent home available to him in both territories, he shall be deemed to be a resident of the territory with which his personal and economic relations are closest (centre of vital interests);

        (ii) if the territory in which he has his centre of vital interests cannot be determined, or if he has not a permanent home available to him in either territory, he shall be deemed to be a resident of the territory in which he has an habitual abode;

        (iii) if he has an habitual abode in both territories or in neither of them, he shall be deemed to be a resident of the territory of which he is a national;

(iv) if he is a national of both territories or of neither of them, the taxation authorities (as defined in Article XVIII) shall settle the question by mutual agreement;

(*i*) Where by reason of the provisions of sub-paragraph (*g*) a person other than an individual is a resident of both territories then it shall be deemed to be a resident of the territory in which its place of effective management is situated;

(*j*) The terms "United Kingdom enterprise" and "Italian enterprise" mean respectively an industrial or commercial enterprise or undertaking carried on by a resident of the United Kingdom and an industrial or commercial enterprise or undertaking carried on by a resident of Italy, and the terms "enterprise of one of the territories" and "enterprise of the other territory" mean a United Kingdom enterprise or an Italian enterprise, as the context requires;

(*k*) The term "permanent establishment" means a branch, management, factory, or other fixed place of business, but does not include an agency unless the agent has, and habitually exercises, a general authority to negotiate and conclude contracts on behalf of an enterprise of one of the territories or has a stock of merchandise from which he regularly fills orders on its behalf. In this connexion—

(i) An enterprise of one of the territories shall not be deemed to have a permanent establishment in the other territory merely because it carries on business dealings in that other territory through a *bona fide* broker or general commission agent acting in the ordinary course of his business as such;

(ii) The fact that an enterprise of one of the territories maintains in the other territory a fixed place of business exclusively for the purchase of goods or merchandise shall not of itself constitute that fixed place of business a permanent establishment of the enterprise;

(iii) The fact that a company which is a resident of one of the territories has a subsidiary company which is a resident of the other territory or which carries on a trade or business in that other territory (whether through a permanent establishment or otherwise) shall not of itself constitute that subsidiary company a permanent establishment of its parent company.

(2) Where under the present Convention income from a source in one of the territories is relieved from tax in that territory if it is subject to tax in the other territory, and, under the law in force in that other territory, the said income is subject to tax by reference to the amount thereof which is remitted to or received in that other territory and not by reference to the full amount thereof, then the relief to be allowed under this Convention in the first-mentioned territory shall apply only to so much of the income as is remitted to or received in the other territory.

(3) In the application of the provisions of the present Convention by one of the Contracting Parties any term not otherwise defined shall, unless the context otherwise requires, have the meaning which it has under the laws in force in the territory of that Party relating to the taxes which are the subject of the present Convention.

Article VI [Shipping and air transport]

Notwithstanding the provisions of Articles III and IV, profits which an enterprise of one of the territories derives from the operation of ships or aircraft registered in that territory shall be exempt from tax in the other territory.

Article III: Taxation of industrial or commercial profits.
Article IV: Taxation of profits of associated enterprises.

Article X [Capital gains]

A resident of one of the territories who does not carry on a trade or business in the other territory through a permanent establishment situated therein shall be exempt in that other territory from any tax on gains from the sale, transfer or exchange of capital assets if he is subject to tax in respect of those gains in the first-mentioned territory.

Article XVIII [Exchange of information]

(1) The taxation authorities of the Contracting Parties shall exchange such information (being information which is at their disposal under their respective taxation laws in the normal course of administration) as is necessary for carrying out the provisions of the present Convention or for the prevention of fraud or for the administration of statutory provisions against legal avoidance in relation to the taxes which are the subject of the present Convention. Any information so exchanged shall be treated as secret and shall not be disclosed to any person other than those concerned with the assessment and collection of the taxes which are the subject of the present Convention. No information as aforesaid shall be exchanged which would disclose any trade, business, industrial or professional secret or trade process.

(2) As used in this Article, the term, "taxation authorities" means, in the case of the United Kingdom, the Commissioners of Inland Revenue or their authorised representatives; in the case of Italy, the Ministry of Finance, General Directorship for Direct Taxation; and, in the case of any territory to which the present Convention is extended under Article XX, the competent authority for the administration in such territory of the taxes to which the present Convention applies.

Article XVIIIA [Mutual agreement procedure]

(1) Where a resident of one of the territories considers that the actions of one or both of the Contracting Parties result or will result for him in taxation not in accordance with this Convention, he may, notwithstanding the remedies provided by the national laws of those Contracting Parties, present his case to the taxation authorities (as defined in Article XVIII) of the territory of which he is a resident. The claim must be lodged within two years from the date on which the tax was notified or withheld at the source whichever is the later.

(2) The taxation authorities shall endeavour, if the objection appears to them to be justified and they are not themselves able to arrive at an appropriate solution, to resolve the case by mutual agreement with the taxation authorities of the other territory, with a view to the avoidance of taxation not in accordance with the Convention.

(3) The taxation authorities of the territories shall endeavour to resolve by mutual agreement any difficulties or doubts arising as to the interpretation or application of the Convention.

(4) The taxation authorities of the territories may communicate with each other directly for the purpose of reaching an agreement in the sense of the preceding paragraphs.

Article XIX [Non-discrimination]

(1) The nationals of one of the Contracting Parties shall not be subjected in the territory of the other Contracting Party to any taxation or any requirement connected therewith which is other, higher, or more burdensome than the taxation and connection requirements to which the nationals of the latter Party are or may be subjected.

(2) The enterprises of one of the territories whether carried on by company, a body of persons or by individuals alone or in partnership, shall not be subjected in the other territory, in respect of income or profits attributable to their permanent establishments in that other territory, to any taxation which is other, higher or more burdensome than the taxation to which the enterprises of that other territory similarly carried on are or may be subjected in respect of the like profits.

(3) Nothing in this Article shall be construed as—

    (a) obliging one of the Contracting Parties to grant to nationals of the other Contracting Party who are not resident in the territory of the former Party the same personal allowances, reliefs and reductions for tax purposes as are granted to its own nationals; or

(b) affecting the imposition in Italy of the tax on companies (*imposta sulle società*) upon foreign partnerships, bodies of persons, etc, which are liable to the tax according to Italian law.

(4) In this Article the term "nationals" means:

(a) in relation to Italy:

all Italian citizens wherever residing, all persons residing in Italy, Italian protected persons and all legal persons, partnership, associations and other entities deriving their status as such from the law in force in any Italian territory to which the Convention applies;

(b) in relation to the United Kingdom:

all British subjects and British protected persons:

(i) residing in the United Kingdom or any British territory to which the present Convention is extended under Article XX, or

(ii) deriving their status as such from connexion with the United Kingdom or any British Territory to which the present Convention is extended under Article XX,

and all legal persons, partnerships, associations and other entities deriving their status as such from the law in force in any British territory to which the Convention applies.

(5) In this Article the term "taxation" means the taxes referred to in Article I of the present Convention.

Article XXII [Entry into force]

Note: Article XXII provided for the entry into force of the 1960 Convention. It takes effect in the UK in its amended form from the year of assessment 1967–68 (income tax and capital gains tax) and from the financial year beginning on 1 April 1967 (corporation tax).

Official languages: The Italian language text and the English language text of this Convention are equally authoritative.

Capital taxes

Convention of 15 February 1966 (SI 1968 No 304)

Article I [Duties covered]

(1) The duties which are the subject of the present Convention are:

(a) in the United Kingdom of Great Britain and Northern Ireland: the estate duty imposed in Great Britain;

(b) in Italy;

the succession duty and the estate duty (*imposta sull'asse ereditario globale*) imposed in Italy.

(2) The present Convention shall also apply to any other duties of a substantially similar character to the duties referred to in paragraph (1) above which may be imposed in Great Britain or Italy subsequently to the date of signature of the present Convention.

Inheritance tax: This Convention covers United Kingdom capital transfer tax (now inheritance tax), by virtue of IHTA 1984, s 158(6), FA 1986, s 100.

Article II [General definitions]

(1) In the present Convention, unless the context otherwise requires:
- (a) the term "United Kingdom" means Great Britain and Northern Ireland;
- (b) the term "Great Britain" means England, Wales and Scotland;
- (c) the term "Italy" means the Italian Republic;
- (d) the term "territory", when used in relation to one or the other Contracting Party, means Great Britain or Italy, as the context requires;
- (e) the term "duty" means the estate duty imposed in Great Britain or the succession duty and estate duty imposed in Italy, as the context requires.

(2) (a) For the purposes of the present Convention, the question whether a deceased person was domiciled at the time of his death in any part of the territory of one of the Contracting Parties shall be determined in accordance with the law in force in that territory.

(b) Where by reason of the provisions of the preceding paragraph a deceased person is deemed to be domiciled in the territory of each of the Contracting Parties, then this case shall be solved in accordance with the following rules:–
- (i) he shall be deemed to be domiciled in the territory of the Contracting Party in which he had a permanent home available to him at the time of his death; if he had a permanent home available to him in the territory of each of the Contracting Parties he shall be deemed to be domiciled in the territory of the Contracting Party with which his personal and economic relations were closest (centre of vital interests);
- (ii) if the Contracting Party in whose territory he had his centre of vital interests cannot be determined, or if he had not a permanent home available to him in the territory of either Contracting Party, he shall be deemed to be domiciled in the territory of the Contracting Party in which he had an habitual abode;
- (iii) if he had an habitual abode in the territory of each of the Contracting Parties, or in the territory of neither, he shall be deemed to be domiciled in that of which he was a national;
- (iv) if he was a national of both territories or of neither of them, the taxation authorities of the Contracting Parties shall determine the question by mutual agreement.

(3) In the application of the provisions of the present Convention by either Contracting Party any term not otherwise defined shall, unless the context otherwise requires, have the meaning which it has under the law in force in the territory of that Party relating to the duties which are the subject of the Convention.

Article III [Situs]

(1) Where a person was at the time of his death domiciled in any part of the territory of one of the Contracting Parties, the situs of any property shall for the purposes of the imposition of duty and for the purposes of Article V and of the credit to be allowed under Article VI be determined exclusively in accordance with the rules in Article IV of the present Convention.

(2) Paragraph (1) of this Article shall apply if, and only if, apart from the said Article IV:
- (a) duty would be imposed on the property under the law of the territory of each of the Contracting Parties; or
- (b) duty would be imposed on the property under the law of the territory of one of

the Contracting Parties and would, but for some specific exemption, also be imposed thereon under the law of the territory of the other Contracting Party.

(3) Paragraph (1) of this Article shall not apply if by reason of its application duty would be imposed in the territory of one of the Contracting Parties on property on which, apart from the said paragraph, duty would not be imposed in that territory.

Article IV [Deemed location of property]

(1)–(8) . . .

(9) Ships and aircraft and shares thereof shall be deemed to be situated at the place of registration of the ship or aircraft.

(10)–(13) . . .

Article V [Deductions]

(1) In determining the amount on which duty is to be computed, permitted deductions shall be allowed in accordance with the law in force in the territory in which the duty is imposed.

(2) Where duty is imposed in the territory of one Contracting Party on the death of a person who at the time of his death was not domiciled in any part of that territory but was domiciled in some part of the territory of the other Contracting Party, no account shall be taken, in determining the amount or rate of such duty, of property situated outside the former territory, provided that this paragraph shall not apply to duty imposed in the territory of a Contracting Party on property passing under a settlement governed by its law.

Article VI [Elimination of double taxation]

(1) Where one Contracting Party imposes duty on any property which is not situated in its territory but is situated in the territory of the other Contracting Party, the former Party shall allow against so much of its duty (as otherwise computed) as is attributable to that property a credit (not exceeding the amount of the duty so attributable) equal to so much of the duty imposed in the territory of the other Contracting Party as is attributable to such property.

(2) For the purposes of this Article, the amount of the duty of a Contracting Party attributable to any property shall be ascertained after taking into account any credit, allowance or relief, or any remission or reduction of duty other than in respect of duty payable in the territory of the other Contracting Party.

Article VII [Time limit]

Any claim for a credit or for a refund of duty founded on the provisions of the present Convention shall be made within five years from the date of the death of the deceased person in respect of whose estate the claim is made, or, where the event causing duty to be payable occurs at some later date, within five years from that date.

Article VIII [Exchange of information]

(1) The taxation authorities of the Contracting Parties shall exchange such information (being information available under the respective taxation laws of the Contracting Parties) as is necessary for carrying out the provisions of the present Convention or for the prevention of fraud or the administration of statutory provisions against avoidance in relation to the duties which are the subject of the present Convention. Any information so exchanged shall be treated as secret and shall not be disclosed to any person other than those concerned with the administration, assessment and collection of the duties which are the subject of the present Convention. No information shall be exchanged which might disclose any trade secret or trade process.

145

(2) As used in this Article, the term "taxation authorities" means—

    (*a*) in the case of Italy, the Ministero delle Finanze, Direzione Generale delle Tasse e Imposte sugli Affari;

    (*b*) in the case of Great Britain, the Commissioners of Inland Revenue or their authorised representative;

    (*c*) in the case of Northern Ireland (to which the present Convention applies under Article X), the Minister of Finance or his authorised representative;

    (*d*) in the case of any territory to which the present Convention is extended under Article XI, the competent authority for the administration in such territory of the duties to which the present Convention applies.

Article XI Entry into force

Note: This Convention applies to estates or inheritances in the case of persons who die after 8 February 1968.

Official languages: The Italian language text and the English language text of this Convention are equally authoritative.

IVORY COAST

Convention of 28 June 1985 (SI 1987 No 169)

Article 1 Personal scope

This Convention shall apply to persons who are residents of one or both of the Contracting States.

Article 2 Taxes covered

(1) This Convention shall apply to taxes on income and on capital gains imposed by a Contracting State irrespective of the manner in which they are levied.

(2) There shall be regarded as taxes on income and on capital gains all taxes imposed on total income, on total capital gains, or on elements of income or of capital gains, including taxes on gains from the alienation of movable or immovable property, as well as taxes on capital appreciation.

(3) The existing taxes which are the subject of this Convention are:

    (*a*) in the United Kingdom of Great Britain and Northern Ireland:

        (i) the income tax;

(ii) the corporation tax; and

(iii) the capital gains tax;

(hereinafter referred to as "United Kingdom tax");

(b) in the Republic of the Ivory Coast:

(i) the tax on industrial and commercial profits and on agricultural profits (*l'impôt sur les bénéfices industriels et commerciaux et sur les bénéfices agricoles*);

(ii) the tax on non-commercial profits (*l'impôt sur les bénéfices non commerciaux*);

(iii) the tax on salaries and wages (*l'impôt sur les traitements et salaires*);

(iv) the tax on income from movable capital (*l'impôt sur le revenu des capitaux mobiliers*); and

(v) the general income tax (*l'impôt général sur le revenu*);

(hereinafter referred to as "Ivory Coast tax").

(4) This Convention shall also apply to any identical or substantially similar taxes which are imposed by either Contracting State after the date of signature of this Convention in addition to, or in place of, the existing taxes. The competent authorities of the Contracting States shall notify each other of any substantial changes which have been made in their respective taxation laws.

Article 3 General definitions

(1) For the purposes of this Convention, unless the context otherwise requires:

(a) the term "United Kingdom" means Great Britain and Northern Ireland, including any area outside the territorial sea of the United Kingdom which in accordance with international law has been or may hereafter be designated, under the laws of the United Kingdom concerning the Continental Shelf, as an area within which the rights of the United Kingdom with respect to the sea-bed and sub-soil and their natural resources may be exercised;

(b) the term "the Ivory Coast" means the national territory of the Republic of the Ivory Coast including any area outside the territorial sea of the Ivory Coast which in accordance with international law has been or may hereafter be designated, under the laws of the Ivory Coast concerning the Continental Shelf, as an area within which the rights of the Ivory Coast with respect to the sea-bed and sub-soil and their natural resources may be exercised;

(c) the term "national" means:

(i) in relation to the United Kingdom, any individual who has under the law in the United Kingdom the status of United Kingdom national, provided he has the right of abode in the United Kingdom; and any legal person, partnership, association or other entity deriving its status as such from the law in force in the United Kingdom;

(ii) in relation to the Ivory Coast, any individual who possesses Ivory Coast nationality and any legal person, partnership, association or other entity deriving its status as such from the law in force in the Ivory Coast;

(d) the terms "a Contracting State" and "the other Contracting State" mean the United Kingdom or the Ivory Coast, as the context requires;

(e) the term "person" comprises an individual, a company and any other body of persons;

(f) the term "company" means any body corporate or any entity which is treated as a body corporate for tax purposes;

(g) the terms "enterprise of a Contracting State" and "enterprise of the other Contracting State" mean respectively an enterprise carried on by a resident of a Contracting State and an enterprise carried on by a resident of the other Contracting State;

(h) the term "international traffic" means any transport by a ship or aircraft operated by an enterprise which has its place of effective management in a Contracting State, except when the ship or aircraft is operated solely between places in the other Contracting State;

147

    (*i*) the term "competent authority" means, in the case of the United Kingdom the Commissioners of Inland Revenue or their authorised representative, and in the case of the Ivory Coast the Minister of Finance (Ministre des Finances) or his authorised representative.

(2) As regards the application of this Convention by a Contracting State any term not otherwise defined shall, unless the context otherwise requires, have the meaning which it has under the laws of that Contracting State relating to the taxes which are the subject of this Convention.

Article 4 Fiscal domicile

(1) For the purposes of this Convention, the term "resident of a Contracting State" means any person who, under the law of that State, is liable to tax therein by reason of his domicile, residence, place of management or any other criterion of a similar nature.

(2) Where by reason of the provisions of paragraph (1) of this Article an individual is a resident of both Contracting States, then his status shall be determined in accordance with the following rules:

    (*a*) he shall be deemed to be a resident of the Contracting State in which he has a permanent home available to him; if he has a permanent home available to him in both States, he shall be deemed to be a resident of the State with which his personal and economic relations are closer (centre of vital interests);

    (*b*) if the State in which he has his centre of vital interests cannot be determined, or if he has not a permanent home available to him in either State, he shall be deemed to be a resident of the State in which he has an habitual abode;

    (*c*) if he has an habitual abode in both States or in neither of them, he shall be deemed to be a resident of the State of which he is a national;

    (*d*) if he is a national of both States or of neither of them, the competent authorities of the Contracting States shall settle the question by mutual agreement.

(3) Where by reason of the provisions of paragraph (1) of this Article a person other than an individual is a resident of both Contracting States, then it shall be deemed to be a resident of the State in which its place of effective management is situated.

Article 6 Income from immovable property

(1) (Taxation of income from immovable property.)

(2) The term "immovable property" shall have the meaning which it has under the law of the Contracting State in which the property in question is situated. The term shall in any case include property accessory to immovable property, livestock and equipment used in agriculture and forestry, rights to which the provisions of general law respecting landed property apply, usufruct of immovable property and rights to variable or fixed payments as consideration for the working of, or the right to work, mineral deposits, sources and other natural resources; ships, boats and aircraft shall not be regarded as immovable property.

    (3) . . .

    (4) . . .

Article 8 Shipping and air transport

(1) Profits from the operation of ships or aircraft in international traffic shall be taxable only in the Contracting State in which the place of effective management of the enterprise is situated.

(2) If the place of effective management of a shipping enterprise is aboard a ship or boat, then it shall be deemed to be situated in the Contracting State in which the home harbour of the ship or boat is situated, or, if there is no such home harbour, in the Contracting State of which the operator of the ship or boat is a resident.

(3) The provisions of paragraph (1) of this Article shall also apply to profits from the participation in a pool, a joint business or an international operating agency.

With respect to profits derived by the air transport company Air-Afrique the provisions of this paragraph and of paragraph (1) of this Article shall only apply to the share of profits attributed to the Ivory Coast.

Article 14 Capital gains

(1) . . .

(2) . . .

(3) Gains from the alienation of ships or aircraft operated in international traffic, or movable property pertaining to the operation of such ships or aircraft shall be taxable only in the Contracting State in which the place of effective management of the enterprise is situated.

(4) . . .

Article 24 Non-discrimination

(1) The nationals of a Contracting State shall not be subjected in the other Contracting State to any taxation or any requirement connected therewith which is other or more burdensome than the taxation and connected requirements to which nationals of that other State in the same circumstances are or may be subjected.

(2) The taxation on a permanent establishment which an enterprise of a Contracting State has in the other Contracting State shall not be less favourably levied in that other State than the taxation levied on enterprises of that other State carrying on the same activities.

(3) Enterprises of a Contracting State, the capital of which is wholly or partly owned or controlled, directly or indirectly, by one or more residents of the other Contracting State, shall not be subjected in the first-mentioned State to any taxation or any requirement connected therewith which is other or more burdensome than the taxation and connected requirements to which other similar enterprises of that first-mentioned State are or may be subjected.

(4) Nothing contained in this Article shall be construed as obliging either Contracting State to grant to individuals not resident in that State any of the personal allowances, reliefs and reductions for tax purposes which are granted to individuals so resident.

(5) Notwithstanding the provisions of this Article the period of exemption from tax on profits, under any relief referred to in paragraph (2)(a) of Article 23 or any relief of a substantially similar character under paragraph (2)(b) of that Article, from which a United Kingdom enterprise established in the Ivory Coast could benefit in the Ivory Coast, shall not under any circumstances exceed 10 years.

(6) In this Article the term "taxation" means taxes referred to in Article 2 of this Convention.

Article 25 Mutual agreement procedure

(1) Where a resident of a Contracting State considers that the actions of one or both of the Contracting States result or will result for him in taxation not in accordance with this Convention, he may, notwithstanding the remedies provided by the domestic law of those States, present his case to the competent authority of the Contracting State of which he is a resident.

(2) The competent authority shall endeavour, if the objection appears to it to be justified and if it is not itself able to arrive at an appropriate solution, to resolve the case by mutual agreement with the competent authority of the other Contracting State, with a view to the avoidance of taxation not in accordance with the Convention.

(3) The competent authorities of the Contracting States shall endeavour to resolve by mutual agreement any difficulties or doubts arising as to the interpretation or application of the Convention.

(4) The competent authorities of the Contracting States may communicate with each other directly for the purpose of reaching an agreement in the sense of the preceding paragraphs.

Article 26 Exchange of information

(1) The competent authorities of the Contracting States shall exchange such information as is necessary for carrying out the provisions of this Convention or of the domestic laws of the Contracting States concerning taxes covered by the Convention insofar as the taxation thereunder is not contrary to the Convention. The exchange of information is not restricted by Article 1. Any information received by a Contracting State shall be treated as secret in the same manner as information obtained under the domestic laws of that State and shall be disclosed only to persons or authorities (including courts and administrative bodies) involved in the assessment or collection of, the enforcement or prosecution in respect of, or the determination of appeals in relation to, the taxes covered by the Convention. Such persons or authorities shall use the information only for such purposes. They may disclose the information in public court proceedings or in judicial decisions.

(2) In no case shall the provisions of paragraph (1) of this Article be construed so as to impose on a Contracting State the obligation:

(a) to carry out administrative measures at variance with the laws and administrative practice of that or of the other Contracting State;

(b) to supply information which is not obtainable under the laws or in the normal course of the administration of that or of the other Contracting State;

(c) to supply information which would disclose any trade, business, industrial, commercial or professional secret or trade process, or information, the disclosure of which would be contrary to public policy (ordre public).

Article 28 Entry into force

Note: This Convention entered into force on 10 February 1987. It takes effect in the Ivory Coast from 1 October 1987 for taxes on commercial profits and from 1 January 1987 for other taxes on income. It takes effect in the United Kingdom for the financial year (or year of assessment) commencing in April 1987.

Official languages: The French language text and the English language text of this Convention are equally authoritative.

JAMAICA

Agreement of 16 March 1973 (SI 1973 No 1329)

Article 1 Taxes covered

(1) The taxes which are the subject of the present Agreement are—

(a) in the United Kingdom of Great Britain and Northern Ireland:

(i) the income tax;

(ii) the capital gains tax; and

(iii) the corporation tax

(hereinafter referred to as "United Kingdom tax");

(b) in Jamaica:

(i) the income tax (including surtax);

(ii) the company profits tax, the additional company profits tax and the investment company profits tax; and

(iii) the transfer tax

(hereinafter referred to as "Jamaican tax").

(2) This Agreement shall also apply to any identical or substantially similar taxes which are subsequently imposed in addition to, or in place of, the existing taxes by either Government or by the Government of any territory to which the present Agreement is extended under Article 28.

Article 2 General definitions

(1) In this Agreement, unless the context otherwise requires—

(a) the term "United Kingdom" means Great Britain and Northern Ireland, including any area outside the territorial sea of the United Kingdom which in accordance with international law has been or may hereafter be designated, under the laws of the United Kingdom concerning the Continental Shelf, as an area within which the rights of the United Kingdom with respect to the sea-bed and sub-soil and their natural resources may be exercised;

(b) (i) the term "Jamaica" means the island of Jamaica, the Morant Cays, the Pedro Cays and their dependencies; and

(ii) when used in a geographical sense the term "Jamaica" includes the territorial waters thereof including any area outside such territorial waters which in accordance with international law and the laws of Jamaica is an area within which the rights of Jamaica with respect to the sea-bed and sub-soil and their natural resources may be exercised;

(c) the terms "one of the territories" and "the other territory" mean the United Kingdom or Jamaica as the context requires;

(d) the term "taxation authorities" means, in the case of the United Kingdom, the Commissioners of Inland Revenue or their authorised representative; in the case of Jamaica, the Commissioner of Income Tax or his authorised representative; and in the case of any territory to which this Agreement is extended under Article 28, the competent authority for the administration in such territory of the taxes to which this agreement applies;

(e) the term "tax" means United Kingdom tax or Jamaican tax, as the context requires;

(f) the term "person" includes any body of persons, corporate or not corporate;

(g) the term "company" means any body corporate or any entity which is treated as a body corporate for tax purposes;

(h) the term "international traffic" includes traffic between places in one country in the course of a voyage which extends over more than one country;

(i) the term "national" means:

(i) in relation to the United Kingdom

(aa) any citizen of the United Kingdom and Colonies who derives his status as such from his connection with the United Kingdom;

(bb) any legal person, partnership or association deriving its status as such from the law in force in the United Kingdom;

(ii) in relation to Jamaica

(aa) any individual who is a citizen of Jamaica;

(bb) any legal person, association or other entity deriving its status as such from the law of Jamaica.

(2) Where under this Agreement any income is exempt from tax or is taxed at a reduced rate in one of the territories and that income is subject to tax in the other territory by reference to the amount thereof which is remitted to or received in that other territory, the exemption or reduction of tax to be allowed under this Agreement in the first-mentioned territory shall apply only to the amount so remitted or received.

(3) In the application of the provisions of the present Agreement by one of the Contracting Governments any term not otherwise defined shall, unless the context otherwise requires, have the meaning which it has under the laws of that Government relating to the taxes which are the subject of the present Agreement.

Article 3 Residence

(1) For the purposes of this Agreement the terms "resident of the United Kingdom" and "resident of Jamaica" mean respectively any person who is resident in the United Kingdom for the purposes of United Kingdom tax and any person who is resident in Jamaica for the purposes of Jamaican tax.

(2) Where by reason of the provisions of paragraph (1) above an individual is a resident of both territories, then his status shall be determined in accordance with the following rules:

(a) he shall be deemed to be a resident of the territory in which he has a permanent home available to him. If he has a permanent home available to him in both territories, he shall be deemed to be a resident of the territory with which his personal and economic relations are closest (hereinafter referred to as his "centre of vital interests");

(b) if the territory in which he has his centre of vital interests cannot be determined, or if he has not a permanent home available to him in either territory, he shall be deemed to be a resident of the territory in which he has an habitual abode;

(c) if he has an habitual abode in both territories or in neither of them, he shall be deemed to be a resident of the territory of which he is a national;

(d) if he is a national of both territories or of neither of them, the taxation authorities of the territories shall determine the question by mutual agreement.

(3) Where by reason of the provisions of paragraph (1) above a legal person is a resident of both territories, then it shall be deemed to be a resident of the territory in which its place of effective management is situated.

(4) The terms "resident of one of the territories" and "resident of the other territory" mean a person who is a resident of the United Kingdom or a person who is a resident of Jamaica, as the context requires.

(5) The terms "United Kingdom enterprise" and "Jamaican enterprise" mean respectively an industrial or commercial enterprise or undertaking carried on by a resident of the United Kingdom and an industrial or commercial enterprise or undertaking carried on by a resident of Jamaica, and the terms "enterprise of one of the territories" and "enterprise of the other territory" mean a United Kingdom enterprise or a Jamaican enterprise, as the context requires.

Article 7 Shipping and air transport

A resident of one of the territories shall be exempt from tax in the other territory on profits from the operation of ships or aircraft other than profits from voyages or ships or aircraft confined solely to places in that other territory.

Article 12 Immovable property

(1) (Taxation of income from immovable property.)

(2) The term "immovable property" shall be defined in accordance with the laws of the territory in which the property in question is situated. The term shall in any case include property accessory to immovable property, livestock and equipment of agricultural and forestry enterprises, rights to which the provisions of general law respecting landed property

apply, usufruct of immovable property and rights to variable or fixed payments as consideration for the working of mineral deposits, sources and other natural resources; ships, boats and aircraft shall not be regarded as immovable property.

(3) . . .

(4) . . .

Article 20 Capital gains

(1) (Taxation of gains from alienation of immovable property.)

(2) . . .

(3) Notwithstanding the provisions of paragraph (1) of this Article, capital gains derived by a resident of one of the territories from the alienation of ships and aircraft operated in international traffic and of movable property pertaining to the operation of such ships and aircraft shall be taxable only in that territory.

(4)–(6) . . .

Article 25 Exchange of information

The taxation authorities of the Contracting Governments shall on request exchange such information (being information which is at their disposal under their respective taxation laws in the normal course of administration) as is necessary for carrying out the provisions of the present Agreement or for the prevention of fraud or for the administration of statutory provisions against legal avoidance in relation to the taxes which are the subject of the present Agreement. Any information so exchanged shall be treated as secret and shall not be disclosed to any persons other than those (including a court or administrative tribunal) concerned with the assessment and collection of the taxes which are the subject of the present Agreement. No information as aforesaid shall be exchanged which would disclose any trade, business, industrial or professional secret or trade process.

Article 26 Consultation

The taxation authorities of the Contracting Governments may communicate with each other directly for the purpose of giving effect to the provisions of this Agreement and for resolving any difficulty or doubt as to application or interpretation of the Agreement.

Article 27 Non-discrimination

(1) The nationals of one of the territories shall not be subjected in the other territory to any taxation or any requirement connected therewith which is other or more burdensome than the taxation and connected requirements to which the nationals of the other territory in the same circumstances are or may be subjected.

(2) The taxation on a permanent establishment which an enterprise of one of the territories has in the other territory shall not be less favourably levied in that other territory than the taxation levied on enterprises of that other territory carrying on the same activities.

(3) Enterprises of one of the territories, the capital of which is wholly or partly owned or controlled, directly or indirectly, by one or more residents of the other territory, shall not be subjected in the first-mentioned territory to any taxation or any requirement connected therewith which is other or more burdensome than the taxation and connected requirements to which other similar enterprises of the first-mentioned territory are or may be subjected.

(4) In this Article the term "taxation" means taxes of every kind and description.

(5) Nothing contained in this Article shall be construed—

　　(a) as obliging either of the Contracting Governments to grant to individuals not resident in its territory those personal allowances and reliefs for tax purposes which are by law available only to persons who are so resident; or

　　(b) as preventing Jamaica from charging a higher rate of income tax under Section 28(3A) of the Income Tax Law 1954 of Jamaica on a life assurance company which is a resident of the United Kingdom than on a Jamaicanized life assurance company; or

(c) as being applicable to any tax of a discriminatory nature which a Contracting Government may impose in pursuance of its programme of economic development and which the Contracting Governments agree should be excluded from the provisions of this Article;

Provided that any such tax as is mentioned in sub-paragraph (b) or (c) of this paragraph shall not be levied less favourably on a resident of the United Kingdom than on a resident of any other territory which is not a member country of the Caribbean Free Trade Association.

Article 29 Entry into force

Note: Article 29 provided for the entry into force of this Agreement. It takes effect in the UK from the year of assessment 1973–74 (income tax and capital gains tax) and from the financial year beginning on 1 April 1973 (corporation tax).

Official language: English.

JAPAN

Convention of 10 February 1969 (SI 1970 No 1948)

(Printed as amended by the Exchange of Notes of 10 February 1969 (SI 1970 No 1948) and the Protocol of 14 February 1980 (SI 1980 No 1530).

Article 1 [Personal scope]

This Convention shall apply to persons who are residents of one or both of the Contracting States.

Article 2 [Taxes covered]

(1) The taxes which are the subject of this Convention are:

(a) in the United Kingdom:
   (i) the income tax;
   (ii) the corporation tax;
   (iii) the capital gains tax;
   (iv) the development land tax; and
   (v) the petroleum revenue tax;

(b) in Japan:
   (i) the income tax;
   (ii) the corporation tax; and

(iii) the local inhabitant taxes.

(2) This Convention shall also apply to any identical or substantially similar taxes, whether national or local, which are imposed in either Contracting State after the date of signature of this Convention in addition to, or in place of, the existing taxes. The competent authorities of the Contracting States shall notify to each other any changes which are made in their respective taxation laws.

(3) With respect to enterprises operating ships or aircraft, this Convention shall also apply to the taxes referred to in paragraph (2) of Article 9.

Article 3 [General definitions]

(1) In this Convention, unless the context otherwise requires:
   (a) the term "United Kingdom" means Great Britain and Northern Ireland;
   (b) the term "Japan" when used in a geographical sense, means the territory in which the laws relating to Japanese tax are in force;
   (c) the term "nationals" means:
      (i) in relation to the United Kingdom, all citizens of the United Kingdom and Colonies who derive their status as such from their connection with the United Kingdom and all legal persons, partnerships and associations deriving their status as such from the law in force in the United Kingdom;
      (ii) in relation to Japan, all individuals possessing the nationality of Japan and all juridical persons created or organised under the laws of Japan and all organisations without juridical personality treated for the purposes of Japanese tax as juridical persons created or organised under the laws of Japan;
   (d) the term "United Kingdom tax" means tax imposed in the United Kingdom being tax to which this Convention applies by virtue of paragraph (1) or paragraph (2) of Article 2; the term "Japanese tax" means tax imposed in Japan being tax to which this Convention applies by virtue of paragraph (1) or paragraph (2) of Article 2;
   (e) the term "tax" means United Kingdom tax or Japanese tax, as the context requires;
   (f) the terms "a Contracting State" and "the other Contracting State" mean the United Kingdom or Japan, as the context requires;
   (g) the term "person" includes a company and any other body of persons;
   (h) the term "company" means any body corporate or any entity which is treated as a body corporate for tax purposes;
   (i) the terms "enterprise of a Contracting State" and "enterprise of the other Contracting State" mean respectively an enterprise carried on by a resident of a Contracting State and an enterprise carried on by a resident of the other Contracting State;
   (j) the term "competent authority" means, in the case of the United Kingdom the Commissioners of Inland Revenue or their authorised representative, and in the case of Japan the Minister of Finance or his authorised representative;
   (k) the term "international traffic" means any voyage of a ship or aircraft other than a voyage solely between places in the Contracting State which is not the Contracting State of which the person deriving the profits from the operation of the ship or aircraft is a resident.

(2) As regards the application of this Convention by a Contracting State any term not otherwise defined shall, unless the context otherwise requires, have the meaning which it has under the laws of that Contracting State relating to the taxes to which this Convention applies.

Article 4 [Fiscal domicile]

(1) For the purposes of this Convention, the term "resident of a Contracting State" means any person who, under the law of that Contracting State, is liable to taxation therein by reason of his domicile, residence, place of head or main office, place of management or any

155

other criterion of a similar nature; the term does not include any individual who is liable to tax in that Contracting State only if he derives income from sources therein. The terms "resident of the United Kingdom" and "resident of Japan" shall be construed accordingly.

(2) Where by reason of the provisions of paragraph (1) of this Article an individual is a resident of both Contracting States, then the competent authorities shall determine by mutual agreement the Contracting State of which that individual shall be deemed to be a resident for the purposes of this Convention.

(3) Where by reason of the provisions of paragraph (1) of this Article a person other than an individual is a resident of both Contracting States, then it shall be deemed to be a resident of the Contracting State in which its head or main office is situated.

Article 7 [Income from immovable property]

(1) (Taxation of income from immovable property.)

(2) (a) The term "immovable property" shall, subject to the provisions of sub-paragraph (b) below, be defined in accordance with the law of the Contracting State in which the property in question is situated.

(b) The term "immovable property" shall in any case include property accessory to immovable property, livestock and equipment used in agriculture and forestry, rights to which the provisions of general law respecting immovable property apply, usufruct of immovable property and rights to variable or fixed payments as consideration for the working of, or the right to work, mineral deposits, sources and other natural resources; ships, boats and aircraft shall not be regarded as immovable property.

(3) . . .

(4) . . .

Article 9 [Shipping and air transport]

(1) Profits from the operation of ships or aircraft in international traffic carried on by an enterprise of a Contracting State shall be exempt from tax in the other Contracting State.

(2) In respect of the operation of ships or aircraft in international traffic carried on by an enterprise of a Contracting State, that enterprise, if an enterprise of the United Kingdom, shall also be exempt from the enterprise tax in Japan and, if an enterprise of Japan, shall also be exempt from any tax similar to the enterprise tax in Japan which may hereafter be imposed in the United Kingdom.

Article 14 [Capital gains]

(1) (Capital gains from the alienation of immovable property.)

(2) Capital gains from the alienation of any property (other than immovable property) forming part of the business property of a permanent establishment which an enterprise of a Contracting State has in the other Contracting State or of any property (other than immovable property) pertaining to a fixed base available to a resident of a Contracting State in the other Contracting State for the purpose of performing professional services, including such gains from the alienation of such a permanent establishment (alone or together with the whole enterprise) or of such a fixed base, may be taxed in that other Contracting State. However, capital gains derived by a resident of a Contracting State from the alienation of ships or aircraft operated in international traffic and any property (other than immovable property) pertaining to the operation of such ships and aircraft shall be taxable only in that Contracting State.

(3) . . .

(4) . . .

Article 25 [Non-discrimination]

(1) The nationals of a Contracting State shall not be subjected in the other Contracting State to any taxation or any requirement connected therewith which is other or more burden-

some than the taxation and connected requirements to which nationals of that other State in the same circumstances are or may be subjected.

(2) The taxation on a permanent establishment which an enterprise of a Contracting State has in the other Contracting State shall not be less favourably levied in that other State than the taxation levied on enterprises of that other State carrying on the same activities.

(3) Enterprises of a Contracting State, the capital of which is wholly or partly owned or controlled, directly or indirectly, by one or more residents of the other Contracting State, shall not be subjected in the first-mentioned Contracting State to any taxation or any requirement connected therewith which is other or more burdensome than the taxation and connected requirements to which other similar enterprises of that first-mentioned State are or may be subjected.

(4) Nothing contained in this Article shall be construed as obliging either Contracting State to grant to individuals not resident in that State any of the personal allowances, reliefs and reductions for tax purposes which are granted to individuals so resident, nor as conferring any exemption from tax in a Contracting State in respect of dividends paid to a company which is a resident of the other Contracting State.

(5) In this Article the term "taxation" means taxes of every kind and description.

Article 26 [Mutual agreement procedure]

(1) Where a resident of a Contracting State considers that the actions of one or both of the Contracting states result or will result for him in taxation not in accordance with this Convention, he may, notwithstanding the remedies provided by the national laws of those States, present his case to the competent authority of the Contracting State of which he is a resident.

(2) The competent authority shall endeavour, if the objection appears to it to be justified and if it is not itself able to arrive at an appropriate solution, to resolve the case by mutual agreement with the competent authority of the other Contracting State, with a view to the avoidance of taxation not in accordance with the Convention.

(3) The competent authorities of the Contracting States shall endeavour to resolve by mutual agreement any difficulties or doubts arising as to the interpretation or application of the Convention.

(4) The competent authorities of the Contracting States may communicate with each other directly for the purpose of reaching an agreement in the sense of the preceding paragraphs.

Article 27 [Exchange of information]

The competent authorities of the Contracting States shall exchange such information (being information which is at their disposal under their respective taxation laws in the normal course of administration) as is necessary for carrying out the provisions of this Convention or for the prevention of fraud or the administration of statutory provisions against legal avoidance in relation to the taxes to which this Convention applies. Any information so exchanged shall be treated as secret but may be disclosed to persons (including a court or administrative body) concerned with assessment, collection, enforcement or prosecution in respect of taxes which are the subject of this Convention. No information shall be exchanged which would disclose any trade, business, industrial or professional secret or any trade process.

Article 29 [Entry into force]

Note: Article 29 provided for the entry into force of the 1969 Convention. It takes effect in the UK in its amended form from the year of assessment 1981–82 (income tax and capital gains tax) and from the financial year beginning on 1 April 1981 (corporation tax).

Official language: The Japanese language text and the English language text of this Convention are equally authoritative.

JERSEY

Arrangement of 24 June 1952 (SI 1952 No 1216)

Paragraph 1 [Taxes covered]

(1) The taxes which are the subject of this Arrangement are:—
    (*a*) In the United Kingdom:
    The income tax (including surtax) and the profits tax (hereinafter referred to as "United Kingdom tax");
    (*b*) In Jersey:
    The income tax (hereinafter referred to as "Jersey tax").

(2) This Arrangement shall also apply to any other taxes of a substantially similar character imposed in the United Kingdom or Jersey after this Arrangement has come into force.

Corporation tax: This Arrangement covers United Kingdom corporation tax, by virtue of ICTA 1988 s 789(1).

Paragraph 2 [General definitions]

(1) In this Arrangement, unless the context otherwise requires:
    (*a*) the term "United Kingdom" means Great Britain and Northern Ireland;
    (*b*) the terms "one of the territories" and "the other territory" mean the United Kingdom or Jersey, as the context requires;
    (*c*) the term "tax" means United Kingdom tax or Jersey tax, as the context requires;
    (*d*) the term "person" includes any body of persons, corporate or not corporate;
    (*e*) the term "company" includes any body corporate;
    (*f*) the terms "resident of the United Kingdom" and "resident of Jersey" mean respectively any person who is resident in the United Kingdom for the purposes of United Kingdom tax and not resident in Jersey for the purposes of Jersey tax and any person who is resident in Jersey for the purposes of Jersey tax and not resident in the United Kingdom for the purposes of United Kingdom tax; and a company shall be regarded as resident in the United Kingdom if its business is managed and controlled in the United Kingdom and as resident in Jersey if its business is managed and controlled in Jersey.
    (*g*) the terms "resident of one of the territories" and "resident of the other territory" mean a person who is a resident of the United Kingdom or a person who is a resident of Jersey, as the context requires;
    (*h*) the terms "United Kingdom enterprise" and "Jersey enterprise" mean respectively an industrial or commercial enterprise or undertaking carried on by a resident of the United Kingdom and an industrial or commercial enterprise or undertaking carried on by a resident of Jersey; and the terms "enterprise of one of the territories" and "enterprise of the other territory" mean a United Kingdom enterprise or Jersey enterprise, as the context requires;
    (*i*) the term "industrial or commercial profits" includes rentals in respect of cinematograph films;
    (*j*) the term "permanent establishment", when used with respect to an enterprise of

one of the territories, means a branch, management or other fixed place of business, but does not include an agency unless the agent has, and habitually exercises, a general authority to negotiate and conclude contracts on behalf of such enterprise or has a stock of merchandise from which he regularly fills orders on its behalf.

An enterprise of one of the territories shall not be deemed to have a permanent establishment in the other territory merely because it carries on business dealings in that other territory through a *bona fide* broker or general commission agent acting in the ordinary course of his business as such.

The fact that an enterprise of one of the territories maintains in the other territory a fixed place of business exclusively for the purchase of goods or merchandise shall not of itself constitute that fixed place of business a permanent establishment of the enterprise. The fact that a company which is a resident of one of the territories has a subsidiary company which is a resident of the other territory or which is engaged in trade or business in that other territory (whether through a permanent establishment or otherwise) shall not of itself constitute that subsidiary company a permanent establishment of its parent company.

(2) Where under this Arrangement any income tax is exempt from tax in one of the territories if (with or without other conditions) it is subject to tax in the other territory, and that income is subject to tax in that other territory by reference to the amount thereof which is remitted to or received in that other territory, the exemption to be allowed under this Arrangement in the first-mentioned territory shall apply only to the amount so remitted or received.

(3) In the application of the provisions of this Arrangement by the United Kingdom or Jersey, any term not otherwise defined shall, unless the context otherwise requires, have the meaning which it has under the laws of the United Kingdom, or, as the case may be, Jersey, relating to the taxes which are the subject of this Arrangement.

Paragraph 5 [Shipping and air transport]

Notwithstanding the provisions of paragraphs 3 and 4, profits which a resident of one of the territories derives from operating ships or aircraft shall be exempt from tax in the other territory.

Paragraph 3: Taxation of industrial or commercial profits.
Paragraph 4: Taxation of profits of associated enterprises.

Paragraph 10 [Exchange of information]

(1) The taxation authorities of the United Kingdom and Jersey shall exchange such information (being information available under their respective taxation laws) as is necessary for carrying out the provisions of this Arrangement or for the prevention of fraud or the administration of statutory provisions against legal avoidance in relation to the taxes which are the subject of this Arrangement. Any information so exchanged shall be treated as secret and shall not be disclosed to any persons other than those concerned with the assessment and collection of the taxes which are the subject of this Arrangement. No information shall be exchanged which would disclose any trade secret or trade process.

(2) As used in this paragraph, the term "taxation authorities" means the Commissioners of Inland Revenue or their authorised representative in the case of the United Kingdom and the Comptroller of Income Tax or his authorised representative in the case of Jersey.

Paragraph 11 [Entry into force]

Note: Paragraph 11 provides for the entry into force of this Convention. It takes effect in the UK from April 1951.

Official language: English.

JORDAN

Agreement of 6 March 1978 (SI 1979 No 300)

Paragraph (1) [Exemption of UK shipping operations]

The Government of the Hashemite Kingdom of Jordan shall exempt from any tax on profits or income which is, or may become, chargeable in Jordan all profits and income derived by United Kingdom undertakings from the business of shipping and air transport.

Paragraph (2) [Exemption of Jordanian shipping operations]

The Government of the United Kingdom shall exempt from income tax, corporation tax, capital gains tax and from any other tax on profits or income which is, or may become, chargeable in the United Kingdom all profits and income derived by Jordanian undertakings from the business of shipping and air transport.

Paragraph (3) [Definition of "the business of shipping and air transport"]

The expression "the business of shipping and air transport" means the business of transporting persons, goods or mail, carried on by the owner or charterer of ships or aircraft.

Paragraph (4) [Definition of "United Kingdom undertakings"]

The expression "United Kingdom undertakings" means the Government of the United Kingdom, physical persons resident in the United Kingdom and not resident in Jordan and corporations and partnerships constituted under the laws in force in the United Kingdom and managed and controlled in the United Kingdom.

Paragraph (5) [Definition of "Jordanian undertakings"]

The expression "Jordanian undertakings" means the Government of the Hashemite Kingdom of Jordan, physical persons resident in Jordan and resident in the United Kingdom and corporations and partnerships constituted under the laws in force in Jordan and managed and controlled in Jordan.

Paragraph (6) [Entry into force]

Note: Paragraph (6) provides for the entry into force of this Agreement. It takes effect as regards profits, income or capital gains arising after 31 March 1977.

Official language: English.

KENYA

Agreement of 31 July 1973 (SI 1977 No 1299)

The Protocol of 20 January 1976 (SI 1977 No 1299) and the Exchange of Notes of 8 February 1977 (SI 1977 No 1299) amend Article 32.

Article 1 Personal scope

This Agreement shall apply to persons who are residents of one or both of the Contracting States.

Article 2 Taxes covered

(1) The taxes which are the subject of this Agreement are:
    (*a*) in the United Kingdom of Great Britain and Northern Ireland:
        (i) the income tax;
        (ii) the corporation tax; and
        (iii) the capital gains tax;
    (*b*) in Kenya:
        (i) the income tax; and
        (ii) the graduated personal tax.

(2) This Agreement shall also apply to any identical or substantially similar taxes which are imposed by either Contracting State after the date of signature of this Agreement in addition to, or in place of, the existing taxes. The competent authorities of the Contracting State shall notify to each other any changes which are made in their respective taxation laws.

Article 3 General definitions

(1) In this Agreement, unless the context otherwise requires:
    (*a*) the term "United Kingdom" means Great Britain and Northern Ireland, including any area outside the territorial sea of the United Kingdom which in accordance with international law has been or may hereafter be designated, under the laws of the United Kingdom concerning the Continental Shelf, as an area within which the rights of the United Kingdom with respect to the sea-bed and sub-soil and their natural resources may be exercised;
    (*b*) the term "Kenya" means the Republic of Kenya, including any area adjacent to the territorial waters of Kenya designated, in accordance with international law, as an area within which Kenya may exercise rights with respect to the sea bed and sub-soil and their natural resources;
    (*c*) the term "nationals" means:
        (i) in relation to the United Kingdom, all citizens of the United Kingdom and Colonies who derive their status as such from their connection with the

161

United Kingdom and all legal persons, partnerships and associations deriving their status as such from the law in force in the United Kingdom;

 (ii) in relation to Kenya, all citizens of the Republic of Kenya and all legal persons, partnerships and associations deriving their status as such from the law in force in Kenya;

(d) the term "United Kingdom tax" means tax imposed by the United Kingdom being tax to which this Agreement applies by virtue of the provisions of Article 2; the term "Kenya tax" means tax imposed by Kenya being tax to which this Agreement applies by virtue of the provisions of Article 2; but neither of these terms are to include any tax payable in the United Kingdom or Kenya which is payable in respect of any default or omission in relation to the taxes which are the subject of this Agreement or which represents a penalty imposed under the law of the United Kingdom or Kenya relating to those taxes;

(e) the term "tax" means United Kingdom tax or Kenya tax, as the context requires;

(f) the terms "a Contracting State" and "the other Contracting State" mean the United Kingdom or Kenya, as the context requires;

(g) the term "persons" means
 (i) in relation to the United Kingdom an individual, a company and any other body of persons;
 (ii) in relation to Kenya an individual, a company and any other body of persons treated as an entity for tax purposes;

(h) the term "company" means any body corporate or any entity which is treated as a body corporate for tax purposes;

(i) the terms "enterprise of a Contracting State" and "enterprise of the other Contracting State" mean respectively an enterprise carried on by a resident of a Contracting State and an enterprise carried on by a resident of the other Contracting State;

(j) the term "competent authority" means, in the case of the United Kingdom the Commissioners of Inland Revenue or their authorised representative, and in the case of Kenya the Minister for Finance or his authorised representative.

(2) As regards the application of this Agreement by a Contracting State any term not otherwise defined shall, unless the context otherwise requires, have the meaning which it has under the laws of that Contracting State relating to the taxes which are the subject of this Agreement.

Article 4 Fiscal domicile

(1) For the purpose of this Agreement, the term "resident of a Contracting State" means, subject to the provisions of paragraphs (2) and (3) of this Article, any person who, under the law of that State, is liable to taxation therein by reason of his domicile, residence, place of management or any other criterion of a similar nature. The terms "resident of the United Kingdom" and "resident of Kenya" shall be construed accordingly.

(2) Where by reason of the provisions of paragraph (1) of this Article an individual is a resident of both Contracting States, then his status shall be determined in accordance with the following rules:

(a) he shall be deemed to be a resident of the Contracting State in which he has a permanent home available to him. If he has a permanent home available to him in both Contracting States, he shall be deemed to be a resident of the Contracting State with which his personal and economic relations are closest (hereinafter referred to as his centre of vital interests);

(b) if the Contracting State in which he has his centre of vital interests cannot be determined, or if he has not a permanent home available to him in either Contracting State, he shall be deemed to be a resident of the Contracting State in which he has an habitual abode;

(c) if he has an habitual abode in both Contracting States or in neither of them, he shall be deemed to be a resident of the Contracting State of which he is a national;

(d) if he is a national of both Contracting States or of neither of them, the competent authorities of the Contracting States shall settle the question by mutual agreement.

(3) Where by reason of the provisions of paragraph (1) of this Article a person other than an individual is a resident of both Contracting States, then it shall be deemed to be a resident of the Contracting State in which its place of effective management is situated.

Article 7 Income from immovable property

(1) (Taxation of income from immovable property.)

(2) (a) The term "immovable property" shall, subject to the provisions of sub-paragraph (b) below be defined in accordance with the law of the Contracting State in which the property in question is situated.

    (b) The term "immovable property" shall in any case include property accessory to immovable property, livestock and equipment used in agriculture and forestry, rights to which the provisions of general law respecting landed property apply, usufruct of immovable property and rights to variable or fixed payments as consideration for the working of, or the right to work, mineral deposits, sources and other natural resources; ships, boats and aircraft shall not be regarded as immovable property.

(3)–(5) . . .

Article 9 Shipping and air transport

A resident of a Contracting State shall be exempt from tax in the other Contracting State on profits from the operation of ships or aircraft other than profits from voyages of ships or aircraft confined solely to places in the other Contracting State.

Article 15 Capital gains

(1) . . .

(2) (Capital gains from alienation of movable business property.)

(3) Notwithstanding the provisions of paragraph (2) of this Article, capital gains derived by a resident of a Contracting State from the alienation of ships and aircraft operated in international traffic and movable property pertaining to the operation of such ships and aircraft shall be taxable only in that Contracting State.

(4) . . .

(5) . . .

Article 25 Capital

(1) . . .

(2) (Taxation of capital represented by movable business property.)

(3) Notwithstanding the provisions of paragraph (2) of this Article, ships and aircraft operated in international traffic and movable property pertaining to the operation of such ships and aircraft shall be taxable only in the Contracting State of which the operator is a resident.

(4) . . .

Article 28 Non-discrimination

(1) The nationals of a Contracting State shall not be subjected in the other Contracting State to any taxation or any requirement connected therewith which is other or more burdensome than the taxation and connected requirements to which nationals of that other State in the same circumstances are or may be subjected.

(2) The taxation on a permanent establishment which an enterprise of a Contracting State has in the other Contracting State shall not be less favourably levied in that other State than the taxation levied on enterprises of that other State carrying on the same activities.

(3) Enterprises of a Contracting State, the capital of which is wholly or partly owned or controlled directly or indirectly, by one or more residents of the other Contracting State, shall not be subjected in the first-mentioned Contracting State to any taxation or any requirement connected therewith which is other or more burdensome than the taxation and connected requirements to which other similar enterprises of that first-mentioned State are or may be subjected.

(4) Nothing contained in this Article shall be construed as obliging either Contracting State to grant to individuals not resident in that State any of the personal allowances, reliefs and reductions for tax purposes which are granted to individuals so resident.

(5) In this Article the term "taxation" means taxes of every kind and description.

Article 29 Mutual agreement procedure

(1) Where a resident of a Contracting State considers that the actions of one or both of the Contracting States result or will result for him in taxation not in accordance with this Agreement, he may, notwithstanding the remedies provided by the national laws of those States, present his case to the competent authority of the Contracting State of which he is a resident.

(2) The competent authority shall endeavour, if the objection appears to it to be justified and if it is not itself able to arrive at an appropriate solution, to resolve the case by mutual agreement with the competent authority of the other Contracting State, with a view to the avoidance of taxation not in accordance with the Agreement.

(3) The competent authorities of the Contracting States shall endeavour to resolve by mutual agreement any difficulties or doubts arising as to the interpretation or application of the Agreement.

(4) The competent authorities of the Contracting States may communicate with each other directly for the purpose of reaching an agreement in the sense of the preceding paragraphs.

Article 30 Exchange of information

The competent authorities of the Contracting States shall exchange such information (being information which is at their disposal under their respective taxation laws in the normal course of administration) as is necessary for carrying out the provisions of this Agreement or for the prevention of fraud or the administration of statutory provisions against legal avoidance in relation to the taxes which are the subject of this Agreement. Any information so exchanged shall be treated as secret but may be disclosed to persons (including a court or administrative body) concerned with assessment, collection, enforcement or prosecution in respect of taxes which are the subject of this Agreement. No information shall be exchanged which would disclose any trade, business, industrial or professional secret or any trade process.

Article 32 Entry into force

Note: Article 32 provides for the entry into force of this Agreement. It takes effect in the UK from the year of assessment 1976–77 (income tax and capital gains tax) and from the financial year beginning on 1 April 1976 (corporation tax).

Official language: English.

KIRIBATI
(Kiribati and Tuvalu: formerly the Gilbert and Ellice Islands)

Arrangement of 10 May 1950 (SI 1950 No 750)

(The Arrangements of 4 March 1968 (SI 1968 No 309) and 25 July 1974 (SI 1974 No 1271) do not amend the paragraphs printed below.)

Paragraph 1 [Taxes covered]

(1) The taxes which are the subject of this Arrangement are—
  (*a*) In the United Kingdom:
      The income tax (including surtax) and the profits tax (hereinafter referred to as "United Kingdom tax").
  (*b*) In the Gilbert and Ellice Islands Colony:
      The normal tax and the surtax (hereinafter referred to as "Colonial tax").
(2) This Arrangement shall also apply to any other taxes of a substantially similar character imposed in the United Kingdom or the Gilbert and Ellice Islands Colony after this Arrangement has come into force.

Corporation tax: This Arrangement covers United Kingdom corporation tax, by virtue of ICTA 1988 s 789(1).

Paragraph 2 [General definitions]

(1) In this Arrangement, unless the context otherwise requires—
  (*a*) The term "United Kingdom" means Great Britain and Northern Ireland, excluding the Channel Islands and the Isle of Man.
  (*b*) The term "the Colony" means the Gilbert and Ellice Islands Colony.
  (*c*) The terms "one of the territories" and "the other territory" mean the United Kingdom or the Colony, as the context requires.
  (*d*) The term "tax" means United Kingdom tax or Colonial tax, as the context requires.
  (*e*) The term "person" includes any body of persons, corporate or not corporate.
  (*f*) The term "company" includes any body corporate.
  (*g*) The terms "resident of the United Kingdom" and "resident of the Colony" mean respectively any person who is resident in the United Kingdom for the purposes of United Kingdom tax and not resident in the Colony for the purposes of Colonial tax and any person who is resident in the Colony for the purposes of Colonial tax and not resident in the United Kingdom for the purposes of United Kingdom tax; and a company shall be regarded as resident in the United Kingdom if its business is managed and controlled in the United Kingdom and as resident in the Colony if its business is managed and controlled in the Colony.
  (*h*) The terms "resident of one of the territories" and "resident of the other territory" mean a person who is a resident of the United Kingdom or a person who is a resident of the Colony, as the context requires.
  (*i*)–(*k*) . . .

(2) Where under the Arrangement any income is exempt from tax in one of the territories if (with or without other conditions) it is subject to tax in the other territory, and that income is subject to tax in that other territory by reference to the amount thereof which is remitted to or received in that other territory, the exemption to be allowed under this Arrangement in the first-mentioned territory shall apply only to the amount so remitted or received.

(3) In the application of the provisions of this Arrangement by the United Kingdom or the Colony, any term not otherwise defined shall, unless the context otherwise requires, have the meaning which it has under the laws of the United Kingdom, or, as the case may be, the Colony, relating to the taxes which are the subject of this Arrangement.

Paragraph 5 [Shipping and air transport]

Notwithstanding the provisions of paragraphs 3 and 4, profits which a resident of one of the territories derives from operating ships or aircraft shall be exempt from tax in the other territory.

Paragraph 3: Taxation of industrial or commercial profits.
Paragraph 4: Taxation of profits of associated enterprises.

Paragraph 14 [Exchange of information]

(1) The taxation authorities of the United Kingdom and the Colony shall exchange such information (being information available under their respective taxation laws) as is necessary for carrying out the provisions of this Arrangement or for the prevention of fraud or the administration of statutory provisions against legal avoidance in relation to the taxes which are the subject of this Arrangement. Any information so exchanged shall be treated as secret and shall not be disclosed to any persons other than those concerned with the assessment and collection of the taxes which are the subject of this Arrangement. No information shall be exchanged which would disclose any trade secret or trade process.

(2) As used in this paragraph, the term "taxation authorities" means the Commissioners of Inland Revenue or their authorised representative in the case of the United Kingdom and the Treasurer or his authorised representative in the case of the Colony.

Paragraph 15 [Entry into force]

Note: Paragraph 15 provided for the entry into force of this Arrangement. It takes effect in the UK from April 1949.

Official language: English.

KOREA

Convention of 21 April 1977 (SI 1978 No 786)

Printed as amended by the Protocol of 21 April 1977 (SI 1978 No 786).

Article 1 Personal scope

This Convention shall apply to persons who are residents of one or both of the Contracting States.

Article 2 Taxes covered

(1) The taxes which are the subject of this Convention are:
    (*a*) in Korea: .
        (i) the income tax; and
        (ii) the corporation tax; and
        (iii) the inhabitant tax;
    (*b*) in the United Kingdom of Great Britain and Northern Ireland:
        (i) the income tax;
        (ii) the corporation tax; and
        (iii) the capital gains tax.

(2) This Convention shall also apply to any identical or substantially similar taxes which are imposed by either Contracting State after the date of signature of this Convention in addition to, or in place of, the existing taxes.

Article 3 General definitions

(1) In this Convention, unless the context otherwise requires:
    (*a*) the term "Korea" means the Republic of Korea and when used in a geographical sense, the term "Korea" means all the territory in which the laws relating to Korean tax are in force. The term also includes the territorial sea thereof, and the sea-bed and sub-soil of the submarine areas adjacent to the coast thereof, but beyond the territorial sea, over which Korea exercises sovereign rights, in accordance with international law, for the purpose of exploration and exploitation of the natural resources of such area;
    (*b*) the term "United Kingdom" means Great Britain and Northern Ireland, including any area outside the territorial sea of the United Kingdom which in accordance with international law has been or may hereafter be designated, under the laws of the United Kingdom concerning the Continental Shelf, as an area within which the rights of the United Kingdom with respect to the sea-bed and sub-soil and their natural resources may be exercised;
    (*c*) the term "national" means:
        (i) in relation to Korea, any individual possessing Korean nationality and any legal person, partnership and association deriving their status as such from the law in force in Korea;
        (ii) in relation to the United Kingdom, any citizen of the United Kingdom and Colonies who derives his status as such from his connection with the United Kingdom and any legal person, association or other entity deriving its status as such from the law in force in the United Kingdom;
    (*d*) the term "Korean tax" means tax imposed by Korea being tax to which this Convention applies by virtue of the provisions of Article 2; the term "United King-

dom tax" means tax imposed by the United Kingdom being tax to which this Convention applies by virtue of the provisions of Article 2;

(e) the term "tax" means Korean tax or United Kingdom tax, as the context requires;

(f) the terms "a Contracting State" and "the other Contracting State" means Korea or the United Kingdom, as the context requires;

(g) the term "person" comprises an individual, a company and any other body of persons;

(h) the term "company" means any body corporate or any entity which is treated as a body corporate for tax purposes;

(i) the terms "enterprise of a Contracting State" and "enterprise of the other Contracting State" mean respectively an enterprise carried on by a resident of a Contracting State and an enterprise carried on by a resident of the other Contracting State;

(j) the term "competent authority" means, in the case of Korea the Minister of Finance or his authorised representative, and in the case of the United Kingdom the Commissioners of Inland Revenue or their authorised representative.

(2) As regards the application of this Convention by a Contracting State any term not otherwise defined shall, unless the context otherwise requires, have the meaning which it has under the laws of that Contracting State relating to the taxes which are the subject of this Convention.

Article 4 Fiscal domicile

(1) For the purposes of this Convention, the term "resident of a Contracting State" means, subject to the provisions of paragraphs (2) and (3) of this Article, any person who, under the law of that State, is liable to taxation therein by reason of his domicile, residence, place of head or main office, place of management or any other criterion of a similar nature; the term does not include any individual who is liable to tax in that Contracting State only if he derives income from sources therein. The terms "resident of Korea" and "resident of the United Kingdom" shall be construed accordingly.

(2) Where by reason of the provisions of paragraph (1) of this Article an individual is a resident of both Contracting States, then his status shall be determined in accordance with the following rules:

(a) he shall be deemed to be a resident of the Contracting State in which he has a permanent home available to him. If he has a permanent home available to him in both Contracting States, he shall be deemed to be a resident of the Contracting State with which his personal economic relations are closer (centre of vital interests);

(b) if the Contracting State in which he has his centre of vital interests cannot be determined, of if he has not a permanent home available to him in either Contracting State, he shall be deemed to be a resident of the Contracting State in which he has an habitual abode;

(c) if he has an habitual abode in both Contracting States or in neither of them, he shall be deemed to be a resident of the Contracting State of which he is a national;

(d) if he is a national of both Contracting States or of neither of them, the competent authorities of the Contracting States shall settle the question by mutual agreement.

(3) Where by reason of the provisions of paragraph (1) of this Article a person other than an individual is a resident of both Contracting States, then it shall be deemed to be a resident of the Contracting State in which its place of effective management is situated. In cases of doubt the competent authorities of the Contracting States shall settle the question by mutual agreement.

Article 6 Income from immovable property

(1) (Taxation of income from immovable property.)

(2) (a) The term "immovable property" shall, subject to the provisions of sub-paragraph

(*b*) below, be defined in accordance with the laws of the Contracting State in which the property in question is situated.

(*b*) The term "immovable property" shall in any case include property accessory to immovable property, livestock and equipment used in agriculture and forestry, rights to which the provisions of general law respecting landed property apply, usufruct of immovable property and rights to variable or fixed payments as consideration for the working of, or the right to work, mineral deposits, sources and other natural resources; ships, boats and aircraft shall not be regarded as immovable property.

(3) . . .

(4) . . .

Article 8 Shipping and air transport

(1) A resident of a Contracting State shall be exempt from tax in the other Contracting State on profits from the operation of ships or aircraft other than profits from voyages of ships or aircraft confined solely to places in the other Contracting State.

(2) (*a*) A resident of Korea shall be exempt from any future United Kingdom tax which is similar to the business tax in Korea in respect of the operation of ships and aircraft on voyages which are not confined solely to places in the United Kingdom.

(*b*) A resident of the United Kingdom shall be exempt from the business tax in Korea in respect of the operation of ships or aircraft on voyages which are not confined solely to places in Korea.

Article 13 Capital gains

(1) . . .

(2) (Taxation of gains from alienation of movable business property.)

(3) Notwithstanding the provisions of paragraph (2) of this Article, capital gains derived by a resident of a Contracting State from the alienation of ships and aircraft operated in international traffic and movable property pertaining to the operation of such ships and aircraft shall be taxable only in that Contracting State.

(4) . . .

Article 22 Non-discrimination

(1) The nationals of a Contracting State shall not be subjected in the other Contracting State to any taxation or any requirement connected therewith which is other or more burdensome than the taxation and connected requirements to which nationals of that other State in the same circumstances are or may be subjected.

(2) The taxation on a permanent establishment which an enterprise of a Contracting State has in the other Contracting State shall not be less favourably levied in that other State than the taxation levied on enterprises of that other State carrying on the same activities.

(3) Enterprises of a Contracting State, the capital of which is wholly or partly owned or controlled, directly or indirectly, by one or more residents of the other Contracting State, shall not be subjected in the first-mentioned Contracting State to any taxation or any requirement connected therewith which is other or more burdensome than the taxation and connected requirements to which other similar enterprises of that first-mentioned State are or may be subjected.

(4) Nothing contained in this Article shall be construed as obliging either Contracting State to grant to individuals not resident in that State any of the personal allowances, reliefs and reductions for tax purposes which are granted to individuals so resident.

(5) In this Article the term "taxation" means taxes of every kind and description.

Article 23 Mutual agreement procedure

(1) Where a resident of a Contracting State considers that the actions of one or both of the Contracting States result or will result for him in taxation not in accordance with this Con-

vention, he may, notwithstanding the remedies provided by the national laws of those States, present his case to the competent authority of the Contracting State of which he is a resident.

(2) The competent authority shall endeavour, if the objection appears to it to be justified and if it is not itself able to arrive at an appropriate solution, to resolve the case by mutual agreement with the competent authority of the other Contracting State, with a view to the avoidance of taxation not in accordance with the Convention.

(3) The competent authorities of the Contracting States shall endeavour to resolve by mutual agreement any difficulties or doubts arising as to the interpretation or application of the Convention.

(4) The competent authorities of the Contracting States may communicate with each other directly for the purpose of reaching an agreement in the sense of the preceding paragraphs.

Article 24 Exchange of information

(1) The competent authorities of the Contracting States shall exchange such information (being information which is at their disposal under their respective taxation laws in the normal course of administration) as is necessary for carrying out the provisions of this Convention or for the prevention of fraud or the administration of statutory provisions against legal avoidance in relation to the taxes which are the subject of this Convention. Any information so exchanged shall be treated as secret but may be disclosed to persons (including a court or administrative body) concerned with assessment, collection, enforcement or prosecution in respect of taxes which are the subject of this Convention. No information shall be exchanged which would disclose any trade, business, industrial or professional secret or any trade process.

(2) The competent authorities of the Contracting States shall notify each other of any amendments of the laws relating to the taxes referred to in paragraph (1) of Article 2 and of the adoption of any taxes referred to in paragraph (2) of Article 2, by transmitting the texts of any amendments or new statutes, if any, at least once a year.

Article 27 Entry into force

Note: Article 27 provided for the entry into force of the 1977 Convention. It takes effect in the UK in its amended form from the year of assessment 1976–77 (income tax and capital gains tax) and from the financial year beginning on 1 April 1976 (corporation tax).

Official languages: The Korean language text and the English language text of this Convention are equally authoritative.

LEBANON

Agreement of 26 February 1964 (SI 1964 No 278)

Paragraph (1) [Exemption of UK undertakings]

The Government of the Lebanon shall exempt all income derived from the business of shipping and air transport between the Republic of the Lebanon and other countries by

United Kingdom undertakings engaged in such business from income tax and all other taxes on income or profits which are or may become chargeable in the Republic of the Lebanon.

Paragraph (2) [Exemption of Lebanese undertakings]

The Government of the United Kingdom shall exempt all income derived from the business of shipping and air transport between the United Kingdom and other countries by Lebanese undertakings engaged in such business from income tax and profits tax and all other taxes on income or profits which are, or may become, chargeable in the United Kingdom and shall take the necessary action under Section 347 of the Act of Parliament of the United Kingdom known as the Income Tax Act 1952, with a view to giving the force of law to the exemption aforesaid. They shall notify the Government of the Lebanon in writing when such action has been taken.

Paragraph (3) [Definition of "the business of shipping and air transport"]

The expression "the business of shipping and air transport" means the business of transporting persons, goods or mail carried on by the owner or charterer of ships or aircraft.

Paragraph (4) [Definition of "United Kingdom undertakings"]

The expression "United Kingdom undertakings" means the Government of the United Kingdom, physical persons resident in the United Kingdom and not resident in the Republic of the Lebanon, and corporations and partnerships constituted under the laws in force in the United Kingdom and managed and controlled in the United Kingdom.

Paragraph (5) [Definition of "Lebanese undertakings"]

The expression "Lebanese undertakings" means the Government of the Lebanon, physical persons resident in the Republic of the Lebanon and not resident in the United Kingdom, and corporations and partnerships constituted under the laws in force in the Republic of the Lebanon and managed and controlled in the Lebanon.

Paragraph (6) [Entry into force]

The exemption provided for in sub-paragraph (1) above shall apply to all income earned as from the 10th of April 1957; the exemption provided for in sub-paragraph (2) shall apply to all income earned from the 6th of April 1957.

Official language: English.

LESOTHO
(formerly Basutoland)

Arrangement of 25 November 1949 (SI 1949 No 2197)

(The Arrangement of 3 July 1968 (SI 1968 No 1868) does not amend the paragraphs printed below.)

LESOTHO

Paragraph 1 [Taxes covered]

(1) The taxes which are the subject of this Arrangement are—

    (*a*) In the United Kingdom:

        The income tax (including surtax) and the profits tax (hereinafter referred to as "United Kingdom tax");

    (*b*) In Lesotho:

        The normal tax and the super-tax (hereinafter referred to as "Lesotho tax").

(2) This Arrangement shall also apply to any other taxes of a substantially similar character imposed in the United Kingdom or Lesotho after this Arrangement has come into force.

Corporation tax: This Arrangement covers United Kingdom corporation tax, by virtue of ICTA 1988 s 789(1).

Paragraph 2 [General definitions]

(1) In this Arrangement, unless the context otherwise requires—

    (*a*) The term "United Kingdom" means Great Britain and Northern Ireland excluding the Channel Islands and the Isle of Man.

    (*b*) The terms "one of the territories" and "the other territory" means the United Kingdom or Lesotho, as the context requires.

    (*c*) The term "tax" means United Kingdom tax or Lesotho tax, as the context requires.

    (*d*) The term "person" includes any body of persons, corporate or not corporate.

    (*e*) The term "company" includes any body corporate.

    (*f*) The terms "resident of the United Kingdom" and "resident of Lesotho" mean respectively any person who is resident in the United Kingdom for the purposes of United Kingdom tax and not resident in Lesotho for the purposes of Lesotho tax and any person who is resident in Lesotho for the purposes of Lesotho tax and not resident in the United Kingdom for the purposes of United Kingdom tax; and a company shall be regarded as resident in the United Kingdom if its business is managed and controlled in the United Kingdom and as resident in Lesotho if its business is managed and controlled in Lesotho.

    (*g*) The terms "resident of one of the territories" and "resident of the other territory" mean a person who is a resident of the United Kingdom or a person who is a resident of Lesotho, as the context requires.

    (*h*)–(*j*) . . .

(2) Where under this Arrangement any income is exempt from tax in one of the territories if (with or without other conditions) it is subject to tax in the other territory, and that income is subject to tax in that other territory by reference to the amount thereof which is remitted to or received in that other territory, the exemption to be allowed under this Arrangement in the first-mentioned territory shall apply only to the amount so remitted or received.

(3) In the application of the provisions of this Arrangement by the United Kingdom or Lesotho, any term not otherwise defined shall, unless the context otherwise requires, have the meaning which it has under the laws of the United Kingdom, or, as the case may be, Lesotho, relating to the taxes which are the subject of this Arrangement.

Paragraph 5 [Shipping and air transport]

Notwithstanding the provisions of paragraphs 3 and 4, profits which a resident of one of the territories derives from operating ships or aircraft shall be exempt from tax in the other territory.

Paragraph 3: Taxation of industrial or commercial profits.
Paragraph 4: Taxation of profits of associated enterprises.

Paragraph 15 [Exchange of information]

(1) The taxation authorities of the United Kingdom and Lesotho shall exchange such information (being information available under their respective taxation laws) as is necessary for carrying out the provisions of this Arrangement or for the prevention of fraud or the administration of statutory provisions against legal avoidance in relation to the taxes which are the subject of this Arrangement. Any information so exchanged shall be treated as secret and shall not be disclosed to any persons other than those concerned with the assessment and collection of the taxes which are the subject of this Arrangement. No information shall be exchanged which would disclose any trade secret or trade process.

(2) As used in this paragraph, the term "taxation authorities" means the Commissioners of Inland Revenue or their authorised representative in the case of the United Kingdom and the Collector of Income Tax or his authorised representative in the case of Lesotho.

Paragraph 16 [Entry into force]

Note: Paragraph 16 provided for the entry into force of this Arrangement. It takes effect in the UK from April 1949.

Official language: English.

LUXEMBOURG

Convention of 24 May 1967 (SI 1968 No 1100)

Printed as amended by the Protocols of 18 July 1978 (SI 1980 No 567) and 28 January 1983 (SI 1984 No 364).

Article I [Personal scope]

This Convention shall apply to persons who are residents of one or both of the Contracting States.

Article II [Taxes covered]

(1) The taxes which are the subject of this Convention are:
  (a) In the United Kingdom of Great Britain and Northern Ireland:
    (i) the income tax;
    (ii) the corporation tax;
    (iii) the petroleum revenue tax;
    (iv) the development land tax; and
    (v) the capital gains tax
      (hereinafter referred to as "United Kingdom tax").
  (b) In Luxembourg:
    (i) the income tax on individuals (*l'impôt sur le revenu des personnes physiques*);
    (ii) the tax on fees of directors of companies (*l'impôt sur les tantièmes*);
    (iii) the corporation tax (*l'impôt sur le revenu des collectivités*);
    (iv) the capital tax (*l'impôt sur la fortune*); and
    (v) the communal trade tax, including tax on the total amount of wages and salaries (*l'impôt commercial communal, y compris l'impôt sur le total des salaires*)
      (hereinafter referred to as "Luxembourg tax").

(2) The Convention shall also apply to any identical or substantially similar taxes which are subsequently imposed in addition to, or in place of, the existing taxes.

Article III [General definitions]

(1) In this Convention, unless the context otherwise requires:
  (a) the term "United Kingdom" means Great Britain and Northern Ireland, including any area outside the territorial sea of the United Kingdom which has been or may hereafter be designated, under the laws of the United Kingdom concerning the Continental Shelf, as an area within which the rights of the United Kingdom with respect to the sea-bed and sub-soil and their natural resources may be exercised;
  (b) the term "Luxembourg" means the Grand Duchy of Luxembourg;
  (c) the terms "a Contracting State" and "the other Contracting State" mean the United Kingdom or Luxembourg, as the context requires;
  (d) the term "competent authority" means, in the case of Luxembourg, the *Ministre du Trésor* or his authorised representative; in the case of the United Kingdom, the Commissioners of Inland Revenue or their authorised representative; and, in the case of any territory to which the Convention is extended under Article XXXI, the competent authority for the administration in such territory of the taxes to which the Convention applies;
  (e) the term "tax" means United Kingdom tax or Luxembourg tax, as the context requires;
  (f) the term "person" comprises an individual, a company and any other body of persons;
  (g) the term "company" means any body corporate or any entity which is treated as a body corporate for tax purposes;
  (h) the terms "enterprise of a Contracting State" and "enterprise of the other Contracting State" means respectively an enterprise carried on by a resident of a Contracting State and an enterprise carried on by a resident of the other Contracting State;
  (i) . . .
  (j) the term "international traffic" includes traffic between places in any State in the course of a voyage which extends over two or more States.

(2) As regards the application of the Convention by a Contracting State any term not otherwise defined shall, unless the context otherwise requires, have the meaning which it has under the laws of that Contracting State relating to the taxes which are the subject of the Convention.

Excluded companies: For companies excluded from this Convention see Article XXX.

Article IV [Fiscal domicile]

(1) For the purposes of this Convention, the term "resident of a Contracting State" means any person who, under the law of that State, is liable to taxation therein by reason of his domicile, residence, place of management or any other criterion of a similar nature.

(2) Where by reason of the provisions of paragraph (1) an individual is a resident of both Contracting States, then this case shall be determined in accordance with the following rules:

(a) he shall be deemed to be a resident of the Contracting State in which he has a permanent home available to him. If he has a permanent home available to him in both Contracting States, he shall be deemed to be a resident of the Contracting State with which his personal and economic relations are closest (centre of vital interests);

(b) if the Contracting State in which he has his centre of vital interests cannot be determined, or if he has not a permanent home available to him in either Contracting State, he shall be deemed to be a resident of the Contracting State in which he has an habitual abode;

(c) if he has an habitual abode in both Contracting States or in neither of them, he shall be deemed to be a resident of the Contracting State of which he is a national;

(d) if he is a national of both Contracting States or of neither of them, the competent authorities of the Contracting States shall settle the question by mutual agreement.

(3) Where by reason of the provisions of paragraph (1) a person other than an individual is a resident of both Contracting States, then it shall be deemed to be a resident of the Contracting State in which its place of effective management is situated.

Article VI [Income from immovable property]

(1) (Taxation of income from immovable property.)

(2) The term "immovable property" shall be defined in accordance with the law of the Contracting State in which the property in question is situated. The term shall in any case include property accessory to immovable property, livestock and equipment used in agriculture and forestry, rights to which the provisions of general law respecting landed property apply, usufruct of immovable property and rights to variable or fixed payments as consideration for the working of, or the right to work, mineral deposits, sources and other natural resources; ships, boats and aircraft shall not be regarded as immovable property.

(3) . . .

(4) . . .

Article VIII [Shipping and air transport]

(1) Profits from the operation of ships or aircraft in international traffic shall be taxable only in the Contracting State in which the place of effective management of the enterprise is situated.

(2) Profits from the operation of boats engaged in inland waterways transport shall be taxable only in the Contracting State in which the place of effective management of the enterprise is situated.

(3) If the place of effective management of a shipping enterprise or of an inland waterways transport enterprise is aboard a ship or boat, then it shall be deemed to be situated in the Contracting State in which the home harbour of the ship or boat is situated, or, if there is no such home harbour, in the Contracting State of which the operator of the ship or boat is a resident.

Article XIII [Capital gains]

(1) (Taxation of gains from alienation of immovable property.)

(2) Gains from the alienation of movable property forming part of the business property of a permanent establishment which an enterprise of a Contracting State has in the other Contracting State, or of movable property pertaining to a fixed base available to a resident of a Contracting State in the other Contracting State for the purpose of performing professional

services, including such gains from the alienation of such a permanent establishment (alone or together with the whole enterprise) or of such a fixed base, may be taxed in the other State. However, gains from the alienation of movable property of the kind referred to in paragraph (3) of Article XXIII shall be taxable only in the Contracting State in which such movable property is taxable according to the said Article.

(3) . . .

(4) . . .

Article XXIII [Capital]

(1) . . .

(2) . . .

(3) Ships and aircraft operated in international traffic and boats engaged in inland waterways transport, and movable property pertaining to the operation of such ships, aircraft and boats, shall be taxable only in the Contracting State in which the place of effective management of the enterprise is situated.

(4) . . .

Article XXVI [Non-discrimination]

(1) The nationals of a Contracting State shall not be subjected in the other Contracting State to any taxation or any requirement connected therewith which is other or more burdensome than the taxation and connected requirements to which nationals of that other State in the same circumstances are or may be subjected.

(2) The term "nationals" means:

(a) in relation to the United Kingdom, all British subjects and British protected persons

  (i) residing in the United Kingdom or any territory to which this Convention is extended under Article XXXI, or

  (ii) deriving their status as such from connection with the United Kingdom or any territory to which the Convention is extended under Article XXXI,

and all legal persons, partnerships and associations deriving their status as such from the law in force in the United Kingdom or in any territory to which the Convention is extended under Article XXXI;

(b) in relation to Luxembourg, all individuals possessing the nationality of Luxembourg and all legal persons, partnerships and associations deriving their status as such from the law in force in Luxembourg.

(3) The taxation on a permanent establishment which an enterprise of a Contracting State has in the other Contracting State shall not be less favourably levied in that other State than the taxation levied on enterprises of that other State carrying on the same activities.

(4) Enterprises of a Contracting State, the capital of which is wholly or partly owned or controlled, directly or indirectly, by one or more residents of the other Contracting State, shall not be subjected in the first-mentioned Contracting State to any taxation or any requirement connected therewith which is other or more burdensome than the taxation and connected requirements to which other similar enterprises of that first-mentioned State are or may be subjected.

(5) This Article shall not be construed as entitling a resident of one of the Contracting States to any personal allowances, reliefs and reductions for taxation purposes on account of civil status or family responsibilities which the law of the other Contracting State grant only to residents of that other Contracting State or as restricting the taxation of dividends paid by a company which is a resident of one of the Contracting States to a company which is a resident of the other Contracting State.

(6) In this Article the term "taxation" means taxes of every kind and description.

Article XXVII [Mutual agreement procedure]

(1) Where a resident of a Contracting State considers that the actions of one or both of the Contracting States result or will result for him in taxation not in accordance with this Con-

vention, he may, notwithstanding the remedies provided by the national laws of those States, present his case to the competent authority of the Contracting State of which he is a resident.

(2) The competent authority shall endeavour, if the objection appears to it to be justified and if it is not itself able to arrive at an appropriate solution, to resolve the case by mutual agreement with the competent authority of the other Contracting State, with a view to the avoidance of taxation not in accordance with the Convention.

(3) The competent authorities of the Contracting States shall endeavour to resolve by mutual agreement any difficulties or doubts arising as to the interpretation or application of the Convention. They may also consult together for the elimination of double taxation in cases not provided for in the Convention.

(4) The competent authorities of the Contracting States may communicate with each other directly for the purpose of reaching an agreement in the sense of the preceding paragraphs or for the purpose of giving effect to the provisions of the Convention and for resolving any difficulty or doubt as to the application or interpretation of the Convention.

Article XXVIII [Exchange of information]

The competent authorities of the Contracting States shall exchange such information (being information which is at their disposal under their respective taxation laws in the normal course of administration) as is necessary for carrying out the provisions of this Convention or for the prevention of fraud or for the administration of statutory provisions against legal avoidance in relation to the taxes which are the subject of the Convention. Any information so exchanged shall be treated as secret and shall not be disclosed to any persons other than persons (including a Court) concerned with the assessment or collection of, or the determination of appeals in relation to, the taxes which are the subject of the Convention. No information as aforesaid shall be exchanged which would disclose any trade, business, industrial or professional secret or trade process.

Article XXX [Holding companies]

This Convention shall not apply to holding companies entitled to any special tax benefit under the Luxembourg laws of 31st July, 1929, or 27th December, 1937, or any similar law enacted by Luxembourg after the signature of the Convention.

Article XXXII [Entry into force]

Note: Article XXXII provided for the entry into force of the 1967 Convention. It takes effect in the UK in its amended form for any year of assessment, financial year or chargeable period beginning after 31 December 1983.

Official languages: The French language text and the English language text of this Convention are equally authoritative.

MALAWI
(formerly part of the Federation of Rhodesia and Nyasaland)

Agreement of 25 November 1955 (SI 1956 No 619)

Continued in force in relation to Malawi by virtue of the Agreement of 1 April 1964 (SI 1964 No 1401).

(The Agreements of 2 April 1968 (SI 1968 No 1101) and 10 February 1978 (SI 1979 No 302) do not amend the Articles printed below.)

MALAWI

Article I [Taxes covered]

(1) The taxes which are the subject of the present Agreement are—

(a) In the United Kingdom of Great Britain and Northern Ireland: the income tax (including surtax), the profits tax and the excess profits levy (hereinafter referred to as "United Kingdom tax").

(b) In the Federation of Rhodesia and Nyasaland: the income tax, supertax and undistributed profits tax (hereinafter referred to as "Federal tax").

(2) The present Agreement shall also apply to any other taxes of a substantially similar character imposed by either Contracting Government subsequently to the date of signature of the present Agreement.

Corporation tax: This Agreement covers United Kingdom corporation tax, by virtue of ICTA 1988 s 789(1).

Article II [General definitions]

(1) In the present Agreement, unless the context otherwise requires:

(a) The term "United Kingdom" means Great Britain and Northern Ireland.

(b) The term "the Federation" means the Federation of Rhodesia and Nyasaland.

(c) The terms "one of the territories" and "the other territory" mean the United Kingdom or the Federation, as the context requires.

(d) The term "tax" means United Kingdom tax or Federal tax, as the context requires.

(e) The term "person" includes any body of persons, corporate or not corporate.

(f) The term "company" includes any body corporate.

(g) The terms "resident of the United Kingdom" and "resident of the Federation" mean respectively any person who is resident in the United Kingdom for the purposes of United Kingdom tax and is not resident in the Federation and any person who is resident in the Federation and is not resident in the United Kingdom for the purposes of United Kingdom tax; and a company shall be regarded as resident in the United Kingdom if its business is managed and controlled in the United Kingdom and as resident in the Federation if its business is managed and controlled in the Federation.

(h) The terms "resident of one of the territories" and "resident of the other territory" mean a person who is a resident of the United Kingdom or a person who is a resident of the Federation, as the context requires.

(i)–(k) . . .

(2) Where under this Agreement any income is exempt from tax in one of the territories if (with or without other conditions) it is subject to tax in the other territory, and that income is subject to tax in that other territory by reference to the amount thereof which is remitted to or received in that other territory, the exemption to be allowed under this Agreement in the first-mentioned territory shall apply only to the amount so remitted or received.

(3) The terms "United Kingdom tax" and "Federation tax", as used in this Agreement, do not include any tax or other amount payable in the United Kingdom or the Federation which is payable in respect of any default or omission in relation to the taxes which are the subject of this Agreement or which represents a penalty imposed under the law of the United Kingdom or the Federation relating to those taxes.

(4) In the application of the provisions of the present Agreement by one of the Contracting Governments any term not otherwise defined shall, unless the context otherwise requires,

have the meaning which it has under the laws of that Contracting Government relating to the taxes which are the subject of the present Agreement.

Article V [Shipping and air transport]

Notwithstanding the provisions of Articles III and IV, profits which a resident of one of the territories derives from operating ships (other than ships operating wholly on inland waters) or aircraft shall be exempt from tax in the other territory.

Article III: Taxation of industrial or commercial profits.
Article IV: Taxation of profits of associated enterprises.

Article XIV [Exchange of information]

(1) The taxation authorities of the Contracting Governments shall exchange such information (being information available under the respective taxation laws of the Contracting Governments) as is necessary for carrying out the provisions of the present Agreement or for the prevention of fraud or the administration of statutory provisions against legal avoidance in relation to the taxes which are the subject of the present Agreement. Any information so exchanged shall be treated as secret and shall not be disclosed to any persons other than those concerned with the assessment and collection of the taxes which are the subject of the present Agreement. No information shall be exchanged which would disclose any trade secret or trade process.

(2) As used in this Article, the term "taxation authorities" means the Commissioner of Taxes or his authorised representative in the case of the Federation, and the Commissioners of Inland Revenue or their authorised representative in the case of the United Kingdom.

Article XV [Entry into force]

Note: Article XV provided for the entry into force of this Agreement. It takes effect in the UK in respect of income or profits which arise after 31 March 1953.

Official language: English.

MALAYSIA

Agreement of 30 March 1973 (SI 1973 No 1330)

The Protocol of 21 July 1987 (SI 1987 No 2056), which amends Articles I, II and III below, had not entered into force on 6 April 1988.

(The Protocol of 30 March 1973 (SI 1973 No 1330) does not amend the Articles printed below.)

Article I Taxes covered

(1) The taxes which are the subject of this Agreement are:
- (a) in Malaysia:
    - (i) the income tax; and
    - (ii) the supplementary income tax, that is, tin profits tax, development tax and timber profits tax
    (hereinafter referred to as "Malaysian tax");
- (b) in the United Kingdom:
    - (i) the income tax (including surtax);
    - (ii) the corporation tax; and
    - (iii) the capital gains tax
    (hereinafter referred to as "United Kingdom tax").

(2) This Agreement shall also apply to any other taxes of a substantially similar character to those referred to in the preceding paragraph imposed in either Contracting State after the date of signature of this Agreement.

Article I(1): The Protocol of 21 July 1987 (SI 1987 No 2056) substitutes the following for paragraph (a):

"(a) in Malaysia:
- (i) the income tax and excess profit tax; and
- (ii) the supplementary income tax, that is, development tax
    (hereinafter referred to as "Malaysian tax");"

and deletes the words "(including surtax)" from paragraph (b)(i).

Article II General definitions

(1) In this Agreement, unless the context otherwise requires:
- (a) the term "Malaysia" means the Federation of Malaysia, and includes any area adjacent to the territorial waters of Malaysia which in accordance with international law has been or may hereafter be designated, under the laws of Malaysia concerning the Continental Shelf, as an area within which the rights of Malaysia with respect to the sea-bed and sub-soil and their natural resources may be exercised;
- (b) the term "United Kingdom" means Great Britain and Northern Ireland, including any area outside the territorial sea of the United Kingdom which in accordance with international law has been or may hereafter be designated, under the laws of the United Kingdom concerning the Continental Shelf, as an area within which the rights of the United Kingdom with respect to the sea bed and sub-soil and their natural resources may be exercised;
- (c) the terms "one of the Contracting States" and "the other Contracting State" mean the United Kingdom or Malaysia, as the context requires;
- (d) the term "tax" means United Kingdom tax or Malaysian tax, as the context requires;
- (e) the term "company" means any body corporate or any entity which is treated as a body corporate for tax purposes;
- (f) the term "individual" means a natural person;
- (g) the term "person" includes an individual, a company and a body of persons, but does not include a partnership, and in the case of Malaysia, also includes a Hundu joint family and a corporation sole;
- (h) the terms "enterprise of one of the Contracting States" and "enterprise of the

other Contracting State" mean respectively an enterprise carried on by a resident of one of the Contracting States and an enterprise carried on by a resident of the other Contracting State;

    (*i*) the term "national" means:
        (i) in relation to Malaysia:
          (*aa*) any individual possessing the citizenship of Malaysia;
          (*bb*) any legal person, partnership, association and other entity deriving its status as such from the law in force in Malaysia;
        (ii) in relation to the United Kingdom:
          (*aa*) any citizen of the United Kingdom and Colonies who derives his status as such from his connection with the United Kingdom;
          (*bb*) any legal person, association or other entity deriving its status as such from the law of the United Kingdom;

    (*j*) the term "competent authority" means, in the case of the United Kingdom, the Commissioners of Inland Revenue or their authorised representative; and in the case of Malaysia, the Minister of Finance or his authorised representative.

(2) In the application of this Agreement by one of the Contracting States, any term not otherwise defined shall, unless the context otherwise requires, have the meaning which it has under the laws of that Contracting State relating to the taxes which are the subject of this Agreement.

Article II(1): The Protocol of 21 July 1987 (SI 1987 No 2056) substitutes the following for paragraphs (*g*) and (*i*)(ii)(*aa*) respectively:
    "(*g*) the term "person" includes an individual, a company and any other body of persons;"
        "(*aa*) any British citizen or any British subject not possessing the citizenship of any other Commonwealth country or territory, provided that he has the right of abode in the United Kingdom;"

Article III Fiscal domicile

(1) In this Agreement, subject to the provisions of paragraphs (2) and (3) of this Article, and unless the context otherwise requires:
    (*a*) the term "resident of Malaysia" means:
        (i) an individual who is ordinarily resident in Malaysia, or
        (ii) a person other than an individual who is resident in Malaysia
    for the basis year for a year of assessment for the purpose of Malaysian tax;
    (*b*) the term "resident of the United Kingdom" means a person who is resident in the United Kingdom for the purposes of United Kingdom tax;
    (*c*) the terms "resident of one of the Contracting States" and "resident of the other Contracting State" mean a resident of the United Kingdom or a resident of Malaysia, as the context requires.

(2) Where by reason of the provisions of paragraph (1) of this Article an individual is a resident of both Contracting States, then his status shall be determined in accordance with the following rules:
    (*a*) he shall be deemed to be a resident of the Contracting State in which he has a permanent home available to him. If he has a permanent home available to him in both Contracting States, he shall be deemed to be a resident of the Contracting State with which his personal and economic relations are closer;
    (*b*) if the Contracting State with which his personal and economic relations are closer cannot be determined, or if he has not a permanent home available to him in either Contracting State, he shall be deemed to be a resident of the Contracting State in which he has an habitual abode;
    (*c*) if he has an habitual abode in both Contracting States or in neither of them, he shall be deemed to be a resident of the Contracting State of which he is a national.
    (*d*) if he is a national of both Contracting States or of neither of them, the competent

authorities of the Contracting States shall determine the question by mutual agreement.

(3) Where by reason of the provisions of paragraph (1) of this Article a person other than an individual is a resident of both Contracting States, then it shall be deemed to be a resident of the Contracting State in which its place of effective management is situated.

Article III(1): The Protocol of 21 July 1987 (SI 1987 No 2056) substitutes the following for paragraph (*a*):

"(*a*) the term 'resident of Malaysia' means a person who is resident in Malaysia for the purpose of Malaysian tax;"

Article VIII Shipping and air transport

A resident of one of the Contracting States shall be exempt from tax in the other Contracting State on income or profits from the operation of ships or aircraft other than income or profits from voyages of ships or aircraft confined solely to places in the other Contracting State.

Article XIX Capital gains

(1) . . .

(2) (Taxation of gains from alienation of movable business property.)

(3) Notwithstanding the provisions of paragraph (2) of this Article, capital gains derived by a resident of a Contracting State from the alienation of ships and aircraft operated in international traffic and movable property pertaining to the operation of such ships and aircraft shall be taxable only in that Contracting State.

(4) . . .

(5) . . .

Article XXII Non-discrimination

(1) The nationals of one of the Contracting States shall not be subjected in the other Contracting State to any taxation or any requirement connected therewith which is other or more burdensome than the taxation and connected requirements to which nationals of that other Contracting State in the same circumstances are or may be subjected.

(2) The taxation on a permanent establishment which an enterprise of one of the Contracting States has in the other Contracting State shall not be less favourably levied in that other Contracting State than the taxation levied on an enterprise of that other Contracting State carrying on the same activities.

(3) Enterprises of one of the Contracting States, the capital of which is wholly or partly owned or controlled, directly or indirectly, by one or more residents of the other Contracting State, shall not be subjected in the first-mentioned Contracting State to any taxation or any requirement connected therewith which is other or more burdensome than the taxation and connected requirements to which other similar enterprises of that first-mentioned Contracting State are or may be subjected.

(4) Nothing contained in this Article shall be construed as obliging either Contracting State to grant to individuals not resident in that Contracting State any of the personal allowances, reliefs and reductions for tax purposes which are granted to individuals so resident.

(5) Moreover nothing contained in this Article shall be construed as obliging a Contracting State to grant to nationals of the other Contracting State not resident in the first-mentioned Contracting State those personal allowances, reliefs and reductions for tax purposes which are by law available on the date of signature of this Agreement only to nationals of the first-mentioned Contracting State or to such other persons specified therein who are not resident in that Contracting State.

(6) In this Article the term "taxation" means taxes which are the subject of this Agreement.

Article XXIII Exchange of information

(1) The competent authorities of the Contracting States shall exchange such information as is necessary for carrying out the provisions of this Agreement or for the prevention of fiscal evasion or for the administration of statutory provisions against tax avoidance in relation to the taxes which are the subject of this Agreement. Any information so exchanged shall be treated as secret and shall not be disclosed to any persons or authorities other than those, including a court or administrative body, concerned with assessment, collection, enforcement or prosecution in respect of those taxes or the determination of appeals in relation thereto.

(2) In no case shall the provisions of paragraph (1) of this Article be construed so as to impose on one of the Contracting States the obligation:

  (a) to carry out administrative measures at variance with the laws or the administrative practice of that or of the other Contracting States;

  (b) to supply particulars which are not obtainable under the laws or in the normal course of the administration of that or of the other Contracting State;

  (c) to supply information which would disclose any trade, business, industrial, commercial or professional secret or trade process, or information the disclosure of which would be contrary to public policy.

Article XXIV Mutual agreement procedure

(1) Where a resident of one of the Contracting States considers that the actions of one or both of the Contracting States result or will result for him in taxation not in accordance with this Agreement, he may, notwithstanding the remedies provided by the taxation laws in force in the Contracting States, present his case to the competent authority of the Contracting State of which he is a resident.

(2) The competent authority of the first-mentioned Contracting State shall endeavour, if the objection appears to it to be justified and if it is not itself able to arrive at an appropriate solution, to resolve that case by mutual agreement with the competent authority of the other Contracting State with a view to the avoidance of taxation which is not in accordance with this Agreement.

(3) The competent authorities of the Contracting States shall endeavour to resolve by mutual agreement any difficulties or doubts arising as to the interpretation or application of this Agreement.

(4) The competent authorities of the Contracting States may communicate with each other directly for the purposes of giving effect to the provisions of this Agreement.

Article XXVI Entry into force

Note: Article XXVI provided for the entry into force of this Agreement. It takes effect in the UK from the year of assessment 1973–74 (income tax and capital gains tax) and from the financial year beginning on 1 April 1973 (corporation tax).

Official language: English.

MALTA

Arrangement of 28 March 1962 (SI 1962 No 639)

Printed as amended by the Agreement of 29 November 1974 (SI 1975 No 426).

MALTA

Paragraph 1 [Taxes covered]

(1) The taxes which are the subject of this Arrangement are:—
   (a) In the United Kingdom (and hereinafter referred to as "United Kingdom tax"):
       The income tax and the corporation tax.
   (b) In the Island of Malta (and hereinafter referred to as "Malta tax"):
       The income tax (including surtax).

(2) This Arrangement shall also apply to any other taxes of a substantially similar character imposed in the United Kingdom or Malta after this Arrangement has come into force.

Paragraph 2 [General definitions]

(1) In this Arrangement, unless the context otherwise requires:
   (a) The term "United Kingdom" means Great Britain and Northern Ireland, including any area outside the territorial sea of the United Kingdom which in accordance with international law has been or may hereafter be designated, under the laws of the United Kingdom concerning the Continental Shelf, as an area within which the rights of the United Kingdom with respect to the sea-bed and sub-soil and their natural resources may be exercised.
   (b) The term "Malta" means the Island of Malta, the Island of Gozo, and the other islands of the Maltese archipelago, including the territorial waters thereof, and any area outside the territorial sea of Malta which, in accordance with international law, has been or may hereafter be designated, under the laws of Malta concerning the Continental Shelf, as an area within which the rights of Malta with respect to the sea-bed and sub-soil and their natural resources may be exercised.
   (c) The terms "one of the territories" and "the other territory" mean the United Kingdom or Malta, as the context requires.
   (d) The term "tax" means United Kingdom tax or Malta tax, as the context requires.
   (e) The term "person" includes any body of persons, corporate or not corporate.
   (f) The term "company" includes any body corporate.
   (g) The term "resident of the United Kingdom" means—
       (i) any company whose business is managed and controlled in the United Kingdom;
       (ii) any other person who is resident in the United Kingdom for the purposes of United Kingdom tax and not resident in Malta for the purposes of Malta tax.
   (h) The term "resident of Malta" means—
       (i) any company whose business is managed and controlled in Malta;
       (ii) any other person who is resident in Malta for the purposes of Malta tax and not resident in the United Kingdom for the purposes of United Kingdom tax.
   (i) The terms "resident of one of the territories" and "resident of the other territory" mean a person who is a resident of the United Kingdom or a person who is a resident of Malta, as the context requires.
   (j)–(l) . . .

(2) Where under this Arrangement any income is exempt from tax or is taxed at a reduced rate in one of the territories and that income is subject to tax in the other territory by reference to the amount thereof which is remitted to or received in that other territory, the exemption or reduction of tax to be allowed under this Arrangement in the first-mentioned territory shall apply only to the amount so remitted or received.

(3) In the application of the provisions of this Arrangement by the United Kingdom or Malta, any term not otherwise defined shall, unless the context otherwise requires, have the meaning which it has under the laws of the United Kingdom, or, as the case may be, Malta, relating to the taxes which are the subject of this Arrangement.

Paragraph 5 [Shipping and air transport]

Notwithstanding the provisions of paragraphs 3 and 4, profits which a resident of one of the territories derives from operating ships or aircraft shall be exempt from tax in the other territory.

Paragraph 3: Taxation of industrial or commercial profits.
Paragraph 4: Taxation of profits of associated enterprises.

Paragraph 14 [Exchange of information]

(1) The taxation authorities of the United Kingdom and Malta shall exchange such information (being information available under their respective taxation laws) as is necessary for carrying out the provisions of this Arrangement or for the prevention of fraud or the administration of statutory provisions against legal avoidance in relation to the taxes which are the subject of this Arrangement. Any information so exchanged shall be treated as secret and shall not be disclosed to any persons other than those concerned with the assessment and collection of the taxes which are the subject of this Arrangement. No information shall be exchanged which would disclose any trade secret or trade process.

(2) As used in this paragraph, the term "taxation authorities" means the Commissioners of Inland Revenue or their authorised representative in the case of the United Kingdom and the Commissioner of Inland Revenue or his authorised representative in the case of Malta.

Paragraph 15 [Entry into force]

Note: Paragraph 15 provided for the entry into force of the 1962 Arrangement. It takes effect in the UK in its amended form from the year of assessment 1973–74 (income tax) and from the financial year beginning on 1 April 1973 (corporation tax).

Official language: English.

MAURITIUS

Convention of 11 February 1981 (SI 1981 No 1121)

(The Protocol of 23 October 1986 (SI 1987 No 467) does not amend the Articles printed below.)

Article 1 Personal scope

This Convention shall apply to persons who are residents of one or both of the Contracting States.

Article 2 Taxes covered

(1) The existing taxes to which this Convention shall apply are:
  (a) in the United Kingdom of Great Britain and Northern Ireland:
    (i) the income tax;
    (ii) the corporation tax; and
    (iii) the capital gains tax;
    (hereinafter referred to as "United Kingdom tax");
  (b) in Mauritius:
    (i) the income tax;
    (ii) the capital gains tax (*morcellement*);
    (hereinafter referred to as "Mauritius tax").

(2) This Convention shall also apply to any identical or substantially similar taxes which are imposed by either Contracting State after the date of signature of this Convention in addition to, or in place of, the existing taxes.

(3) The competent authorities of the Contracting States shall notify each other of any substantial changes which are made in their respective taxation laws.

Article 3 General definitions

(1) For the purposes of this Convention, unless the context otherwise requires:
  (a) the term "United Kingdom" means Great Britain and Northern Ireland, including any area outside the territorial sea of the United Kingdom which in accordance with international law has been or may hereafter be designated, under the laws of the United Kingdom concerning the Continental Shelf, as an area within which the rights of the United Kingdom with respect to the sea-bed and sub-soil and their natural resources may be exercised;
  (b) the term "Mauritius" means all the territories, including all the islands, which, in accordance with the laws of Mauritius, constitute the State of Mauritius and includes:
    (i) the territorial sea of Mauritius; and
    (ii) any area outside the territorial sea of Mauritius which in accordance with international law has been or may hereafter be designated, under the laws of Mauritius concerning the Continental Shelf, as an area within which the rights of Mauritius with respect to the sea bed and sub-soil and their natural resources may be exercised;
  (c) the term "national" means:
    (i) in relation to the United Kingdom, any citizen of the United Kingdom and Colonies, or any British subject not possessing that citizenship or the citizenship of any other Commonwealth country or territory, provided that in either case he has the right of abode in the United Kingdom; and any legal person, partnership, association or other entity deriving its status as such from the law in force in the United Kingdom;
    (ii) in relation to Mauritius, any individual who is a citizen of Mauritius and any legal person, partnership, association or other entity deriving its status as such from the law in force in Mauritius;
  (d) the terms "a Contracting State" and "the other Contracting State" mean the United Kingdom or Mauritius as the context requires;
  (e) the term "person" comprises an individual, a company and any other body of persons, corporate or not corporate;
  (f) the term "company" means any body corporate or any entity which is treated as a company or body corporate for tax purposes;
  (g) the terms "enterprise of a Contracting State" and "enterprise of the other Contracting State" mean respectively an industrial, mining, commercial, plantation or agricultural enterprise or similar undertaking carried on by a resident of a Contracting State and an industrial, mining, commercial, plantation or agricultural

enterprise or similar undertaking carried on by a resident of the other Contracting State;

(h) the term "international traffic" means any transport by a ship or aircraft operated by an enterprise which has its place of effective management in a Contracting State, except when the ship or aircraft is operated solely between places in the other Contracting State;

(i) the term "competent authority" means, in the case of the United Kingdom the Commissioners of Inland Revenue or their authorised representative, and in the case of Mauritius the Commissioner of Income Tax or his authorised representative;

(j) the term "tax" means United Kingdom tax or Mauritius tax as the context requires.

(2) In the application of the provisions of this Convention by a Contracting State, any term not otherwise defined shall, unless the context otherwise requires, have the meaning which it has under the laws of that Contracting State relating to the taxes which are the subject of this Convention.

Article 4 Residence

(1) For the purposes of this Convention, the term "resident of a Contracting State" means, subject to the provisions of paragraphs (2) and (3) of this Article, any person who, under the law of that State, is liable to taxation therein by reason of his domicile, residence, place of management or any other criterion of a similar nature. The terms "resident of the United Kingdom" and "resident of Mauritius" shall be construed accordingly.

(2) Where by reason of the provisions of paragraph (1) of this Article an individual is a resident of both Contracting States, then his status shall be determined in accordance with the following rules:

(a) he shall be deemed to be a resident of the Contracting State in which he has a permanent home available to him. If he has a permanent home available to him in both Contracting States, he shall be deemed to be a resident of the Contracting State with which his personal and economic relations are closer (centre of vital interests);

(b) if the Contracting State in which he has his centre of vital interests cannot be determined, or if he has not a permanent home available to him in either Contracting State, he shall be deemed to be a resident of the Contracting State in which he has an habitual abode;

(c) if he has an habitual abode in both Contracting States or in neither of them, he shall be deemed to be a resident of the Contracting State of which he is a national;

(d) if he is a national of both Contracting States or of neither of them, the competent authorities of the Contracting States shall determine the question by mutual agreement.

(3) Where by reason of the provisions of paragraph (1) of this Article a person other than an individual is a resident of both Contracting States, then it shall be deemed to be a resident of the Contracting State in which its place of effective management is situated.

Article 6 Income from immovable property

(1) (Taxation of income from immovable property.)

(2) (a) The term "immovable property" shall, subject to the provisions of sub-paragraph (b) below, be defined in accordance with the law of the Contracting State in which the property in question is situated.

(b) The term "immovable property" shall in any case include property accessory to immovable property, livestock and equipment used in agriculture and forestry, rights to which the provisions of general law respecting landed property apply, usufruct of immovable property and rights to variable or fixed payments as consideration for the working of, or the right to work, mineral deposits, sources and other natural resources; ships, boats and aircraft shall not be regarded as immovable property.

(3)–(5) . . .

Article 8 Shipping and air transport

(1) Profits from the operation of ships or aircraft in international traffic shall be taxable only in the Contracting State in which the place of effective management of the enterprise is situated.

(2) If the place of effective management of a shipping enterprise is aboard a ship then it shall be deemed to be situated in the Contracting State in which the home harbour of the ship is situated, or, if there is no such home harbour, in the Contracting State of which the operator of the ship is a resident.

(3) The provisions of paragraph (1) of this Article shall also apply to profits from the participation in a pool, a joint business or an international operating agency.

Article 13 Capital gains

(1) . . .

(2) (Taxation of gains from alienation of movable business property.)

(3) Notwithstanding the provisions of paragraph (2) of this Article, capital gains from the alienation of ships and aircraft operated in international traffic and movable property pertaining to the operation of such ships and aircraft shall be taxable only in the Contracting State in which the place of effective management of the enterprise is situated.

(4) . . .

(5) . . .

Article 26 Non-discrimination

(1) The nationals of a Contracting State shall not be subjected in the other Contracting State to any taxation or any requirement connected therewith which is other or more burdensome than the taxation and connected requirements to which nationals of that other State in the same circumstances are or may be subjected.

(2) The taxation on a permanent establishment which an enterprise of a Contracting State has in the other Contracting State shall not be less favourably levied in that other State than the taxation levied on enterprises of that other State carrying on the same activities.

(3) Enterprises of a Contracting State, the capital of which is wholly or partly owned or controlled, directly or indirectly, by one or more residents of the other Contracting State, shall not be subjected in the first-mentioned Contracting State to any taxation or any requirement connected therewith which is other or more burdensome than the taxation and connected requirements to which other similar enterprises of that first-mentioned State are or may be subjected.

(4) Nothing contained in this Article shall be considered as obliging either Contracting State to grant to individuals not resident in that State any of the personal allowances, reliefs and reductions for tax purposes which are granted to individuals so resident, nor as obliging Mauritius to grant to a company which is not a resident of Mauritius any deduction in the computation of its chargeable income in respect of dividends paid by the company.

(5) In this Article the term "taxation" means taxes of every kind and description.

Article 27 Mutual agreement procedure

(1) Where a resident of a Contracting State considers that the actions of one or both of the Contracting States result or will result for him in taxation not in accordance with this Convention, he may, notwithstanding the remedies provided by the national laws of those States, present his case to the competent authority of the Contracting State of which he is a resident.

(2) The competent authority shall endeavour, if the objection appears to it to be justified

and if it is not itself able to arrive at an appropriate solution, to resolve the case by mutual agreement with the competent authority of the other Contracting State, with a view to the avoidance of taxation not in accordance with the Convention.

(3) The competent authorities of the Contracting States shall endeavour to resolve by mutual agreement any difficulties or doubts arising as to the interpretation or application of the Convention, with the object of facilitating any appropriate adjustment of liability.

(4) The competent authorities of the Contracting States may communicate with each other directly for the purpose of reaching an agreement in the sense of the preceding paragraphs.

Article 28 Exchange of information

The competent authorities of the Contracting States shall exchange such information (being information which is at their disposal under their respective taxation laws in the normal course of administration) as is necessary for carrying out the provisions of this Convention or for the prevention of fraud or for the administration of statutory provisions against legal avoidance in relation to the taxes which are the subject of this Convention. Any information so exchanged shall be treated as secret but may be disclosed to persons (including a court or administrative body) concerned with assessment, collection, enforcement or prosecution in respect of the taxes which are the subject of this Convention. No information shall be exchanged which would disclose any trade, business, industrial or professional secret or any trade process.

Article 30 Entry into force

Note: Article 30 provided for the entry into force of this Convention. It takes effect in the UK from the year of assessment 1981–82 (income tax and capital gains tax) and from the financial year beginning on 1 April 1981 (corporation tax).

Official language: English.

MONTSERRAT

Arrangement of 19 December 1947 (SR & O 1947 No 2869)

Printed as amended by the Arrangement of 8 April 1968 (SI 1968 No 576).

Paragraph 1 [Taxes covered]

(1) The taxes which are the subject of this Arrangement are—
    (*a*) In the United Kingdom:
        The income tax (including surtax) and the profits tax (hereinafter referred to as "United Kingdom tax").
    (*b*) In the Presidency of Montserrat:

The income tax (hereinafter referred to as "Presidential tax").

(2) This Arrangement shall also apply to any other taxes of a substantially similar character imposed in the United Kingdom or the Presidency after this Arrangement has come into force.

Corporation tax: This Arrangement covers United Kingdom corporation tax, by virtue of ICTA 1988 s 789(1).

Paragraph 2 [General definitions]

(1) In this Arrangement, unless the context otherwise requires—
- (a) The term "United Kingdom" means Great Britain and Northern Ireland, excluding the Channel Islands and the Isle of Man.
- (b) . . .
- (c) The terms "one of the territories" and "the other territory" mean the United Kingdom or the Presidency, as the context requires.
- (d) The term "tax" means United Kingdom tax or Presidential tax, as the context requires.
- (e) The term "person" includes any body of persons, corporate or not corporate.
- (f) The term "company" includes any body corporate.
- (g) The terms "resident of the United Kingdom" and "resident of the Presidency" mean respectively any person who is resident in the United Kingdom for the purposes of United Kingdom tax and not resident in the Presidency for the purposes of Presidential tax and any person who is resident in the Presidency for the purposes of Presidential tax and not resident in the United Kingdom for the purposes of United Kingdom tax; and a company shall be regarded as resident in the United Kingdom if its business is managed and controlled in the United Kingdom and as resident in the Presidency if its business is managed and controlled in the Presidency.
- (h) The terms "resident of one of the territories" and "resident of the other territory" mean a person who is a resident of the United Kingdom or a person who is a resident of the Presidency, as the context requires.
- (i)–(k) . . .

(2) Where under this Arrangement any income is exempt from tax in one of the territories if (with or without other conditions) it is subject to tax in the other territory, and that income is subject to tax in that other territory by reference to the amount thereof which is remitted to or received in that other territory, the exemption to be allowed under this Arrangement in the first-mentioned territory shall apply only to the amount so remitted or received.

(3) In the application of the provisions of this Arrangement by the United Kingdom or the Presidency, any term not otherwise defined shall, unless the context otherwise requires, have the meaning which it has under the laws of the United Kingdom, or, as the case may be, the Presidency, relating to the taxes which are the subject of this Arrangement.

Paragraph 5 [Shipping and air transport]

Notwithstanding the provisions of paragraphs 3 and 4, profits which a resident of one of the territories derives from operating ships or aircraft shall be exempt from tax in the other territory.

Paragraph 3: Taxation of industrial or commercial profits.
Paragraph 4: Taxation of profits of associated enterprises.

Paragraph 14 [Exchange of information]

(1) The taxation authorities of the United Kingdom and the Presidency shall exchange such information (being information available under their respective taxation laws) as is

necessary for carrying out the provisions of this Arrangement or for the prevention of fraud or the administration of statutory provisions against legal avoidance in relation to the taxes which are the subject of this Arrangement. Any information so exchanged shall be treated as a secret and shall not be disclosed to any persons other than those concerned with the assessment and collection of the taxes which are the subject of this Arrangement. No information shall be exchanged which would disclose any trade secret or trade process.

(2) As used in this paragraph, the term "taxation authorities" means the Commissioners of Inland Revenue or their authorised representative in the case of the United Kingdom and the Income Tax Commissioners or their authorised representative in the case of the Presidency.

Paragraph 15 [Entry into force]

Note: Paragraph 15 provided for the entry into force of the 1947 Arrangement. It takes effect in the UK in its amended form the year of assessment 1968–69 (income tax) and from the financial year beginning on 1 April 1968 (corporation tax).

Official language: English.

MOROCCO

Convention of 8 September 1981 (SI 1981/Draft)

Article 1 Personal scope

This Convention shall apply to persons who are residents of one or both of the Contracting States.

Article 2 Taxes covered

(1) The taxes which are the subject of this Convention are:
    (*a*) in the Kingdom of Morocco:
        (i) the business profits tax and the investment reserve (*l'impôt sur les bénéfices professionnels et la réserve d'investissement*);
        (ii) the tax on public and private salaries, emoluments, fees, wages, pensions and life annuities (*le prélèvement sur les traitements publics et privés, les indemnités et émoluments, les salaires, les pensions et les rentes viagères*);
        (iii) the tax on urban real property and taxes related thereto (*la taxe urbaine et les taxes qu iy sont rattachées*);

   (iv) the agricultural tax (*l'impôt agricole*);

   (v) the complementary tax on the total income of individuals (*la contribution complémentaire sur le revenu global des personnes physiques*);

   (vi) the tax on income from shares or corporate rights and assimilated income (*la taxe sur les produits des actions ou parts sociales et revenus assimilés*);

   (vii) the tax on gains from real property (*la taxe sur les profits immobiliers*);

   (viii) the tax on urban land (*l'impôt sur les terrains urbains*); and

   (ix) the national solidarity tax (*la participation à la solidarité nationale*);

   (hereinafter referred to as "Moroccan tax");

  (*b*) in the United Kingdom of Great Britain and Northern Ireland:

   (i) the income tax;

   (ii) the corporation tax; and

   (iii) the capital gains tax;

   (hereinafter referred to as "United Kingdom tax").

(2) This Convention shall also apply to any identical or substantially similar taxes which are imposed by either Contracting State after the date of signature of this Convention in addition to, or in place of, the existing taxes. The competent authorities of the Contracting States shall notify each other of any changes which are made in their respective taxation laws.

Article 3 General definitions

(1) In this Convention, unless the context otherwise requires:

  (*a*) the term "Morocco" means the Kingdom of Morocco and, where used in a geographical sense, the territory of Morocco as well as any area adjacent to the territorial waters of Morocco and designated a national area for tax purposes, and in which Morocco may exercise, in accordance with international law, its rights with respect to the sea-bed and sub-soil and their natural resources (Continental Shelf);

  (*b*) the term "United Kingdom" means Great Britain and Northern Ireland, including any area outside the territorial sea of the United Kingdom which in accordance with international law has been or may hereafter be designated, under the laws of the United Kingdom concerning the Continental Shelf, as an area within which the rights of the United Kingdom with respect to the sea-bed and sub-soil and their natural resources may be exercised;

  (*c*) the term "national" means:

   (i) in relation to the Kingdom of Morocco, any individual possessing Moroccan nationality in accordance with the Moroccan Nationality Code, published on 6 September 1958, as well as any legal person, partnership or other association or entity deriving its status from the law in force in the Kingdom of Morocco;

   (ii) in relation to the United Kingdom, any individual who has under the law in the United Kingdom the status of United Kingdom national, provided he has the right of abode in the United Kingdom; and any legal person, partnership, association or other entity deriving its status as such from the law in force in the United Kingdom;

  (*d*) the term "tax" means United Kingdom or Moroccan tax, as the context requires;

  (*e*) the terms "a Contracting State" and "the other Contracting State" mean the United Kingdom or the Kingdom of Morocco, as the context requires;

  (*f*) the term "person" comprises an individual, a company and any other body of persons;

  (*g*) the term "company" means any body corporate or any entity which is treated as a body corporate for tax purposes;

  (*h*) the terms "enterprise of a Contracting State" and "enterprise of the other Contracting State" mean respectively an enterprise carried on by a resident of a Contracting State and an enterprise carried on by a resident of the other Contracting State;

  (*i*) the term "competent authority" means, in the case of Morocco, the Minister of Finance or his representative duly delegated or authorised and, in the case of the

United Kingdom, the Commissioners of Inland Revenue or their authorised representative;

(j) the term "international traffic" includes any voyage of a ship or aircraft other than a voyage solely between places in the Contracting State which is not the Contracting State of which a person deriving the profits of the operation of a ship or aircraft is a resident.

(2) As regards the application of this Convention by a Contracting State, any term not otherwise defined shall, unless the context otherwise requires, have the meaning which it has under the laws of that Contracting State relating to the taxes which are the subject of this Convention.

Article 4 Fiscal residence

(1) For the purposes of this Convention and subject to the provisions of Article 26 the term "resident of a Contracting State" means any person who, under the law of that State, is liable to taxation therein by reason of his domicile, residence, place of management or any other criterion of a similar nature.

(2) Where by reason of the provisions of paragraph (1) of this Article an individual is a resident of both Contracting States, then his status shall be determined in accordance with the following rules:

(a) he shall be deemed to be a resident of the Contracting State in which he has a permanent home available to him. If he has a permanent home available to him in both Contracting States, he shall be deemed to be a resident of the Contracting State with which his personal and economic relations are closer (centre of vital interests);

(b) if the Contracting State in which he has his centre of vital interests cannot be determined, or if he has not a permanent home available to him in either Contracting State, he shall be deemed to be a resident of the Contracting State in which he has an habitual abode;

(c) if he has an habitual abode in both Contracting States or in neither of them, he shall be deemed to be a resident of the Contracting State of which he is a national;

(d) if he is a national of both Contracting States or of neither of them, the competent authorities of the Contracting States shall settle the question by mutual agreement.

(3) Where by reason of the provisions of paragraph (1) of this Article a person other than an individual is a resident of both Contracting States, then it shall be deemed to be a resident of the Contracting State in which its place of effective management is situated.

Article 6 Income from immovable property

(1) (Taxation of income from immovable property.)

(2) (a) The term "immovable property" shall be defined in accordance with the law of the Contracting State in which the property in question is situated.

(b) The term "immovable property" shall in any case include property accessory to immovable property, livestock and equipment used in agriculture and forestry, rights to which the provisions of general law respecting landed property apply, usufruct of immovable property and rights to variable or fixed payments as consideration for the working of, or the right to work, mineral deposits, sources and other natural resources; ships, boats and aircraft shall not be regarded as immovable property.

(3) . . .

(4) . . .

Article 8 Shipping and air transport

Profits which an enterprise of one of the Contracting States derives from the operation of ships or aircraft in international traffic shall be taxable only in that State.

Article 13 Capital gains

(1) . . .

(2) Capital gains from the alienation of movable property forming part of the business property of a permanent establishment which an enterprise of a Contracting State has in the other Contracting State or of movable property pertaining to a fixed base available to a resident of a Contracting State in the other Contracting State for the purpose of performing professional services, including such gains from the alienation of such a permanent establishment (alone or together with the whole enterprise) or of such a fixed base, may be taxed in the other State. However, capital gains derived by a resident of a Contracting State from the alienation of ships and aircraft operated in international traffic and movable property pertaining to the operation of such ships and aircraft shall be taxable only in the Contracting State.

(3) . . .

(4) . . .

Article 23 Non-discrimination

(1) The nationals of a Contracting State shall not be subjected in the other Contracting State to any taxation or any requirement connected therewith which is other or more burdensome than the taxation and connected requirements to which nationals of that other State in the same circumstances are or may be subjected.

(2) The taxation on a permanent establishment which an enterprise of a Contracting State has in the other Contracting State shall not be less favourably levied in that other State than the taxation levied on enterprises of that other State carrying on the same activities.

(3) Nothing contained in this Article shall be construed as obliging either Contracting State to grant to individuals not resident in that State any of the personal allowances, reliefs and reductions for tax purposes which it grants to its own residents.

(4) Enterprises of a Contracting State, the capital of which is wholly or partly owned or controlled, directly or indirectly, by one or more residents of the other Contracting State, shall not be subjected in the first-mentioned Contracting State to any taxation or any requirement connected therewith which is other or more burdensome than the taxation and connected requirements to which other similar enterprises of that first-mentioned State are or may be subjected.

(5) In this Article the term "taxation" means taxes of every kind and description.

Article 24 Mutual agreement procedure

(1) Where a resident of a Contracting State considers that the actions of one or both of the Contracting States result or will result for him in taxation not in accordance with this Convention, he may, notwithstanding the remedies provided by the national laws of those States, present his case to the competent authority of the Contracting State of which he is a resident.

(2) The competent authority shall endeavour, if the objection appears to it to be justified and if it is not itself able to arrive at an appropriate solution, to resolve the case by mutual agreement with the competent authority of the other Contracting State, with a view to the avoidance of taxation not in accordance with the Convention.

(3) The competent authorities of the Contracting States shall endeavour to resolve by mutual agreement any difficulties or doubts arising as to the interpretation or application of the Convention.

(4) The competent authorities of the Contracting States may communicate with each other directly for the purpose of reaching an agreement in the sense of the preceding paragraphs.

Article 25 Exchange of information

(1) The competent authorities of the Contracting States shall exchange such information as is necessary for carrying out the provisions of this Convention, or for the prevention of fraud, or for the administration of statutory provisions against legal avoidance in relation to

the taxes which are the subject of the Convention. Any information so exchanged shall be treated as secret and shall not be disclosed to any persons other than persons (including a court or administrative body) concerned with the assessment or collection of, or prosecution in respect of, or the determination of appeals in relation to, the taxes which are the subject of the Convention.

(2) In no case shall the provisions of paragraph (1) of this Article be construed so as to impose on the competent authorities of either Contracting State the obligation:

(a) to carry out administrative measures at variance with the laws or administrative practice prevailing in either Contracting State;

(b) to supply information which is not obtainable under the laws or in the normal course of the administration of that or of the other Contracting State; or

(c) to supply information which would disclose any trade, business, industrial, commercial or professional secret or trade process, or information the disclosure of which would be contrary to public policy (*ordre public*).

Article 27 Entry into force

Note: This Convention had not entered into force on 6 April 1988.

NAMIBIA

(South West Africa)

South African Convention of 28 May 1962 (SI 1962 No 2352)

Extended to South West Africa by the Extension of 8 August 1962 (SI 1962 No 2788).
(The Protocol of 14 June 1967 (SI 1967 No 1489), extended by the Extension of 14 June 1967 (SI 1967 No 1490), does not amend the Articles printed below.)

Article I [Taxes covered]

(1) The taxes which are the subject of the present Convention are:

(a) In South West Africa:
the normal tax, the super tax, the non-resident shareholders' tax, the undistributed profits tax and the diamond profits tax (hereinafter referred to as "South West African tax").

(b) In the United Kingdom of Great Britain and Northern Ireland:
  (i) the income tax (including surtax); and
  (ii) the profits tax
(hereinafter referred to as "United Kingdom tax").

(2) This Convention shall also apply to any identical or substantially similar taxes which are subsequently imposed in addition to, or in place of, the existing taxes.

Corporation tax: This Convention covers United Kingdom corporation tax, by virtue of ICTA 1988 s 789(1).

Article II [General definitions]

(1) In the present Convention, unless the context otherwise requires:

    (*a*) the term "United Kingdom" means Great Britain and Northern Ireland;

    (*b*) the term "South West Africa" means the territory of South West Africa;

    (*c*) the terms "one of the territories" and "the other territory" mean the United Kingdom or South West Africa, as the context requires;

    (*d*) the term "taxation authorities" means, in the case of South West Africa, the Commissioner for Inland Revenue or his authorised representative; in the case of the United Kingdom, the Commissioners of Inland Revenue or their authorised representative; and, in the case of any territory to which this Convention is extended under Article XXIV, the competent authority for the administration in such territory of the taxes to which this Convention applies;

    (*e*) the term "tax" means United Kingdom tax or South West African tax, as the context requires;

    (*f*) the term "person" includes any body of persons, corporate or not corporate;

    (*g*) the term "company" means any body corporate;

    (*h*) (i) the terms "resident of the United Kingdom" and "resident of South West Africa" mean respectively any person who is resident in the United Kingdom for the purposes of United Kingdom tax and any person who is resident in South West Africa for the purposes of South West African tax; but

       (ii) where by reason of the provisions of sub-paragraph (i) an individual is a resident of both territories, then this case shall be solved in accordance with the following rules:

          (*aa*) he shall be deemed to be a resident of the territory in which he has a permanent home available to him; if he has a permanent home available to him in both territories, he shall be deemed to be a resident of the territory with which his personal and economic relations are closest (hereinafter referred to as "his centre of vital interests");

          (*bb*) if the territory in which he has his centre of vital interests cannot be determined, or if he has not a permanent home available to him in either territory, he shall be deemed to be a resident of the territory in which he has an habitual abode;

          (*cc*) if he has an habitual abode in both territories or in neither of them, he shall be deemed to be a resident of the territory of which he is a national;

          (*dd*) if he is a national of both territories or of neither of them, the taxation authorities of the territories shall determine the question by mutual agreement;

       (iii) where by reason of the provisions of sub-paragraph (i) a legal person is a resident of both territories, then it shall be deemed to be a resident of the territory in which its place of effective management is situated; the same provisions shall apply to partnerships and associations which under the national laws by which they are governed are not legal persons;

    (*i*) the terms "resident of one of the territories" and "resident of the other territory" mean a person who is a resident of the United Kingdom or a person who is a resident of South West Africa, as the context requires;

    (*j*) the terms "United Kingdom enterprise" and "South West African enterprise" mean respectively an industrial or commercial enterprise or undertaking carried on by a resident of the United Kingdom and an industrial or commercial enterprise or undertaking carried on by a resident of South West Africa, and the terms "enterprise of one of the territories" and "enterprise of the other territory" mean a United Kingdom enterprise or a South West African enterprise, as the context requires;

(k) (i) the term "permanent establishment" means a fixed place of business in which the business of the enterprise is wholly or partly carried on;

   (ii) a permanent establishment shall include especially:

      (*aa*) a place of management;

      (*bb*) a branch;

      (*cc*) an office;

      (*dd*) a factory;

      (*ee*) a workshop;

      (*ff*) a mine, quarry or other place of extraction of natural resources;

      (*gg*) a building site or construction or assembly project which exists for more than twelve months;

   (iii) the term "permanent establishment" shall not be deemed to include:

      (*aa*) the use of facilities solely for the purpose of storage, display or delivery of goods or merchandise belonging to the enterprise;

      (*bb*) the maintenance of a stock of goods or merchandise belong to the enterprise solely for the purpose of storage, display or delivery;

      (*cc*) the maintenance of a stock of goods or merchandise belonging to the enterprise solely for the purpose of processing by another enterprise;

      (*dd*) the maintenance of a fixed place of business solely for the purpose of purchasing goods or merchandise, or for collecting information, for the enterprise;

      (*ee*) the maintenance of a fixed place of business solely for the purpose of advertising, for the supply of information, for scientific research or for similar activities which have a preparatory or auxiliary character, for the enterprise;

   (iv) an enterprise of one of the territories shall be deemed to have a permanent establishment in the other territory if it carries on the activity of providing the services of public entertainers or of athletes referred to in Article XV, in that other territory;

   (v) a person acting in one of the territories on behalf of an enterprise of the other territory—other than an agent of an independent status to whom sub-paragraph (vi) applies—shall be deemed to be a permanent establishment in the first-mentioned territory if he has, and habitually exercises in that territory, an authority to conclude contracts in the name of the enterprise, unless his activities are limited to the purchase of goods or merchandise for the enterprise;

   (vi) an enterprise of one of the territories shall not be deemed to have a permanent establishment in the other territory merely because it carries on business in that other territory through a broker, general commission agent or any other agent of an independent status, where such persons are acting in the ordinary course of their business;

   (vii) the fact that a company which is a resident of one of the territories controls or is controlled by a company which is a resident of the other territory, or which carries on business in that other territory (whether through a permanent establishment or otherwise), shall not of itself constitute either company a permanent establishment of the other;

(*l*) the term "international traffic" includes traffic between places in one country in the course of a voyage which extends over more than one country.

(2) Where under this Convention any income is exempt from tax, or is to be granted relief from tax, in one of the territories if (with or without other conditions) it is subject to tax in the other territory and that income is subject to tax in that other territory by reference to the amount thereof which is remitted to or received in that other territory, the exemption or relief

to be allowed under this Convention in the first-mentioned territory shall apply only to the amount so remitted or received.

(3) In the application of the provisions of this Convention by one of the Contracting Parties any term not otherwise defined shall, unless the context otherwise requires, have the meaning which it has under the laws in force in the territory of that Party relating to the taxes which are the subject of this Convention.

Article V [Shipping and air transport]

Notwithstanding the provisions of Article III and IV, income from the operation of ship, or aircraft in international traffic shall be taxable only in the territory in which the place of effective management of the enterprise is situated.

Article III: Taxation of industrial or commercial profits.
Article IV: Taxation of profits of associated enterprises.

Article X [Income from immovable property]

(1) (Taxation of income from immovable property.)

(2) The term "immovable property" shall be construed in accordance with the laws of the territory in which the property in question is situated. The term shall in any case include property accessory to immovable property, livestock and equipment of agricultural and forestry enterprises, rights to which the provisions of general law respecting landed property apply, usufruct of immovable property and rights to variable or fixed payments as consideration for the working of mineral deposits, sources and other natural resources; ships, boats and aircraft shall not be regarded as immovable property.

(3) . . .

(4) . . .

Article XXI [Exchange of information]

The taxation authorities of the Contracting Parties shall exchange such information (being information which is at their disposal under their respective taxation laws in the normal course of administration) as is necessary for carrying out the provisions of the present Convention or for the prevention of fraud or for the administration of statutory provisions against legal avoidance in relation to the taxes which are the subject of this Convention. Any information so exchanged shall be treated as secret and shall not be disclosed to any persons other than those concerned with the assessment and collection of the taxes which are the subject of this Convention. No information as aforesaid shall be exchanged which would disclose any trade, business, industrial or professional secret or trade process.

Article XXII [Communication between taxation authorities]

The taxation authorities of the Contracting Parties may communicate with each other directly for the purpose of giving effect to the provisions of the present Convention and for resolving any difficulty or doubt as to the application or interpretation of this Convention.

Article XXIII [Non-discrimination]

(1) The nationals of one of the Contracting Parties shall not be subjected in the territory of the other Contracting Party to any taxation or any requirement connected therewith which is other or more burdensome than the taxation and connected requirements to which the nationals of the latter Party in the same circumstances are or may be subjected.

(2) In this Article the term "nationals" means—

(a) in relation to South West Africa:

all South West African citizens and all legal persons, partnerships and associations deriving their status as such from the law in force in South West Africa;

(b) in relation to the United Kingdom, all British subjects and British protected persons

 (i) residing in the United Kingdom or any territory to which the present Convention is extended under Article XXIV, or

 (ii) deriving their status as such from connection with the United Kingdom or any territory to which this Convention is extended under Article XXIV,

and all legal persons, partnerships and associations deriving their status as such from the law in force in the United Kingdom or in any territory to which the Convention is extended under Article XXIV.

(3) The taxation on a permanent establishment which an enterprise of one of the territories has in the other territory shall not be less favourably levied in that other territory than the taxation levied on enterprises of that other territory carrying on the same activities.

This provision shall not be construed as obliging one of the Contracting Parties to grant to residents of the other Contracting Party any personal allowances, reliefs and reductions for taxation purposes on account of civil status or family responsibilities which it grants to its own residents.

(4) Enterprises of one of the territories, the capital of which is wholly or partly owned or controlled, directly or indirectly, by one or more residents of the other territory, shall not be subjected in the first-mentioned territory to any taxation or any requirement connected therewith which is other or more burdensome than the taxation and connected requirements to which other similar enterprises of that first-mentioned territory are or may be subjected.

(5) In this Article the term "taxation" means the taxes which are the subject of this Convention.

Article XXV [Entry into force]

Note: Article XXV provides for the entry into force of this Convention. It takes effect in the UK from the year of assessment 1968–69 (income tax and capital gains tax) and from the financial year beginning on 1 April 1968 (corporation tax).

Official languages: The Afrikaans language text and the English language text of this Convention are equally authoritative.

NETHERLANDS

Convention of 7 November 1980 (SI 1980 No 1961)

The Protocol of 12 July 1983 (SI 1983 No 1902), which inserts Article 22A, had not entered into force on 6 April 1988.

NETHERLANDS

Article 1 Personal scope

This Convention shall apply to persons who are residents of one or both of the States.

Article 2 Taxes covered

(1) The taxes which are the subject of this Convention are:
    (a) in the United Kingdom of Great Britain and Northern Ireland:
        (i) the income tax;
        (ii) the corporation tax;
        (iii) the capital gains tax;
        (iv) the petroleum revenue tax; and
        (v) the development land tax;
        (hereinafter referred to as "United Kingdom tax");
    (b) in the Netherlands:
        (i) the income tax (*inkomstenbelasting*);
        (ii) the wages tax (*loonbelasting*);
        (iii) the company tax (*vennootschapsbelasting*); and
        (iv) the dividend tax (*dividendbelasting*);
        (hereinafter referred to as "Netherlands tax").

(2) This Convention shall also apply to any identical or substantially similar taxes which are imposed by either State after the date of signature of this Convention in addition to, or in place of, the existing taxes. The competent authorities of the States shall notify each other of substantial changes which have been made in their respective taxation laws.

Article 3 General definitions

(1) In this Convention, unless the context otherwise requires:
    (a) the term "United Kingdom" means Great Britain and Northern Ireland, including any area outside the territorial sea of the United Kingdom which in accordance with international law has been or may hereafter be designated, under the laws of the United Kingdom concerning the Continental Shelf, as an area within which the rights of the United Kingdom with respect to the sea-bed and sub-soil and their natural resources may be exercised;
    (b) the term "Netherlands" comprises the part of the Kingdom of the Netherlands that is situated in Europe and the part of the sea bed and its sub-soil under the North Sea over which the Kingdom of the Netherlands has sovereign rights in accordance with international law;
    (c) the term "State" means the United Kingdom or the Netherlands, as the context requires; the term "States" means the United Kingdom and the Netherlands;
    (d) the term "national" means:
        (i) in relation to the United Kingdom, any citizen of the United Kingdom and Colonies, or any British subject not possessing that citizenship or the citizenship of any other Commonwealth country or territory, provided in either case he has the right of abode in the United Kingdom, and any legal person, partnership or association deriving its status as such from the law in force in the United Kingdom;
        (ii) in relation to the Netherlands, any individual possessing the nationality of the Netherlands and any legal person, partnership or association deriving its status as such from the law in force in the Netherlands;
    (e) the term "tax" means United Kingdom tax or Netherlands tax, as the context requires;

(*f*) the term "person" comprises an individual, a company and any other body of persons;

(*g*) the term "company" means any body corporate or any entity which is treated as a body corporate for tax purposes;

(*h*) the term "enterprise of one of the States" and "enterprise of the other State" mean respectively an enterprise carried on by a resident of one of the States and an enterprise carried on by a resident of the other State;

(*i*) the term "international traffic" means any transport by a ship or aircraft operated by an enterprise which has its place of effective management in a State, except when the ship or aircraft is operated solely between places in the other State;

(*j*) the term "political subdivision", in relation to the United Kingdom, includes Northern Ireland;

(*k*) the term "competent authority" means in the case of the United Kingdom the Commissioners of Inland Revenue or their authorised representative, and in the case of the Netherlands the Minister of Finance or his authorised representative.

(2) As regards the application of the Convention by one of the States any term not defined therein shall, unless the context otherwise requires, have the meaning which it has under the law of that state concerning the taxes to which the Convention applies.

Article 6 Income from immovable property

(1) (Taxation of income from immovable property.)

(2) The term "immovable property" shall have the meaning which it has under the law of the State in which the property in question is situated. The term shall in any case include property accessory to immovable property, livestock and equipment used in agriculture and forestry, rights to which the provisions of general law respecting landed property apply, usufruct of immovable property and rights to variable or fixed payments as consideration for the working of, or the right to work, mineral deposits, sources and other natural resources; ships, boats and aircraft shall not be regarded as immovable property.

(3) . . .

(4) . . .

Article 8 Shipping and air transport

(1) Profits from the operation of ships or aircraft in international traffic shall be taxable only in the State in which the place of effective management of the enterprise is situated.

(2) If the place of effective management of a shipping enterprise is aboard a ship then it shall be deemed to be situated in the State in which the home harbour of the ship is situated, or, if there is no such home harbour, in the State of which the operator of the ship is a resident.

(3) Where profits within paragraph (1) of this Article are derived by an enterprise from participation in a pool, a joint business or an international operating agency, the profits attributable to that enterprise shall be taxable only in the State in which the place of effective management of that enterprise is situated. For the purposes of this paragraph the expression "a pool, a joint business or an international agency" shall not include a person, as defined in Article 3 of this Convention.

Offshore activities: See Article 22A(4) in relation to offshore activities.

Article 13 Capital gains

(1) . . .

(2) . . .

(3) Gains from the alienation of ships or aircraft operated in international traffic, or movable property pertaining to the operation of such ships or aircraft shall be taxable only in the States in which the place of effective management of the enterprise is situated.

(4) . . .

(5) . . .

[Article 22A Miscellaneous rules applicable to certain offshore activities

Notwithstanding any other provision of this Convention:

(1) An enterprise of one of the States which carries on activities offshore in the other State in connection with the exploration or exploitation of the sea bed and sub-soil and their natural resources situated in that other State shall, subject to paragraphs (2) and (4) of this Article, be deemed to be carrying on, in respect of those activities, business in that other State through a permanent establishment situated therein.

(2) The provisions of paragraph (1) of this Article shall not apply where the activities referred to therein are carried on in the other State for a period or periods not exceeding in the aggregate 30 days in any period of 12 months. For the purposes of this paragraph:

(a) where an enterprise carrying on activities referred to in paragraph (1) of this Article in the other State is associated with another enterprise carrying on substantially similar activities there, the former enterprise shall be deemed to be carrying on all such activities of the latter enterprise, except to the extent that those activities are carried on at the same time as its own activities;

(b) an enterprise shall be regarded as associated with another enterprise if one participates directly or indirectly in the management, control or capital of the other or if the same persons participate directly or indirectly in the management, control or capital of both enterprises.

(3) . . .

(4) Profits from the transportation of supplies or personnel to a location where activities in connection with the exploration or exploitation of the sea bed and sub-soil and their natural resources are being carried on in one of the States, or from the operation of tugboats and similar vessels in connection with such activities, shall be taxable only in the State in which the place of effective management of the enterprise is situated.

(5)–(8) . . .]

Article 22A: Added by the Protocol of 12 July 1983 (SI 1983 No 1902) which had not entered into force on 6 April 1988.

Article 23 Non-discrimination

(1) Nationals of one of the States shall not be subjected in the other State to any taxation or any requirement connected therewith, which is other or more burdensome than the taxations and connected requirements to which nationals of that other State in the same circumstances are or may be subjected.

(2) The taxation on a permanent establishment which an enterprise of one of the States has in the other State shall not be less favourably levied in that other State than the taxation levied on enterprises of that other State carrying on the same activities.

(3) Nothing contained in this Article shall be construed as obliging either State to grant to individuals not resident in that State any of the personal allowances, reliefs and reductions for tax purposes which are granted to individuals so resident, nor as conferring any exemption from tax in one of the States in respect of dividends paid to a company which is a resident of the other State.

(4) Enterprises of one of the States, the capital of which is wholly or partly owned or controlled, directly or indirectly, by one or more residents of the other State, shall not be subjected in the first-mentioned State to any taxation or any requirement connected therewith which is other or more burdensome than the taxation and connected requirements to which other similar enterprises of the first-mentioned State are or may be subjected.

(5) The provisions of this Article shall apply to taxes of every kind and description.

Article 24 Mutual agreement procedure

(1) Where a person considers that the actions of one or both of the States result or will result for him in taxation not in accordance with the provisions of this Convention, he may, irrespective of the remedies provided by the domestic law of those States, present his case to the competent authority of the State of which he is a resident, or, if his case comes under paragraph (1) of Article 23 and he is a resident of one of the States and a national of the other State, to that of the State of which he is a national. The case must be presented within six years from the first notification of the action resulting in taxation not in accordance with the provisions of the Convention.

(2) The competent authority shall endeavour, if the objection appears to it to be justified and if it is not itself able to arrive at a satisfactory solution, to resolve the case by mutual agreement with the competent authority of the other State, with a view to the avoidance of taxation which is not in accordance with the Convention.

(3) The competent authorities of the States shall endeavour to resolve by mutual agreement any difficulties or doubts arising as to the interpretation or application of the Convention. They may also consult together to consider measures to counteract improper use of the provisions of the Convention.

(4) The competent authorities of the States may communicate with each other directly for the purpose of reaching an agreement in the sense of the preceding paragraphs.

Article 25 Exchange of information

(1) The competent authorities of the States shall exchange such information as is necessary for carrying out the provisions of this Convention or of the domestic laws of the States concerning taxes covered by the Convention insofar as the taxation thereunder is not contrary to the Convention. Any information received by one of the States shall be treated as secret in the same manner as information obtained under the domestic laws of that State and shall be disclosed only to persons or authorities (including courts and administrative bodies) involved in the assessment or collection of, the enforcement or prosecution in respect of, or the determination of appeals in relation to, the taxes covered by the Convention. Such persons or authorities shall use the information only for such purposes. They may disclose the information in public court proceedings or in judicial decisions.

(2) In no case shall the provisions of paragraph (1) of this Article be construed so as to impose on one of the States the obligation:

(a) to carry out administrative measures at variance with the laws or administrative practice of that or of the other State;

(b) to supply information which is not obtainable under the laws or in the normal course of the administration of that or of the other State;

(c) to supply information which would disclose any trade, business, industrial, commercial or professional secret or trade process, or information, the disclosure of which would be contrary to public policy (*ordre public*).

Article 29 Entry into force

Note: Article 29 provided for the entry into force of this Convention. It takes effect from 6 April 1981.

Official languages: The Netherlands language text and the English language text of this Convention are equally authoritative.

NETHERLANDS

Capital taxes

Convention of 11 December 1979 (SI 1980 No 706)

Article 1 Scope

(1) This Convention shall apply:
- (a) to estates of and gifts made by persons domiciled in one or both of the States, at their death or at the time of the gift, as the case may be;
- (b) to property comprised in settlements made by persons domiciled in either State at the time when the settlement was made.

Article 2 Taxes covered

(1) The taxes which are the subject of this Convention are:
- (a) in the United Kingdom, the capital transfer tax (hereinafter referred to as "United Kingdom tax");
- (b) in the Netherlands, the succession duty (*het recht van successie*), the gift duty (*het recht van schenking*) and the transfer duty (*het recht van overgang*) (hereinafter referred to as "Netherlands tax").

(2) This Convention shall apply also to any identical similar taxes which are imposed after the date of signature of the Convention in addition to, or in place of, the existing taxes. The competent authorities of the States shall notify each other of any substantial changes which have been made in their respective taxation laws.

Inheritance tax: United Kingdom capital transfer tax is known as inheritance tax by virtue of FA 1986, s 100.

Article 3 General definitions

(1) In this Convention, unless the context otherwise requires:
- (a) the term "United Kingdom" means Great Britain and Northern Ireland;
- (b) the term "the Netherlands" means the part of the Kingdom of the Netherlands that is situated in Europe;
- (c) the term "State" means the United Kingdom or the Netherlands as the context requires and the term "States" means the United Kingdom and the Netherlands;
- (d) the term "national" means:
  - (i) in relation to the United Kingdom, any citizen of the United Kingdom and

Colonies, or any British subject not possessing that citizenship or the citizenship of any other Commonwealth country or territory, provided in either case he had the right of abode in the United Kingdom at the time of the death or gift or any other material time;

    (ii) in relation to the Netherlands, any individual possessing the Netherlands nationality;

(e) the term "tax" means United Kingdom tax or Netherlands tax as the context requires:

(f) the term "person" includes an individual, a company and any other body of persons;

(g) the term "competent authority" means, in the case of the United Kingdom, the Commissioners of Inland Revenue or their authorised representative and, in the case of the Netherlands, the Minister of Finance or his authorised representative;

(h) the term "gift" means in the United Kingdom a transfer of value other than one made on death and the term "donor" shall be construed accordingly.

(2) As regards the application of the Convention by one of the States any term not defined therein shall, unless the context otherwise requires, have the meaning which it has under the law of that State concerning the taxes to which the Convention applies.

Article 4 Fiscal domicile

(1) For the purposes of this Convention, a person was domiciled:

(a) in the United Kingdom, if he was domiciled in the United Kingdom in accordance with its law or is treated as so domiciled for the purposes of a tax which is the subject of this Convention;

(b) in the Netherlands, if he was a resident of or is treated as a resident of the Netherlands for the purposes of a tax which is the subject of this Convention;

provided that a person shall not be deemed to be domiciled in one of the States if on the death or gift that State imposes tax only by reference to property situated in that State.

(2) Where by reason of the provisions of paragraph (1) of this Article an individual was domiciled in both States, then, subject to the provisions of paragraph (3) of this Article, his status shall be determined as follows:

(a) he shall be deemed to be domiciled in the State in which he had a permanent home available to him; if he had a permanent home available to him in both States, the domicile shall be deemed to be in the State with which his personal and economic relations were closer (centre of vital interests);

(b) if the State in which he had his centre of vital interests cannot be determined, or if he had not a permanent home available to him in either State, the domicile shall be deemed to be in the State in which he had an habitual abode;

(c) if he had an habitual abode in both States or in neither of them, the domicile shall be deemed to be in the State of which he was a national;

(d) if he was a national of both States or neither of them, the competent authorities of the States shall settle the question by mutual agreement.

(3) Notwithstanding the provisions of paragraph (2) of this Article, where by reason of the provisions of paragraph (1) of this Article an individual was at the time his domicile falls to be determined domiciled in both States and

(a) was at that time a national of one of the States but not of the other, and

(b) was resident in that other State but had been so resident for less than seven years out of the ten years immediately preceding that time, and

(c) did not intend to remain indefinitely in that other State,

then he shall be deemed to be domiciled at the time in the State of which he was a national.

For the purposes of this paragraph where that other State is the United Kingdom the question whether a person was resident there shall be determined as for income tax purposes, but without regard to any dwelling-house available to him in the United Kingdom for his use, and "years" shall be taken to mean income tax years of assessment ending with the year of assessment in which death or the making of a gift occurs.

Article 5 Immovable property

(1) (Taxation of immovable property).

(2) The term "immovable property" shall have the meaning which it has under the law of the State in which the property in question is situated. The term shall in any case include property accessory to immovable property, livestock and equipment used in agriculture and forestry, rights to which the provisions of general law respecting landed property apply, an interest in the proceeds of sale of land which is held on trust for sale, usufruct of immovable property and rights to variable or fixed payments as consideration for the working of, or the right to work, mineral deposits, sources and other natural resources; ships, boats, aircraft and debts secured by mortgage or otherwise shall not be regarded as immovable property.

(3) . . .

Article 7 Ships and aircraft

Ships and aircraft operated in international traffic and boats engaged in inland waterways transport, and movable property pertaining to the operation of such ships, aircraft and boats, may be taxed in the State in which the place of effective management of the enterprise is situated.

Article 10 Deductions

In determining the amount on which tax is to be computed, deductions shall be allowed in accordance with the law of the State in which the tax is imposed.

Article 11 Subsidiary taxing rights

(1) If the deceased or the donor was domiciled in one of the States at the time of the death or gift and was at that time a national of the other State and had been domiciled in that other State at any time within the ten years immediately preceding the death or gift, that other State may impose tax according to its domestic law.

(2) The United Kingdom may impose tax by reference to property comprised in a settlement unless at the time when the settlement was made the settlor was:

    (a) domiciled in the Netherlands; and

    (b) not a national of the United Kingdom who had been domiciled in the United Kingdom at any time within the immediately preceding ten years.

(3) If under the provisions of Article 8 any property would be taxable only in the Netherlands and the deceased or donor is either a national of the United Kingdom and not a national of the Netherlands or is treated for the purposes of Netherlands tax as a resident of the Netherlands under its unilateral 10-year rule, the United Kingdom may also impose tax, according to its law, by reference to such property, if the competent authority of the Netherlands notifies the competent authority of the United Kingdom that the Netherlands tax chargeable with respect to such property has not been paid (otherwise than as a result of a specific exemption, deduction, credit or allowance).

Article 12 Exemptions

(1) Where property other than community property passes from a deceased person who was domiciled in the Netherlands to his or her spouse, and that property may be taxed in the United Kingdom solely by reason of Articles 5, 6 or 7, and the spouse was not domiciled in the United Kingdom but the transfer would have been wholly exempt if the spouse had been so domiciled, the United Kingdom shall exempt the property from tax to the extent of not less than 50 per cent of the value transferred, calculated as a value on which no tax is payable and after taking account of all exemptions except those for transfers between spouses.

(2) Where property other than community property passes from a deceased person who was domiciled in the United Kingdom to his or her spouse and that property may be taxed in the Netherlands solely by reason of Articles 5, 6 or 7, the Netherlands shall exempt from tax

such property to the extent that 50 per cent of its value exceeds the amount of the personal exemption which under the law of the Netherlands is given to a surviving spouse. If however the deceased person was a resident of the Netherlands under its domestic law the preceding sentence shall apply only to the extent that it is shown that the tax so computed is not less than the tax which would have been imposed if the deceased person had been domiciled in the Netherlands for the purposes of this Convention.

(3) Paragraph (2) shall not apply if at the time of death the United Kingdom under its domestic law taxes property passing from a deceased person to his or her spouse, who has the same domicile as that of the deceased person, to the extent of more than 50 per cent of its value.

Article 13 Credit provisions

(1) Where one of the States imposes tax in connection with any event by reference to any property which the other State may tax in accordance with Articles 5, 6 or 7, the former State shall allow against so much of its tax (as otherwise computed) as is attributable to such property a credit (not exceeding the amount of tax so attributable) equal to so much of the tax imposed in the other State in connection with the same event as is attributable to such property.

(2) Subject to paragraph (3) of this Article, where both States impose tax in connection with any event by reference to any property not being property referred to in Articles 5, 6 or 7, the State which imposes tax by virtue of paragraph (1) of Article 11 shall allow against so much of its tax (as otherwise computed) as is attributable to such property a credit (not exceeding the amount of the tax so attributable) equal to so much of the tax imposed in the other State by virtue of Article 8 in connection with the same event as is attributable to such property.

(3) Where by virtue of paragraph (2) of Article 11 the United Kingdom imposes tax in connection with any event by reference to any property comprised in a settlement not being property referred to in Articles 5, 6 or 7, the United Kingdom shall allow against so much of its tax (as otherwise computed) as is attributable to such property a credit (not exceeding the amount of tax so attributable) equal to so much of the tax imposed in the Netherlands in connection with the same event as is attributable to such property.

(4) For the purposes of this Article,
   (a) the tax attributable to any property imposed in one of the States is tax as reduced by the amount of any credit allowed by that State in respect of tax attributable to that property imposed in a territory other than one of the States;
   (b) where tax is imposed on the death of a person by reason of a gift made within 3 years preceding the death, whether in consequence of the fact that the gift is deemed to be derived from his estate or otherwise with respect to that gift, that tax shall be treated as if it were imposed in connection with that gift;
   (c) tax is imposed in one of the States if it is chargeable under the law of that State and duly paid.

Article 14 Time limit

Any claim for a credit or for a repayment of tax founded on the provisions of this Convention shall be made within six years from the date of the event giving rise to a liability to tax or, where later, within one year from the last date on which tax for which credit is given is due.

Article 15 Non-discrimination

(1) The nationals of one of the States shall not be subjected in the other State to any taxation or any requirement connected therewith which is other or more burdensome than the taxation and connected requirements to which nationals of that other State in the same circumstances are or may be subjected.

(2) The taxation on a permanent establishment which an enterprise of one of the States has in the other State shall not be less favourably levied in that other State than the taxation levied on enterprises of that other State carrying on the same activities.

(3) Enterprises of one of the States, the capital of which is wholly or partly owned or controlled, directly or indirectly, by one or more residents of the other State, shall not be subjected in the first-mentioned State to any taxation or any requirement connected therewith which is other or more burdensome than the taxation and connected requirements to which other similar enterprises of that first-mentioned State are or may be subjected.

(4) Nothing contained in this Article shall be construed as obliging either State to grant to individuals not resident in that State any of the personal allowances, reliefs and reductions for tax purposes which are granted to individuals so resident.

Article 16 Mutual agreement procedure

(1) Where a person considers that the actions of one or both of the States result or will result for him in taxation not in accordance with the provisions of this Convention, he may, irrespective of the remedies provided by the domestic laws of those States, present his case to the competent authority of either State. The case must be presented within three years for the first notification of the action resulting in taxation not in accordance with the provisions of the Convention.

(2) The competent authority shall endeavour, if the objection appears to it to be justified and if it is not itself able to arrive at a satisfactory solution, to resolve the case by mutual agreement with the competent authority of the other State, with a view to the avoidance of taxation which is not in accordance with the provisions of the Convention.

(3) The competent authorities of the States shall endeavour to resolve by mutual agreement any difficulties or doubts arising as to the interpretation or application of the Convention.

(4) The competent authorities of the States may communicate with each other directly for the purpose of reaching an agreement in the sense of the preceding paragraphs.

Article 17 Exchange of information

(1) The competent authorities of the States shall exchange such information as is necessary for carrying out the provisions of this Convention or of the domestic laws of the States concerning taxes covered by the Convention in so far as the taxation thereunder is not contrary to the Convention. Any information received by one of the States shall be treated as secret in the same manner as information obtained under the domestic laws of that State and shall be disclosed only to persons or authorities (including courts and administrative bodies) involved in the assessment or collection of, the enforcement or prosecution in respect of, or the determination of appeals in relation to, the taxes covered by the Convention. Such persons or authorities shall use the information only for such purposes. They may disclose the information in public court proceedings or in judicial decisions.

(2) In no case shall the provisions of paragraph (1) of this Article be construed so as to impose on one of the States the obligation:

    (a) to carry out administrative measures at variance with the laws and administrative practice of that or of the other State;

    (b) to supply information which is not obtainable under the laws or in the normal course of the administration of that or of the other State;

    (c) to supply information which would disclose any trade, business, industrial, commercial or professional secret or trade process, or information, the disclosure of which would be contrary to public policy (ordre public).

Article 20 Entry into force

Note: This Convention applies in respect of property by reference to which there is a charge to tax which arises after 16 June 1980 (subject to transitional relief in respect of deaths occurring before 27 March 1981 where greater relief would have been afforded under the 1948 Convention).

Official languages: The Dutch language text and the English language text of this Convention are equally authoritative.

NETHERLANDS ANTILLES

Netherlands Convention of 31 October 1967 (SI 1968 No 577)

Printed as amended by the Extending Arrangement of 24 July 1970 (SI 1970 No 1949).

Article 1 Persons covered

This Convention shall apply to persons who are residents of one or both of the States.

Article 2 Taxes covered

(1) The taxes which are the subject of this Convention are:
  (a) In the United Kingdom of Great Britain and Northern Ireland:
      the income tax including surtax, the corporation tax and the capital gains tax
      (hereinafter referred to as "United Kingdom tax").
  (b) In the Netherlands Antilles:
      the income tax (*inkomstenbelasting*), the profits tax (*winstbelasting*) and the sur-
      taxes on the income and profits taxes
      (hereinafter referred to as "Netherlands Antilles tax").

(2) This Convention shall also apply to any identical or substantially similar future taxes which are imposed in addition to, or in place of, the existing taxes by either State. The taxation authorities of the States shall notify to each other any substantial changes which have been made in their taxation laws.

Article 3 General definitions

(1) In this Convention, unless the context otherwise requires—
  (a) the term "United Kingdom" means Great Britian and Northern Ireland, including any area outside the territorial sea of the United Kingdom which in accordance with international law has been or may hereafter be designated, under the laws of the United Kingdom concerning the Continental Shelf, as an area within which the rights of the United Kingdom with respect to the sea-bed and sub-soil and their natural resources may be exercised;
  (b) the term "Netherlands Antilles" means the part of the Kingdom of the Netherlands that is situated in the Caribbean area and consisting of the islands Aruba, Bonaire, Curaçao, Saba, St. Eustatius and St. Martin (Dutch part) and the part of the sea bed and its sub-soil under the Caribbean Sea over which the Kingdom of the Netherlands has sovereign rights in accordance with international law;
  (c) the term "State" means the United Kingdom or the Netherlands Antilles, as the context requires; the term "States" means the United Kingdom and the Netherlands Antilles;

209

(*d*) the term "person" comprises an individual, a company and any other body of persons;

(*e*) the term "company" means any body corporate or any entity which is treated as a body corporate for tax purposes;

(*f*) the term "enterprise of one of the States" and "enterprise of the other State" mean respectively an enterprise carried on by a resident of one of the States and an enterprise carried on by a resident of the other State;

(*g*) the term "taxation authorities" means, in the case of the United Kingdom, the Commissioners of Inland Revenue or their authorised representative; in the case of the Netherlands Antilles the Minister of Finance (*de Minister van Financiën*) or his authorised representative;

(*h*) the term "tax" means United Kingdom tax or Netherlands Antilles tax as the context requires;

(*i*) the term "international traffic" includes any voyage of a ship or aircraft other than a voyage solely between places in the State which is not the State of which the person deriving the profits from the operation of the ship or aircraft is a resident.

(2) As regards the application of the Convention by one of the States any term not otherwise defined shall, unless the context otherwise requires, have the meaning which it has under the laws of that State relating to the taxes which are the subject of the Convention.

Article 4 Residence

(1) For the purposes of this Convention, the term "resident of one of the States" means any person who, under the law of that State, is liable to taxation therein by reason of his domicile, residence, place of management or any other criterion of a similar nature but the term does not include any person who is liable to tax in that State only if he derives income from sources therein. The terms "resident of the United Kingdom" and "resident of the Netherlands Antilles" shall be construed accordingly.

(2) Where by reason of the provisions of paragraph (1) an individual is a resident of both States, then his status shall be determined in accordance with the following rules:

(*a*) he shall be deemed to be a resident of the State in which he has a permanent home available to him. If he has a permanent home available to him in both States, he shall be deemed to be a resident of the State with which his personal and economic relations are closest (centre of vital interests);

(*b*) if the State in which he has his centre of vital interests cannot be determined, or if he has not a permanent home available to him in either State, he shall be deemed to be a resident of the State in which he has an habitual abode;

(*c*) if he has an habitual abode in both States or in neither of them, he shall be deemed to be a resident of the State of which he is a national;

(*d*) if he is a national of both States or of neither of them, the taxation authorities of the States shall settle the question by mutual agreement.

(3) Where by reason of the provisions of paragraph (1) a person other than an individual is a resident of both States, then it shall be deemed to be a resident of the State in which its place of effective management is situated.

Article 7 Immovable property

(1) (Taxation of income from immovable property.)

(2) (*a*) The term "immovable property" shall, subject to sub-paragraph (*b*) below, be defined in accordance with the law of the State in which the property in question is situated.

(*b*) The term "immovable property" shall in any case include property accessory to immovable property, livestock and equipment used in agriculture and forestry, rights to which the provisions of general law respecting landed property apply, usufruct of immovable property and rights to variable or fixed payments as consideration for the working of, or the right to work, mineral deposits, sources and other natural resources; ships, boats and aircraft shall not be regarded as immovable property.

(3) . . .

(4) . . .

Article 9 Shipping and air transport

Profits which a resident of one of the States derives from the operation of ships or aircraft in international traffic shall be taxable only in that State.

Article 15 Capital gains

(1) (Taxation of gains from alienation of business property.)

(2) Notwithstanding paragraph (1) of this Article, gains derived by a resident of one of the States from the alienation of ships and aircraft operated in international traffic and movable property pertaining to the operation of such ships and aircraft shall be taxable only in that State.

(3) . . .

(4) . . .

Article 24 Capital

(1) . . .

(2) (Taxation of capital represented by movable property.)

(3) Notwithstanding paragraph (2) of this Article, ships and aircraft operated in international traffic and immovable property pertaining to the operation of such ships and aircraft shall be taxable only in the State of which the operator is a resident.

(4) . . .

Article 27 Non-discrimination

(1) The nationals of one of the States shall not be subjected in the other State to any taxation or any requirement connected therewith which is other or more burdensome than the taxation and connected requirements to which nationals of that other State in the same circumstances are or may be subjected.

(2) The term "national" means:

(*a*) in relation to the United Kingdom:

(i) all British subjects deriving their status as such from connection with the United Kingdom and all British subjects and British protected persons residing in the United Kingdom;

(ii) all legal persons, partnerships, associations and other entities deriving their status as such from the law of the United Kingdom;

(*b*) in relation to the Netherlands Antilles:

(i) all individuals possessing the Netherlands nationality;

(ii) all legal persons, partnerships, associations and other entities deriving their status as such from the law in force in the Netherlands Antilles.

(3) The taxation on a permanent establishment which an enterprise of one of the states has in the other State shall not be less favourably levied in that other State than the taxation levied on enterprises of that other State carrying on the same activities.

Nothing contained in this paragraph shall be construed as obliging either State to grant to individuals not resident in that State any of the personal allowances and reliefs for tax purposes which are granted to individuals so resident, nor as conferring any exemption from tax in a State in respect of dividends paid to a company which is a resident of the other State.

(4) Enterprises of one of the States, the capital of which is wholly or partly owned or controlled, directly or indirectly, by one or more residents of the other State, shall not be subjected in the first-mentioned State to any taxation or any requirement connected therewith

which is other or more burdensome than the taxation and connected requirements to which other similar enterprises of that first-mentioned State are or may be subjected.

(5) In determining for the purposes of United Kingdom tax whether a company is a close company, the term "recognized stock exchange" shall include any stock exchange in the Netherlands Antilles which is a stock exchange within the meaning of the Netherlands Antilles law relating to stock exchanges.

(6) In this Article the term "taxation" means taxes of every kind and description.

Article 28 Mutual agreement

(1) Where a resident of one of the States considers that the actions of one or both of the States result or will result for him in taxation not in accordance with this Convention, he may, notwithstanding the remedies provided by the national laws of those States, present his case to the taxation authority of the State of which he is a resident or a national.

(2) The taxation authority shall endeavour, if the objection appears to it to be justified and if it is not itself able to arrive at an appropriate solution, to resolve the case by mutual agreement with the taxation authority of the other state, with a view to the avoidance of taxation not in accordance with the Convention.

(3) The taxation authorities of the States shall endeavour to resolve by mutual agreement any difficulties or doubts arising as to the interpretation or application of the Convention. . . .

Article 29 Exchange of information

(1) The taxation authorities of the States shall exchange such information (being information which such authorities have at their disposal) as is necessary for carrying out the provisions of this Convention or for the prevention of fraud or for the administration of statutory provisions against legal avoidance in relation to the taxes which are the subject of the Convention. Any information so exchanged shall be treated as secret and shall not be disclosed to any persons other than persons (including a Court or administrative body) concerned with the assessment or collection of, or prosecution in respect of, or the determination of appeals in relation to, the taxes which are the subject of the Convention.

(2) In no case shall the provisions of paragraph (1) be construed so as to impose on the taxation authority of either State the obligation:

(a) to carry out administrative measures at variance with the laws or administrative practice prevailing in that or the other State;

(b) to supply particulars which are not obtainable under the laws or in the normal course of the administration in that or the other State; or

(c) to supply information which would disclose any trade, business, industrial, commercial or professional secret or trade process, or information the disclosure of which would be contrary to public policy in that or the other State.

SI 1970 No 1949 Sch (3), (4) Entry into force

Note: Paragraphs (3) and (4) provided for the entry into force of the 1968 Convention as extended by the 1970 Arrangement. It takes effect in the UK from the year of assessment 1970–71 (income tax and capital gains tax) and from the financial year beginning on 1 April 1970 (corporation tax).

Official languages: The Netherlands language text and the English language text of this Convention are equally authoritative.

NEW ZEALAND

Convention of 4 August 1983 (SI 1984 No 365)

Article 1 Personal scope

This Convention shall apply to persons who are residents of one or both of the Contracting States.

Article 2 Taxes covered

(1) The taxes which are the subject of this Convention are:
    (*a*) in the United Kingdom:
        (i) the income tax;
        (ii) the corporation tax;
        (iii) the capital gains tax; and
        (iv) the petroleum revenue tax;
        (hereinafter referred to as "United Kingdom tax");
    (*b*) in New Zealand:
        (i) the income tax; and
        (ii) the excess retention tax;
        (hereinafter referred to as "New Zealand tax").

(2) Notwithstanding the provisions of paragraph (1) of this Article, the terms "United Kingdom tax" and "New Zealand tax" do not include any amount which represents a penalty or interest imposed under the law of either Contracting State relating to the taxes to which this Convention applies.

(3) This Convention shall also apply to any identical or substantially similar taxes which are imposed by either Contracting State after the date of signature of this Convention in addition to, or in place of, the existing taxes. The competent authorities of the Contracting States shall notify each other of any significant changes which are made in their respective taxation laws.

Article 3 General definitions

(1) In this Convention, unless the context otherwise requires:
    (*a*) the term "United Kingdom" means Great Britain and Northern Ireland, including any area outside the territorial sea of the United Kingdom which in accordance with international law has been or may hereafter be designated, under the laws of the United Kingdom concerning the Continental Shelf, as an area within which the rights of the United Kingdom with respect to the sea-bed and sub-soil and their natural resources may be exercised;
    (*b*) the term "New Zealand" means the territory of New Zealand but does not include Tokelau or the Associated Self Governing States of the Cook Islands and Niue; it also includes any area beyond the territorial sea which by New Zealand

legislation and in accordance with international law has been, or may hereafter be, designated as an area in which the rights of New Zealand with respect to natural resources may be exercised;

(c) the term "national" means:

    (i) in relation to the United Kingdom, any individual who has under the law of the United Kingdom the status of United Kingdom national provided he has the right of abode in the United Kingdom, and any legal person or other entity deriving its status as such from the law in force in the United Kingdom;

    (ii) in relation to New Zealand, any individual who is a New Zealand citizen and any legal person or other entity deriving its status as such from the law in force in New Zealand;

(d) the terms "a Contracting State" and "the other Contracting State" mean, as the context requires, the United Kingdom or New Zealand;

(e) the term "person" includes an individual, a company and any other body of persons;

(f) the term "company" means any body corporate or any entity which is treated as a body corporate for tax purposes;

(g) the terms "enterprise of a Contracting State" and "enterprise of the other Contracting State" mean respectively an enterprise carried on by a resident of a Contracting State and an enterprise carried on by a resident of the other Contracting State;

(h) the term "international traffic" means any transport by a ship or aircraft operated by an enterprise of a Contracting State, except when such transport is solely between places in the other Contracting State;

(i) the term "competent authority" means, in the case of the United Kingdom, the Commissioners of Inland Revenue or their authorised representative, and in the case of New Zealand, the Commissioner of Inland Revenue or his authorised representative.

(2) As regards the application of this Convention by a Contracting State any term not defined herein shall, unless the context otherwise requires, have the meaning which it has under the laws of that State relating to the taxes to which the Convention applies.

Article 4 Residence

(1) For the purposes of this Convention the term "resident of a Contracting State" means, as the context requires:

    (a) any person who is resident in the United Kingdom for the purposes of United Kingdom tax; or

    (b) any person who is resident in New Zealand for the purposes of New Zealand tax.

(2) Where by reason of the provisions of paragraph (1) of this Article an individual is a resident of both Contracting States, then his status shall be determined in accordance with the following rules:

    (a) he shall be deemed to be a resident of the State in which he has a permanent home available to him; if he has a permanent home available to him in both States, he shall be deemed to be a resident of the State with which his personal and economic relations are closer (centre of vital interests);

    (b) if the State in which he has his centre of vital interests cannot be determined, or if he has not a permanent home available to him in either State, he shall be deemed to be a resident of the State in which he has an habitual abode;

    (c) if he has an habitual abode in both States or in neither of them, he shall be deemed to be a resident of the State of which he is a national;

    (d) if he is a national of both States or of neither of them, the competent authorities of the Contracting States shall settle the question by mutual agreement.

(3) Where by reason of the provisions of paragraph (1) of this Article a person other than an individual is a resident of both Contracting States, then it shall be deemed to be a resident of the State in which its place of effective management is situated.

Article 7 Income from immovable property

(1) (Taxation of income from immovable property.)

(2) The term "immovable property" shall have the meaning which it has under the law of the Contracting State in which the property in question is situated. The term shall in any case include property accessory to immovable property, livestock and equipment used in agriculture and forestry, rights to which the provisions of general law respecting landed property apply, usufruct of immovable property and rights to variable or fixed payments as consideration for the working of, or the right to work, mineral deposits, sources and other natural resources; ships, boats and aircraft shall not be regarded as immovable property.

(3) . . .

(4) . . .

Article 9 Shipping and air transport

(1) Profits of an enterprise of a Contracting State from the operation of ships or aircraft in international traffic shall be taxable only in that State.

(2) Where profits referred to in paragraph (1) of this Article are derived by an enterprise of a Contracting State from participation in a pool, a joint business or an international operating agency, the profits attributable to that enterprise shall be taxable only in that State.

(3) Profits of an enterprise of a Contracting State referred to in paragraphs (1) and (2) of this Article from the rental of ships or aircraft or from the use, maintenance, or rental of containers (including trailers, barges, and related equipment for the transport of containers) shall be taxable only in that State to the extent that those ships, aircraft or containers are used in international traffic and such profits are incidental to the profits of the enterprise.

Article 23 Non-discrimination

(1) Nationals of a Contracting State shall not be subjected in the other Contracting State to any taxation or any requirement connected therewith which is other or more burdensome than the taxation and connected requirements to which nationals of that other State in the same circumstances are or may be subjected.

(2) The taxation on a permanent establishment which an enterprise of a Contracting State has in the other Contracting State shall not be less favourably levied in that other State than the taxation levied on enterprises of that other State carrying on the same activities: provided that this paragraph shall not prevent a Contracting State from imposing on the profits attributable to a permanent establishment in that State of a company which is a resident of the other Contracting State a tax not exceeding 5 per cent of those profits in addition to the tax which would be chargeable on those profits if they were the profits of a company which was a resident of the first-mentioned State.

(3) Enterprises of a Contracting State, the capital of which is wholly or partly owned or controlled, directly or indirectly, by one or more residents of the other Contracting State, shall not be subjected in the first-mentioned State to any taxation or any requirement connected therewith which is other or more burdensome than the taxation and connected requirements to which enterprises of the first-mentioned State carrying on the same activities, the capital of which is owned or controlled by residents of the first-mentioned State, are or may be subjected.

(4) Except where the provisions of Article 10, paragraph (8) of Article 12, or paragraph (6) of Article 13, apply, interest, royalties and other disbursements paid by an enterprise of a Contracting State to a resident of the other Contracting State shall, for the purpose of determining the taxable profits of such enterprise, be deductible under the same conditions as if they had been paid to a resident of the first-mentioned State.

(5) Nothing contained in this Article shall be construed as obliging a Contracting State to grant to persons not resident in that State any exemption, relief, reduction or allowance for tax purposes which is granted to persons resident in that State.

(6) In this Article, the term "taxation" means the taxes to which this Convention applies.

Article 24 Mutual agreement procedure

(1) Where a resident of a Contracting State considers that the actions of one or both of the Contracting States result or will result for him in taxation not in accordance with the provisions of this Convention, he may, irrespective of the remedies provided by the domestic law of those States, present his case to the competent authority of the Contracting State of which he is a resident.

(2) The competent authority shall endeavour, if the objection appears to it be justified and if it is not itself able to arrive at a satisfactory solution, to resolve the case by mutual agreement with the competent authority of the other Contracting State, with a view to the avoidance of taxation which is not in accordance with the Convention.

(3) The competent authorities of the Contracting States shall endeavour to resolve by mutual agreement any difficulties or doubts arising as to the interpretation or application of the Convention.

(4) The competent authorities of the Contracting States may communicate with each other directly for the purpose of reaching an agreement in the sense of the preceding paragraphs.

Article 25 Exchange of information

(1) The competent authorities of the Contracting States shall exchange such information as is necessary for carrying out the provisions of this Convention or of the domestic laws of the Contracting States concerning taxes covered by the Convention insofar as the taxation thereunder is not contrary to the Convention. Any information received by a Contracting State shall be treated as secret and shall be disclosed only to persons or authorities (including courts and administrative bodies) involved in the assessment or collection of, the enforcement or prosecution in respect of, or the determination of appeals in relation to, the taxes covered by the Convention. Such persons or authorities shall use the information only for such purposes. They may disclose the information in public court proceedings or in judicial decisions.

(2) In no case shall the provisions of paragraph (1) of this Article be construed so as to impose on the competent authority of either Contracting State the obligation:

> (a) to carry out administrative measures at variance with laws and administrative practice prevailing in either Contracting State;
>
> (b) to supply information which is not obtainable under laws or in the normal course of the administration of either Contracting State;
>
> (c) to supply information which would disclose any trade, business, industrial, commercial or professional secret or trade process, or information the disclosure of which would be contrary to public policy.

Article 27 Entry into force

Note: Article 27 provided for the entry into force of this Convention. It takes effect in the UK from the year of assessment 1984–85 (income tax and capital gains tax) and from the financial year beginning on 1 April 1984 (corporation tax).

Official language: English.

NIGERIA

Agreement of 9 June 1987 (SI 1987 No 2057)

Article 1 Personal scope

This Agreement shall apply to persons who are residents of one or both of the Contracting States.

Article 2 Taxes covered

(1) The taxes which are the subject of this Agreement are:
  (a) in the United Kingdom:
     (i) the income tax;
     (ii) the corporation tax;
     (iii) the capital gains tax; and
     (iv) the petroleum revenue tax;
     (hereinafter referred to as "United Kingdom tax");
  (b) in Nigeria:
     (i) the personal income tax;
     (ii) the companies income tax;
     (iii) the capital gains tax; and
     (iv) the petroleum profits tax;
     (hereinafter referred to as "Nigeria tax").

(2) This Agreement shall also apply to any identical or substantially similar taxes which are imposed by either Contracting State after the date of signature of this Agreement in addition to, or in place of, the existing taxes. The competent authorities of the Contracting States shall notify each other of any substantial changes which have been made in their respective taxation laws.

Article 3 General definitions

(1) In this Agreement, unless the context otherwise requires:
  (a) the term "United Kingdom" means Great Britain and Northern Ireland, including any area outside the territorial sea of the United Kingdom which in accordance with international law has been or may hereafter be designated, under the laws of the United Kingdom concerning the Continental Shelf, as an area within which the rights of the United Kingdom with respect to the sea-bed and sub-soil and their natural resources may be exercised;
  (b) the term "Nigeria" means the Federal Republic of Nigeria, including any area outside the territorial waters of the Federal Republic of Nigeria which in accordance with international law has been or may hereafter be designated, under the laws of the Federal Republic of Nigeria concerning the Continental Shelf, as an area within which the rights of the Federal Republic of Nigeria with respect to the sea bed and sub-soil and their natural resources may be exercised;
  (c) the term "national" means:
     (i) in relation to the United Kingdom, any individual who has under the law in the United Kingdom the status of United Kingdom national, provided he has the right of abode in the United Kingdom; and any legal person, partnership, association or other entity deriving its status as such from the law in force in the United Kingdom;

217

(ii) in relation to Nigeria, any citizen of Nigeria and any legal person, partnership, association or other entity deriving its status as such from the law in force in Nigeria;

(*d*) the terms "a Contracting State" and "the other Contracting State" mean the United Kingdom or Nigeria as the context requires;

(*e*) the term "person" means an individual, a company or any other body of persons;

(*f*) the term "company" means any body corporate or any entity which is treated as a body corporate for tax purposes under the laws of a Contracting State;

(*g*) the terms "enterprise of a Contracting State" and "enterprise of the other Contracting State" mean respectively an enterprise carried on by a resident of a Contracting State and an enterprise carried on by a resident of the other Contracting State;

(*h*) the term "international traffic" means any transport by a ship or aircraft operated by an enterprise of a Contracting State, except when the ship or aircraft is operated solely between places in the other Contracting State;

(*i*) the term "competent authority" means, in the case of the United Kingdom, the Board of Inland Revenue or its authorised representative, and in the case of Nigeria, the Honourable Minister of Finance or his authorised representative.

(2) As regards the application of this Agreement by a Contracting State any term not defined shall, unless the context otherwise requires, have the meaning which it has under the laws of that Contracting State relating to the taxes which are the subject of this Agreement.

Article 4 Fiscal domicile

(1) For the purposes of this Agreement, the term "resident of a Contracting State" means any person who, under the laws of that State, is liable to tax therein by reason of his domicile, residence, place of incorporation, place of management or any other criterion of a similar nature.

(2) Where by reason of the provisions of paragraph (1) of this Article an individual is a resident of both Contracting States, then his status shall be determined in accordance with the following rules:

(*a*) he shall be deemed to be a resident of the State in which he has a permanent home available to him; if he has a permanent home available to him in both States, he shall be deemed to be a resident of the State with which his personal and economic relations are closer (centre of vital interests);

(*b*) if the State in which he has his centre of vital interests cannot be determined, or if he has not a permanent home available to him in either State, he shall be deemed to be a resident of the State in which he has an habitual abode;

(*c*) if he has an habitual abode in both States or in neither of them, he shall be deemed to be a resident of the State of which he is a national;

(*d*) if he is a national of both States or of neither of them, the competent authorities of the Contracting States shall settle the question by mutual agreement.

(3) Where by reason of the provisions of paragraph (1) of this Article a person other than an individual is a resident of both Contracting States, then the competent authorities of the Contracting States shall settle the question by mutual agreement.

Article 6 Income from immovable property

(1) (Taxation of income from immovable property.)

(2) The term "immovable property" shall have the meaning which it has under the law of the Contracting State in which the property in question is situated. The term shall in any case include property accessory to immovable property, livestock and equipment used in agriculture and forestry, rights to which the provisions of general law respecting landed property apply, usufruct of immovable property and rights to variable or fixed payments as consideration for the working of, or the right to work, mineral deposits, sources and other natural resources; ships and aircraft shall not be regarded as immovable property.

(3) . . .
(4) . . .

Article 8 Shipping and air transport

(1) A resident of a Contracting State shall be exempt from tax in the other Contracting State in respect of profits or gains derived from the operation of ships or aircraft in international traffic.

(2) The provisions of paragraph (1) of this Article shall also apply to profits derived from the participation in a pool, a joint business or an international operating agency.

Article 13 Capital gains

Except as provided in Article 8 of this Agreement (Shipping and air transport), each Contracting State may tax capital gains in accordance with the provision of its domestic law.

Article 23 Non-discrimination

(1) Nationals of a Contracting State shall not be subjected in the other Contracting State to any taxation or any requirement connected therewith which is other or more burdensome than the taxation and connected requirements to which nationals of that other State in the same circumstances are or may be subjected.

(2) The taxation on a permanent establishment which an enterprise of a Contracting State has in the other Contracting State shall not be less favourably levied in that other State than the taxation levied on enterprises of that other State carrying on the same activities.

(3) Enterprises of a Contracting State, the capital of which is wholly or partly owned or controlled, directly or indirectly, by one or more residents of the other Contracting State, shall not be subjected in the first-mentioned State to any taxation or any requirement connected therewith which is other or more burdensome than the taxation and connected requirements to which other similar enterprises of that first-mentioned State are or may be subjected.

(4) Nothing contained in this Article shall be construed as obliging either Contracting State to grant to individuals not resident in that State any of the personal allowances, reliefs and reductions for tax purposes, which are granted to individuals so resident.

(5) In this Article the term "taxation" means taxes of every kind and description.

Article 24 Mutual agreement procedure

(1) Where a resident of a Contracting State considers that the actions of one or both of the Contracting States result or will result for him in taxation not in accordance with this Agreement, he may, irrespective of the remedies provided by the domestic law of those States, present his case to the competent authority of the Contracting State of which he is a resident.

(2) The competent authority shall endeavour, if the objection appears to it to be justified and if it is not itself able to arrive at a satisfactory solution, to resolve the case by mutual agreement with the competent authority of the other Contracting State, with a view to the avoidance of taxation not in accordance with the Agreement.

(3) The competent authorities of the Contracting States shall endeavour to resolve by mutual agreement any difficulties or doubts arising as to the interpretation or application of the Agreement.

(4) The competent authorities of the Contracting States may communicate with each other directly for the purpose of reaching an agreement in the sense of the preceding paragraphs.

Article 25 Exchange of information

The competent authorities of the Contracting States shall exchange such information (being information which is at their disposal under their respective taxation laws in the normal course of administration) as is necessary for carrying out the provisions of this Agreement or for the prevention of fraud or for the administration of statutory provisions against legal avoidance in relation to the taxes which are the subject of this Agreement. Any information so exchanged shall be treated as secret and shall not be disclosed to any persons other than those (including a court or administrative body) concerned with the assessment, collection, enforcement or prosecution in respect of taxes which are the subject of this Agreement. No information shall be exchanged which would disclose any trade, business, industrial or professional secret or trade process.

Article 27 Entry into force

Each of the Contracting States shall notify to the other the completion of the procedures required by its law for the bringing into force of this Agreement. The Agreement shall enter into force thirty days after the date of the later of these notifications and shall thereupon have effect:

> (a) in the United Kingdom:
>> (i) in respect of income tax and capital gains tax, for any year of assessment beginning on or after 6 April in the calendar year next following that in which the Agreement enters into force;
>> (ii) in respect of corporation tax, for any financial year beginning on or after 1st April in the calendar year next following that in which the Agreement enters into force;
>> (iii) in respect of petroleum tax, for any chargeable period beginning on or after 1 January in the calendar year next following that in which the Agreement enters into force;
> (b) in Nigeria:
>> (i) in respect of withholding tax on income and taxes on capital gains derived by a non-resident, in relation to income and capital gains derived on or after 1 January in the calendar year next following that in which the Agreement enters into force;
>> (ii) in respect of other taxes, in relation to income of any basis period beginning on or after 1 January in the calendar year next following that in which the Agreement enters into force.

Note: This Agreement entered into force on 27 December 1987.
Official language: English.

NORWAY

Convention of 3 October 1985 (SI 1985 No 1998)

Article 1 Personal scope

This Convention shall apply to persons who are residents of one or both of the Contracting States.

Article 2 Taxes covered

(1) This Convention shall apply to taxes on income and on capital imposed on behalf of a Contracting State or its political subdivisions or local authorities, irrespective of the manner in which they are levied.

(2) There shall be regarded as taxes on income and on capital all taxes imposed on total income, on total capital, or on elements of income or of capital, including trades on gains from the alienation of movable or immovable property, taxes on the total amounts of wages or salaries paid by enterprises, as well as taxes on capital appreciation.

(3) The existing taxes to which the Convention shall apply are in particular:
- (a) in the United Kingdom of Great Britain and Northern Ireland:
    - (i) the income tax;
    - (ii) the corporation tax;
    - (iii) the capital gains tax;
    - (iv) the petroleum revenue tax; and
    - (v) the development land tax;
    - (hereinafter referred to as "United Kingdom tax");
- (b) in Norway:
    - (i) the national tax on income (*inntektsskatt til staten*);
    - (ii) the county municipal tax on income (*inntektsskatt til fylkeskommunen*);
    - (iii) the municipal tax on income (*inntektsskatt til kommunen*);
    - (iv) the national contributions to the Tax Equalisation Fund (*fellesskatt til Skattefordelingsfondet*);
    - (v) the national tax on capital (*formuesskatt til staten*);
    - (vi) the municipal tax on capital (*formuesskat til kommunen*);
    - (vii) the national tax relating to income and capital from the exploration for and the exploitation of submarine petroleum resources and activities and work relating thereto, including pipeline transport of petroleum produced (*skatt til staten vedrørende inntekt og formue i forbindelse med undersøkelse etter og utnyttelse av undersjøiske petroleumsforekomster og dertil knyttet virksomhet og arbeid, herunder rørledningstransport av utvunnet petroleum*);
    - (viii) the national dues on remuneration to non-resident artistes (*avgift til staten av honorarer som tilfaller kunstnere bosatt i utlandet*);
    - (ix) the seamen's tax (*sjømannsskatt*);
    - (hereinafter referred to as "Norwegian tax").

(4) This Convention shall also apply to any identical or substantially similar taxes which are imposed by either Contracting State after the date of signature of this Convention in addition to, or in place of, the existing taxes.

Article 3 General definitions

(1) In this Convention, unless the context otherwise requires:
- (a) the term "United Kingdom" means Great Britain and Northern Ireland, including any area outside the territorial sea of the United Kingdom which in accordance with international law has been or may hereafter be designated, under the laws of

the United Kingdom concerning the Continental Shelf, as an area within which the rights of the United Kingdom with respect to the sea-bed and sub-soil and their natural resources may be exercised;

(b) the term "Norway" means the Kingdom of Norway, including any area outside the territorial waters of the Kingdom of Norway where the Kingdom of Norway, according to Norwegian legislation and in accordance with international law, may exercise her right with respect to the sea-bed and sub-soil and their natural resources; the term does not comprise Svalbard, Jan Mayen and the Norwegian dependencies ("biland");

(c) the term "national" means:

   (i) in relation to the United Kingdom, any British citizen or any British subject not possessing the citizenship of any other Commonwealth country or territory, provided he has the right of abode in the United Kingdom; and any legal person, partnership, association or other entity deriving its status as such from the law in force in the United Kingdom;

   (ii) in relation to Norway all individuals possessing Norwegian nationality and all legal persons, partnerships and associations deriving their status as such from the law in force in Norway;

(d) the term "tax" means United Kingdom tax or Norwegian tax, as the context requires;

(e) the terms "a Contracting State" and "the other Contracting State" mean the United Kingdom or Norway, as the context requires;

(f) the term "person" comprises an individual, a company and any other body of persons;

(g) the term "company" means any body corporate or any entity which is treated as a body corporate for tax purposes;

(h) the terms "enterprise of a Contracting State" and "enterprise of the other Contracting State" mean respectively an enterprise carried on by a resident of a Contracting State and an enterprise carried on by a resident of the other Contracting State;

(i) the term "international traffic" means any transport by a ship or aircraft operated by an enterprise which has its place of effective management in a Contracting State, except when the ship or aircraft is operated solely between places in the other Contracting State;

(j) the term "political subdivision", in relation to the United Kingdom, includes Northern Ireland;

(k) the term "competent authority" means in the case of the United Kingdom the Commissioners of Inland Revenue or their authorised representative, and in the case of Norway the Minister of Finance and Customs or his authorised representative.

(2) As regards the application of the Convention by a Contracting State any term not defined therein shall, unless the context otherwise requires, have the meaning which it has under the law of that State concerning the taxes to which the Convention applies.

Article 6 Income from immovable property

(1) (Taxation of income from immovable property.)

(2) The term "immovable property" shall have the meaning which it has under the law of the Contracting State in which the property in question is situated. The term shall in any case include property accessory to immovable property, livestock and equipment used in agriculture and forestry, rights to which the provisions of general law respecting landed property apply, usufruct of immovable property and rights to variable or fixed payments as consideration for the working of, or the right to work, mineral deposits, sources and other natural resources; ships, boats and aircraft shall not be regarded as immovable property.

(3) . . .

(4) . . .

Article 8 Shipping and air transport

(1) Profits from the operation of ships or aircraft in international traffic shall be taxable only in the Contracting State in which the place of effective management of the enterprise is situated.

(2) If the place of effective management of a shipping enterprise is aboard a ship then it shall be deemed to be situated in the Contracting State in which the home harbour of the ship is situated, or, if there is no such home harbour, in the State of which the operator of the ship is a resident.

(3) Where profits within the meaning of paragraph (1) of this Article are derived by an enterprise from participation in a pool, a joint business or an international operating agency, the profits attributable to that enterprise shall be taxable only in the Contracting State in which the place of effective management of that enterprise is situated.

(4) Notwithstanding the provisions of Article 7 of this Convention profits of an enterprise of a Contracting State from the use, maintenance or rental of containers (including trailers and related equipment for the transport of containers) used for the transport of goods or merchandise shall be taxable only in the Contracting State in which the place of effective management of that enterprise is situated except insofar as those containers or trailers and related equipment are used for transport solely between places within the other Contracting State.

(5) Notwithstanding the preceding provisions of this Article, where ships or aircraft are operated in international traffic by a partnership which includes one or more partners resident in a Contracting State and one or more partners resident in the other Contracting State profits shall be taxable, in proportion to the share of the said partners, only in the State of which each such partner is a resident.

(6) With respect to profits derived by the Danish, Norwegian and Swedish air transport consortium, known as the Scandinavian Airlines System (SAS) the provisions of paragraphs (1) and (4) of this Article shall only apply to such part·of the profits as corresponds to the shareholding in the consortium held by Det Norske Luftfartselskap (DNL) the Norwegian partner of Scandinavian Airlines System (SAS).

Article 7: Taxation of business profits.
Offshore activities: See Article 23(9) in relation to offshore activities.

Article 13 Capital gains

(1) . . .

(2) . . .

(3) Gains from the alienation of ships or aircraft operated in international traffic, or movable property pertaining to the operation of such ships or aircraft shall be taxable only in the Contracting State in which the profits of the enterprise are taxable according to Article 8 of this Convention.

(4)–(6) . . .

Article 22 Capital

(1) . . .

(2) . . .

(3) Capital represented by ships and aircraft operated in international traffic, and by movable property pertaining to the operation of such ships and aircraft, shall be taxable only in the Contracting State in which the profits are taxable according to Article 8 of this Convention.

(4) . . .

(5) . . .

Article 23 Miscellaneous rules applicable to certain offshore activities

(1) The provisions of this Article shall apply notwithstanding any other provision of this Convention.

(2) In this Article the term "offshore activities" means activities which are carried on off-shore in connection with the exploration or exploitation of the seabed and subsoil and their natural resources situated in a Contracting State.

(3)–(8) . . .

(9) Profits derived by a resident of a Contracting State from the operation, in connection with offshore activities, of ships or aircraft which are in their existing state designed primarily for the purpose of transporting supplies or personnel, or of tugboats or anchor handling vessels, shall be taxable only in that State. However, the provisions of this paragraph shall not apply to profits derived during any period in which such a ship or aircraft is contracted to be used mainly for purposes other than to transport supplies or personnel to or between places where offshore activities are being carried on.

(10) . . .

(11) . . .

Article 28 Non-discrimination

(1) Nationals of a Contracting State shall not be subjected in the other Contracting State to any taxation or any requirement connected therewith, which is other or more burdensome than the taxation and connected requirements to which nationals of that other State in the same circumstances are or may be subjected.

(2) The taxation on a permanent establishment which an enterprise of a Contracting State has in the other Contracting State shall not be less favourably levied in that other State than the taxation levied on enterprises of that other State carrying on the same activities. This paragraph shall not be construed as preventing Norway from taxing the total profits attributable to a permanent establishment maintained in Norway by a company which is a resident of the United Kingdom at a rate at which the undistributed profits of a Norwegian company may be taxed. However, if a company which is a resident of the United Kingdom whose profits are wholly attributable to a permanent establishment in Norway makes allocations for reserve funds equivalent at least to those required in the case of Norwegian company law for Norwegian companies, the amount of tax shall not exceed the tax which would have been imposed on a Norwegian corporation wholly owned by shareholders who are residents of the United Kingdom and on those shareholders having regard to the limitations laid down in Norwegian tax and company legislation as to dividend distribution and deductibility of such distribution and to the provisions of this Convention.

(3) Nothing contained in this Article shall be construed as obliging either Contracting State to grant to individuals not resident in that State any of the personal allowances, reliefs and reductions for tax purposes which are granted to individuals so resident.

(4) The provisions of this Article shall not be construed as obliging Norway to grant to nationals of the United Kingdom, not being nationals of Norway, the exceptional tax relief which is accorded to Norwegian nationals and individuals born of parents having Norwegian nationality pursuant to Section 22 of Norwegian Taxation Act.

(5) Enterprises of a Contracting State, the capital of which is wholly or partly owned or controlled, directly or indirectly, by one or more residents of the other Contracting State, shall not be subjected in the first-mentioned State to any taxation or any requirement connected therewith which is other or more burdensome than the taxation and connected requirements to which other similar enterprises of the first-mentioned State are or may be subjected.

(6) The provisions of this Article shall apply to taxes of every kind and description.

Article 29 Mutual agreement procedure

(1) Where a person considers that the actions of one or both of the Contracting States result or will result for him in taxation not in accordance with the provisions of this Convention, he may, irrespective of the remedies provided by the domestic law of those States, present his case to the competent authority of the Contracting State of which he is a resident. The case must be presented within three years from the first notification of the action resulting in taxation not in accordance with the provisions of the Convention.

(2) The competent authority shall endeavour, if the objection appears to it to be justified and if it is not itself able to arrive at a satisfactory solution, to resolve the case by mutual agreement with the competent authority of the other Contracting State, with a view to the avoidance of taxation which is not in accordance with the Convention.

(3) The competent authorities of the Contracting States shall endeavour to resolve by mutual agreement any difficulties or doubts arising as to the interpretation or application of the Convention. They may also consult together to consider measures to counteract improper use of the provisions of the Convention.

(4) The competent authorities of the Contracting States may communicate with each other directly for the purpose of reaching an agreement in the sense of the preceding paragraphs.

Article 30 Exchange of information

(1) The competent authorities of the Contracting States shall exchange such information as is necessary for carrying out the provisions of this Convention or of the domestic laws of the Contracting State concerning taxes covered by the Convention insofar as the taxation thereunder is not contrary to the Convention. Any information received by a Contracting State shall be treated as secret in the same manner as information obtained under the domestic laws of that State and shall be disclosed only to persons or authorities (including courts and administrative bodies) involved in the assessment or collection of, the enforcement or prosecution in respect of, or the determination of appeals in relation to, the taxes covered by the Convention. Such persons or authorities shall use the information only for such purposes. They may disclose the information in public court proceedings or in judicial decisions.

(2) In no case shall the provision of paragraph (1) of this Article be construed so as to impose on a Contracting State the obligation:

    (*a*) to carry out administrative measures at variance with the laws and administrative practice of that or of the other Contracting State;

    (*b*) to supply information which is not obtainable under the laws or in the normal course of the administration of that or of the other Contracting State;

    (*c*) to supply information which would disclose any trade, business, industrial, commercial or professional secret or trade process, or information the disclosure of which would be contrary to public policy (*ordre public*).

Article 33 Entry into force

Note: Article 33 provided for the entry into force of this Convention. It takes effect in the UK from the year of assessment 1986–87 (income tax and capital gains tax) and from the financial year beginning on 1 April 1986 (corporation tax).

Official languages: The Norwegian language text and the English language text of this Convention are equally authoritative.

PAKISTAN

Convention of 24 November 1986 (SI 1987 No 2058)

PAKISTAN

Article 1 Personal scope

This Convention shall apply to persons who are residents of one or both of the Contracting States.

Article 2 Taxes covered

(1) The taxes which are the subject of this Convention are:
  (a) in the United Kingdom of Great Britain and Northern Ireland:
    (i) the income tax;
    (ii) the corporation tax;
    (iii) the capital gains tax;
    (hereinafter referred to as "United Kingdom tax");
  (b) in the Islamic Republic of Pakistan:
    (i) the income tax;
    (ii) the super tax;
    (iii) the surcharge;
    (hereinafter referred to as "Pakistan tax").

(2) This Convention shall also apply to any identical or substantially similar taxes which are imposed by either Contracting State after the date of signature of this Convention in addition to, or in place of, the taxes referred to in paragraph (1) of this Article. The competent authorities of the Contracting States shall notify each other of any substantial changes which are made in their respective taxation laws.

Article 3 General definitions

(1) For the purposes of this Convention, unless the context otherwise requires:
  (a) the term "United Kingdom" means Great Britain and Northern Ireland, including any area outside the territorial sea of the United Kingdom which in accordance with international law has been or may hereinafter be designated, under the laws of the United Kingdom concerning the Continental Shelf, as an area within which the rights of the United Kingdom with respect to the sea-bed and sub-soil and their natural resources may be exercised;
  (b) the term "Pakistan" used in the geographical sense means Pakistan as defined in the Constitution of the Islamic Republic of Pakistan and also includes any area outside the territorial waters of Pakistan which under the laws of Pakistan and international law is an area within which the rights of Pakistan with respect to the sea bed and sub-soil and their natural resources may be exercised;
  (c) the term "national" means:
    (i) in relation to the United Kingdom, any British citizen or any British subject not possessing the citizenship of any other Commonwealth country or territory, provided he has the right of abode in the United Kingdom; and any legal person, partnership, association or other entity deriving its status as such from the law in force in the United Kingdom;
    (ii) in relation to Pakistan, any individual possessing the nationality of Pakistan; and any legal person, partnership or association deriving its status as such from the law in force in Pakistan;

226

(*d*) the terms "a Contracting State" and "the other Contracting State" mean the United Kingdom or Pakistan, as the context requires;

(*e*) the term "person" means an individual, a company and any other body of persons;

(*f*) the term "company" means any body corporate or any entity which is treated as a body corporate for tax purposes;

(*g*) the terms "enterprise of a Contracting State" and "enterprise of the other Contracting State" mean respectively an enterprise carried on by a resident of a Contracting State and an enterprise carried on by a resident of the other Contracting State;

(*h*) the term "international traffic" means any transport by a ship or aircraft operated by an enterprise which has its place of effective management in a Contracting State, except when the ship or aircraft is operated solely between places in the other Contracting State;

(*i*) the term "competent authority" means, in the case of the United Kingdom, the Commissioners of Inland Revenue or their authorised representative, and, in the case of Pakistan, the Central Board of Revenue or its authorised representative.

(2) As regards the application of this Convention by a Contracting State any term not otherwise defined shall, unless the context otherwise requires, have the meaning which it has under the laws of that Contracting State relating to the taxes which are the subject of this Convention.

Article 4 Fiscal domicile

(1) For the purposes of this Convention, the term "resident of a Contracting State" means any person who, under the laws of that State, is liable to tax therein by reason of his domicile, residence, place of management or any other criterion of a similar nature.

(2) Where by reason of the provisions of paragraph (1) of this Article an individual is a resident of both Contracting States, then his status shall be determined in accordance with the following rules:

(*a*) he shall be deemed to be a resident of the Contracting State in which he has a permanent home available to him; if he has a permanent home available to him in both Contracting States, he shall be deemed to be a resident of the Contracting State with which his personal and economic relations are closer (centre of vital interests);

(*b*) if the Contracting State in which he has his centre of vital interests cannot be determined, or if he has no permanent home available to him in either Contracting State, he shall be deemed to be a resident of the Contracting State in which he has an habitual abode;

(*c*) if he has an habitual abode in both Contracting States or in neither of them, he shall be deemed to be a resident of the Contracting State of which he is a national;

(*d*) if he is a national of both Contracting States or of neither of them, the competent authorities of the Contracting States shall settle the question by mutual agreement.

(3) Where by reason of the provision of paragraph (1) of this Article a person other than an individual is a resident of both Contracting States, then it shall be deemed to be a resident of the State in which its place of effective management is situated.

Article 6 Income from immovable property

(1) (Taxation of income from immovable property.)

(2) The term "immovable property" shall have the meaning which it has under the law of the Contracting State in which the property in question is situated. The term shall in any case include property accessory to immovable property, livestock and equipment used in agriculture and forestry, rights to which the provisions of general law respecting landed property apply, usufruct of immovable property and rights to variable or fixed payments as consideration for the working of, or the right to work, mineral deposits, sources and other natural resources; ships, boats and aircraft shall not be regarded as immovable property.

(3) . . .
(4) . . .

Article 8 Shipping and air transport

(1) Profits from the operation of ships or aircraft in international traffic shall be taxable only in the Contracting State in which the place of effective management of the enterprise is situated.

(2) If the place of effective management of a shipping enterprise is aboard a ship, then it shall be deemed to be situated in the Contracting State in which the home harbour of the ship is situated, or, if there is no such home harbour, in the Contracting State of which the operator of the ship is a resident.

(3) The provisions of this Article shall also apply to profits derived from participation in a pool, a joint business or an international operating agency.

Article 14 Capital gains

(1) . . .

(2) Gains from the alienation of ships or aircraft operated in international traffic and any property, other than immovable property, pertaining to the operation of such ships or aircraft shall be taxable only in the Contracting State in which the place of effective management of the enterprise is situated.

Article 24 Non-discrimination

(1) Nationals of a Contracting State shall not be subjected in the other Contracting State to any taxation or any requirement connected therewith, which is other or more burdensome than the taxation and connected requirements to which nationals of that other State in the same circumstances are or may be subjected.

(2) The taxation on a permanent establishment which an enterprise of a Contracting State has in the other Contracting State shall not be less favourably levied in that other State than the taxation levied on enterprises of that other State carrying on the same activities.

(3) Except where the provisions of Article 9, paragraph (7) of Article 11, paragraph (6) of Article 12 or paragraph (6) of Article 13 of this Convention apply, interest, royalties and other disbursements paid by an enterprise of a Contracting State to a resident of the other Contracting State shall, for the purpose of determining the taxable profits of such enterprise, be deductible under the same conditions as if they had been paid to a resident of the first-mentioned State.

(4) Enterprises of a Contracting State, the capital of which is wholly or partly owned or controlled, directly or indirectly, by one or more residents of the other Contracting State, shall not be subject in the first-mentioned State to any taxation or any requirement connected therewith which is other or more burdensome than the taxation and connected requirements to which the similar enterprises of the first-mentioned State are or may be subjected.

(5) Nothing contained in this Article shall be construed:

(a) as obliging either Contracting State to grant to individuals not resident in that State any of the personal allowances, reliefs and reductions for tax purposes which are granted to individuals so resident; or

(b) as affecting the provisions of the Pakistan law providing for a higher allowance or rebate of super-tax to those companies which make the prescribed arrangements for the declaration and payment of dividends.

(6) In this Article the term "taxation" means the taxes to which this Convention applies.

Article 25 Mutual agreement procedure

(1) Where a resident of a Contracting State considers that the actions of one or both of the Contracting States result or will result for him in taxation not in accordance with the pro-

visions of this Convention, he may, irrespective of the remedies provided by the domestic law of those States, present his case to the competent authority of the Contracting State of which he is resident.

(2) The competent authority shall endeavour, if the objection appears to it to be justified and if it is not itself able to arrive at a satisfactory solution, to resolve the case by mutual agreement with the competent authority of the other Contracting State, with a view to the avoidance of taxation not in accordance with the Convention.

(3) The competent authorities of the Contracting States shall endeavour to resolve by mutual agreement any difficulties or doubts arising as to the interpretation or application of the Convention.

(4) The competent authorities of the Contracting States may communicate with each other directly for the purpose of reaching an agreement in the sense of the preceding paragraphs.

Article 26 Exchange of information

(1) The competent authorities of the Contracting States shall exchange such information as is necessary for carrying out the provisions of this Convention or for the prevention of fraud or the administration of statutory provisions against legal avoidance in relation to the taxes covered by this Convention insofar as the taxation thereunder is not contrary to this Convention. Any information received by a Contracting State shall be treated as secret and shall be disclosed only to persons or authorities (including courts and administrative bodies) involved in the assessment or collection of, the enforcement or prosecution in respect of, or the determination of appeals in relation to, the taxes covered by this Convention. Such persons or authorities shall use the information only for such purposes. They may disclose the information in public court proceedings or in judicial decisions.

(2) In no case shall the provisions of paragraph (1) of this Article be construed so as to impose on the competent authority of either Contracting State the obligation:

   (a) to carry out administrative measures at variance with the laws and administrative practice prevailing in either Contracting State;
   (b) to supply information which is not obtainable under the laws or in the normal course of the administration of either Contracting State;
   (c) to supply information which would disclose any trade, business, industrial, commercial or professional secret or trade process, or information the disclosure of which would be contrary to public policy (*ordre public*).

Article 28 Entry into force

(1) Each of the Contracting States shall notify to the other the completion of the procedures required by its law from the bringing into force of this Convention. This Convention shall enter into force on the date of the later of these notifications and shall thereupon have effect:

   (a) in relation to payments referred to in Article 13 of this Convention to amounts paid on or after 1 July 1985;
   (b) in relation to all other provisions of this Convention;
      (i) in the United Kingdom:
         (aa) in respect of income tax and capital gains tax, for any year of assessment beginning on or after 6 April in the calendar year next following that in which the Convention enters into force;
         (bb) in respect of corporation tax, for any financial year beginning on or after 1 April in the calendar year next following that in which the Convention enters into force;
      (ii) in Pakistan:
         for any year of assessment beginning on or after 1 July in the calendar year next following that in which the Convention enters into force.

(2) Subject to the provisions of paragraph (3) of this Article, the Agreement between the

Government of the United Kingdom of Great Britain and Northern Ireland and the Government of Pakistan for the Avoidance of Double Taxation and the Prevention of Fiscal Evasion with respect to Taxes on Income signed at London on 24 April 1961 (hereinafter referred to as "the 1961 Agreement") shall terminate and cease to be effective from the date upon which this Convention has effect in respect of the taxes to which this Convention applies in accordance with the provisions of paragraph (1) of this Article.

(3) Where any provision of the 1961 Agreement would have afforded any greater relief from tax than is due under this Convention, any such provision as aforesaid shall continue to have effect:

(a) in the United Kingdom, for any year of assessment or financial year; and

(b) in Pakistan, for any year of assessment;

beginning in either case before the entry into force of this Convention.

Note: This Convention entered into force on 8 December 1987.
Official language: English.

Capital taxes

Agreement of 8 June 1957 (SI 1957 No 1522)

Article I [Duties covered]

(1) The duties which are the subject of the present Agreement are—

(a) in the United Kingdom, the estate duty imposed in Great Britain, and

(b) in Pakistan, the estate duty imposed in Pakistan by or under the law of the Central Government.

(2) The present Agreement shall also apply to any other duties of a substantially similar character imposed by either Contracting Government subsequently to the date of signature of the present Agreement or by the Government of any territory to which the present Agreement is extended under Article IX or applies under Article X.

Inheritance tax: This Agreement covers United Kingdom capital transfer tax (now inheritance tax), by virtue of IHTA 1984, s 158(6), FA 1986, s 100.

Article II [General definitions]

(1) In the present Agreement, unless the context otherwise requires—

(a) the term "United Kingdom" means Great Britain and Northern Ireland;

(b) the term "Pakistan" means the Provinces of Pakistan and the Capital of the Federation;

(c) the term "Great Britain" means England, Wales and Scotland, and does not include the Channel Islands and the Isle of Man;

(d) the term "territory" when used in relation to one or the other Contracting Government means Great Britain or Pakistan, as the context requires;

(e) the term "duty" means the estate duty imposed in Great Britain or the estate duty imposed in Pakistan by the Central Government, as the context requires.

(2) For the purposes of the present Agreement, the question whether a deceased person was at the time of his death domiciled in any part of Great Britain or in any part of Pakistan shall be determined in accordance with the law in force in Great Britain and Pakistan respectively.

(3) In the application of the provisions of the present Agreement by either Contracting Government any term not otherwise defined shall, unless the context otherwise requires, have the meaning which it has under the law of that Contracting Government relating to the duties which are the subject of the present Agreement.

Article III [Situs]

(1) Where a person was at the time of his death domiciled in any part of the territory of one of the Contracting Governments, the situs of any property which for the purposes of duty passes or is deemed to pass on his death shall for the purposes of the imposition of duty and for the purposes of Article V and of credit to be allowed under Article VI be determined exclusively in accordance with the rules in Article IV.

(2) Paragraph (1) of this Article shall apply if, and only if, apart from the said Article IV—

(a) duty would be imposed on the property under the law of each of the Contracting Governments; or

(b) duty would be imposed on the property under the law of one of the Contracting Governments and would, but for some specific exemption, also be imposed thereon under the law of the other Contracting Government.

(3) Paragraph (1) of this Article shall not apply if by reason of its application duty would be imposed in the territory of one of the Contracting Governments on property on which, apart from the said paragraph, duty would not be imposed in that territory.

Article IV [Deemed location of property]

The rules referred to in paragraph (1) of Article III are—

(a)–(i) . . .

(j) Ships and aircraft and shares thereof shall be deemed to be situated at the place of registration of the ship or aircraft;

(k)–(o) . . .

Article V [General taxing rights]

(1) Where a person at the time of his death was domiciled in some part of Great Britain and was not domiciled in some part of Pakistan, duty shall not be imposed in Pakistan on any property which for the purposes of duty passes or is deemed to pass on his death unless that property—

(a) is situated in Pakistan, or

(b) is settled property of which the deceased was life tenant where the settlor was domiciled in some part of Pakistan at the date on which the settlement took effect, or

(c) passes under a devolution regulated by the law of some part of Pakistan;

and, in determining the amount or rate of duty payable in Pakistan, property not falling within sub-paragraph (a), (b) or (c) shall be disregarded.

(2) Where a person at the time of his death was domiciled in some part of Pakistan and was not domiciled in some part of Great Britain, duty shall not be imposed in Great Britain on any property which for the purposes of duty passes or is deemed to pass on his death unless that property—

(a) is situated in Great Britain, or

(b) passes under a disposition or devolution regulated by the law of some part of Great Britain;

and, in determining the amount or rate of duty payable in Great Britain, property not falling within sub-paragraph (a) or (b) shall be disregarded.

(3) In determining the amount on which duty is to be imposed, permitted deductions shall be allowed in accordance with the law in force in the territory in which the duty is imposed.

Article VI [Elimination of double taxation]

(1) Where one Contracting Government imposes duty on any property which is not situated in its territory but is situated in the territory of the other Contracting Government, the former Government shall allow against so much of its duty (as otherwise computed) as is attributable to that property a credit (not exceeding the amount of the duty so attributable) equal to so much of the duty imposed by the other Contracting Government as is attributable to such property.

(2) Where each Contracting Government imposes duty on any property which is situated—

(a) in the territories of both Governments, or

(b) outside those territories,

each Government shall allow against so much of its duty (as otherwise computed) as is attributable to that property a credit which bears the same proportion to the amount of its duty so attributable or to the amount of duty imposed by the other Contracting Government and attributable to the same property, whichever is less, as the former amount bears to the sum of both amounts.

(3) For the purposes of this Article, the amount of duty imposed by a Contracting Government and attributable to any property shall be ascertained after taking into account any credit, allowance or relief or any remission or reduction of duty, otherwise than in respect of duty payable in the territory of the other Contracting Government.

Article VII [Time limit]

(1) Any claim for a credit or for a refund of duty founded on the provisions of the present Agreement shall be made within six years from the date of the death of the deceased person in respect of whose estate the claim is made, or, in the case of a reversionary interest where payment of duty is deferred until the date on which the interest falls into possession, within six years from that date.

(2) Any such refund shall be made without payment of interest on the amount so refunded.

Article VIII [Exchange of information]

(1) The taxation authorities of the Contracting Government shall exchange such information (being information which is available under their respective taxation laws in the normal course of administration) as is necessary for carrying out the provisions of the present Agreement or for the prevention of fraud or for the administration of statutory provisions against legal avoidance in relation to the duties which are the subject of the present Agreement. Any information so exchanged shall be treated as secret and shall not be disclosed to any person other than those concerned with the assessment and collection of the duties which are the subject of the present Agreement. No information as aforesaid shall be exchanged which would disclose any trade, business, industrial or professional secret or trade process.

(2) The taxation authorities of the Contracting Governments may consult together as may be necessary, for the purpose of carrying out the provisions of the present Agreement and in particular the provisions of Articles III and IV.

(3) As used in this Article, the term "taxation authorities" means, in the case of Great Britain, the Commissioners of Inland Revenue or their authorised representative; in the case

of Pakistan, the Central Board of Revenue or their authorised representative; in the case of Northern Ireland, to which the present Agreement applies under Article X, the Minister of Finance or his authorised representative; and, in the case of any territory to which the present Agreement is extended under Article IX, the competent authority for the administration in such territory of the duties to which the present Agreement applies.

Article XI [Entry into force]

Note: This Agreement applies to the estates of persons dying after 23 September 1957 or, where the personal representatives so elect, to the estates of persons who died after 4 December 1951 and before 24 September 1957.

Official language: English.

PHILIPPINES

Convention of 10 June 1976 (SI 1978 No 184)

Article 1 Personal scope

(1) This Convention shall apply to persons who are residents of one or both of the Contracting States.

(2) However, nothing in this Convention shall prevent the Philippines from taxing its own citizens, who are not residents of the Philippines, in accordance with Philippine laws but the United Kingdom shall not be bound to give credit for such tax.

Article 2 Taxes covered

(1) The taxes which are the subject of this Convention are:
  (a) in the United Kingdom of Great Britain and Northern Ireland:
     (i) the income tax;
     (ii) the corporation tax; and
     (iii) the capital gains tax;
  (b) in the Philippines:
     the income tax imposed by the Government of the Republic of the Philippines except the tax on gross billings in respect of international carriers (Section 24, Paragraph (b), sub-paragraph (2), Internal Revenue Code).
(2) This Convention shall also apply to any identical or substantially similar taxes which

233

are imposed by either Contracting State after the date of signature of this Convention in addition to or in place of, the existing taxes. The Contracting States shall notify each other of the changes which have been made to their respective taxation laws.

Article 3 General definitions

(1) In this Convention, unless the context otherwise requires:

(a) the term "United Kingdom" means Great Britain and Northern Ireland, including any area outside the territorial sea of the United Kingdom which in accordance with international law has been or may hereafter be designated, under the laws of the United Kingdom concerning the Continental Shelf, as an area within which the rights of the United Kingdom with respect to the sea-bed and sub-soil and their natural resources may be exercised;

(b) the term "Philippines" means the national territory comprising the Republic of the Philippines;

(c) the term "national" means:

(i) in relation to the United Kingdom, any citizen of the United Kingdom and Colonies who derives his status as such from his connection with the United Kingdom and any legal person, association or other entity deriving its status as such from the law in force in the United Kingdom;

(ii) in relation to the Philippines, any citizen of the Philippines who derives his status as such and any legal person, association or other entity deriving its status as such from the law in force in the Philippines;

(d) the term "United Kingdom tax" means tax imposed by the United Kingdom being tax to which this Convention applies by virtue of the provisions of Article 2; the term "Philippine tax" means tax imposed by the Philippines being tax to which this Convention applies by virtue of the provisions of Article 2;

(e) the term "tax" means United Kingdom tax or Philippine tax, as the context requires;

(f) the terms "a Contracting State" and "the other Contracting State" mean the United Kingdom or the Philippines, as the context requires;

(g) the term "person" comprises an individual, a company and any other body of persons;

(h) the term "company" means any body corporate or any entity which is treated as a body corporate for tax purposes;

(i) the terms "enterprise of a Contracting State" and "enterprise of the other Contracting State" mean respectively an enterprise carried on by a resident of a Contracting State and an enterprise carried on by a resident of the other Contracting State;

(j) the term "competent authority" means, in the case of the United Kingdom the Commissioners of Inland Revenue or their authorised representative, and in the case of the Philippines the Secretary of Finance or his duly authorised representative.

(2) As regards the application of this Convention by a Contracting State any term not otherwise defined shall, unless the context otherwise requires, have the meaning which it has under the law of that Contracting State relating to the taxes which are the subject of this Convention.

(3) An enterprise of a Contracting State shall likewise be deemed to have a permanent establishment in the other Contracting State if:

(a) it carries on supervisory activities within that other Contracting State for more than 183 days in connection with a building site, or a construction or assembly project which is being undertaken, in that other Contracting State; or

(b) it furnishes services, including consultancy services, in that other Contracting State through its employees or other personnel (other than agents of an independent status within the meaning of paragraph (7) of this Article) for a period exceeding in the aggregate 183 days within any twelve-month period.

(4) The term "permanent establishment" shall not be deemed to include:

(*a*) the use of facilities solely for the purpose of storage, display or delivery of goods or merchandise belonging to the enterprise;

(*b*) the maintenance of a stock of goods or merchandise belonging to the enterprise solely for the purpose of storage, display or delivery;

(*c*) the maintenance of a stock of goods or merchandise belonging to the enterprise solely for the purpose of processing by another enterprise;

(*d*) the maintenance of a fixed place of business solely for the purpose of purchasing goods or merchandise, or for collecting information for the enterprise;

(*e*) the maintenance of a fixed place of business solely for the purpose of advertising, for the supply of information, for scientific research or for similar activities which have a preparatory or auxiliary character, for the enterprise.

(5) A person acting in a Contracting State on behalf of an enterprise of the other Contracting State—other than an agent of an independent status to whom the provisions of paragraph (7) of this Article apply—shall be deemed to be a permanent establishment in the first-mentioned State if:

(*a*) he has, and habitually exercises in that first-mentioned State, an authority to conclude contracts in the name of the enterprise, unless his activities are limited to the purchase of goods or merchandise for the enterprise; or

(*b*) he has no such authority but habitually maintains in that first-mentioned State a stock of goods or merchandise belonging to the enterprise from which he regularly delivers goods or merchandise on behalf of that enterprise.

(6) . . .

(7) An enterprise of a Contracting State shall not be deemed to have a permanent establishment in the other Contracting State merely because it carries on business in that other State through a broker, general commission agent or any other agent of an independent status, where such persons are acting in the ordinary course of their business. However, when the activities of such an agent are devoted wholly or almost wholly on behalf of that enterprise, he shall not be considered an agent of an independent status within the meaning of this paragraph.

(8) The fact that a company which is a resident of a Contracting State controls or is controlled by a company which is a resident of the other Contracting State, or which carries on business in that other State (whether through a permanent establishment or otherwise), shall not of itself constitute either company a permanent establishment of the other.

Article 4 Fiscal domicile

(1) For the purposes of this Convention, the term "resident of a Contracting State" means, subject to the provisions of paragraphs (2) and (3) of this Article, any person who, under the law of that State, is liable to taxation therein by reason of his domicile, residence, place of management or any other criterion of a similar nature; an individual who is a member of the diplomatic, consular or permanent mission of a Contracting State which is situated in the other Contracting State and who is subject to tax in that other State only if he derives income from sources therein, shall not be deemed to be a resident of that other State. The terms "resident of the United Kingdom" and "resident of the Philippines" shall be construed accordingly.

(2) Where by reason of the provisions of paragraph (1) of this Article an individual is a resident of both Contracting States, then his status shall be determined in accordance with the following rules:

(*a*) he shall be deemed to be a resident of the Contracting State in which he has a permanent home available to him. If he has a permanent home available to him in both Contracting States, he shall be deemed to be a resident of the Contracting State with which his personal and economic relations are closer (centre of vital interests);

(*b*) if the Contracting State in which he has his centre of vital interests cannot be determined, or if he has not a permanent home available to him in either Contracting

State, he shall be deemed to be a resident of the Contracting State in which he has an habitual abode;

(c) if he has an habitual abode in both Contracting States or in neither of them, he shall be deemed to be a resident of the Contracting State of which he is a national;

(d) if he is a national of both Contracting States or of neither of them, the competent authorities of the Contracting States shall settle the question by mutual agreement.

(3) Where by reason of the provisions of paragraph (1) of this Article a person other than an individual is a resident of both Contracting States, then it shall be deemed to be a resident of the Contracting State in which its place of effective management is situated.

Article 6 Income from immovable property

(1) (Taxation of income from immovable property.)

(2)(a) The term "immovable property" shall, subject to the provisions of sub-paragraph (b) below, be defined in accordance with the law of the Contracting State in which the property in question is situated.

(b) The term "immovable property" shall in any case include property accessory to immovable property, livestock and equipment used in agriculture and forestry, rights to which the provisions of general law respecting landed property apply, usufruct of immovable property and rights to variable or fixed payments as consideration for the working of, or right to work, mineral deposits, sources and other natural resources; ships, boats and aircraft shall not be regarded as immovable property.

(3) . . .

(4) . . .

Article 7 Business profits

(1) The profits of an enterprise of a Contracting State shall be taxable only in that State unless the enterprise carries on business in the other Contracting State through a permanent establishment situated therein. If the enterprise carries on business as aforesaid, the profits of the enterprise may be taxed in the other State but only so much of them as is directly or indirectly attributable to that permanent establishment.

(2) Subject to the provisions of paragraph (3) and (4) of this Article, where an enterprise of a Contracting State carries on business in the other Contracting State through a permanent establishment situated therein, shall in each Contracting State be attributed to that permanent establishment the profits which it might be expected to make if it were a distinct and separate enterprise engaged in the same or similar activities under the same or similar conditions and dealing at arm's length with the enterprise of which it is a permanent establishment.

(3) In the determination of the profits of a permanent establishment:

(a) there shall be allowed as deductions expenses of the enterprises which are incurred for the purposes of the permanent establishment, including executive and general administrative expenses insofar as they are reasonably connected to the permanent establishment, whether incurred in the State in which the permanent establishment is situated or elsewhere;

(b) there shall not be allowed any deduction for payments by that permanent establishment to the head office or any other part of the enterprise, by way of royalties, fees or other similar payments for the use of patents or other rights or by way of commission for specific services or for management or (except in the case of a banking enterprise) by way of interest on moneys lent to the permanent establishment, unless such payments reimburse expenses actually incurred by the enterprise.

(4) In determining the profits of a permanent establishment amounts receivable by the permanent establishment from the head office or any other part of the enterprise by way of royalties, fees or other similar payments in return for the use of patents or other rights, or by way of commission for specific services performed, or for management, or (except in the case of a banking enterprise) by way of interest on moneys lent to the head office or any other part

of the enterprise shall not be included in the receipts of the permanent establishment except insofar as they represent reimbursement of allowable expenses which it has actually incurred.

(5) No profits shall be attributed to a permanent establishment by reason of the mere purchase by that permanent establishment of goods or merchandise for the enterprise.

(6) For the purpose of the preceding paragraphs, the profits to be attributed to the permanent establishment shall be determined by the same method year by year, unless there is good and sufficient reason to the contrary.

(7) Where profits include terms which are dealt with separately in other Articles of this Convention, then the provisions of those Articles shall not be affected by the provisions of this Article.

Article 12 Gains from the alienation of property

(1) . . .

(2) (Taxation of gains from alienation of immovable business property.)

(3) Notwithstanding the provisions of paragraph (2) of this Article, capital gains derived by a resident of a Contracting State from the alienation of ships, and aircraft operated in international traffic and movable property pertaining to the operation of such ships and aircraft shall be taxable only in that Contracting State.

(4) . . .

(5) . . .

Article 22 Non-discrimination

(1) The nationals of a Contracting State shall not be subjected in the other Contracting State to any taxation or any requirement connected therewith which is other or more burdensome than the taxation and connected requirements to which nationals of that other State in the same circumstances are or may be subjected.

(2) The taxation on a permanent establishment which an enterprise of a Contracting State has in the other Contracting State shall not be less favourably levied in that other State than the taxation levied on enterprises of that other State carrying on the same activities.

(3) Enterprises of a Contracting State, the capital of which is wholly or partly owned or controlled, directly or indirectly, by one or more residents of the other Contracting State, shall not be subjected in the first-mentioned Contracting State to any taxation or any requirement connected therewith which is other or more burdensome than the taxation and connected requirements to which other similar enterprises of that first-mentioned State are or may be subjected.

(4) Nothing contained in this Article shall be construed as obliging either Contracting State to grant to individuals not resident in that State any of the personal allowances, reliefs and reductions for tax purposes which are granted to individuals so resident.

(5) In this Article, the term "Taxation" means taxes which are the subject of this Convention.

(6) Nothing in this Article shall be construed so as to prevent the Philippines from limiting to its nationals the enjoyment of tax incentives granted by law. However, such incentives which are available to nationals of any third State shall likewise be available to nationals of the United Kingdom.

Article 23 Mutual agreement procedure

(1) Where a resident of a Contracting State considers that the actions of one or both of the Contracting States result or will result for him in taxation not in accordance with this Convention, he may, notwithstanding the remedies provided by the national laws of those States, present his case in writing to the competent authority of the Contracting State of which he is a resident or, if his case comes under paragraph 1 of Article 22, to that of the Contracting State of which he is a national. This case must be presented within three years from the first notification of the action giving rise to taxation not in accordance with the Convention.

(2) The competent authority shall endeavour, if the objection appears to it to be justified and if it is not itself able to arrive at an appropriate solution, to resolve the case by mutual agreement with the competent authority of the other Contracting State, with a view to the avoidance of taxation not in accordance with the Convention.

(3) The competent authorities of the Contracting States shall endeavour to resolve by mutual agreement any difficulties or doubts arising as to the interpretation or application of the Convention.

(4) The competent authorities of the Contracting States may communicate with each other directly for the purpose of reaching an agreement in the sense of the preceding paragraphs.

Article 24 Exchange of information

(1) The competent authorities of the Contracting States shall exchange such information as is necessary for the carrying out of the provisions of this Convention and of the domestic laws of the Contracting States concerning taxes covered by this Convention, in particular, for the prevention of fraud or evasion of such taxes. Any information so exchanged shall be treated as secret, but may be disclosed to persons (including a court or administrative body) concerned with the assessment, collection, enforcement or prosecution in respect of the taxes which are the subject of the Convention.

(2) In no case shall the provisions of paragraph (1) be construed so as to impose on one of the Contracting States the obligations:

> (a) to carry out administrative measures at variance with the laws or the administrative practice of that or of the other Contracting State;
>
> (b) to supply particulars which are not obtainable under the laws or in the normal course of the administration of that or of the other Contracting State;
>
> (c) to supply information which would disclose any trade, business, industrial, commercial or professional secret or trade process, or information, the disclosure of which would be contrary to public policy.

Article 27 Entry into force

Note: Article 27 provides for the entry into force of this Convention. It takes effect in the UK from the year of assessment 1977–78 (income tax and capital gains tax) and from the financial year beginning on 1 April 1977 (corporation tax).

Official language: English.

POLAND

Convention of 16 December 1976 (SI 1978 No 282)

Article 1 Personal scope

This Convention shall apply to persons who are residents of one or both of the Contracting States.

Article 2 Taxes covered

(1) The taxes which are the subject of this Convention are:
- (a) in the United Kingdom of Great Britain and Northern Ireland:
  - (i) the income tax;
  - (ii) the corporation tax; and
  - (iii) the capital gains tax;
  - (hereinafter referred to as "United Kingdom tax");
- (b) in Poland:
  - (i) the income tax (*podatek dochodowy*);
  - (ii) the tax on wages or salaries (*podatek od wynagrodzen*); and
  - (iii) the surcharge on the income tax or on the tax on wages or salaries (*podatek wyrownawczy*);
  - (hereinafter referred to as "Polish tax").

(2) This Convention shall also apply to any identical or substantially similar taxes which are imposed by either Contracting State after the date of signature of this Convention in addition to, or in place of, the existing taxes. The competent authorities of the Contracting States shall notify to each other any substantial changes which have been made in their respective taxation laws.

Article 3 General definitions

(1) In this Convention, unless the context otherwise requires:
- (a) the term "United Kingdom" means Great Britain and Northern Ireland, including any area outside the territorial sea of the United Kingdom which in accordance with international law is an area within which the rights of the United Kingdom with respect to the sea-bed and sub-soil and their natural resources may be exercised;
- (b) the term "Poland" means the Polish People's Republic and includes any area outside the territorial sea of Poland which in accordance with international law is an area within which the rights of Poland with respect to the sea bed and sub-soil and their natural resources may be exercised;
- (c) the terms "a Contracting State" and "the other Contracting State" mean the United Kingdom, or Poland, as the context requires;
- (d) the term "person" comprises an individual, a company and any other body of persons;
- (e) the term "company" means any body corporate or any entity which is treated as a body corporate for tax purposes;
- (f) the terms "enterprise of a Contracting State" and "enterprise of the other Contracting State" mean respectively an enterprise carried on by a resident of a Contracting State and an enterprise carried on by a resident of the other Contracting State;
- (g) the term "competent authority" means, in the case of the United Kingdom the Commissioners of Inland Revenue or their authorised representative; and in the case of Poland the Minister of Finance or his authorised representative;
- (h) the term "national" means:
  - (i) in relation to the United Kingdom, any individual possessing the national

239

status of citizen under the law of the United Kingdom by virtue of his connection with the United Kingdom and any legal person, association or other entity deriving its status as such from the law in force in the United Kingdom;

(ii) in relation to Poland, any individual having the nationality of Poland and any legal person or association or other entity created under the law in force in Poland;

(*i*) the term "international traffic" means any transport by a ship or aircraft or a railway or road vehicle operated by an enterprise which has its place of effective management in a Contracting State, except when such transport is made solely between places in the other Contracting State;

(*j*) the term "tax" means United Kingdom tax or Polish tax, as the context requires.

(2) As regards the application of this Convention by a Contracting State any term not otherwise defined shall, unless the context otherwise requires, have the meaning which it has under the laws of that Contracting State relating to the taxes which are the subject of this Convention.

Article 4 Fiscal domicile

(1) For the purposes of this Convention, the term "resident of a Contracting State" means, subject to the provisions of paragraphs (2) and (3) of this Article, any person who, under the law of that State, is liable to taxation therein by reason of his domicile, residence, place of management or any other criterion of a similar nature; the term does not include any individual who is liable to tax in that Contracting State only if he derives income from sources therein. The terms "resident of the United Kingdom" and "resident of Poland" shall be construed accordingly.

(2) Where by reason of the provisions of paragraph (1) of this Article an individual is a resident of both Contracting States, then this case shall be determined in accordance with the following rules:

(*a*) he shall be deemed to be a resident of the Contracting State in which he has a permanent home available to him. If he has a permanent home available to him in both Contracting States, he shall be deemed to be a resident of the Contracting State with which his personal and economic relations are closer (centre of vital interests);

(*b*) if the Contracting State in which he has his centre of vital interests cannot be determined, or if he has not a permanent home available to him in either Contracting State, he shall be deemed to be a resident of the Contracting State in which he has an habitual abode;

(*c*) if he has an habitual abode in both Contracting States or if he has not an habitual abode in either Contracting State, he shall be deemed to be a resident of the Contracting State of which he is a national;

(*d*) if the question of residence cannot be determined according to the provisions of sub-paragraphs (*a*), (*b*) and (*c*) of this paragraph, the competent authorities of the Contracting States shall settle the question by mutual agreement.

(3) Where by reason of the provisions of paragraph (1) of this Article a person other than an individual is a resident of both Contracting States, then it shall be deemed to be a resident of the Contracting State in which its place of effective management is situated.

Article 6 Income from immovable property

(1) (Taxation of income from immovable property.)

(2) The term "immovable property" shall be defined in accordance with the law of the Contracting State in which the property is situated. The term shall in any case include property accessory to immovable property, livestock and equipment used in agriculture and forestry, rights to which the provisions of general law respecting landed property apply, usufruct of immovable property and rights to variable or fixed payments as consideration for the working of, or the right to work, mineral deposits, sources and other natural resources. Ships, boats and aircraft shall not be regarded as immovable property.

(3) . . .
(4) . . .

Article 8 International transport

(1) Profits from the operation of ships, aircraft, or railway and road vehicles in international traffic shall be taxable only in the Contracting State in which the place of effective management of the enterprise is situated.

(2) If the place of effective management of an enterprise carrying on shipping in international traffic is aboard a ship, then it shall be deemed to be situated in the Contracting State in which the home harbour of the ship is situated, or, if there is no such home harbour, in the Contracting State of which the operator is a resident.

(3) (*a*) For the purposes of this Article, profits from the operation of ships or aircraft in international traffic include profits derived from the rental on a bareboat basis of ships or aircraft operated in international traffic if such rental income is incidental to other income described in paragraph (1) of this Article.

    (*b*) Notwithstanding the provisions of Article 7 (Business profits), profits of an enterprise of a Contracting State from the use, maintenance or rental of containers (including trailers and related equipment for the transport of containers) used for the transport of goods or merchandise in international traffic shall be taxable only in that State.

(4) The provisions of this Article shall also apply to profits derived from the participation in a pool, a joint business or in an international operating agency.

Article 13 Capital gains

(1) . . .

(2) (Taxation of gains from alienation of movable business property.)

(3) Notwithstanding the provisions of paragraph (2) of this Article, capital gains derived by a resident of a Contracting State from the alienation of ships and aircraft operated in international traffic and movable property pertaining to the operation of such ships and aircraft shall be taxable only in that Contracting State.

(4) . . .

Article 24 Non-discrimination

(1) The nationals of a Contracting State shall not be subjected in the other Contracting State to any taxation or any requirement connected therewith which is other or more burdensome than the taxation and connected requirements to which nationals of that other State in the same circumstances are or may be subjected.

(2) The taxation on a permanent establishment which an enterprise of a Contracting State has in the other Contracting State shall not be less favourably levied in that other State than the taxation levied on enterprises of that other State carrying on the same activities.

(3) Enterprises of a Contracting State, the capital of which is wholly or partly owned or controlled, directly or indirectly, by one or more residents of the other Contracting State, shall not be subjected in the first-mentioned Contracting State to any taxation or any requirement connected therewith which is other or more burdensome than the taxation and connected requirements to which other similar enterprises of that first-mentioned State are or may be subjected.

(4) Nothing contained in this Article shall be construed as obliging either Contracting State to grant to individuals not resident in that State any of the personal allowances, reliefs and reductions for tax purposes which are granted to individuals so resident.

(5) In this Article the term "taxation" means taxes of every kind and description other than the Polish residence-registration fee (*Oplata Skarbowa za Zameldowanie*) and the Polish fee for a permit to open an enterprise (*Oplata Skarbowa za Zezwolenie*).

(6) The taxes on income and capital and payments from profits to the budget (*Wplaty z*

Zysku) which under Polish law are chargeable on Polish socialised enterprises (*Jednostki Gospodarki Uspolecznionej*) shall be chargeable only on such enterprises and shall not be treated as "taxation" for the purposes of this Article.

Article 25 Mutual agreement procedure

(1) Where a resident of a Contracting State considers that the actions of one or both of the Contracting States result or will result for him in taxation not in accordance with this Convention, he may, notwithstanding the remedies provided by the national laws of those States, present his case to the competent authority of the Contracting State of which he is a resident.

(2) The competent authority shall endeavour, if the objection appears to it to be justified and if it is not itself able to arrive at an appropriate solution, to resolve the case by mutual agreement with the competent authority of the other Contracting State, with a view to the avoidance of taxation not in accordance with the Convention.

(3) The competent authorities of the Contracting States shall endeavour to resolve by mutual agreement any difficulties or doubts arising as to the interpretation or application of the Convention.

(4) The competent authorities of the Contracting States may communicate with each other directly for the purpose of reaching an agreement in the sense of the preceding paragraphs.

Article 26 Exchange of information

(1) The competent authorities of the Contracting States shall exchange such information as is necessary for the carrying out of this Convention and of the domestic laws of the Contracting States concerning taxes covered by this Convention insofar as the taxation thereunder is in accordance with this Convention. Any information so exchanged shall be treated as secret and shall not be disclosed to any persons other than persons (including a Court or administrative body) concerned with the assessment or collection of, or prosecution in respect of, or the determination of appeals in relation to, the taxes which are the subject of the Convention.

(2) In no case shall the provisions of paragraph (1) of this Article be construed so as to impose on the competent authority of either Contracting State the obligation:

(*a*) to carry out administrative measures at variance with the laws or administrative practice of that or the other Contracting State;

(*b*) to supply particulars which are not obtainable under the laws or in the normal course of the administration of that or the other Contracting State;

(*c*) to supply information which would disclose any trade, business, industrial, commercial or professional secret or trade process, or information, the disclosure of which would be contrary to public policy (*ordre public*).

Article 28 Entry into force

Note: Article 28 provided for the entry into force of this Convention. It takes effect in the UK from the year of assessment 1975–76 (income tax and capital gains tax) and from the financial year beginning on 1 April 1975 (corporation tax).

Official languages: The Polish language text and the English language text of this Convention are equally authoritative.

PORTUGAL

Convention of 27 March 1968 (SI 1969 No 599)

Article 1 Persons covered

This Convention shall apply to persons who are residents of one or both of the Contracting States.

Article 2 Taxes covered

(1) The taxes which are the subject of this Convention are:—
    (*a*) In the United Kingdom of Great Britain and Northern Ireland:
        (i) the income tax (including surtax);
        (ii) the capital gains tax; and
        (iii) the corporation tax
        (hereinafter referred to as "United Kingdom tax").
    (*b*) In Portugal:
        (i) the property tax (*contribuição predial*);
        (ii) the agricultural tax (*imposto sobre a indústria agrícola*);
        (iii) the industrial tax (*contribuição industrial*);
        (iv) the tax on income from movable capital (*imposto de capitais*);
        (v) the professional tax (*imposto profissional*);
        (vi) the complementary tax (*imposto complementar*);
        (vii) the tax for overseas defence and development (*imposto para a defesa e valorização do Ultramar*);
        (viii) the tax on capital gains (*imposto de mais-valias*);
        (ix) any surcharges on the preceding taxes; and
        (x) other taxes charged by reference to the taxes referred to in heads (i) to (viii) for the benefit of local authorities and the corresponding surcharges
        (hereinafter referred to as "Portuguese tax").

(2) The Convention shall also apply to any identical or substantially similar future taxes which are imposed in addition to, or in place of, the existing taxes by either Contracting State.

Article 3 General definitions

(1) In this Convention, unless the context otherwise requires:
    (*a*) the term "United Kingdom" means Great Britain and Northern Ireland, including any area outside the territorial sea of the United Kingdom which, in accordance with international law, has been or may hereafter be designated, under the laws of

243

the United Kingdom concerning the Continental Shelf, as an area within which the rights of the United Kingdom with respect to the sea-bed and sub-soil and their natural resources may be exercised;

(b) the term "Portugal" means European Portugal comprising the continental territory and the archipelagoes of Azores and Madeira and includes any area outside the territorial sea of Portugal which, in accordance with international law, has been or may hereafter be designated, under the laws of Portugal concerning the Continental Shelf, as an area within which the rights of Portugal with respect to the sea-bed and sub-soil and their natural resources may be exercised;

(c) the terms "a Contracting State" and "the other Contracting State" mean the United Kingdom or Portugal as the context requires;

(d) the term "competent authority" means, in the case of the United Kingdom, the Commissioners of Inland Revenue or their authorized representative; in the case of Portugal, the Director-General of Taxation (*Director-Geral das Contribuições e Impostos*) or his authorized representative;

(e) the term "tax" means United Kingdom tax or Portuguese tax as the context requires;

(f) the term "person" comprises an individual, a company and any other body of persons;

(g) the term "company" means any body corporate or any entity which is treated as a body corporate for tax purposes;

(h) the terms "enterprise of a Contracting State" and "enterprise of the other Contracting State" mean respectively an enterprise carried on by a resident of a Contracting State and an enterprise carried on by a resident of the other Contracting State;

(i) the term "international traffic" includes any voyage of a ship or aircraft other than a voyage solely between places in the Contracting State which is not the Contracting State of which a person deriving the profits of the operation of a ship or aircraft is a resident.

(2) Where under the Convention a person is entitled to exemption or relief from tax in a Contracting State on certain income if (with or without further conditions) he is subject to tax in the other Contracting State in respect thereof and he is subject to tax there by reference to the amount of that income which is remitted to, or received in, that other Contracting State the amount of that income on which exemption or relief is to be allowed in the first-mentioned Contracting State shall be limited to the amount so remitted or received.

(3) As regards the application of the Convention by a Contracting State any term not otherwise defined shall, unless the context otherwise requires, have the meaning which it has under the laws of that Contracting State relating to the taxes which are the subject of the Convention.

Article 4 Residence

(1) For the purposes of this Convention, the term "resident of a Contracting State" means any person who, under the law of that State, is liable to taxation therein by reason of his domicile, residence, place of management or any other criterion of a similar nature, and the terms "resident of the United Kingdom" and "resident of Portugal" shall be construed accordingly.

(2) Where by reason of the provisions of paragraph (1) an individual is a resident of both Contracting States, then his status shall be determined in accordance with the following rules:

(a) he shall be deemed to be a resident of the Contracting State in which he has a permanent home available to him. If he has a permanent home available to him in both Contracting States, he shall be deemed to be a resident of the Contracting State with which his personal and economic relations are closest (centre of vital interests);

(b) if the Contracting State in which he has his centre of vital interests cannot be determined, or if he has not a permanent home available to him in either Contracting

State, he shall be deemed to be a resident of the Contracting State in which he has an habitual abode;

    (c) if he has an habitual abode in both Contracting States or in neither of them, he shall be deemed to be a resident of the Contracting State of which he is a national;

    (d) if he is a national of both Contracting States or of neither of them, the competent authorities of the Contracting States shall settle the question by mutual agreement.

(3) Where by reason of the provisions of paragraph (1) a person other than an individual is a resident of both Contracting States, then it shall be deemed to be a resident of the Contracting State in which its place of effective management is situated.

Article 6 Income from immovable property

(1) (Taxation of income from immovable property.)

(2) (a) The term "immovable property" shall, subject to sub-paragraph (b) below, be defined in accordance with the law of the Contracting State in which the property in question is situated.

    (b) The term "immovable property" shall in any case include property accessory to immovable property, livestock and equipment used in agriculture and forestry, rights to which the provisions of general law respecting landed property apply, usufruct of immovable property and rights to variable or fixed payments as consideration for the working of, or the right to work, mineral deposits, sources and other natural resources; ships and aircraft shall not be regarded as immovable property.

(3) . . .

(4) . . .

Article 8 Shipping and air transport

(1) Profits which a resident of a Contracting State derives from the operation of ships or aircraft in international traffic shall be taxable only in that Contracting State.

(2) The agreement between the Contracting States for the Avoidance of Double Taxation on Income derived from Sea and Air Transport, signed at Lisbon on 31st July, 1961, shall, in relation to any tax for any period for which the present Convention has effect as respects that tax, cease to have effect so far as it exempts from United Kingdom tax or Portuguese tax, profits derived from the operation of ships or aircraft by, respectively, Portuguese undertakings or United Kingdom undertakings as therein defined.

Article 13 Capital gains

(1) . . .

(2) (Taxation of gains from alienation of movable business property.)

(3) Notwithstanding paragraph (2) of this Article, gains from the alienation of ships and aircraft operated in international traffic and movable property pertaining to the operation of such ships and aircraft shall be taxable only in the Contracting State of which the alienator is a resident.

(4) . . .

Article 23 Non-discrimination

(1) The nationals of a Contracting State shall not be subjected in the other Contracting State to any taxation or any requirement connected therewith which is other or more burdensome than the taxation and connected requirements to which nationals of that other State in the same circumstances are or may be subjected.

(2) The term "nationals" means:

    (a) in relation to the United Kingdom:

        (i) all citizens of the United Kingdom and Colonies other than those citizens who derive their status as such from connection with any territory to which this Convention may be extended under Article 27 but has not been so extended;

(ii) all legal persons and associations deriving their status as such from the laws of the United Kingdom or any territory for whose international relations the United Kingdom is responsible to which this Convention is extended under Article 27;

(b) in relation to Portugal: all individuals possessing the nationality of Portugal and all legal persons and associations deriving their status as such from the laws of Portugal.

(3) The taxation on a permanent establishment which an enterprise of a Contracting State has in the other Contracting State shall not be less favourably levied in that other State than the taxation levied on enterprises of that other State carrying on the same activities.

(4) Enterprises of a Contracting state, the capital of which is wholly or partly owned or controlled, directly or indirectly, by one or more residents of the other Contracting State, shall not be subjected in the first-mentioned Contracting State to any taxation or any requirement connected therewith which is other or more burdensome than the taxation and connected requirements to which other similar enterprises of that first-mentioned State are or may be subjected.

Article 24 Mutual agreement

(1) Where a resident of a Contracting State considers that the actions of one or both of the Contracting States result or will result for him in taxation not in accordance with this Convention, he may, notwithstanding the remedies provided by the national laws of those States, present his case to the competent authority of the Contracting State of which he is a resident.

(2) The competent authority shall endeavour, if the objection appears to it to be justified and if it is not itself able to arrive at an appropriate solution, to resolve the case by mutual agreement with the competent authority of the other Contracting State, with a view to the avoidance of taxation not in accordance with the Convention.

(3) The competent authorities of the Contracting States shall endeavour to resolve by mutual agreement any difficulties or doubts arising as to the interpretation or application of the Convention.

(4) The competent authorities of the Contracting States may communicate with each other directly for the purpose of reaching an agreement in the sense of the preceding paragraphs or for the purpose of giving effect to the provisions of the Convention.

Article 25 Exchange of information

(1) The competent authorities of the Contracting States shall exchange such information as is necessary for the carrying out of this Convention and of the domestic laws of the Contracting States concerning taxes covered by this Convention insofar as the taxation thereunder is in accordance with this Convention. Any information so exchanged shall be treated as secret and shall not be disclosed to any persons or authorities other than those (including a court or administrative body) concerned with the assessment or collection of, or prosecution in respect of, or the determination of appeals in relation to, the taxes which are the subject of the Convention.

(2) In no case shall the provisions of paragraph (1) be construed so as to impose on one of the Contracting States the obligation:

(a) to carry out administrative measures at variance with the laws or the administrative practice of that or of the other Contracting State;

(b) to supply particulars which are not obtainable under the laws or in the normal course of the administration of that or of the other Contracting State;

(c) to supply information which would disclose any trade, business, industrial, commercial or professional secret or trade process, or information, the disclosure of which would be contrary to public policy (ordre public).

(3) The competent authorities of the Contracting States shall notify to each other any changes which have been made in their respective taxation laws.

Article 28 Entry into force

Note: Article 28 provided for the entry into force of this Convention. It takes effect in the UK from the year of assessment 1970–71 (income tax and capital gains tax) and from the financial year beginning on 1 April 1970 (corporation tax).

Official languages: The Portuguese language text and the English language text of this Convention are equally authoritative.

ROMANIA

Convention of 18 September 1975 (SI 1977 No 57)

(The Exchange of Notes of 3 February 1976 (SI 1976 No 57) does not amend the Articles printed below.)

Article 1 Personal scope

This Convention shall apply to persons who are residents of one or both of the Contracting States.

Article 2 Taxes covered

(1) The taxes which are the subject of this Convention are:
   (a) in the United Kingdom of Great Britain and Northern Ireland:
       (i) the income tax;
       (ii) the corporation tax; and
       (iii) the capital gains tax;
       (hereinafter referred to as "United Kingdom tax");
   (b) in Romania:
       (i) tax on incomes derived by individuals and corporate bodies;
       (ii) tax on the profits of joint companies constituted with the participation of some Romanian economic organisations and some foreign partners; and
       (iii) tax on income realised from agricultural activities;
       (hereinafter referred to as "Romanian tax").

(2) This Convention shall also apply to any identical or substantially similar taxes which are imposed by either Contracting State after the date of signature of this Convention in addition to, or in place of, the existing taxes.

Article 3 General definitions

(1) In this Convention, unless the context otherwise requires:
   (a) the term "United Kingdom" means Great Britain and Northern Ireland, including any area outside the territorial sea of the United Kingdom which in accordance with international law is or may hereafter be designated, under the laws of the

247

United Kingdom concerning the Continental Shelf, as an area within which the rights of the United Kingdom with respect to the sea-bed and sub-soil and their natural resources may be exercised;

(b) the term "Romania" means the territory of the Socialist Republic of Romania and the sea-bed and sub-soil of the submarine areas beyond the territorial sea, over which Romania exercises sovereign rights, in accordance with international law and with its own law, for the purpose of exploration for and exploitation of the natural resources of such areas;

(c) the term "national" means:

(i) in relation to the United Kingdom, any individual possessing the national status of citizen under the law of the United Kingdom by virtue of his connection with the United Kingdom and any legal person, association or other entity deriving its status as such from the law in force in the United Kingdom;

(ii) in relation to the Socialist Republic of Romania, any individual having the citizenship of the Socialist Republic of Romania and any legal person or other entity created under the law in force in the Socialist Republic of Romania;

(d) the term "tax" means United Kingdom tax or Romanian tax, as the context requires;

(e) the terms "a Contracting State" and "the other Contracting State" mean the United Kingdom or Romania, as the context requires;

(f) the term "person" comprises an individual, a company and any other body of persons;

(g) the term "company" means any body corporate, including a joint company (*societate mixtă*) incorporated under Romanian law, or any entity which is treated as a body corporate for tax purposes;

(h) the terms "enterprise of a Contracting State" and "enterprise of the other Contracting State" mean respectively an enterprise carried on by a resident of a Contracting State and an enterprise carried on by a resident of the other Contracting State;

(i) the term "international traffic" means any transport by a ship or an aircraft or a railway or road vehicle operated by an enterprise which has its place of effective management in a Contracting State, except when such transport is made solely between places in the other Contracting State;

(j) the term "competent authority" means:

(i) in the case of the United Kingdom, the Commissioners of Inland Revenue or their authorised representative;

(ii) in the case of Romania, the Minister of Finance or his authorised representative.

(2) As regards the application of this Convention by a Contracting State any term not otherwise defined shall, unless the context otherwise requires, have the meaning which it has under the laws of that Contracting State relating to the taxes which are the subject of this Convention.

Article 4 Fiscal domicile

(1) For the purposes of this Convention, the term "resident of a Contracting State" means, subject to the provisions of paragraphs (2) and (3) of this Article, any person who, under the law of that State, is liable to taxation there by reason of his domicile, residence, place of management or any other criterion of a similar nature. The terms "resident of the United Kingdom" and "resident of Romania" shall be construed accordingly.

(2) Where by reason of the provisions of paragraph (1) of this Article an individual is a resident of both Contracting States, then his status shall be determined in accordance with the following rules:

(a) he shall be deemed to be a resident of the Contracting State in which he has a permanent home available to him. If he has a permanent home available to him in both Contracting States, he shall be deemed to be a resident of the Contracting

State with which his personal and economic relations are closer (centre of vital interests);

(b) if the Contracting State in which he has his centre of vital interests cannot be determined, or if he has not a permanent home available to him in either Contracting State, he shall be deemed to be a resident of the Contracting State in which he has an habitual abode;

(c) if he has an habitual abode in both Contracting States or in neither of them, he shall be deemed to be a resident of the Contracting State of which he is a national (*cetăţean*);

(d) if he is a national (*cetăţean*) of both Contracting States or of neither of them, the competent authorities of the Contracting States shall settle the question by mutual agreement.

(3) Where by reason of the provisions of paragraph (1) of this Article a person other than an individual is a resident of both Contracting States, then it shall be deemed to be a resident of the Contracting State in which its place of effective management is situated.

Article 6 Income from immovable property

(1) (Taxation of income from immovable property.)

(2) (a) The term "immovable property" shall, subject to the provisions of sub-paragraph (b) below, be defined in accordance with the law of the Contracting State in which the property in question is situated.

(b) The term "immovable property" shall in any case include property accessory to immovable property, livestock and equipment used in agriculture and forestry, rights to which the provisions of general law respecting landed property apply, usufruct of immovable property and rights to variable or fixed payments as consideration for the working of, or the right to work, mineral deposits, sources and other natural resources; ships, boats and aircraft shall not be regarded as immovable property.

(3) . . .

(4) . . .

Article 8 International transport

Profits from the operation of ships, aircraft, or railway and road vehicles in international traffic shall be taxable only in the Contracting State in which the place of effective management of the enterprise is situated.

Article 14 Capital gains

(1) . . .

(2) (Taxation of gains from alienation of movable business property.)

(3) Notwithstanding the provisions of paragraph (2) of this Article, capital gains from the alienation of ships, aircraft and railway and road vehicles operated in international traffic and movable property pertaining to the operation of such ships, aircraft and railway and road vehicles shall be taxable only in the Contracting State in which, under the provisions of Article 8, profits from such activities are taxable.

(4) . . .

Article 25 Non-discrimination

(1) The nationals (*cetăţenii*) of a Contracting State shall not be subjected in the other Contracting State to any taxation or any requirement connected therewith which is other or more burdensome than the taxation and connected requirements to which nationals of that other State in the same circumstances are or may be subjected.

(2) The taxation on a permanent establishment which an enterprise of a Contracting State has in the other Contracting State shall not be less favourably levied in that other State than the taxation levied on enterprises of that other State carrying on the same activities.

(3) Enterprises of a Contracting State, the capital of which is wholly or partly owned or controlled, directly or indirectly, by one or more residents of the other Contracting State, shall not be subjected in the first-mentioned Contracting State to any taxation or any requirement connected therewith which is other or more burdensome than the taxation and connected requirements to which other similar enterprises of that first-mentioned State are or may be subjected.

(4) Nothing contained in this Article shall be construed as obliging either Contracting State to grant to individuals not resident in that State any of the personal allowances, reliefs and reductions for tax purposes which are granted to individuals so resident.

(5) In this Article the term "taxation" means taxes of every kind and description.

(6) The taxes on income, profits and capital and the payments from profits to the State budget (*vărsăminte din beneficii la bugetul de stat*) which under Romanian law are chargeable on socialist units (*unități socialiste*) shall be chargeable only on such units.

Article 26 Mutual agreement procedure

(1) Where a resident of a Contracting State considers that the actions of one or both of the Contracting States result or will result in taxation not in accordance with this Convention, he may, notwithstanding the remedies provided by the national laws of those States, present his case to the competent authority of the Contracting State of which he is a resident.

(2) The competent authority shall endeavour, if the objection appears to it to be justified and if it is not itself able to arrive at an appropriate solution, to resolve the case by mutual agreement with the competent authority of the other Contracting State, with a view to the avoidance of taxation not in accordance with this Convention.

(3) The competent authorities of the Contracting States shall endeavour to resolve by mutual agreement any difficulties or doubts arising as to the interpretation or application of this Convention.

(4) The competent authorities of the Contracting States may communicate with each other directly for the purpose of reaching an agreement in the sense of the preceding paragraphs.

Article 27 Exchange of information

(1) The competent authorities of the Contracting States shall exchange such information as is necessary for the carrying out of this Convention and of the domestic laws of the Contracting States concerning taxes covered by this Convention. Any information so exchanged shall be treated as secret and shall not be disclosed to any persons other than persons (including a court or administrative body) concerned with the assessment or collection of, or prosecution in respect of, or the determination of appeals in relation to, the taxes which are the subject of this Convention.

(2) In no case shall the provisions of paragraph (1) be construed so as to impose on the competent authority of either Contracting State the obligation:

    (*a*) to carry out administrative measures at variance with the laws or administrative practice prevailing in either Contracting State;

    (*b*) to supply particulars which are not obtainable under the laws or in the normal course of the administration of that or of the other Contracting State;

    (*c*) to supply information which would disclose any trade, business, industrial, commercial or professional secret or trade process, or information, the disclosure of which would be contrary to public policy (*ordre public*).

Article 29 Entry into force

Note: Article 29 provided for the entry into force of this Convention. It takes effect in the UK from the year of assessment 1976–77 (income tax and capital gains tax) and from the financial year beginning on 1 April 1976 (corporation tax).

Official languages: The Romanian language text and the English language text of this Convention are equally authoritative.

ST CHRISTOPHER (ST KITTS) AND NEVIS

Arrangement of 19 December 1947 (SR & O 1947 No 2872)

(The status of association with the UK under the West Indies Act 1967 s 1 terminated on 19 September 1983, from which date St Christopher and Nevis has fully responsible government status within the Commonwealth.)

Paragraph 1 [Taxes covered]

(1) The taxes which are the subject of this Arrangement are—
    (a) In the United Kingdom:
        The income tax (including surtax) and the profits tax (hereinafter referred to as "United Kingdom tax").
    (b) In the Presidency of St. Christopher and Nevis:
        The income tax (hereinafter referred to as "Presidential tax").

(2) This Arrangement shall also apply to any other taxes of a substantially similar character imposed in the United Kingdom or the Presidency after this Arrangement has come into force.

Corporation tax: This Arrangement covers United Kingdom corporation tax, by virtue of ICTA 1988 s 789(1).

Paragraph 2 [General definitions]

(1) In this Arrangement, unless the context otherwise requires—
    (a) The term "United Kingdom" means Great Britain and Northern Ireland, excluding the Channel Islands and the Isle of Man.
    (b) The term "the Presidency" means the Presidency of St. Christopher and Nevis.
    (c) The terms "one of the territories" and "the other territory" mean the United Kingdom or the Presidency, as the context requires.
    (d) The term "tax" means United Kingdom tax or Presidential tax, as the context requires.
    (e) The term "person" includes any body of persons, corporate or not corporate.
    (f) The term "company" includes any body corporate.
    (g) The terms "resident of the United Kingdom" and "resident of the Presidency" mean respectively any person who is resident in the United Kingdom for the purposes of United Kingdom tax and not resident in the Presidency for the purposes of Presidential tax and any person who is resident in the Presidency for the purposes of Presidential tax and not resident in the United Kingdom for the purposes of United Kingdom tax; and a company shall be regarded as resident in the United Kingdom if its business is managed and controlled in the United Kingdom and as resident in the Presidency if its business is managed and controlled in the Presidency.
    (h) The terms "resident of one of the territories" and "resident of the other territory" mean a person who is a resident of the United Kingdom or a person who is a resident of the Presidency, as the context requires.

(i)–(k) . . .

(2) Where under this Arrangement any income is exempt from tax in one of the territories if (with or without other conditions) it is subject to tax in the other territory, and that income is subject to tax in that other territory by reference to the amount thereof which is remitted to or received in that other territory, the exemption to be allowed under this Arrangement in the first-mentioned territory shall apply only to the amount so remitted or received.

(3) In the application of the provisions of this Arrangement by the United Kingdom or the Presidency, any term not otherwise defined shall, unless the context otherwise requires, have the meaning which it has under the laws of the United Kingdom, or, as the case may be, the Presidency, relating to the taxes which are the subject of this Arrangement.

Paragraph 5 [Shipping and air transport]

Notwithstanding the provisions of paragraphs 3 and 4, profits which a resident of one of the territories derives from operating ships or aircraft shall be exempt from tax in the other territory.

Paragraph 3: Taxation of industrial or commercial profits.
Paragraph 4: Taxation of profits of associated enterprises.

Paragraph 14 [Exchange of information]

(1) The taxation authorities of the United Kingdom and the Presidency shall exchange such information (being information available under their respective taxation laws) as is necessary for carrying out the provisions of this Arrangement or for the prevention of fraud or the administration of statutory provisions against legal avoidance in relation to the taxes which are the subject of this Arrangement. Any information so exchanged shall be treated as secret and shall not be disclosed to any persons other than those concerned with the assessment and collection of the taxes which are the subject of this Arrangement. No information shall be exchanged which would disclose any trade secret or trade process.

(2) As used in this paragraph, the term "taxation authorities" means the Commissioners of Inland Revenue or their authorised representative in the case of the United Kingdom and the Income Tax Commissioners or their authorised representative in the case of the Presidency.

Paragraph 15 [Entry into force]

Note: Paragraph 15 provided for the entry into force of this Arrangement. It takes effect in general from 1947–48.

Official language: English.

ST LUCIA

The Arrangement of 4 March 1949 (SI 1949 No 366), which was amended by the Agreement of 5 April 1968 (SI 1968 No 1102), was terminated by notice given by St Lucia in October 1986. The termination took effect in St Lucia from 1 January 1988 and in the UK from 1 April 1988 in respect of corporation tax and 6 April 1988 in respect of income tax.

A new Agreement is under consideration.

ST VINCENT AND THE GRENADINES

The Arrangement of 4 March 1949 (SI 1949 No 367), which was amended by the Agreement of 1 April 1968 (SI 1968 No 1103), was terminated by notice given by St Vincent and the Grenadines in June 1986. The termination took effect in St Vincent and the Grenadines from 1 January 1987 and in the UK from 1 April 1987 in respect of corporation tax and 6 April 1987 in respect of income tax.

A new Agreement is under consideration.

SIERRA LEONE

Arrangement of 19 December 1947 (SR & O No 1947 No 2873)

Printed as amended by the Agreement of 18 March 1968 (SI 1968 No 1104).

Paragraph 1 [Taxes covered]

(1) The taxes which are the subject of this Arrangement are—
   (a) In the United Kingdom:
   The income tax (including surtax) and the profits tax (hereinafter referred to as "United Kingdom tax").
   (b) In Sierra Leone:
   The income tax, the duty on profits charged under the Concessions Ordinance, 1931, the diamond industry profit tax, and the profits tax charged under the Tonkolili Agreement Ordinance, 1937 (hereinafter referred to as "Sierra Leone tax").

(2) This Arrangement shall also apply to any other taxes of a substantially similar character imposed in the United Kingdom or Sierra Leone after this Arrangement has come into force.

Corporation tax: This Arrangement covers United Kingdom corporation tax, by virtue of ICTA 1988 s 789(1).

Paragraph 2 [General definitions]

(1) In this Arrangement, unless the context otherwise requires—
   (a) The term "United Kingdom" means Great Britain and Northern Ireland, excluding the Channel Islands and the Isle of Man.
   (b) . . .
   (c) The terms "one of the territories" and "the other territory" mean the United Kingdom or Sierra Leone, as the context requires.
   (d) The term "tax" means United Kingdom tax or Sierra Leone tax as the context requires.

253

(e) The term "person" includes any body of persons, corporate or not corporate.

(f) The term "company" includes any body corporate.

(g) The terms "resident of the United Kingdom" and "resident of Sierra Leone" mean respectively any person who is resident in the United Kingdom for the purposes of United Kingdom tax and not resident in Sierra Leone for the purposes of Sierra Leone tax and any person who is resident in Sierra Leone for the purposes of Sierra Leone tax and not resident in the United Kingdom for the purposes of United Kingdom tax; and a company shall be regarded as resident in the United Kingdom if its business is managed and controlled in the United Kingdom and as resident in Sierra Leone if its business if managed and controlled in Sierra Leone.

(h) The terms "resident of one of the territories" and "resident of the other territory" mean a person who is a resident of the United Kingdom or a person who is a resident of Sierra Leone, as the context requires.

(i)–(k) . . .

(2) Where under this Arrangement any income is exempt from tax in one of the territories if (with or without other conditions) it is subject to tax in the other territory, and that income is subject to tax in that other territory by reference to the amount thereof which is remitted to or received in that other territory, the exemption to be allowed under this Arrangement in the first-mentioned territory shall apply only to the amount so remitted or received.

(3) In the application of the provisions of this Arrangement by the United Kingdom or Sierra Leone, any term not otherwise defined shall, unless the context otherwise requires, have the meaning which it has under the laws of the United Kingdom, or, as the case may be, Sierra Leone, relating to the taxes which are the subject of this Arrangement.

Paragraph 5 [Shipping and air transport]

Notwithstanding the provisions of paragraphs 3 and 4, profits which a resident of one of the territories derives from operating ships or aircraft shall be exempt from tax in the other territory.

Paragraph 3: Taxation of industrial or commercial profits.
Paragraph 4: Taxation of profits of associated enterprises.

Paragraph 14 [Exchange of information]

(1) The taxation authorities of the United Kingdom and Sierra Leone shall exchange such information (being information available under their respective taxation laws) as is necessary for carrying out the provisions of this Arrangement or for the prevention of fraud or the administration of statutory provisions against legal avoidance in relation to the taxes which are the subject of this Arrangement. Any information so exchanged shall be treated as secret and shall not be disclosed to any persons other than those concerned with the assessment and collection of the taxes which are the subject of this Arrangement. No information shall be exchanged which would disclose any trade secret or trade process.

(2) As used in this paragraph, the term "taxation authorities" means the Commissioners of Inland Revenue or their authorised representative in the case of the United Kingdom and the Commissioner for Income Tax or his authorised representative in the case of Sierra Leone.

Paragraph 15 [Entry into force]

Note: Paragraph 15 provided for the entry into force of the 1947 Arrangement. It takes effect in the UK in its amended form from the year of assessment 1968–69 (income tax) and from the financial year beginning on 1 April 1968 (corporation tax).

Official language: English.

SINGAPORE

Agreement of 1 December 1966 (SI 1967 No 483)

Printed as amended by the Protocol of 21 July 1975 (as amended by the Exchange of Notes of 27 December 1975, 12 March 1976 and 23 July 1977). The amended Protocol was contained in SI 1978 No 787.

Article 1 [Taxes covered]

(1) The taxes which are the subject of this Agreement are—
  (a) in the Republic of Singapore:
    the income tax (hereinafter referred to as "Singapore tax"); and
  (b) in the United Kingdom of Great Britain and Northern Ireland:
    the income tax (including surtax), the profits tax, the corporation tax and the capital gains tax (hereinafter referred to as "United Kingdom tax").

(2) This Agreement shall also apply to the other taxes of a substantially similar character imposed in Singapore or the United Kingdom subsequently to the date of signature of this Agreement.

Article 2 [General definitions]

(1) In this Agreement, unless the context otherwise requires—
  (a) the term "Singapore" means the Republic of Singapore;
  (b) the term "United Kingdom" means Great Britain and Northern Ireland, including any area outside the territorial waters of the United Kingdom which has been designated, under the laws of the United Kingdom concerning the Continental Shelf, as an area within which the rights of the United Kingdom with respect to the sea-bed and sub-soil and their natural resources may be exercised;
  (c) the terms "one of the Contracting States" and "the other Contracting State" mean Singapore or the United Kingdom, as the context requires;
  (d) the term "tax" means Singapore tax or United Kingdom tax, as the context requires;
  (e) the term "company" means any body corporate;
  (f) the term "person" includes any body of persons, corporate or not corporate;
  (g) (i) the term "resident of Singapore" means any person who is resident in Singapore for the purposes of Singapore tax; and the term "resident of the United Kingdom" means any person who is resident in the United Kingdom for the purposes of United Kingdom tax;
    (ii) where by reason of the provisions of sub-paragraph (i) above an individual is a resident of both Contracting States, then his residence shall be determined in accordance with the following rules—
      (aa) he shall be deemed to be a resident of the Contracting State in which he has a permanent home available to him. If he has a permanent home available to him in both Contracting States, he shall be deemed to be a resident of the Contracting State with which his personal and economic relations are closest;
      (bb) if the Contracting State, with which his personal and economic relations

are closest, cannot be determined, or if he has not a permanent home available to him in either Contracting State, he shall be deemed to be a resident of the Contracting State in which he has an habitual abode;

(cc) if he has an habitual abode in both Contracting States or in neither of them, the competent authorities of the Contracting States shall settle the question by mutual agreement;

(iii) where by reason of the provisions of sub-paragraph (i) above a person other than an individual is a resident of both Contracting States, then it shall be deemed to be a resident of the Contracting State in which it is managed and controlled;

(h) the terms "resident of one of the Contracting States" and "resident of the other Contracting State" mean a resident of Singapore or a resident of the United Kingdom, as the context requires;

(i) the terms "Singapore enterprise" and "United Kingdom enterprise" mean, respectively, an industrial, mining, commercial, plantation or agricultural enterprise or undertaking carried on by a resident of Singapore and an industrial, mining, commercial, plantation or agricultural enterprise or undertaking carried on by a resident of the United Kingdom;

(j) the terms "enterprise of one of the Contracting States" and "enterprise of the other Contracting State" mean a Singapore enterprise or a United Kingdom enterprise, as the context requires;

(k) the terms "profits of a Singapore enterprise" and "profits of a United Kingdom enterprise" do not include rents or royalties in respect of motion picture films or of tapes for telecasting or of mines, oil wells, quarries or other places of extraction of natural resources, or income in the form of dividends, interest, rents, royalties, or capital gains, or fees or other remuneration derived from the management, control or supervision of the trade, business or other activity of another enterprise or concern, or remuneration for labour or personal services, or profits derived from the operation of ships or aircraft;

(l) (i) subject to the provisions of this sub-paragraph, the term "permanent establishment" means a fixed place of business in which the business of the enterprise is wholly or partly carried on;

(ii) a permanent establishment shall include especially—

(aa) a place of management;

(bb) a branch;

(cc) an office;

(dd) a factory;

(ee) a workshop;

(ff) a mine, oil well, quarry or other place of extraction of natural resources;

(gg) a building site or construction or assembly project which exists for more than six months;

(hh) a farm or plantation;

(iii) the term "permanent establishment" shall not be deemed to include—

(aa) the use of facilities solely for the purpose of storage, display or delivery of goods or merchandise belonging to the enterprise;

(bb) the maintenance of a stock of goods or merchandise belonging to the enterprise solely for the purpose of storage, display or delivery;

(cc) the maintenance of a stock of goods or merchandise belonging to the enterprise solely for the purpose of processing by another enterprise;

(dd) the maintenance of a fixed place of business solely for the purpose of purchasing goods or merchandise, or for collecting information, for the enterprise;

(ee) the maintenance of a fixed place of business solely for the purpose of advertising, for the supply of information, for scientific research or for similar activities which have a preparatory or auxiliary character, for the enterprise;

       (iv) an enterprise of one of the Contracting States shall be deemed to have a permanent establishment in the other Contracting State if—

          (*aa*) it carries on supervisory activities in that other Contracting State for more than six months in connection with a construction, installation or assembly project which is being undertaken in that other Contracting State;

          (*bb*) it carries on a business which consists of providing the services of public entertainers referred to in paragraph (3) of Article 12 in that other Contracting State;

       (v) a person acting in one of the Contracting States on behalf of an enterprise of the other Contracting State (other than an agent of independent status to whom sub-paragraph (*l*) (vi) of this Article applies) shall be deemed to be a permanent establishment in the former Contracting State if—

          (*aa*) he has, and habitually exercises in that former Contracting State, an authority to conclude contracts in the name of the enterprise, unless his activities are limited to the purchase of goods or merchandise for the enterprise; or

          (*bb*) he maintains in that former Contracting State a stock of goods or merchandise belonging to the enterprise from which he regularly fills orders on behalf of the enterprise;

       (vi) an enterprise of one of the Contracting States shall not be deemed to have a permanent establishment in the other Contracting State merely because it carries on business in that other Contracting State through a broker, general commission agent or any other agent of independent status, where such person is acting in the ordinary course of his business;

       (vii) the fact that a company which is a resident of one of the Contracting States controls or is controlled by a company which is a resident of the other Contracting State, or which carries on business in that other Contracting State (whether through a permanent establishment or otherwise), shall not of itself constitute either company a permanent establishment of the other;

   (*m*) the term "competent authorities" means, in the case of Singapore, the Minister for Finance or his authorised representative; and in the case of the United Kingdom, the Commissioners of Inland Revenue or their authorised representative.

(2) In the application of the provisions of this Agreement by the Government of one of the Contracting States, any term not otherwise defined shall, unless the context otherwise requires, have the meaning which it has under the laws of that Contracting State relating to the taxes which are the subject of this Agreement.

Article 6 [Shipping and air transport]

(1) Profits which an enterprise of one of the Contracting States derives from the operation of ships or aircraft in international traffic in respect of carriage of passengers, mails, livestock or goods shall be exempt from tax in the other Contracting State.

(2) The term "international traffic" means all movements by a ship or aircraft operated by an enterprise of one of the Contracting States, other than movements solely between places in the other Contracting State or solely between such places and one or more structures used for the exploration or extraction of natural resources situated in waters adjacent to the territorial waters of that other Contracting State.

(3) This Article shall likewise apply to the share in respect of participation in shipping or aircraft pools of any kind by such enterprise engaged in shipping or air transport.

Article 19 [Exchange of information]

The competent authorities of the Contracting States shall exchange such information (being information which is available under their respective taxation laws in the normal course of administration) as is necessary for carrying out the provisions of this Agreement or for the prevention of fraud or underpayment of tax by reasons other than fraud or for the administration of statutory provisions against legal avoidance in relation to the taxes which are the subject of this Agreement. Any information so exchanged shall be treated as secret and shall not be disclosed to any persons other than persons, including a court, concerned with the assessment and collection of those taxes or the determination of appeals in relation thereto. No information shall be exchanged which would disclose any trade secret or trade process.

Article 20 [Non-discrimination]

(1) Residents of one of the Contracting States shall not be subjected in the other Contracting State to any taxation or any requirement connected therewith which is other or more burdensome than the taxation and connected requirements to which the residents of that other Contracting State in the same circumstances are or may be subjected.

(2) The taxation on a permanent establishment which an enterprise of one of the Contracting States has in the other Contracting State shall not be less favourably levied in that other Contracting State than the taxation levied on enterprises of that other Contracting State carrying on the same activities.

(3) Enterprises of one of the Contracting States, the capital of which is wholly or partly owned or controlled, directly or indirectly, by one or more residents of the other Contracting State, shall not be subjected in the former Contracting State to any taxation or any requirement connected therewith which is other or more burdensome than the taxation and connected requirements to which other similar enterprises of the former Contracting State are or may be subjected.

(4) Nothing in this Article shall be construed as obliging the Government of either Contracting State to grant to persons not resident in its territory, any personal allowances, reliefs and reductions for tax purposes, which are, by law, available only to persons who are so resident, nor as restricting the deduction of United Kingdom income tax from dividends paid to a permanent establishment in the United Kingdom of a company which is a resident of Singapore.

(5) In this Article the term "taxation" means taxes which are the subject of this Agreement.

Article 21 [Mutual agreement procedure]

(1) Where a taxpayer considers that the action of the taxation authorities of the Contracting Governments has resulted or will result in taxation contrary to the provisions of this Agreement, he shall be entitled to present his case to the Government of the Contracting State of which he is a resident. Should the taxpayer's claim be deemed worthy of consideration, the taxation authorities of the Government to which the claim is made shall endeavour to come to an agreement with the taxation authorities of the other Government with a view to a satisfactory adjustment.

(2) The taxation authorities of the Contracting States may communicate with each other directly for the purpose of giving effect to the provisions of this Agreement and for resolving any difficulty or doubt as to the application or interpretation of this Agreement . . .

(3) . . .

(4) . . .

Article 23 [Entry into force]

Note: Article 23 provided for the entry into force of the 1966 Agreement. It takes effect in the UK in its amended form from the year of assessment 1973–74 (income tax and capital gains tax) and from the financial year beginning on 1 April 1973 (corporation tax).

Official language: English.

SOLOMON ISLANDS

Arrangement of 10 May 1950 (SI 1950 No 748)

(The Arrangement of 8 April 1968 (SI 1968 No 574) and the Supplementary Arrangement of 25 July 1974 (SI 1974 No 1270) do not amend the paragraphs printed below.)

Paragraph 1 [Taxes covered]

(1) The taxes which are the subject of this Arrangement are—
    (a) In the United Kingdom:
        The income tax (including surtax) and the profits tax (hereinafter referred to as "United Kingdom tax").
    (b) In the British Solomon Islands Protectorate:
        The normal tax and the surtax (hereinafter referred to as "Protectorate tax").

(2) This Arrangement shall also apply to any other taxes of a substantially similar character imposed in the United Kingdom or the British Solomon Islands Protectorate after this Arrangement has come into force.

Corporation tax: This Arrangement covers United Kingdom corporation tax, by virtue of ICTA 1988 s 789(1).

Paragraph 2 [General definitions]

(1) In this Arrangement, unless the context otherwise requires—
    (a) The term "United Kingdom" means Great Britain and Northern Ireland, excluding the Channel Islands and the Isle of Man.
    (b) The term "the Protectorate" means the British Solomon Islands Protectorate.
    (c) The terms "one of the territories" and "the other territory" mean the United Kingdom or the Protectorate, as the context requires.
    (d) The term "tax" means United Kingdom tax or Protectorate tax, as the context requires.
    (e) The term "person" includes any body of persons, corporate or not corporate.
    (f) The term "company" includes any body corporate.
    (g) The terms "resident of the United Kingdom" and "resident of the Protectorate" mean respectively any person who is resident in the United Kingdom for the purposes of United Kingdom tax and not resident in the Protectorate for the purposes of Protectorate tax and any person who is resident in the Protectorate for the purposes of Protectorate tax and not resident in the United Kingdom for the purposes of United Kingdom tax; and a company shall be regarded as resident in the United Kingdom if its business is managed and controlled in the United Kingdom and as resident in the Protectorate if its business is managed and controlled in the Protectorate.
    (h) The terms "resident of one of the territories" and "resident of the other territory" mean a person who is a resident of the United Kingdom or a person who is a resident of the Protectorate, as the context requires.
    (i)–(k) . . .

(2) Where under this Arrangement any income is exempt from tax in one of the territories

if (with or without other conditions) it is subject to tax in the other territory, and that income is subject to tax in that other territory by reference to the amount thereof which is remitted to or received in that other territory, the exemption to be allowed under this Arrangement in the first-mentioned territory shall apply only to the amount so remitted or received.

(3) In the application of the provisions of this Arrangement by the United Kingdom or the Protectorate, any term not otherwise defined shall, unless the context otherwise requires, have the meaning which it has under the laws of the United Kingdom, or, as the case may be, the Protectorate, relating to the taxes which are the subject of this Arrangement.

Paragraph 5 [Shipping and air transport]

Notwithstanding the provisions of paragraphs 3 and 4, profits which a resident of one of the territories derives from operating ships or aircraft shall be exempt from tax in the other territory.

Paragraph 3: Taxation of industrial or commercial profits.
Paragraph 4: Taxation of profits of associated enterprises.

Paragraph 14 [Exchange of information]

(1) The taxation authorities of the United Kingdom and the Protectorate shall exchange such information (being information available under their respective taxation laws) as is necessary for carrying out the provisions of this Arrangement or for the prevention of fraud or the administration of statutory provisions against legal avoidance in relation to the taxes which are the subject of this Arrangement. Any information so exchanged shall be treated as secret and shall not be disclosed to any persons other than those concerned with the assessment and collection of the taxes which are the subject of this Arrangement. No information shall be exchanged which would disclose any trade secret or trade process.

(2) As used in this paragraph, the term "taxation authorities" means the Commissioners of Inland Revenue or their authorised representative in the case of the United Kingdom and the Treasurer or his authorised representative in the case of the Protectorate.

Paragraph 15 [Entry into force]

Note: Paragraph 15 provides for the entry into force of this Arrangement. It takes effect from the year 1949–50.

Official language: English.

SOUTH AFRICA

Convention of 21 November 1968 (SI 1969 No 864)

Article 1 [Taxes covered]

(1) The taxes which are the subject of this Convention are:
- (a) in South Africa:
  - (i) the normal tax;
  - (ii) the non-resident shareholders' tax;
  - (iii) the undistributed profits tax;
  - (iv) the non-residents' tax on interest; and
  - (v) the provincial income and personal taxes
  (hereinafter referred to as "South African tax");
- (b) in the United Kingdom of Great Britain and Northern Ireland:
  - (i) the income tax (including surtax);
  - (ii) the corporation tax; and
  - (iii) the capital gains tax
  (hereinafter referred to as "United Kingdom tax").

(2) This Convention shall also apply to any identical or substantially similar taxes which are subsequently imposed in addition to, or in place of, the existing taxes.

Article 2 [General definitions]

(1) In this Convention, unless the context otherwise requires:
- (a) the term "United Kingdom" means Great Britain and Northern Ireland;
- (b) the term "South Africa" means the Republic of South Africa;
- (c) the terms "a Contracting State" and "the other Contracting State" mean the United Kingdom or South Africa, as the context requires;
- (d) the term "taxation authorities" means, in the case of the United Kingdom, the Commissioners of Inland Revenue or their authorised representative; in the case of South Africa, the Secretary for Inland Revenue or his authorised representative; and in the case of any territory to which this Convention is extended under Article 26, the competent authority for the administration in such territory of the taxes to which this Convention applies;
- (e) the term "tax" means United Kingdom tax or South African tax, as the context requires;
- (f) the term "person" includes any body of persons, corporate or not corporate;
- (g) the term "company" means any body corporate;
- (h) the terms "United Kingdom enterprise" and "South African enterprise" mean respectively an industrial or commercial enterprise or undertaking carried on by a resident of the United Kingdom and an industrial or commercial enterprise or undertaking carried on by a resident of South Africa, and the terms "enterprise of a Contracting State" and "enterprise of the other Contracting State" mean a United Kingdom enterprise or a South African enterprise, as the context requires;
- (i) the term "international traffic" includes traffic between places in one country in the course of a voyage which extends over more than one country.

(2) Where under this Convention any income is exempt from tax, or is to be granted relief from tax, in a Contracting State if (with or without other conditions) it is subject to tax in the other Contracting State and that income is subject to tax in that other Contracting State by reference to the amount thereof which is remitted to or received in that other Contracting State, the exemption or relief to be allowed under this Convention in the first-mentioned Contracting State shall apply only to the amount so remitted or received.

(3) In the application of the provisions of this Convention by a Contracting State any

term not otherwise defined shall, unless the context otherwise requires, have the meaning which it has under the laws in force in the territory of that Contracting State relating to the taxes which are the subject of this Convention.

Article 3 [Fiscal domicile]

(1) For the purposes of this Convention the term "resident of a Contracting State" means any person who, under the law of that State, is liable to taxation therein by reason of his domicile, residence, place of management or any other criterion of a similar nature. The terms "resident of the United Kingdom" and "resident of South Africa" shall be construed accordingly.

(2) Where by reason of the provisions of paragraph (1) of this Article an individual is a resident of both Contracting States, then his status shall be determined in accordance with the following rules:

> (a) He shall be deemed to be a resident of the Contracting State in which he has a permanent home available to him; if he has a permanent home available to him in both Contracting States, he shall be deemed to be a resident of the Contracting State with which his personal and economic relations are closest (hereinafter referred to as "his centre of vital interests").
>
> (b) If the Contracting State in which he has his centre of vital interests cannot be determined, or if he has not a permanent home available to him in either Contracting State, he shall be deemed to be a resident of the Contracting State in which he has an habitual abode.
>
> (c) If he has an habitual abode in both Contracting States or in neither of them, he shall be deemed to be a resident of the Contracting State of which he is a national.
>
> (d) If he is a national of both Contracting States or of neither of them, the taxation authorities of the Contracting States shall determine the question by mutual agreement.

(3) Where by reason of the provisions of paragraph (1) of this Article, a person other than an individual is a resident of both Contracting States, then it shall be deemed to be a resident of the Contracting State in which its place of effective management is situated.

Article 5 [Income from immovable property]

(1) (Taxation of income from immovable property.)

(2) (a) The term "immovable property" shall, subject to sub-paragraph (b) below, be defined in accordance with the law of the Contracting State in which the property in question is situated.

> (b) The term "immovable property" shall in any case include property accessory to immovable property, livestock and equipment used in agriculture and forestry, rights to which the provisions of general law respecting landed property apply, usufruct of immovable property and rights to variable or fixed payments as consideration for the working of, or the right to work, mineral deposits, sources and other natural resources; ships, boats and aircraft shall not be regarded as immovable property.

(3) . . .

(4) . . .

Article 7 [Shipping and air transport]

A resident of a Contracting State shall be exempt from tax in the other Contracting State on profits from the operation of ships and aircraft other than profits from voyages of ships or aircraft confined solely to places in the other Contracting State.

Article 12 [Capital gains]

(1) (Taxation of gains from alienation of business property.)

(2) Notwithstanding paragraph (1) of the Article, capital gains derived by a resident of a

Contracting State from the alienation of ships and aircraft operated in international traffic and movable property pertaining to the operation of such ships and aircraft shall be taxable only in that Contracting State.

(3) . . .

(4) . . .

Article 23 [Non-discrimination]

(1) The nationals of a Contracting State shall not be subjected in the territory of the other Contracting State to any taxation or any requirement connected therewith which is other or more burdensome than the taxation and connected requirements to which the nationals of the other State in the same circumstances are or may be subjected.

(2) In this Article the term "nationals" means:

(a) in relation to South Africa:
all South African citizens and all legal persons, partnerships and associations deriving their status as such from the law in force in South Africa;

(b) in relation to the United Kingdom:
all British subjects and British protected persons
 (i) residing in the United Kingdom or any territory to which this Convention is extended under Article 26, or
 (ii) deriving their status as such from connection with the United Kingdom or any territory to which this Convention is extended under Article 26,
and all legal persons, partnerships and associations deriving their status as such from the law in force in the United Kingdom or in any territory to which the Convention is extended under Article 26.

(3) The taxation on a permanent establishment which an enterprise of a Contracting State has in the other Contracting State shall not be less favourably levied in that other State than the taxation levied on enterprises of that other State carrying on the same activities.

(4) Enterprises of a Contracting State, the capital of which is wholly or partly owned or controlled, directly or indirectly, by one or more residents of the other Contracting State, shall not be subjected in the first-mentioned Contracting State to any taxation or any requirement connected therewith which is other or more burdensome than the taxation and connected requirements to which other similar enterprises of that first-mentioned State are or may be subjected.

(5) Nothing contained in this Article shall be construed as obliging either Contracting State to grant to individuals not resident in that State any of the personal allowances and reliefs for tax purposes which are granted to individuals so resident, nor as conferring any exemption from tax in a State in respect of dividends paid to a company which is a resident of the other State.

(6) In determining for the purpose of United Kingdom tax whether a company is a close company, the term "recognised stock exchange" shall include the Johannesburg Stock Exchange.

(7) In this Article the term "taxation" means the taxes which are the subject of this Convention.

Article 24 [Communication]

The taxation authorities of the Contracting States may communicate with each other directly for the purpose of giving effect to the provisions of this Convention and for resolving any difficulty or doubt as to the application or interpretation of this Convention.

Article 25 [Exchange of information]

The taxation authorities of the Contracting States shall exchange such information (being information which is at their disposal under their respective taxation laws in the normal course of administration) as is necessary for carrying out the provisions of this Convention or for the prevention of fraud or for the administration of statutory provisions against legal avoidance in relation to the taxes which are the subject of this Convention. Any information so exchanged shall be treated as secret but may be disclosed to persons (including a court or administrative body) concerned with assessment, collection, enforcement or prosecution in respect of taxes which are the subject of this Convention. No information shall be exchanged which would disclose any trade, business, industrial or professional secret or any trade process.

Article 27 [Entry into force]

Note: Article 27 provided for the entry into force of this Convention. It takes effect in the UK from the year of assessment 1968–69 (income tax and capital gains tax) and from the financial year beginning on 1 April 1968 (corporation tax).

Official languages: The Afrikaans language text and the English language text of this Convention are equally authoritative.

Capital taxes

Convention of 31 July 1978 (SI 1979 No 576)

Article 1 Scope

This Convention shall apply to any person who is within the scope of a tax which is the subject of this Convention.

Article 2 Taxes covered

(1) The taxes which are the subject of this Convention are:
    (*a*) in the United Kingdom, the capital transfer tax;
    (*b*) in South Africa, the estate duty and the donations tax.
(2) This Convention shall also apply to any identical or substantially similar taxes which are imposed by either Contracting State after the date of signature of this Convention in addition to, or in place of, the existing taxes.

Inheritance tax: United Kingdom capital transfer tax is known as inheritance tax by virtue of FA 1986, s 100.

Article 3 General definitions

(1) In this Convention, unless the context otherwise requires:

    (*a*) the term "United Kingdom" means Great Britain and Northern Ireland;

    (*b*) the term "South Africa" means the Republic of South Africa;

    (*c*) the term "nationals" means:

        (i) in relation to the United Kingdom, any citizen of the United Kingdom and Colonies, or any British subject not possessing that citizenship or the citizenship of any other Commonwealth country or territory, provided in either case he had the right of abode in the United Kingdom at the time of the death or the transfer or other material time;

        (ii) in relation to South Africa, any citizen of South Africa;

    (*d*) the term "tax" means:

        (i) the capital transfer tax imposed in the United Kingdom; or

        (ii) the estate duty or the donations tax imposed in South Africa; or

        (iii) any other tax imposed by a Contracting State to which this Convention applies by virtue of the provisions of paragraph (1) of Article 2, as the context requires.

    (*e*) the terms "a Contracting State" and "the other Contracting State" mean the United Kingdom or South Africa, as the context requires;

    (*f*) the term "competent authority" means, in the case of the United Kingdom, the Commissioners of Inland Revenue or their authorised representative, and in the case of South Africa, the Secretary for Inland Revenue or his authorised representative;

    (*g*) the term "transfer" includes, in the case of South Africa, a donation and the term "transferor" shall be construed accordingly.

(2) As regards the application of this Convention by a Contracting State any term not otherwise defined shall, unless the context otherwise requires, have the meaning which it has under the law of that Contracting State relating to the taxes which are the subject of this Convention.

Article 4 Fiscal domicile

(1) For the purposes of this Convention an individual was domiciled:

    (*a*) in the United Kingdom if he was domiciled in the United Kingdom in accordance with the law of the United Kingdom or is treated as so domiciled for the purposes of a tax which is the subject of this Convention;

    (*b*) in South Africa if he was ordinarily resident in South Africa.

(2) Subject to the provisions of paragraph (4) of this Article, where by reason of the provisions of paragraph (1) of this Article an individual was at any time domiciled in both Contracting States, and

    (*a*) was a national of the United Kingdom but not of South Africa; and

    (*b*) had not been resident or ordinarily resident in South Africa in seven or more of the ten income tax years of assessment immediately preceding that time,

then he shall be deemed to be domiciled at that time in the United Kingdom.

(3) Subject to the provisions of paragraph (4) of this Article, where by reason of the provisions of paragraph (1) of this Article an individual was at any time domiciled in both Contracting States, and

    (*a*) was a national of South Africa but not of the United Kingdom; and

    (*b*) had not been resident or ordinarily resident in the United Kingdom in seven or more of the ten income tax years of assessment ending with the year of assessment in which that time falls,

then he shall be deemed to be domiciled at the time in South Africa. For the purposes of this paragraph the question whether an individual was resident or ordinarily resident in the United Kingdom shall be determined as for the purposes of income tax, but without regard to any dwelling-house available in the United Kingdom for his use.

(4) An individual shall not, by virtue of paragraph (2) or (3) of this Article, be deemed to be domiciled at any time in a Contracting State if, under the law of that Contracting State other than its law relating to a tax which is the subject of this Convention, he had ceased to be domiciled in that Contracting State more than three years before that time.

(5) Where by reason of the provisions of paragraph (1) of this Article an individual was domiciled in both Contracting States, then, subject to the provisions of paragraphs (2), (3) and (4) of this Article, his status shall be determined as follows:

(a) he shall be deemed to be domiciled in the Contracting State in which he had a permanent home available to him. If he had a permanent home available to him in both Contracting States, the domicile shall be deemed to be in the Contracting State with which his personal and economic relations were closer (centre of vital interests);

(b) if the Contracting State in which he had his centre of vital interests cannot be determined, or if he had not a permanent home available to him in either Contracting State, the domicile shall be deemed to be in the Contracting State in which he had an habitual abode;

(c) if he had an habitual abode in both Contracting States or in neither of them, the domicile shall be deemed to be in the Contracting State of which he was a national; and

(d) if he was a national of both Contracting States or of neither of them, the competent authorities of the Contracting States shall settle the question by mutual agreement.

Article 5 General taxing rights

(1) Subject to the provisions of Articles 6, 7, 8 and 9 and the following paragraphs of this Article, if the deceased or the transferor was domiciled in one of the Contracting States at the time of the death or transfer, property shall not be taxable in the other Contracting State unless he had been domiciled in the other Contracting State within the ten years immediately preceding the death or transfer.

(2) Paragraph (1) of this Article shall not apply in the United Kingdom to property comprised in a settlement; but, subject to the provisions of Articles 6, 7, 8 and 9, such property shall not be taxable in the United Kingdom if at the time when the settlement was made the settlor was domiciled in South Africa and had not been domiciled in the United Kingdom within the immediately preceding ten years.

(3) If by reason of paragraph (1) of this Article any property would be taxable only in one Contracting State and tax, though chargeable, is not paid (otherwise than as a result of a specific exemption, deduction, credit or allowance) in that Contracting State, tax may be imposed by reference to that property in the other Contracting State notwithstanding that paragraph.

Article 6 Immovable property

(1) (Taxation of immovable property.)

(2) The term "immovable property" shall have the meaning which it has under the law of the Contracting State in which the property in question is situated provided always that debts secured by mortgage or otherwise shall not be regarded as immovable property. The term shall in any case include property accessory to immovable property, livestock and equipment used in agriculture and forestry, rights to which the provisions of general law respecting landed property apply, usufruct of immovable property and rights to variable or fixed payments as consideration for the working of, or the right to work, mineral deposits, sources and other natural resources; ships, boats and aircraft shall not be regarded as immovable property.

(3) . . .

Article 8 Ships and aircraft

Ships and aircraft operated in international traffic and movable property pertaining to the operation of such ships and aircraft may be taxed in the Contracting State in which the place of effective management of the enterprise is situated.

Article 11 Deductions, allowances etc

(1) In determining the amount on which tax is to be computed permitted deductions shall be allowed in accordance with the law in force in the territory in which the tax is imposed.

(2) Nothing contained in this Convention shall be construed as obliging either Contracting State to grant to individuals not domiciled in that Contracting State, or to the estates of such individuals, any of the personal allowances, reliefs, and reductions for tax purposes which are granted to individuals so domiciled, or to their estates.

Article 12 Credit provisions

(1) Where a Contracting State imposes tax in connection with any event by reference to any property which the other Contracting State may tax in accordance with Articles 6, 7, 8 or 9, the former Contracting State shall allow against so much of its tax (as otherwise computed) as is attributable to such property a credit (not exceeding the amount of tax so attributable) equal to so much of the tax imposed in the other Contracting State in connection with the same event as is attributable to such property.

(2) Subject to paragraph (3) of this Article, where a Contracting State imposes tax in connection with any event by reference to any property not referred to in paragraph (1) of this Article and the deceased or transferor was domiciled in the other Contracting State at the time of the death or transfer, the first-mentioned Contracting State shall allow against so much of its tax (as otherwise computed) as is attributable to such property a credit (not exceeding the amount of tax so attributable) equal to so much of the tax imposed in the other Contracting State in connection with the same event as is attributable to such property.

(3) Where
- (a) under paragraph (2) of Article 5 the United Kingdom imposes tax in connection with any event by reference to any property which is not referred to in paragraph (1) of this Article and which is comprised in a settlement in which an interest in possession subsists; and
- (b) at the time of the event giving rise to the liability to tax the individual entitled to that interest was domiciled in South Africa,

the United Kingdom shall allow against so much of its tax (as otherwise computed) as is attributable to such property a credit (not exceeding the amount of tax so attributable) equal to so much of the tax imposed in South Africa in connection with the same event as is attributable to such property.

(4) For the purposes of this Article:
- (a) the tax attributable to any property imposed in a Contracting State is tax as reduced by the amount of any credit allowed by that Contracting State in respect of tax attributable to that property imposed in a territory other than a Contracting State;
- (b) tax is imposed on a Contracting State if it is chargeable under the law of that Contracting State and duly paid; and
- (c) where tax is imposed on the death of a transferor by reason of a transfer made within three years immediately preceding the death, whether in consequence of the inclusion of property affected by the transfer in the transferor's estate or otherwise with respect to the transfer, that tax shall be treated as if it were imposed in connection with that transfer.

Article 13 Time limit

Any claim for a credit or for a repayment of tax founded on the provisions of this Convention shall be made within six years from the date of the event giving rise to a liability to tax or, where later, within one year from the last date on which tax for which credit is given is due. The competent authority of a Contracting State may, in appropriate circumstances, extend this time limit where the final determination or the payment of tax in the other Contracting State is delayed.

Article 14 Non-discrimination

(1) The nationals of a Contracting State shall not be subjected in the other Contracting State to any taxation or any requirement connected therewith which is other or more burdensome than the taxation and connected requirements to which nationals of that other Contracting State in the same circumstances are or may be subjected.

(2) The taxation of a permanent establishment which an enterprise of a Contracting State has in the other Contracting State shall not be less favourably levied in that other Contracting State than the taxation levied on enterprises of that other Contracting State carrying on the same activities.

(3) Enterprises of a Contracting State, the capital of which is wholly or partly owned or controlled, directly or indirectly, by one or more residents of the other Contracting State, shall not be subjected in the first-mentioned Contracting State to any taxation or any requirement connected therewith which is other or more burdensome than the taxation and connected requirements to which other similar enterprises of that first-mentioned State are or may be subjected.

(4) Nothing contained in this Article shall be construed as restricting the provisions of paragraph (2) of Article 11.

(5) In this Article the term "taxation" means taxes covered by this Convention.

Article 15 Mutual agreement procedure

(1) Where a person considers that the actions of one or both of the Contracting States result or will result for him in taxation not in accordance with the provisions of this Convention, he may, irrespective of the remedies provided by the domestic laws of those Contracting States, present his case to the competent authority of either Contracting State.

(2) The competent authority shall endeavour, if the objection appears to it to be justified and if it is not itself able to arrive at a satisfactory solution, to resolve the case by mutual agreement with the competent authority of the other Contracting State, with a view to the avoidance of taxation which is not in accordance with the provisions of this Convention.

(3) The competent authorities of the Contracting States shall endeavour to resolve by mutual agreement any difficulties or doubts arising as to the interpretation or application of this Convention.

(4) The competent authorities of the Contracting States may communicate with each other directly for the purpose of reaching an agreement in the sense of the preceding paragraphs.

Article 16 Exchange of information

(1) The competent authorities of the Contracting States shall exchange such information as is necessary for carrying out the provisions of this Convention or for the prevention of fraud or the administration of statutory provisions against legal avoidance in relation to the taxes which are the subject of this Convention. Any information so exchanged shall be treated as secret and shall not be disclosed to any persons other than persons (including a Court or administrative body) concerned with the assessment or collection of, or prosecution in respect of, or the determination of appeals in relation to, the taxes which are the subject of this Convention.

(2) In no case shall the provisions of paragraph (1) of this Article be construed so as to impose on the competent authority of either Contracting State the obligation:

    (*a*) to carry out administrative measures at variance with the laws or administrative practice prevailing in either Contracting State;

    (*b*) to supply particulars which are not obtainable under the laws or in the normal course of the administration of that or of the other Contracting State;

    (*c*) to supply information which would disclose any trade, business, industrial, commercial or professional secret or trade process, or information, the disclosure of which would be contrary to public policy.

Article 18 Entry into force

Note: This Convention applies in the UK in respect of property by reference to which there is a charge to tax which arises after 31 December 1978 (subject to transitional provisions in respect of deaths after 31 December 1977 and before 6 May 1979 and, in certain circumstances, in respect of deaths after 6 May 1979 and before 27 March 1981, where the 1946 Convention would have afforded greater relief).

Official languages: The Afrikaans language text and the English language text of this Convention are equally authoritative.

SPAIN

Convention of 21 October 1975 (SI 1976 No 1919)

Article 1 Personal scope

This Convention shall apply to persons who are residents of one or both of the Contracting States.

Article 2 Taxes covered

(1) The taxes which are the subject of this Convention are:
    (*a*) in the United Kingdom of Great Britain and Northern Ireland:
        (i) the income tax;
        (ii) the corporation tax; and
        (iii) the capital gains tax;
        (hereinafter referred to as "United Kingdom tax");
    (*b*) in Spain:
        (i) the general income tax on individuals (*el impuesto general sobre la Renta de las personas físicas*);
        (ii) the general corporation tax (*el impuesto general sobre la Renta de Sociedades y demás entidades jurídicas*);
        (iii) the following prepayments: the tax on rural land, the tax on urban land, the tax on earned income, the tax on income from capital, the tax on business and industrial activities (*los siguientes impuestos a cuenta: la Contribución Territorial sobre la Riqueza Rústica y Pecuaria, la Contribución Territorial sobre la Riqueza Urbana, el impuesto sobre los Rendimientos del Trabajo Personal, el impuesto sobre las Rentas del Capital y el impuesto sobre Actividades y beneficios comerciales e industriales*);

(iv) In Sahara, the income taxes on earned income and on income from capital and the taxes on profits of the enterprises (*en Sahara, los impuestos sobre la renta sobre los rendimientos del trabajo y del patrimonio y sobre los beneficios de las empresas*);

(v) The "surface royalty" and the tax on corporation profits, regulated by the Law of 27 June 1974 applicable to enterprises engaged in prospecting and exploiting oil wells (*el Canon de superficie y el impuesto sobre los beneficios, regulados por la Ley de 27 de Junio de 1974 aplicabel a las empresas que se dedican a la investigación y explotación de hidrocarburos*); and

(vi) the local taxes on income and capital (*los impuestos locales sobre la renta y el partimonio*);

(hereinafter referred to as "Spanish tax").

(2) This Convention shall also apply to any identical or substantially similar taxes which are imposed by either Contracting State after the date of signature of this Convention in addition to, or in place of, the existing taxes. At the end of each year, the competent authorities of the Contracting States shall notify to each other any changes which have been made in their respective taxation laws.

Article 3 General definitions

(1) In this Convention, unless the context otherwise requires:

(a) the term "United Kingdom" means Great Britain and Northern Ireland, including any area outside the territorial sea of the United Kingdom which in accordance with international law has been or may hereafter be designated, under the laws of the United Kingdom concerning the Continental Shelf, as an area within which the rights of the United Kingdom with respect to the sea-bed and sub-soil and their natural resources may be exercised;

(b) the term "Spain" means the Spanish State and, when used in a geographical sense, Peninsular Spain, the Balearic and Canary Islands, and the Spanish towns and territories in Africa, including any area outside the territorial sea of Spain which in accordance with international law has been or may hereafter be designated, under the laws of Spain concerning the Continental Shelf, as an area within which the rights of Spain with respect to the sea bed and sub-soil and their natural resources may be exercised;

(c) the term "national" means:

(i) in relation to the United Kingdom, any citizen of the United Kingdom and Colonies who derives his status as such from his connection with the United Kingdom and any legal person, association or other entity deriving its status as such from the law in force in the United Kingdom;

(ii) in relation to Spain, any individual possessing the nationality of Spain and any legal person, partnership or association deriving its status as such from the law in force in Spain;

(d) the term "international traffic" means any transport by a ship or aircraft operated by an enterprise of a Contracting State, except when the ship or aircraft is operated solely between places in the other Contracting State;

(e) the terms "a Contracting State" and "the other Contracting State" mean the United Kingdom or Spain as the context requires;

(f) the term "person" comprises an individual, a company and any other body of persons;

(g) the term "company" means any body corporate or any entity which is treated as a body corporate for tax purposes;

(h) the terms "enterprises of a Contracting State" and "enterprise of the other Contracting State" mean respectively an enterprise carried on by a resident of a Contracting State and an enterprise carried on by a resident of the other Contracting State;

(i) the term "competent authority" means, in the case of the United Kingdom, the Commissioners of Inland Revenue or their authorised representative and, in the case of Spain, the Minister of Finance, the Technical General Secretary or any other authority to whom the Minister delegates.

(2) As regards the application of this Convention by a Contracting State any term not otherwise defined shall, unless the context otherwise requires, have the meaning which it has under the laws of that Contracting State relating to the taxes which are the subject of this Convention.

Article 4 Fiscal domicile

(1) For the purposes of this Convention, the term "resident of a Contracting State" means, subject to the provisions of paragraphs (2) and (3) of this Article, any person who, under the law of that State, is liable to taxation therein by reason of his domicile, residence, place of management or any other criterion of a similar nature; the term does not include any individual who is liable to tax in that Contracting State only if he derives income from sources therein. The terms "resident of the United Kingdom" and "resident of Spain" shall be construed accordingly.

(2) Where by reason of the provisions of paragraph (1) of this Article an individual is a resident of both Contracting States, then his status shall be determined in accordance with the following rules:

(a) he shall be deemed to be a resident of the Contracting State in which he has a permanent home available to him. If he has a permanent home available to him in both Contracting States, he shall be deemed to be a resident of the Contracting State with which his personal and economic relations are closer (centre of vital interests);

(b) if the Contracting State in which he has his centre of vital interests cannot be determined, or if he has not a permanent home available to him in either Contracting State, he shall be deemed to be a resident of the Contracting State in which he has an habitual abode;

(c) if he has an habitual abode in both Contracting States or in neither of them, he shall be deemed to be a resident of the Contracting state of which he is a national;

(d) if he is a national of both Contracting States or of neither of them, the competent authorities of the Contracting States shall settle the question by mutual agreement.

(3) Where by reason of the provisions of paragraph (1) of this Article a person other than an individual is a resident of both Contracting States, then it shall be deemed to be a resident of the Contracting State in which its place of effective management is situated.

Article 6 Income from immovable property

(1) (Taxation of income from immovable property.)

(2) The term "immovable property" shall be defined in accordance with the law of the Contracting State in which the property in question is situated. The term shall in any case include property accessory to immovable property, livestock and equipment used in agriculture and forestry, rights to which the provisions of general law respecting landed property apply, usufruct of immovable property and rights to variable or fixed payments as consideration for the working of, or the right to work, mineral deposits, sources and other natural resources; ships, boats and aircraft shall not be regarded as immovable property.

(3) . . .

(4) . . .

Article 8 Shipping and air transport

(1) A resident of a Contracting State shall be exempt from tax in the other Contracting State on profits from the operation of ships or aircraft other than profits from voyages of ships or aircraft confined solely to places in the other Contracting State.

(2) The provisions of paragraph (1) shall also apply to profits derived from a participation in a pool, a joint business or an international operating agency.

Article 13 Capital gains

(1) . . .

(2) (Taxation of gains from alienation of movable business property.)

(3) Notwithstanding the provisions of paragraph (2) of this Article, capital gains derived by a resident of a Contracting State from the alienation of ships and aircraft operated in international traffic and movable property pertaining to the operation of such ships and aircraft shall be taxable only in that Contracting State.

(4) . . .

Article 23 Capital

(1) . . .

(2) (Taxation of capital represented by movable business property.)

(3) Notwithstanding the provisions of paragraph (2) of this Article, ships and aircraft operated in international traffic and movable property pertaining to the operation of such ships and aircraft shall be taxable only in the Contracting State of which the operator is a resident.

(4) . . .

Article 25 Non-discrimination

(1) The nationals of a Contracting State shall not be subjected in the other Contracting State to any taxation or any requirement connected therewith which is other or more burdensome than the taxation and connected requirements to which nationals of that other State in the same circumstances are or may be subjected.

(2) Stateless persons who are residents of one of the Contracting States shall not be subjected in either Contracting State to any taxation or any requirement connected therewith which is other or more burdensome than the taxation and connected requirements to which nationals of the State concerned in the same circumstances are or may be subjected.

(3) Subject to the provisions of paragraph (7) of Article 10, the taxation on a permanent establishment which an enterprise of a Contracting State has in the other Contracting State shall not be less favourably levied in that other State than the taxation levied on enterprises of that other State carrying on the same activities.

(4) Enterprises of a Contracting State, the capital of which is wholly or partly owned or controlled, directly or indirectly, by one or more residents of the other Contracting State, shall not be subjected in the first-mentioned Contracting State to any taxation or any requirement connected therewith which is other or more burdensome than the taxation and connected requirements to which other similar enterprises of the first-mentioned State are or may be subjected.

(5) Nothing in this Article shall be construed as obliging either Contracting State to grant to individuals not resident in that State any of the personal allowances, reliefs and reductions for tax purposes which are granted to individuals so resident.

(6) In this Article the term "taxation" means taxes of every kind and description.

Article 26 Mutual agreement procedure

(1) Where a resident of a Contracting State considers that the actions of one or both of the Contracting States result or will result for him in taxation not in accordance with this Convention, he may, notwithstanding the remedies provided by the national laws of those States, present his case to the competent authority of the Contracting State of which he is a resident.

(2) The competent authority shall endeavour, if the objection appears to it to be justified and if it is not itself able to arrive at an appropriate solution, to resolve the case by mutual agreement with the competent authority of the other Contracting State, with a view to the avoidance of taxation not in accordance with the Convention.

(3) The competent authorities of the Contracting States shall endeavour to resolve by mutual agreement any difficulties or doubts arising as to the interpretation or application of the Convention.

(4) The competent authorities of the Contracting States may communicate with each other directly for the purpose of reaching an agreement in the sense of the preceding paragraphs.

Article 27 Exchange of information

(1) The competent authorities of the Contracting States shall exchange such information as is necessary for carrying out the provisions of this Convention or for the prevention of fraud or for the administration of statutory provisions against legal avoidance in relation to the taxes which are the subject of this Convention. Any information so exchanged shall be treated as secret and shall not be disclosed to any persons other than persons (including a court or administrative body) concerned with the assessment or collection of, or prosecution in respect of, or the determination of appeals in relation to, the taxes which are the subject of the Convention.

(2) In no case shall the provisions of paragraph (1) be construed so as to impose on the competent authority of either Contracting State the obligation:

- (a) to carry out administrative measures at variance with the laws or administrative practice prevailing in either Contracting State;
- (b) to supply particulars which are not obtainable under the laws or in the normal course of the administration of that or of the other Contracting State;
- (c) to supply information which would disclose any trade, business, industrial, commercial or professional secret or trade process, or information, the disclosure of which would be contrary to public policy (*ordre public*).

Article 30 Entry into force

Note: Article 30 provided for the entry into force of this Convention. It takes effect in the UK from the year of assessment 1976–77 (income tax and capital gains tax) and from the financial year beginning on 1 April 1976 (corporation tax).

Official languages: The Spanish language text and the English language text of this Convention are equally authoritative.

SRI LANKA

Convention of 21 June 1979 (SI 1980 No 713)

(The Exchange of Notes of 13 February 1980 (SI 1980 No 713) does not amend the Articles printed below.)

SRI LANKA

Article 1 Personal scope

This Convention shall apply to persons who are residents of one or both of the Contracting States.

Article 2 Taxes covered

(1) The taxes which are the subject of this Convention are:
  (a) in the United Kingdom of Great Britain and Northern Ireland:
    (i) the income tax;
    (ii) the corporation tax; and
    (iii) the capital gains tax;
    (hereinafter referred to as "United Kingdom tax")
  (b) in Sri Lanka:
    the income tax;
    (hereinafter referred to as "Sri Lanka tax").

(2) This Convention shall also apply to any identical or substantially similar taxes which are imposed by either Contracting State after the date of signature of this Convention in addition to, or in place of, the existing taxes. The competent authorities of the Contracting States shall notify each other of any substantial changes which have been made in their respective taxation laws.

Article 3 General definitions

(1) In this Convention, unless the context otherwise requires:
  (a) the term "United Kingdom" means Great Britain and Northern Ireland, including any area outside the territorial sea of the United Kingdom which in accordance with international law has been or may hereafter be designated, under the laws of the United Kingdom concerning the Continental Shelf, as an area within which the rights of the United Kingdom with respect to the sea-bed and sub-soil and the natural resources may be exercised;
  (b) the term "Sri Lanka" means the Democratic Socialist Republic of Sri Lanka;
  (c) the term "national" means:
    (i) in relation to the United Kingdom, any citizen of the United Kingdom and Colonies, or any British subject not possessing that citizenship or the citizenship of any other Commonwealth country or territory, provided in either case he has the right of abode in the United Kingdom, and any legal person, partnership and association deriving its status as such from the law in force in the United Kingdom;
    (ii) in relation to Sri Lanka, any natural person who, under the law in force in Sri Lanka, is a citizen of Sri Lanka, and any legal person, partnership and association deriving its status as such from the law in force in Sri Lanka;
  (d) the term "tax" means United Kingdom tax or Sri Lanka tax, as the context requires;
  (e) the terms "a Contracting State" and "the other Contracting State" mean the United Kingdom or Sri Lanka, as the context requires;
  (f) the term "person" comprises an individual, a company and any other body of persons;
  (g) the term "company" means any body corporate or any entity which is treated as a body corporate for tax purposes;
  (h) the term "international traffic" includes traffic between places in one Contracting State in the course of a voyage which extends over more than one Contracting State;
  (i) the terms "enterprise of a Contracting State" and "enterprise of the other Contracting State" mean respectively an enterprise carried on by a resident of a Contracting State and an enterprise carried on by a resident of the other Contracting State;

(*j*) the term "competent authority" means, in the case of the United Kingdom the Commissioners of Inland Revenue or their authorised representative, and in the case of Sri Lanka the Commissioner General of Inland Revenue or his authorised representative.

(2) As regards the application of this Convention by a Contracting State any term not otherwise defined shall, unless the context otherwise requires, have the meaning which it has under the laws of that Contracting State relating to the taxes which are the subject of this Convention.

Article 4 Residence

(1) For the purposes of this Convention the term "resident of a Contracting State" means, subject to the provisions of paragraphs (2) and (3) of this Article, any person who, under the law of that State, is liable to taxation therein by reason of his domicile, residence, place of management or any other criterion of a similar nature; this term does not include any person who is liable to tax in that Contracting State in respect only of income from sources therein.

(2) Where by reason of the provisions of paragraph (1) of this Article an individual is a resident of both Contracting States, then his status shall be determined in accordance with the following rules:

(*a*) He shall be deemed to be a resident of the Contracting State in which he has a permanent home available to him. If he has a permanent home available to him in both Contracting States, he shall be deemed to be a resident of the Contracting State with which his personal and economic relations are closer (centre of vital interests).

(*b*) If the Contracting State in which he has his centre of vital interests cannot be determined, or if he has not a permanent home available to him in either Contracting State, he shall be deemed to be a resident of the Contracting State in which he has an habitual abode.

(*c*) If he has an habitual abode in both Contracting States or in neither of them, he shall be deemed to be a resident of the Contracting State of which he is a national.

(*d*) If he is a national of both Contracting States or of neither of them, the competent authorities of the Contracting States shall endeavour to settle the question by mutual agreement.

(3) Where by reason of the provisions of paragraph (1) of this Article a person other than an individual is a resident of both Contracting States, then it shall be deemed to be a resident of the Contracting State in which its place of effective management is situated.

Article 6 Income from immovable property

(1) (Taxation of income from immovable property.)

(2) (*a*) The term "immovable property" shall, subject to the provisions of sub-paragraph (*b*) below, be defined in accordance with the law of the Contracting State in which the property in question is situated.

(*b*) The term "immovable property" shall in any case include property accessory to immovable property, livestock and equipment used in agriculture and forestry, rights to which the provisions of general law respecting landed property apply, usufruct of immovable property and rights to variable or fixed payments as consideration for the working of, or the right to work, mineral deposits, sources and other natural resources; ships, boats and aircraft shall not be regarded as immovable property.

(3) . . .

(4) . . .

Article 8 Shipping and air transport

(1) A resident of one of the Contracting States shall be exempt from tax in the other Contracting State on profits from the operation of ships or aircraft in international traffic.

(2) The provisions of paragraph (1) of this Article shall likewise apply to profits derived from participation in a pool, a joint business or an international operating agency.

Article 13 Capital gains

(1) . . .

(2) (Taxation of gains from alienation of movable business property.)

(3) Notwithstanding the provisions of paragraph (2) of this Article, capital gains derived by a resident of a Contracting State from the alienation of ships and aircraft operated in international traffic and movable property pertaining to the operation of such ships and aircraft shall be taxable only in that Contracting State.

(4) . . .

Article 22 Non-discrimination

(1) The nationals of a Contracting State shall not be subjected in the other Contracting State to any taxation or any requirement connected therewith which is other or more burdensome than the taxation and connected requirements to which nationals of that other State in the same circumstances are or may be subjected.

(2) The taxation on a permanent establishment which an enterprise of a Contracting State has in the other Contracting State shall not be less favourably levied in that other State than the taxation levied on enterprises of that other State carrying on the same activities.

(3) Enterprises of a Contracting State, the capital of which is wholly or partly owned or controlled, directly or indirectly, by one or more residents of the other Contracting State, shall not be subjected in the first-mentioned Contracting State to any taxation or any requirements connected therewith which is other or more burdensome than the taxation and connected requirements to which other similar enterprises of that first-mentioned State are or may be subjected.

(4) Nothing contained in this Article shall be construed as obliging either Contracting State to grant to individuals not resident in that State any of the personal allowances, reliefs and reductions for tax purposes which are granted to individuals so resident.

(5) The additional rate of tax chargeable under subsection (4) of Section 26 of the Sri Lanka Inland Revenue Act No 4 of 1963 and Section 37 of the Sri Lanka Inland Revenue Act No 28 of 1979 (insofar as these provisions are in force on the date of signature of this Convention or have been modified only in minor respects so as not to affect their general character) shall not, in the case of companies which are residents of the United Kingdom, exceed 6 per cent in respect of any year of assessment commencing before 1 April 1979 and 5 per cent in respect of any year of assessment commencing on or after 1 April 1979.

(6) In this Article the term "taxation" means taxes which are the subject of this Convention.

Article 23 Mutual agreement procedure

(1) Where a resident of a Contracting State considers that the actions of one or both of the Contracting States result or will result for him in taxation not in accordance with this Convention, he may, notwithstanding the remedies provided by the national laws of those States, present his case to the competent authority of the Contracting State of which he is a resident.

(2) The competent authority shall endeavour, if the objection appears to it to be justified and if it is not itself able to arrive at an appropriate solution, to resolve the case by mutual agreement with the competent authority of the other Contracting State, with a view to the avoidance of taxation not in accordance with the Convention.

(3) The competent authorities of the Contracting States shall endeavour to resolve by mutual agreement any difficulties or doubts arising as to the interpretation or application of the Convention.

(4) The competent authorities of the Contracting States may communicate with each other directly for the purpose of reaching an agreement in the sense of the preceding paragraphs.

Article 24 Exchange of information

The competent authorities of the Contracting States shall exchange such information (being information which is at their disposal under their respective taxation laws in the normal course of administration) as is necessary for carrying out the provisions of this Convention or for the prevention of fraud or the administration of statutory provisions against legal avoidance in relation to the taxes which are the subject of this Convention. Any information so exchanged shall be treated as secret but may be disclosed to persons (including a court or administrative body) concerned with assessment, collection, enforcement or prosecution in respect of taxes which are the subject of this Convention. No information shall be exchanged which would disclose any trade, business, industrial or professional secret or any trade process.

Article 25 Entry into force

Note: Article 25 provides for the entry into force of this Convention. It takes effect in the UK from the year of assessment 1977–78 (income tax and capital gains tax) and from the financial year beginning on 1 April 1977 (corporation tax).

Official languages: The Sinhala language text and the English language text of this Convention are equally authoritative.

SUDAN

Convention of 8 March 1975 (SI 1977 No 1719)

Article 1 Personal scope

This Convention shall apply to persons who are residents of one or both of the Contracting States.

Article 2 Taxes covered

(1) The taxes which are the subject of this Convention are:
    (a) in the United Kingdom of Great Britain and Northern Ireland:
        (i) the income tax;
        (ii) the corporation tax; and
        (iii) the capital gains tax;

(b) in the Sudan:
- (i) the income tax
- (ii) the capital gains tax.

(2) This Convention shall also apply to any identical or substantially similar taxes which are imposed by either Contracting State after the date of signature of this Convention in addition to, or in place of, the existing taxes. The competent authorities of the Contracting States shall notify to each other any changes which are made in their respective taxation laws.

Article 3 General definitions

(1) In this Convention, unless the context otherwise requires:

(a) the term "United Kingdom" means Great Britain and Northern Ireland, including any area outside the territorial sea of the United Kingdom which in accordance with international law has been or may hereafter be designated, under the laws of the United Kingdom concerning the Continental Shelf, as an area within which the rights of the United Kingdom with respect to the sea-bed and sub-soil and their natural resources may be exercised;

(b) the term "the Sudan" means the Democratic Republic of the Sudan, including any area outside the territorial sea of the Democratic Republic of the Sudan which in accordance with international law has been or may hereafter be designated, under the laws of the Democratic Republic of the Sudan concerning the Continental Shelf, as an area within which the rights of the Democratic Republic of the Sudan with respect to the sea bed and sub-soil and their natural resources may be exercised;

(c) the term "nationals" means:
- (i) in relation to the United Kingdom all citizens of the United Kingdom and Colonies who derive their status as such from their connection with the United Kingdom and all legal persons, partnerships and associations deriving their status as such from the law in force in the United Kingdom;
- (ii) in relation to the Sudan, all citizens of the Democratic Republic of the Sudan who derive their status as such from their connection with the Democratic Republic of the Sudan and all legal persons, partnerships and associations deriving their status as such from the law in force in the Democratic Republic of the Sudan;

(d) the term "United Kingdom tax" means tax imposed by the United Kingdom, being tax to which this Convention applies by virtue of the provisions of Article 2; the term "Sudan tax" means tax imposed by the Sudan, being tax to which this Convention applies by virtue of the provisions of Article 2;

(e) the term "tax" means United Kingdom tax or Sudan tax, as the context requires;

(f) the terms "a Contracting State" and "the other Contracting State" mean the United Kingdom or the Sudan, as the context requires;

(g) the term "person" comprises an individual, a company and any other body of persons;

(h) the term "company" means any body corporate or any entity which is treated as a body corporate for tax purposes;

(i) the terms "enterprise of a Contracting State" and "enterprise of the other Contracting State" mean respectively an enterprise carried on by a resident of a Contracting State and an enterprise carried on by a resident of the other Contracting State;

(j) the term "competent authority" means, in the case of the United Kingdom the Commissioners of Inland Revenue or their authorised representative, and in the case of the Sudan the Director of Taxation or his authorised representative.

(2) As regards the application of this Convention by a Contracting State any term not otherwise defined shall, unless the context otherwise requires, have the meaning which it has under the laws of that Contracting State relating to the taxes which are the subject of this Convention.

278

Article 4 Fiscal domicile

(1) For the purposes of this Convention, the term "resident of a Contracting State" means, subject to the provisions of paragraphs (2) and (3) of this Article, any person who, under the law of that State, is liable to taxation therein by reason of his domicile, residence, place of management or any other criterion of a similar nature. The terms "resident of the United Kingdom" and "resident of the Sudan" shall be construed accordingly.

(2) Where by reason of the provisions of paragraph (1) of this Article an individual is a resident of both Contracting States, then his status shall be determined in accordance with the following rules:

(a) He shall be deemed to be a resident of the Contracting State in which he has a permanent home available to him. If he has a permanent home available to him in both Contracting States, he shall be deemed to be a resident of the Contracting State with which his personal and economic relations are closest (centre of vital interests).

(b) If the Contracting State in which he has his centre of vital interests cannot be determined, or if he has not a permanent home available to him in either Contracting State, he shall be deemed to be a resident of the Contracting State in which he has an habitual abode.

(c) If he has an habitual abode in both Contracting States or in neither of them, he shall be deemed to be a resident of the Contracting State of which he is a national.

(d) If he is a national of both Contracting States or of neither of them, the competent authorities of the Contracting States shall settle the question by mutual agreement.

(3) Where by reason of the provisions of paragraph (1) of this Article a person other than an individual is a resident of both Contracting States, then it shall be deemed to be a resident of the Contracting State in which its place of effective management is situated.

Article 6 Income from immovable property

(1) (Taxation of income from immovable property.)

(2) (a) The term "immovable property" shall, subject to the provisions of sub-paragraph (b) below, be defined in accordance with the law of the Contracting State in which the property in question is situated.

(b) The term "immovable property" shall in any case include property accessory to immovable property, livestock and equipment used in agriculture and forestry, rights to which the provisions of general law respecting landed property apply, usufruct of immovable property and rights to variable or fixed payments as consideration for the working of, or the right to work, mineral deposits, sources and other natural resources; ships, boats and aircraft shall not be regarded as immovable property.

(3)–(5) . . .

Article 8 Shipping and air transport

(1) Profits derived from the operation of ships or aircraft in international traffic by an enterprise of a Contracting State shall be exempt from tax in the other Contracting State.

(2) The provisions of paragraph (1) of this Article shall likewise apply to the share in respect of participation in shipping or aircraft pools of any kind by such an enterprise engaged in shipping or air transport.

(3) Profits from voyages of ships or aircraft confined solely to places within a Contracting State may be taxed in that State.

Article 13 Capital gains

(1) . . .

(2) (Taxation of gains from alienation of movable business property.)

(3) Notwithstanding the provisions of paragraph (2) of this Article, capital gains derived

279

by a resident of a Contracting State from the alienation of ships and aircraft operated in international traffic and movable property pertaining to the operation of such ships and aircraft shall be taxable only in that Contracting State.

(4) . . .

(5) . . .

Article 22 Capital

(1) . . .

(2) (Taxation of capital represented by movable business property.)

(3) Notwithstanding the provisions of paragraph (2) of this Article, ships and aircraft operated in international traffic and movable property pertaining to the operation of such ships and aircraft shall be taxable only in the Contracting State of which the operator is a resident.

(4) . . .

Article 25 Non-discrimination

(1) The nationals of a Contracting State shall not be subjected in the other Contracting State to any taxation or any requirement connected therewith which is other or more burdensome than the taxation and connected requirements to which nationals of that other State in the same circumstances are or may be subjected.

(2) The taxation on a permanent establishment which an enterprise of a Contracting State has in the other Contracting State shall not be less favourably levied in that other State than the taxation levied on enterprises of that other State carrying on the same activities.

(3) Enterprises of a Contracting State, the capital of which is wholly or partly owned or controlled, directly or indirectly, by one or more residents of the other Contracting State, shall not be subjected in the first-mentioned Contracting State to any taxation or any requirement connected therewith which is other or more burdensome than the taxation and connected requirements to which other similar enterprises of that first-mentioned State are or may be subjected.

(4) Nothing contained in this Article shall be construed as obliging either Contracting State to grant to individuals not resident in that State any of the personal allowances, reliefs and reductions for tax purposes which are granted to individuals so resident.

(5) In this Article the term "taxation" means taxes of every kind and description.

Article 26 Mutual agreement procedure

(1) Where a resident of a Contracting State considers that the actions of one or both of the Contracting States result or will result for him in taxation not in accordance with this Convention, he may, notwithstanding the remedies provided by the national laws of those States, present his case to the competent authority of the Contracting State of which he is a resident.

(2) The competent authority shall endeavour, if the objection appears to it to be justified and if it is not itself able to arrive at an appropriate solution, to resolve the case by mutual agreement with the competent authority of the other Contracting State, with a view to the avoidance of taxation not in accordance with the Convention.

(3) The competent authorities of the Contracting States shall endeavour to resolve by mutual agreement any difficulties or doubts arising as to the interpretation or application of the Convention.

(4) The competent authorities of the Contracting States may communicate with each other directly for the purpose of reaching an agreement in the sense of the preceding paragraphs.

Article 27 Exchange of information

(1) The competent authorities of the Contracting States shall exchange such information as is necessary for carrying out the provisions of this Convention or for the prevention of

fraud or the administration of statutory provisions against legal avoidance in relation to the taxes which are the subject of this Convention. Any information so exchanged shall be treated as secret but may be disclosed to persons (including a court or administrative body) concerned with assessment, collection, enforcement or prosecution in respect of taxes which are the subject of this Convention.

(2) In no case shall the provisions of paragraph (1) be construed so as to impose on the competent authority of either Contracting State the obligation:

(*a*) to carry out administrative measures at variance with the laws or administrative practice of that or of the other Contracting State

(*b*) to supply particulars which are not obtainable under the laws or in the normal course of the administration of that or of the other Contracting State

(*c*) to supply information which would disclose any trade, business, industrial, commercial or professional secret or trade process, or information, the disclosure of which would be contrary to public policy.

Article 29 Entry into force

Note: Article 29 provides for the entry into force of this Convention. It takes effect in the UK from the year of assessment 1975–76 (income tax and capital gains tax) and from the financial year beginning on 1 April 1975 (corporation tax).

Official language: English.

SWAZILAND

Agreement of 26 November 1968 (SI 1969 No 380)

Article 1 Persons covered

This Agreement shall apply to persons who are residents of one or both of the Contracting States.

Article 2 Taxes covered

(1) The taxes which are the subject of this Agreement are—

(*a*) in the United Kingdom of Great Britain and Northern Ireland—

(i) the income tax (including surtax);

(ii) the corporation tax; and

(iii) the capital gains tax;

(*b*) in Swaziland—

         (i) the normal tax;

         (ii) the non-resident shareholders' tax; and

         (iii) the non-residents' tax on interest.

(2) This Agreement shall also apply to any identical or substantially similar taxes which are imposed by either Contracting State after the date of signature of this Agreement in addition to, or in place of, the existing taxes. The competent authorities of the Contracting States shall notify to each other any changes which are made in their respective taxation laws.

Article 3 General definitions

(1) In this Agreement, unless the context otherwise requires—

    (a) the term "United Kingdom" means Great Britain and Northern Ireland, including any area outside the territorial sea of the United Kingdom which in accordance with international law has been or may hereafter be designated, under the laws of the United Kingdom concerning the Continental Shelf, as an area within which the rights of the United Kingdom with respect to the sea-bed and sub-soil and their natural resources may be exercised;

    (b) the term "Swaziland" means the Kingdom of Swaziland;

    (c) the term "nationals" means—

        (i) in relation to the United Kingdom, all citizens of the United Kingdom and Colonies who derive their status as such from their connection with the United Kingdom and all legal persons, partnerships and associations deriving their status as such from the law in force in the United Kingdom;

        (ii) in relation to Swaziland, all Swaziland citizens and all legal persons, partnerships and associations deriving their status as such from the law in force in Swaziland;

    (d) the term "United Kingdom tax" means tax imposed by the United Kingdom being tax to which this Agreement applies by virtue of Article 2; the term "Swaziland tax" means tax imposed by Swaziland being tax to which this Agreement applies by virtue of Article 2;

    (e) the term "tax" means United Kingdom tax or Swaziland tax, as the context requires;

    (f) the terms "a Contracting State" and "the other Contracting State" mean the United Kingdom or Swaziland, as the context requires;

    (g) the term "person" comprises an individual, a company and any other body of persons;

    (h) the term "company" means any body corporate or any entity which is treated as a body corporate for tax purposes;

    (i) the terms "enterprise of a Contracting State" and "enterprise of the other Contracting State" mean respectively an enterprise carried on by a resident of a Contracting State and an enterprise carried on by a resident of the other Contracting State;

    (j) the term "competent authority" means, in the case of the United Kingdom the Commissioners of Inland Revenue or their authorised representative, and in the case of Swaziland, the Collector of Income Tax or his authorised representative.

(2) As regards the application of this Agreement by a Contracting State any term not otherwise defined shall, unless the context otherwise requires, have the meaning which it has under the laws of that Contracting State relating to the taxes which are the subject of this Agreement.

Article 4 Fiscal domicile

(1) For the purposes of this Agreement, the term "resident of a Contracting State" means subject to paragraphs (2) and (3) of this Article, any person who, under the law of that State, is liable to taxation therein by reason of his domicile, residence, place of management or any other criterion of a similar nature; the term does not include any individual who is liable to tax

in that Contracting State only if he derives income from sources therein. The terms "resident of the United Kingdom" and "resident of Swaziland" shall be construed accordingly.

(2) Where by reason of the provisions of paragraph (1) of this Article an individual is a resident of both Contracting States, then his status shall be determined in accordance with the following rules—

    (a) he shall be deemed to be a resident of the Contracting State in which he has a permanent home available to him. If he has a permanent home available to him in both Contracting States, he shall be deemed to be a resident of the Contracting State with which his personal and economic relations are closest (centre of vital interests);

    (b) if the Contracting State in which he has his centre of vital interests cannot be determined, or if he has not a permanent home available to him in either Contracting State, he shall be deemed to be a resident of the Contracting State in which he has an habitual abode;

    (c) if he has an habitual abode in both Contracting States or in neither of them, he shall be deemed to be a resident of the Contracting State of which he is a national;

    (d) if he is a national of both Contracting States or of neither of them, the competent authorities of the Contracting States shall settle the question by mutual agreement.

(3) Where by reason of the provisions of paragraph (1) of this Article a person other than an individual is a resident of both Contracting States, then it shall be deemed to be a resident of the Contracting State in which its place of effective management is situated.

Article 7 Income from immovable property

(1) (Taxation of income from immovable property.)

(2) (a) The term "immovable property" shall, subject to sub-paragraph (b) below, be defined in accordance with the law of the Contracting State in which the property in question is situated;

    (b) the term "immovable property" shall in any case include property accessory to immovable property, livestock and equipment used in agriculture and forestry, rights to which the provisions of general law respecting landed property apply, usufruct of immovable property and rights to variable or fixed payments as consideration for the working of, or the right to work, mineral deposits, sources and other natural resources; ships, boats and aircraft shall not be regarded as immovable property.

(3) . . .

(4) . . .

Article 9 Shipping and air transport

A resident of a Contracting State shall be exempt from tax in the other Contracting State on profits from the operation of ships or aircraft other than profits from voyages of ships or aircraft confined solely to places in the other Contracting State.

Article 23 Non-discrimination

(1) The nationals of a Contracting State shall not be subjected in the other Contracting State to any taxation or any requirement connected therewith which is other or more burdensome than the taxation and connected requirements to which nationals of that other State in the same circumstances are or may be subjected.

(2) The taxation on a permanent establishment which an enterprise of a Contracting State has in the other Contracting State shall not be less favourably levied in that other State than the taxation levied on enterprises of that other State carrying on the same activities.

(3) Enterprises of a Contracting State, the capital of which is wholly or partly owned or controlled, directly or indirectly, by one or more residents of the other Contracting State, shall not be subjected in the first-mentioned Contracting State to any taxation or any require-

ment connected therewith which is other or more burdensome than the taxation and connected requirements to which other similar enterprises of that first-mentioned State are or may be subjected.

(4) Nothing contained in this Article shall be construed as obliging either Contracting State to grant to individuals not resident in that State any of the personal allowances, reliefs and reductions for tax purposes which are granted to individuals so resident, nor as conferring any exemption from tax in a Contracting State in respect of dividends paid to a company which is a resident of the other Contracting State.

(5) In this Article the term "taxation" means the taxes which are the subject of this Agreement.

Article 24 Mutual agreement procedure

(1) Where a resident of a Contracting State considers that the actions of one or both of the Contracting States result or will result for him in taxation not in accordance with this Agreement, he may, notwithstanding the remedies provided by the national laws of those States, present his case to the competent authority of the Contracting State of which he is a resident.

(2) The competent authority shall endeavour, if the objection appears to it to be justified and if it is not itself able to arrive at an appropriate solution, to resolve the case by mutual agreement with the competent authority of the other Contracting State, with a view to the avoidance of taxation not in accordance with the Agreement.

(3) The competent authorities of the Contracting States shall endeavour to resolve by mutual agreement any difficulties or doubts arising as to the interpretation or application of the Agreement.

(4) The competent authorities of the Contracting States may communicate with each other directly for the purpose of reaching an agreement in the sense of the preceding paragraphs.

Article 25 Exchange of information

The competent authorities of the Contracting States shall exchange such information (being information which is at their disposal under their respective taxation laws in the normal course of administration) as is necessary for carrying out the provisions of this Agreement or for the prevention of fraud or the administration of statutory provisions against legal avoidance in relation to the taxes which are the subject of this Agreement. Any information so exchanged shall be treated as secret but may be disclosed to persons (including a court or administrative body) concerned with assessment, collection, enforcement or prosecution in respect of taxes which are the subject of this Agreement. No information shall be exchanged which would disclose any trade, business, industrial or professional secret or any trade process.

Article 27 Entry into force

Note: Article 27 provided for the entry into force of this Agreement. It takes effect in the UK from the year of assessment 1968–69 (income tax and capital gains tax) and from the financial year beginning on 1 April 1968 (corporation tax).

Official language: English.

SWEDEN

Convention of 30 August 1983 (SI 1984 No 366)

Article 1 Personal scope

This Convention shall apply to persons who are residents of one or both of the Contracting States.

Article 2 Taxes covered

(1) The taxes which are the subject of this Convention are:
  (a) in the United Kingdom of Great Britain and Northern Ireland:
    (i) the income tax;
    (ii) the corporation tax;
    (iii) the capital gains tax;
    (iv) the petroleum revenue tax; and
    (v) the development land tax;
    (hereinafter referred to as "United Kingdom tax");
  (b) in the case of Sweden:
    (i) the State income tax (*statlig inkomstskatt*), including sailors' tax (*sjomansskatt*) and coupon tax (*kupongskatt*);
    (ii) the tax on undistributed profits of companies (*ersättningsskatt*);
    (iii) the tax on distributed income of companies (*utskiftningsskatt*);
    (iv) the tax on public entertainers (*bevillningsavgift för vissa offentliga föreställningar*);
    (v) the communal income tax (*kommunal inkomstskatt*);
    (hereinafter referred to as "Swedish tax").

(2) This Convention shall also apply to any identical or substantially similar taxes which are imposed by either Contracting State after the date of signature of this Convention in addition to, or in place of, the existing taxes. The competent authorities of the Contracting States shall notify each other of substantial changes which have been made in their respective taxation laws.

Article 3 General definitions

(1) In this Convention, unless the context otherwise requires:
  (a) the term "United Kingdom" means Great Britain and Northern Ireland, including any area outside the territorial sea of the United Kingdom which in accordance with international law has been or may hereafter be designated, under the laws of the United Kingdom concerning the Continental Shelf, as an area within which the rights of the United Kingdom with respect to the sea-bed and sub-soil and their natural resources may be exercised;

(*b*) the term "Sweden" means the Kingdom of Sweden and includes any area outside the territorial sea of Sweden within which under the laws of Sweden and in accordance with international law the rights of Sweden with respect to the exploitation and exploration of the natural resources on the sea-bed or in its sub-soil may be exercised;

(*c*) the term "national" means:

   (i) in relation to the United Kingdom, any individual who has under the law of the United Kingdom the status of United Kingdom national provided he has the right of abode in the United Kingdom, and any legal person, partnership, association or other entity deriving its status as such from the law in force in the United Kingdom;

   (ii) in relation to Sweden, any individual possessing the nationality of Sweden and any legal person, partnership or association deriving its status as such from the law in force in Sweden;

(*d*) the term "tax" means United Kingdom tax or Swedish tax, as the context requires;

(*e*) the terms "a Contracting State" and "the other Contracting State" mean the United Kingdom or Sweden, as the context requires;

(*f*) the term "person" comprises an individual, a company and any other body of persons;

(*g*) the term "company" means any body corporate or any entity which is treated as a body corporate for tax purposes;

(*h*) the terms "enterprise of a Contracting State" and "enterprise of the other Contracting State" mean respectively an enterprise carried on by a resident of a Contracting State and an enterprise carried on by a resident of the other Contracting State;

(*i*) the term "international traffic" means any transport by a ship or aircraft operated by an enterprise which has its place of effective management in a Contracting State, except when the ship or aircraft is operated solely between places in the other Contracting State;

(*j*) the term "political subdivision", in relation to the United Kingdom, includes Northern Ireland;

(*k*) the term "competent authority" means, in the case of the United Kingdom, the Commissioners of Inland Revenue or their authorised representative, and in the case of Sweden, the Minister of Finance or his authorised representative.

(2) As regards the application of the Convention by a Contracting State any term not defined therein shall, unless the context otherwise requires, have the meaning which it has under the law of that State concerning the taxes to which the Convention applies.

Article 6 Income from immovable property

(1) (Taxation of income from immovable property.)

(2) The term "immovable property" shall have the meaning which it has under the law of the Contracting State in which the property in question is situated. The term shall in any case include property accessory to immovable property, livestock and equipment used in agriculture and forestry, rights to which the provisions of general law respecting landed property apply, usufruct of immovable property and rights to variable or fixed payments as consideration for the working of, or the right to work, mineral deposits, sources and other natural resources; ships, boats and aircraft shall not be regarded as immovable property.

(3) . . .

(4) . . .

Article 8 Shipping and air transport

(1) Profits from the operation of ships or aircraft in international traffic shall be taxable only in the Contracting State in which the place of effective management of the enterprise is situated.

(2) If the place of effective management of a shipping enterprise is aboard a ship then it shall be deemed to be situated in the Contracting State in which the home harbour of the ship is situated, or, if there is no such home harbour, in the State of which the operator of the ship is a resident.

(3) Where profits within paragraph (1) of this Article are derived by an enterprise from participation in a pool, a joint business or an international operating agency, the profits attributable to that enterprise shall be taxable only in the Contracting State in which the place of effective management of that enterprise is situated. For the purposes of this paragraph the expression "a pool, a joint business or an international operating agency" shall not include a person, as defined in Article 3 of this Convention.

(4) With respect to profits derived by the Danish, Norwegian and Swedish air transport consortium, known as the Scandinavian Airlines System (SAS), the provisions of paragraphs (1) and (3) of this Article shall only apply to such part of the profits as corresponds to the shareholding in the consortium held by AB Aerotransport (ABA), the Swedish partner of Scandinavian Airlines System (SAS).

Offshore activities: See Article 28(5) in relation to offshore activities.

Article 13 Capital gains

(1)–(3) . . .

(4) Gains from the alienation of ships or aircraft operated in international traffic, or movable property pertaining to the operation of such ships or aircraft shall be taxable only in the Contracting State in which the place of effective management of the enterprise is situated. With respect to gains derived by the Swedish, Danish and Norwegian air transport consortium, known as Scandinavian Airlines System (SAS), the provisions of this paragraph shall only apply to such proportion of the gains as corresponds to the shareholding in that consortium held by AB Aerotransport (ABA), the Swedish partner of Scandinavian Airlines System (SAS).

(5) Gains from the alienation of ships or aircraft used for the transportation of supplies or personnel to a location where activities in connection with the exploration or exploitation of the sea-bed and subsoil and their natural resources are being carried on in a Contracting State or from the alienation of tugboats or anchor handling vessels operated in connection with such activities shall be taxable in the Contracting State in which the place of effective management of the enterprise is situated.

(6) . . .

(7) . . .

Article 23 Non-discrimination

(1) Nationals of a Contracting State shall not be subjected in the other Contracting State to any taxation or any requirement connected therewith, which is other or more burdensome than the taxation and connected requirements to which nationals of that other State in the same circumstances are or may be subjected.

(2) The taxation on a permanent establishment which an enterprise of a Contracting State has in the other Contracting State shall not be less favourably levied in that other State than the taxation levied on enterprises of that other State carrying on the same activities.

(3) Nothing contained in this Article shall be construed as obliging either Contracting State to grant to individuals not resident in that State any of the personal allowances, reliefs and reductions for tax purposes which are granted to individuals so resident.

(4) Except where the provisions of paragraph (1) of Article 9, paragraphs (4) and (5) of Article 11, or paragraph (4) of Article 12, apply, interest, royalties and other disbursements paid by an enterprise of a Contracting State to a resident of the other Contracting State shall, for the purpose of determining the taxable profits of such enterprise, be deductible under the same conditions as if they had been paid to a resident of the first-mentioned State. Similarly,

any debts of an enterprise of a Contracting State to a resident of the other Contracting State shall, for the purpose of determining the taxable capital of such enterprise, be deductible under the same conditions as if they had been contracted to a resident of the first-mentioned State.

(5) Enterprises of a Contracting State, the capital of which is wholly or partly owned or controlled, directly or indirectly by one or more residents of the other Contracting State, shall not be subjected in the first-mentioned State to any taxation or any requirement connected therewith which is other or more burdensome than the taxation and connected requirements to which the similar enterprises of the first-mentioned State are or may be subjected.

(6) The provisions of this Article shall apply to taxes of every kind and description.

Article 24 Mutual agreement procedure

(1) Where a person considers that the actions of one or both of the Contracting States result or will result for him in taxation not in accordance with the provisions of this Convention, he may, irrespective of the remedies provided by the domestic law of those States, present his case to the competent authority of the Contracting State of which he is a resident.

(2) The competent authority shall endeavour, if the objection appears to it to be justified and if it is not itself able to arrive at a satisfactory solution, to resolve the case by mutual agreement with the competent authority of the other Contracting State, with a view to the avoidance of taxation which is not in accordance with the Convention.

(3) The competent authorities of the Contracting States shall endeavour to resolve by mutual agreement any difficulties or doubts arising as to the interpretation or application of the Convention. They may also consult together to consider measures to counteract improper use of the provisions of the Convention.

(4) The competent authorities of the Contracting States may communicate with each other directly for the purpose of reaching an agreement in the sense of the preceding paragraphs.

Article 25 Exchange of information

(1) The competent authorities of the Contracting States shall exchange such information as is necessary for carrying out the provisions of this Convention or of the domestic laws of the Contracting States concerning taxes covered by the Convention insofar as the taxation thereunder is not contrary to the Convention. Any information received by a Contracting State shall be treated as secret in the same manner as information obtained under the domestic laws of that State and shall be disclosed only to persons or authorities (including courts and administrative bodies) involved in the assessment or collection of, the enforcement or prosecution in respect of, or the determination of appeals in relation to, the taxes covered by the Convention. Such persons or authorities shall use the information only for such purposes. They may disclose the information in public court proceedings or in judicial decisions.

(2) In no case shall the provisions of paragraph (1) of this Article be construed so as to impose on a Contracting State the obligation:

    (a) to carry out administrative measures at variance with the laws and administrative practice of that or of the other Contracting State;

    (b) to supply information which is not obtainable under the laws or in the normal course of the administration of that or of the other Contracting State;

    (c) to supply information which would disclose any trade, business, industrial, commercial or professional secret or trade process, or information, the disclosure of which would be contrary to public policy (ordre public).

Article 28 Miscellaneous rules applicable to certain offshore activities

(1) The provisions of this Article shall apply notwithstanding any other provision of this Convention where activities (in this Article called "relevant activities") are carried on offshore in connection with the exploration or exploitation of the sea-bed and subsoil and their natural resources situated in a Contracting State.

(2)–(4) . . .

(5) Profits derived by an enterprise of a Contracting State from the transportation of supplies or personnel by a ship or aircraft to a location where relevant activities are being carried on, or from the operation of tugboats or anchor handling vessels in connection with such activities, shall be taxable only in the Contracting State in which the place of effective management of the enterprise is situated.

(6) . . .

Article 29 Entry into force

Note: Article 29 provides for the entry into force of this Convention. It takes effect in the UK from the year of assessment 1985–86 (income tax and capital gains tax) and from the financial year beginning on 1 April 1985 (corporation tax).

Official languages: The Swedish language text and the English language text of this Convention are equally authoritative.

Capital taxes

Convention of 8 October 1980 (SI 1981 No 840)

Article 1 Personal scope

This Convention shall apply to any person who is within the scope of a tax which is the subject of this Convention.

Article 2 Taxes covered

(1) The taxes which are the subject of this Convention are:
(*a*) in the United Kingdom, the capital transfer tax;
(*b*) in Sweden, the inheritance tax and the gift tax.
(2) This Convention shall also apply to any identical or substantially similar taxes which are imposed by either Contracting State after the date of signature of this Convention in addition to, or in place of, the existing taxes.

Inheritance tax: United Kingdom capital transfer tax is known as inheritance tax by virtue of FA 1986, s 100.

Article 3 General definitions

(1) In this Convention, unless the context otherwise requires:
- (a) the term "United Kingdom" means Great Britain and Northern Ireland;
- (b) the term "Sweden" means the Kingdom of Sweden;
- (c) the term "national" means:
  - (i) in relation to the United Kingdom, any citizen of the United Kingdom and Colonies, or any British subject not possessing that citizenship or the citizenship of any other Commonwealth country or territory, provided in either case he had the right of abode in the United Kingdom at the time of the death or transfer or at any other time at which his domicile falls to be determined;
  - (ii) in relation to Sweden, any individual possessing Swedish nationality;
- (d) the term "tax" means:
  - (i) the capital transfer tax imposed in the United Kingdom, or
  - (ii) the inheritance tax or the gift tax imposed in Sweden, or
  - (iii) any other tax imposed by a Contracting State to which this Convention applies by virtue of the provisions of paragraph (2) of Article 2, as the context requires;
- (e) the terms "a Contracting State" and "the other Contracting State" mean the United Kingdom or Sweden as the context requires;
- (f) the term "competent authority" means, in the case of the United Kingdom, the Commissioners of Inland Revenue or their authorised representative, and in the case of Sweden, the Minister of the Budget or his authorised representative.

(2) As regards the application of this Convention by a Contracting State any term not otherwise defined shall, unless the context otherwise requires, have the meaning which it has under the law of that Contracting State relating to the taxes which are the subject of this Convention.

Article 4 Fiscal domicile

(1) For the purposes of this Convention, the question whether an individual was domiciled in a Contracting State shall be determined by whether he was domiciled in that Contracting State in accordance with the law of that Contracting State or is treated as so domiciled for the purposes of a tax which is the subject of this Convention.

(2) Where by reason of the provisions of paragraph (1) of this Article an individual was domiciled in both Contracting States, then his status shall be determined as follows:
- (a) he shall be deemed to be domiciled in the Contracting State in which he had a permanent home available to him. If he had a permanent home available to him in both Contracting States, the domicile shall be deemed to be in the Contracting State with which his personal and economic relations were closer (centre of vital interests);
- (b) if the Contracting State in which he had his centre of vital interests cannot be determined, or if he had not a permanent home available to him in either Contracting State, the domicile shall be deemed to be in the Contracting State in which he had an habitual abode;
- (c) if he had an habitual abode in both Contracting States or in neither of them, the domicile shall be deemed to be in the Contracting State of which he was a national; and
- (d) if he was a national of both Contracting States or of neither of them, the competent authorities of the Contracting States shall settle the question by mutual agreement.

Article 5 General taxing rights

(1) Subject to the provisions of Articles 6, 7 and 8 and the following provisions of this Article, if the deceased or the transferor was domiciled in a Contracting State at the time of

the death or transfer, property shall not be taxable in the other Contracting State unless he was a national of that other State at the time of the death or transfer and had been domiciled in that other State within the ten years immediately preceding that time.

(2) Paragraph (1) of this Article shall not apply where at the time of the death or transfer the deceased or the transferor was domiciled in Sweden and he

    (a) had not been domiciled in Sweden in accordance with the law of Sweden in seven or more of the ten years immediately preceding that time; and

    (b) was at that time a national of the United Kingdom but not of Sweden; and

    (c) was at that time domiciled in the United Kingdom in accordance with the law of the United Kingdom or treated as so domiciled for the purposes of a tax which is the subject of this Convention;

but in such a case, subject to the provisions of Articles 6, 7 and 8, property shall not be taxable in Sweden.

(3) Paragraph (1) of this Article shall not apply where at the time of the death or transfer the deceased or the transferor was domiciled in the United Kingdom and he

    (a) had not been resident in the United Kingdom in seven or more of the ten income tax years of assessment ending with the year of assessment in which the time falls; and

    (b) was at that time a national of Sweden but not of the United Kingdom; and

    (c) had been domiciled in Sweden within the ten years immediately preceding that time;

but in such a case, subject to the provisions of Articles 6, 7 and 8 and of paragraph (4) of this Article, property shall not be taxable in the United Kingdom.

For the purposes of this paragraph the question whether an individual was resident in the United Kingdom shall be determined as for the purposes of income tax, but without regard to any dwelling-house available in the United Kingdom for his use.

(4) Paragraphs (1) and (3) of this Article shall not apply in the United Kingdom to property comprised in a settlement; but, subject to the provisions of Articles 6, 7 and 8, such property shall not be taxable in the United Kingdom if at the time when the settlement was made the settlor was domiciled in Sweden unless he was at that time a national of the United Kingdom and had been domiciled in the United Kingdom within the immediately preceding ten years.

(5) If by reason of any of the preceding paragraphs of this Article any property would be taxable only in one Contracting State and tax, though chargeable, is not paid (otherwise than as a result of a specific exemption, deduction, credit or allowance) in that Contracting State, tax may be imposed by reference to that property in the other Contracting State notwithstanding that paragraph.

Article 6 Immovable property

(1) (Taxation of immovable property.)

(2) The term "immovable property" shall have the meaning which it has under the law of the Contracting State in which the property in question is situated provided always that debts secured by mortgage or otherwise shall not be regarded as immovable property. The term shall in any case include property accessory to immovable property, livestock and equipment used in agriculture and forestry, rights to which the provisions of general law respecting landed property apply, an interest in the proceeds of sale of land which is held on a trust for sale, usufruct of immovable property and rights to variable or fixed payments as consideration for the working of, or the right to work, mineral deposits, sources and other natural resources; ships, boats and aircraft shall not be regarded as immovable property.

(3) . . .

Article 8 Ships and aircraft

Ships and aircraft operated in international traffic and boats engaged in inland waterways transport, and movable property pertaining to the operation of such ships, aircraft and boats, may be taxed in the Contracting State in which the place of effective management of the enterprise is situated.

Article 9 Conflict as to the nature of property

(1) If the deceased or the transferor was domiciled in a Contracting State at the time of death or transfer, and

(a) by the law of that Contracting State any right or interest is regarded as property not falling within Articles 6, 7 or 8, but

(b) by the law of the other Contracting State that right or interest is regarded as property falling within those Articles,

then the Article of the Convention under which the property falls shall be determined by the law of the other Contracting State.

(2) If the deceased or the transferor was domiciled in neither Contracting State at the time of the death or transfer, and each Contracting State would regard any property as situated in its territory and in consequence tax would be imposed in both Contracting States, the competent authorities shall determine the situs of the property by mutual agreement.

Article 10 Deductions

In determining the amount on which tax is to be computed permitted deductions shall be allowed in accordance with the law in force in the Contracting State in which the tax is imposed.

Article 11 Spouse transfers

(1) Property which passes to the spouse from a deceased person who was domiciled in or a national of Sweden and which may be taxed in the United Kingdom shall, where

(a) the spouse was not domiciled in the United Kingdom but the transfer would have been wholly exempt had the spouse been so domiciled, and

(b) a greater exemption for transfers between spouses would not have been given under the law of the United Kingdom apart from this Convention,

be exempt from tax in the United Kingdom to the extent of 50 per cent of all value transferred, calculated as a value on which no tax is payable after taking account of all exemptions except those for transfers between spouses.

(2) Where property passes to a spouse from a deceased person who was domiciled in or a national of the United Kingdom and the property rights of the spouse are not regulated by Swedish general law regarding matrimonial property, then Swedish tax on such property shall, if the surviving spouse so requests, be assessed as if the provisions of Swedish law regulating matrimonial property rights were applicable to such property.

Article 12 Credit provisions

(1) Where under this Convention the United Kingdom may impose tax by reference to any property other than property which the United Kingdom is entitled to tax in accordance with Articles 6, 7 or 8, then double taxation shall be avoided in the following manner:

(a) Where Sweden imposes tax by reference to property in accordance with the said Articles 6, 7, or 8, the United Kingdom shall allow against the tax calculated according to its law by reference to that property a credit equal to the tax paid in Sweden by reference to that property.

(b) Where Sweden imposes tax by reference to property not referred to in subparagraph (a) of this paragraph and

(i) except where the property was comprised in a settlement if the deceased or transferor was a national of the United Kingdom and was domiciled in Sweden at the time of the death or transfer; or

(ii) where the property was comprised in a settlement, if at the time when the settlement was made the settlor was a national of the United Kingdom and was domiciled in Sweden, then the United Kingdom shall allow against the tax calculated according to its law by reference to that property a credit equal to the tax paid in Sweden by reference to that property.

(2) Where under this Convention Sweden may impose tax by reference to any property other than property which Sweden is entitled to tax in accordance with the said Articles 6, 7 or 8, then double taxation shall be avoided in the following manner:

    (*a*) Where the United Kingdom imposes tax by reference to property in accordance with the said Articles 6, 7 or 8, Sweden shall allow against the tax calculated according to its law by reference to that property a credit equal to the tax paid in the United Kingdom by reference to that property.

    (*b*) Where the United Kingdom imposes tax by reference to property not referred to in sub-paragraph (*a*) of this paragraph and the deceased or transferor was a national of Sweden and was domiciled in the United Kingdom at the time of the death or transfer, Sweden shall allow against the tax calculated according to its law by reference to that property a credit equal to the tax paid in the United Kingdom by reference to that property.

(3) Any credit allowed in a Contracting State under paragraphs (1) or (2) of this Article shall not exceed the part of the tax imposed in that Contracting State which is attributable to the property by reference to which the credit is given.

(4) For the purposes of this Article:

    (*a*) the tax attributable to any property imposed in a Contracting State is tax as reduced by the amount of any credit allowed by that Contracting State in respect of tax attributable to that property imposed outside Sweden or the United Kingdom; and

    (*b*) tax is imposed in a Contracting State if it is chargeable under the law of that Contracting State and duly paid.

Article 13 Time limit

Any claim for a credit or for a refund of tax founded on the provisions of this Convention shall be made within six years from the date of the event giving rise to a liability to tax or, where later, within one year from the last date on which tax for which credit is given is due. The competent authority of a Contracting State may, in appropriate circumstances, extend this time limit where the final determination or the payment of tax in the other Contracting State is delayed.

Article 14 Mutual agreement procedure

(1) Where a person considers that the actions of one or both of the Contracting States result or will result for him in taxation not in accordance with the provisions of this Convention, he may, irrespective of the remedies provided by the domestic laws of those Contracting States, present his case to the competent authority of either Contracting State.

(2) The competent authority shall endeavour, if the objection appears to it to be justified and if it is not itself able to arrive at a satisfactory solution, to resolve the case by mutual agreement with the competent authority of the other Contracting State, with a view to the avoidance of taxation which is not in accordance with the provisions of this Convention.

(3) The competent authorities of the Contracting States shall endeavour to resolve by mutual agreement any difficulties or doubts arising as to the interpretation or application of this Convention.

(4) The competent authorities of the Contracting States may communicate with each other directly for the purpose of reaching an agreement in the sense of the preceding paragraphs.

Article 15 Exchange of information

(1) The competent authorities of the Contracting States shall exchange such information as is necessary for carrying out the provisions of this Convention or for the prevention of

fraud or the administration of statutory provisions against legal avoidance in relation to the taxes which are the subject of this Convention. Any information so exchanged shall be treated as secret and shall not be disclosed to any persons other than persons (including a Court or administrative body) concerned with the assessment or collection of, or prosecution in respect of, or the determination of appeals in relation to, the taxes which are the subject of this Convention.

(2) In no case shall the provisions of paragraph (1) of this Article be construed so as to impose on the competent authority of either Contracting State the obligation:

(a) to carry out administrative measures at variance with the laws or administrative practice prevailing in either Contracting State;

(b) to supply particulars which are not obtainable under the laws or in the normal course of the administration of that or of the other Contracting State;

(c) to supply information which would disclose any trade, business, industrial, commercial or professional secret or trade process, or information, the disclosure of which would be contrary to public policy.

Article 17 Entry into force

Note: This Convention applies in the UK in respect of property by reference to which there is a charge to tax which arises after 19 June 1981 (subject to transitional provisions in respect of deaths before 27 March 1981 where the 1964 Convention would have afforded greater relief).

Official languages: The Swedish language text and the English language text of this Convention are equally authoritative.

SWITZERLAND

Convention of 8 December 1977 (SI 1978 No 1408)

(The Protocol of 5 March 1981 (SI 1982 No 714) does not amend the Articles printed below.)

Article 1 Personal scope

This Convention shall apply to persons who are residents of one or both of the Contracting States.

Article 2 Taxes covered

(1) The taxes which are the subject of this Convention are:
  (a) in the United Kingdom of Great Britain and Northern Ireland:
        the income tax, the corporation tax, the capital gains tax, the development land tax and the petroleum revenue tax
      (hereinafter referred to as "United Kingdom tax");
  (b) in Switzerland:
        the federal, cantonal and communal taxes on income (total income, earned-income, income from capital, industrial and commercial profits, capital gains and other items of income)
      (hereinafter referred to as "Swiss tax").

(2) The Convention shall also apply to any identical or substantially similar taxes which are imposed by a Contracting State or a political sub-division or a local authority thereof after the date of signature of the Convention in addition to, or in place of, the existing taxes. The competent authorities of the Contracting States shall notify each other of any substantial changes which have been made in their respective taxation laws.

(3) . . .

Article 3 General definitions

(1) In this Convention, unless the context otherwise requires:
  (a) the term "United Kingdom" means Great Britain and Northern Ireland, including any area outside the territorial sea of the United Kingdom which in accordance with international law has been or may hereafter be designated, under the laws of the United Kingdom concerning the Continental Shelf, as an area within which the rights of the United Kingdom with respect to the sea-bed and sub-soil and their natural resources may be exercised;
  (b) the term "Switzerland" means the Swiss Confederation;
  (c) the terms "a Contracting State" and "the other Contracting State" mean the United Kingdom or Switzerland, as the context requires;
  (d) the term "tax" means United Kingdom tax or Swiss tax, as the context requires;
  (e) the term "person" includes any individual, company, unincorporated body of persons, and any other entity with or without juridical personality;
  (f) the term "company" means any body corporate or any entity which is treated as a body corporate for tax purposes;
  (g) the terms "enterprise of a Contracting State" and "enterprise of the other Contracting State" mean respectively an enterprise carried on by a resident of a Contracting State and an enterprise carried on by a resident of the other Contracting State;
  (h) the term "national" means:
      (i) in relation to the United Kingdom, any citizen of the United Kingdom and Colonies, or any British subject not possessing that citizenship or the citizenship of any other Commonwealth country or territory, provided in either case he has the right of abode in the United Kingdom, and any legal person, partnership, association or other entity deriving its status as such from the law in force in the United Kingdom;
      (ii) in relation to Switzerland, any Swiss citizen and any legal person, partnership, association or other entity deriving its status as such from the law in force in Switzerland;
  (i) the term "international traffic" means any transport by a ship or aircraft operated by an enterprise which has its place of effective management in a Contracting State, except when the ship or aircraft is operated solely between places in the other Contracting State;
  (j) the term "competent authority" means in the United Kingdom, the Commissioners of Inland Revenue or their authorised representative and in Switzer-

land, the Director of the Federal Tax Administration or his authorised representative.

Article 6 Income from immovable property

(1) (Taxation of income from immovable property.)

(2) The term "immovable property" shall have the meaning which it has under the law of the Contracting State in which the property in question is situated. The term shall in any case include property accessory to immovable property, livestock and equipment used in agriculture and forestry, rights to which the provisions of general law respecting landed property apply, usufruct of immovable property and rights to variable or fixed payments as consideration for the working of, or the right to work, mineral deposits, sources and other natural resources; ships, boats and aircraft shall not be regarded as immovable property.

(3) . . .

(4) . . .

Article 8 Shipping, inland waterways transport and air transport

(1) Profits from the operation of ships or aircraft in international traffic shall be taxable only in the Contracting State in which the place of effective management of the enterprise is situated.

(2) Profits from the operation of boats engaged in inland waterways transport shall be taxable only in the Contracting State in which the place of effective management of the enterprise is situated.

(3) If the place of effective management of a shipping enterprise or of an inland waterways transport enterprise is aboard a ship or boat, then it shall be deemed to be situated in the Contracting State in which the home harbour of the ship or boat is situated, or, if there is no such home harbour, in the Contracting State of which the operator of the ship or boat is a resident.

(4) The provisions of paragraph (1) shall also apply to profits from the participation in a pool, a joint business or an international operating agency.

Article 13 Capital gains

(1) . . .

(2) . . .

(3) Gains from the alienation of ships or aircraft operated in international traffic, boats engaged in inland waterways transport or movable property pertaining to the operation of such ships, aircraft or boats, shall be taxable only in the Contracting State in which the place of effective management of the enterprise is situated.

(4) . . .

(5) . . .

Article 23 Non-discrimination

(1) Nationals of a Contracting State shall not be subjected in the other Contracting State to any taxation or any requirement connected therewith, which is other or more burdensome than the taxation and connected requirements to which nationals of that other State in the same circumstances are or may be subjected.

(2) The taxation on a permanent establishment which an enterprise of a Contracting State has in the other Contracting State shall not be less favourably levied in that other State than the taxation levied on enterprises of that other State carrying on the same activities.

(3) Nothing contained in this Article shall be construed as obliging a Contracting State to grant to individuals not resident in that State any of the personal allowances and reliefs which are granted to individuals so resident.

(4) Except where the provisions of paragraph (1) of Article 9, paragraph (4) of Article 11, or paragraph (4) of Article 12 apply, interest, royalties and other disbursements paid by an

enterprise of a Contracting State to a resident of the other Contracting State shall, for the purpose of determining the taxable profits of such enterprise, be deductible under the same conditions as if they had been paid to a resident of the first-mentioned State.

(5) Enterprises of a Contracting State, the capital of which is wholly or partly owned or controlled, directly or indirectly, by one or more residents of the other Contracting State, shall not be subjected in the first-mentioned State to any taxation or any requirement connected therewith which is other or more burdensome than the taxation and connected requirements to which other similar enterprises of the first-mentioned State are or may be subjected.

(6) The provisions of this Article shall apply to taxes of every kind and description.

Article 24 Mutual agreement procedure

(1) Where a person considers that the actions of one or both of the Contracting States result or will result for him in taxation not in accordance with the provisions of this Convention, he may, irrespective of the remedies provided by the domestic law of those States, present his case to the competent authority of the Contracting State of which he is a resident.

(2) The competent authority shall endeavour, if the objection appears to it to be justified and if it is not itself able to arrive at a satisfactory solution, to resolve the case by mutual agreement with the competent authority of the other Contracting State, with a view to the avoidance of taxation which is not in accordance with the Convention.

(3) The competent authorities of the Contracting State shall endeavour to resolve by mutual agreement any difficulties or doubts arising as to the interpretation or application of the Convention. They may also consult together to consider measures to counteract improper use of the provisions of the Convention.

(4) The competent authorities of the Contracting States may communicate with each other directly for the purpose of reaching an agreement in the sense of the preceding paragraphs.

Article 25 Exchange of information

(1) The competent authorities of the Contracting States shall exchange such information (being information which is at their disposal under their respective taxation laws in the normal course of administration) as is necessary for carrying out the provisions of this Convention in relation to the taxes which are the subject of the Convention. Any information so exchanged shall be treated as secret and shall not be disclosed to any persons other than those concerned with the assessment and collection of the taxes which are the subject of the Convention. No information as aforesaid shall be exchanged which would disclose any trade, business, banking, industrial or professional secret or trade process.

(2) In no case shall the provisions of this Article be construed as imposing upon either Contracting State the obligation to carry out administrative measures at variance with the regulations and practice of either Contracting State or which would be contrary to its sovereignty, security or public policy (ordre public) or to supply particulars which are not procurable under its own laws or those of the State making the application.

Article 28 Entry into force

Note: Article 28 provides for the entry into force of this Convention. It takes effect in the UK from the year of assessment 1978–79 (income tax and capital gains tax) and from the financial year beginning on 1 April 1978 (corporation tax).

Official languages: The French language text and the English language text of this Convention are equally authoritative.

Capital taxes

Convention of 12 June 1956 (SI 1957 No 426)

Article I [Taxes covered]

(1) The taxes which are the subject of the present Convention are:—
    (*a*) In the United Kingdom:
        The estate duty imposed in Great Britain;
    (*b*) In Switzerland:
        The cantonal and communal taxes imposed on estates and inheritances.

(2) The present Convention shall apply in relation to the estate duty imposed in Northern Ireland as it applies in relation to the estate duty imposed in Great Britain.

(3) The present Convention shall also apply to any other taxes of a substantially similar character to the taxes referred to in paragraphs (1) and (2) which may be imposed in Great Britain, Northern Ireland or Switzerland subsequent to the date of signature of the present Convention.

Inheritance tax: This Convention covers United Kingdom capital transfer tax (now inheritance tax) by virtue of IHTA 1984, s 158(6), FA 1986, s 100.

Article II [General definitions]

(1) In the present Convention, unless the context otherwise requires:—
    (*a*) The term "United Kingdom" means Great Britain and Northern Ireland;
    (*b*) The term "Great Britain" means England, Wales and Scotland, and does not include the Channel Islands and the Isle of Man;
    (*c*) The term "Switzerland" means the Swiss Confederation;
    (*d*) The term "territory", when used in relation to one or the other Contracting Party, means Great Britain or Switzerland, as the context requires;
    (*e*) The term "tax" means the estate duty imposed in Great Britain or any of the cantonal and communal taxes imposed in Switzerland on estates and inheritances, as the context requires.

(2) For the purposes of the present Convention, the question whether a deceased person was domiciled in any part of the territory of one of the Contracting Parties at the time of his death shall be determined in accordance with the law in force in that territory; and a person who was not domiciled in Switzerland at the time of his death shall be treated as having been so domiciled if Swiss civil law requires the succession to be opened in Switzerland.

(3) In the application of the provisions of the present Convention by either Contracting Party any term not otherwise defined shall, unless the context otherwise requires, have the meaning which it has under the law in force in the territory of that Party relating to the taxes which are the subject of the Convention.

Article III [Situs]

(1) Where a person dies domiciled in Switzerland and does not die domiciled in some part of Great Britain, the situs of any of the rights or interests, legal or equitable, enumerated in Article VI of this Convention shall, so far as their situs is relevant for the purpose of imposing

tax in Great Britain, be determined exclusively in accordance with the rules in the said Article IV; provided, however, that if, apart from this paragraph, tax would be imposed in Great Britain on any property, Article IV shall not apply to such property unless tax is imposed or would but for some specific exemption be imposed on such property in Switzerland.

(2) Where a person dies domiciled in some part of Great Britain and does not die domiciled in Switzerland, the situs of any of the rights or interests, legal or equitable, enumerated in Article IV of this Convention shall, so far as their situs is relevant for the purpose of imposing tax in Switzerland, be determined exclusively in accordance with the rules in the said Article IV; provided, however, that if, apart from this paragraph, tax would be imposed in Switzerland on any property, Article IV shall not apply to such property unless tax is imposed or would but for some specific exemption be imposed on such property in Great Britain.

(3) If by reason of the application of Article IV tax would be imposed in the territory of one Contracting Party on property on which, apart from the said Article IV, tax would not be imposed in that territory, that Article shall not apply to such property.

(4) Nothing in this Article shall prevent the imposition of tax in Great Britain on any right or interest which passes under a disposition or devolution regulated by the law of some part of Great Britain.

Article IV [Deemed situation of rights etc]

The rules referred to in paragraphs (1) and (2) of Article III are:—

(a)–(e) . . .

    (f) Ships and aircraft and shares thereof shall be deemed to be situated at the place of registration of the ship or aircraft;

(g)–(k) . . .

Article V [Determination of tax]

(1) In determining the amount on which tax is to be computed, permitted deductions shall be allowed in accordance with the law in force in the territory in which the tax is imposed.

(2) Where in the territory of one Contracting Party tax is imposed on any property on the death of a person who at the time of his death was not domiciled in any part of that territory but was domiciled in some part of the territory of the other Contracting Party, no account shall be taken, in determining the amount or rate of such tax, of any other property, so far as that other property is situated outside the former territory; but this paragraph shall not apply:—

    (a) to tax imposed in Switzerland on immovable property (including the contents thereof) situated in Switzerland;

    (b) to tax imposed in Great Britain in so far as the other property referred to in this paragraph passes under a disposition or devolution regulated by the law of some part of Great Britain.

Article VI [Time limit]

(1) Any claim for a refund of tax founded on the provisions of the present Convention shall be made within five years from the date of the death of the deceased person in respect of whose estate the claim is made, or, in the case of an interest in expectancy where payment of tax is deferred until the date on which the interest falls into possession, within five years from that date.

(2) Any such refund shall be made without payment of interest on the amount so refunded.

Article VII [Direct communications]

(1) The competent authorities of the two Contracting Parties may communicate with each other directly for the purpose of resolving any difficulty or doubt as to the application or interpretation of this Convention.

(2) In this Article, the term "competent authorities" means in the case of Great Britain, the Commissioners of Inland Revenue, or their authorised representative; in the case of Switzerland, the Director of the Federal Tax Administration or his authorised representative; in the case of Northern Ireland, the Minister of Finance or his authorised representative; . . .

Article IX [Entry into force]

Note: This Convention applies to estates or inheritances in the case of persons who died after 24 February 1957.

Official languages: The French language text and the English language text of this Convention are equally authoritative.

THAILAND

Convention of 18 February 1981 (SI 1981 No 1546)

Article 1 Personal scope

This Convention shall apply to persons who are residents of one or both of the Contracting States.

Article 2 Taxes covered

(1) The existing taxes which are the subject of this Convention are:
　(a) in the United Kingdom:
　　(i) the income tax;
　　(ii) the corporation tax;
　　(iii) the capital gains tax;
　　(iv) the development land tax; and
　　(v) the petroleum revenue tax;
　　(hereinafter referred to as "United Kingdom tax");
　(b) in Thailand:
　　(i) the income tax; and
　　(ii) the petroleum income tax;
　　(hereinafter referred to as "Thai tax").
(2) The Convention shall also apply to any tax which is subsequently imposed by either Contracting State in addition to, or in place of, the existing taxes provided that it is agreed by the competent authorities of the Contracting States to be identical or substantially similar to

the taxes existing at the date of signature of the Convention. The competent authorities of the Contracting States shall notify each other of any changes which are made in their respective taxation laws.

Article 3 General definitions

(1) In this Convention, unless the context otherwise requires:

(*a*) the term "United Kingdom" means Great Britain and Northern Ireland, including any area outside the territorial sea of the United Kingdom which in accordance with international law has been or may hereafter be designated, under the laws of the United Kingdom concerning the Continental Shelf, as an area within which the rights of the United Kingdom with respect to the sea-bed and sub-soil and their natural resources may be exercised;

(*b*) the term "Thailand" means the Kingdom of Thailand and any area adjacent to the territorial waters of the Kingdom of Thailand which by Thai legislation, and in accordance with international law, has been or may hereafter be designated as an area within which the rights of the Kingdom of Thailand with respect to the sea bed and subsoil and their natural resources may be exercised;

(*c*) the term "nationals" means:

(i) in relation to the United Kingdom, citizens of the United Kingdom and Colonies and British subjects not possessing that citizenship or the citizenship of any other Commonwealth country or territory, provided in all cases they are patrial within the meaning of the Immigration Act 1971(a), and all legal persons, partnerships, associations or other entities deriving their status as such from the law in force in the United Kingdom;

(ii) in relation to Thailand, all individuals possessing the nationality of Thailand and all legal persons, partnerships and associations deriving their status as such from the law in force in Thailand;

(*d*) the term "tax" means United Kingdom tax or Thai tax, as the context requires;

(*e*) the terms "a Contracting State" and "the other Contracting State" mean the United Kingdom or Thailand, as the context requires;

(*f*) the term "person" comprises an individual, a company and any body of persons which is treated as an entity for tax purposes;

(*g*) the term "company" means any body corporate or any entity which is treated as a body corporate for tax purposes;

(*h*) the terms "enterprise of a Contracting State" and "enterprise of the other Contracting State" mean respectively an enterprise carried on by a resident of a Contracting State and an enterprise carried on by a resident of the other Contracting State;

(*i*) the term "competent authority" means, in the case of the United Kingdom the Commissioners of Inland Revenue or their authorised representative, and in the case of Thailand, the Minister of Finance or his authorised representative;

(*j*) the term "international traffic" means any transport by a ship or aircraft operated by an enterprise which has its place of effective management in a Contracting State, except when the ship or aircraft is operated solely between places in the other Contracting State;

(*k*) the term "political subdivision", in relation to the United Kingdom, includes Northern Ireland.

(2) As regards the application of this Convention by a Contracting State any term not otherwise defined shall, unless the context otherwise requires, have the meaning which it has under the laws of that Contracting State relating to the taxes which are the subject of this Convention.

Article 4 Fiscal domicile

(1) For the purposes of this Convention, the term "resident of a Contracting State" means, subject to the provisions of paragraphs (2) and (3) of this Article, any person who,

under the law of that State, is liable to taxation therein by reason of his domicile, residence, place of management, place of incorporation, or any other criterion of a similar nature.

(2) Where by reason of the provisions of paragraph (1) of this Article an individual is a resident of both Contracting States, then his status shall be determined in accordance with the following rules:

(a) he shall be deemed to be a resident of the Contracting State in which he has a permanent home available to him. If he has a permanent home available to him in both Contracting States, he shall be deemed to be a resident of the Contracting State with which his personal and economic relations are closer (centre of vital interests);

(b) if the Contracting State in which he has his centre of vital interests cannot be determined, or if he has not a permanent home available to him in either Contracting State, he shall be deemed to be a resident of the Contracting State in which he has an habitual abode;

(c) if he has an habitual abode in both Contracting States or in neither of them, he shall be deemed to be a resident of the Contracting State of which he is national;

(d) if he is a national of both Contracting States or of neither of them, the competent authorities of the Contracting States shall endeavour to settle the question by mutual agreement.

(3) Where by reason of the provisions of paragraph (1) of this Article a person other than an individual is a resident of both Contracting States, then the competent authorities of the Contracting States shall endeavour to settle the question by mutual agreement.

Article 7 Income from immovable property

(1) (Taxation of income from immovable property.)

(2) (a) The term "immovable property" shall, subject to the provisions of sub-paragraph (b) below, be defined in accordance with the law of the Contracting State in which the property in question is situated.

(b) The term "immovable property" shall in any case include property accessory to immovable property, livestock and equipment used in agriculture and forestry, rights to which the provisions of general law respecting landed property apply, usufruct of immovable property and rights to variable or fixed payments as consideration for the working of, or the right to work, mineral deposits, sources and other natural resources; ships, boats and aircraft shall not be regarded as immovable property.

(3) . . .

(4) . . .

Article 8 Business profits

(1) The profits of an enterprise of a Contracting State shall be taxable only in that State unless the enterprise carries on business in the other Contracting State through a permanent establishment situated therein. If the enterprise carries on business as aforesaid, the profits of the enterprise may be taxed in the other State but only so much of them as is attributable to that permanent establishment.

(2) Where an enterprise of a Contracting State carries on business in the other Contracting State through a permanent establishment situated therein, there shall in each Contracting State be attributed to that permanent establishment the profits which it might be expected to make if it were a distinct and separate enterprise engaged in the same or similar activities under the same or similar conditions and dealing wholly independently with the enterprise of which it is a permanent establishment.

(3) In the determination of the profits of a permanent establishment there shall be allowed as deductions expenses of the enterprise (other than expenses which would not be deductible if the permanent establishment were a separate enterprise) which are incurred for the purposes of, and are related to, the permanent establishment, including executive and general adminis-

trative expenses so incurred, whether in the State in which the permanent establishment is situated or elsewhere.

(4) Insofar as it has been customary in a Contracting State to determine the profits to be attributed to a permanent establishment on the basis of an apportionment of the total profits of the enterprise to its various parts or, in the case of a person who does not claim taxation on the basis of the actual net profits of the permanent establishment, on the basis of a certain reasonable percentage of the gross receipts of the permanent establishment, nothing in paragraph (2) of this Article shall preclude such State from determining the profits to be taxed by such a method. The method adopted shall, however, be such that the result shall be in accordance with the principles laid down in this Article.

(5) No profits shall be attributed to a permanent establishment by reason of the mere purchase by that permanent establishment of goods or merchandise for the enterprise.

(6) For the purposes of the preceding paragraphs, the profits to be attributed to the permanent establishment shall be determined by the same method year by year unless there is good and sufficient reason to the contrary.

(7) Where profits include items which are dealt with separately in other Articles of this Convention, then the provisions of those Articles shall not be affected by the provisions of this Article.

(8) For the purposes of this Article the term "profits" does not include income from the operation of ships.

Article 14 Capital gains

(1) . . .

(2) (Taxation of gains from alienation of movable business property.)

(3) Notwithstanding the provisions of paragraph (2) of this Article, capital gains derived by a resident of a Contracting State from the alienation of ships and aircraft operated in international traffic and movable property pertaining to the operation of such ships and aircraft shall be taxable only in that Contracting State.

(4) . . .

(5) . . .

Article 24 Non-discrimination

(1) The nationals of a Contracting State shall not be subjected in the other Contracting State to any taxation or any requirement connected therewith which is other or more burdensome than the taxation and connected requirements to which nationals of that other State in the same circumstances are or may be subjected.

(2) The taxation on a permanent establishment which an enterprise of a Contracting State has in the other Contracting State shall not be less favourably levied in that other State than the taxation levied on enterprises of that other State carrying on the same activities.

(3) Enterprises of a Contracting State, the capital of which is wholly or partly owned or controlled, directly or indirectly, by one or more residents of the other Contracting State, shall not be subjected in the first-mentioned Contracting State to any taxation or any requirement connected therewith which is other or more burdensome than the taxation and connected requirements to which other similar enterprises of that first-mentioned State are or may be subjected.

(4) Nothing contained in this Article shall be construed as obliging either Contracting State to grant to individuals not resident in that State any of the personal allowances, reliefs and reductions for tax purposes which are granted to individuals so resident.

(5) In this Article the term "taxation" means taxes of every kind and description.

Article 25 Mutual agreement procedure

(1) Where a resident of a Contracting State considers that the actions of one or both of the Contracting States result or will result for him in taxation not in accordance with this Con-

vention, he may, notwithstanding the remedies provided by the national laws of those States, present his case to the competent authority of the Contracting State of which he is a resident.

(2) The competent authority shall endeavour, if the objection appears to it to be justified and if it is not itself able to arrive at an appropriate solution, to resolve the case by mutual agreement with the competent authority of the other Contracting State, with a view to the avoidance of taxation not in accordance with the Convention.

(3) The competent authorities of the Contracting States shall endeavour to resolve by mutual agreement any difficulties or doubts arising as to the interpretation or application of the Convention.

(4) The competent authorities of the Contracting States may communicate with each other directly for the purpose of reaching an agreement in the sense of the preceding paragraphs.

Article 26 Exchange of information

(1) The competent authorities of the Contracting States shall exchange such information as is necessary for the carrying out of this Convention or for the prevention of fraud or for the administration of the domestic laws of the Contracting States concerning taxes covered by this Convention insofar as the taxation thereunder is in accordance with this Convention. Any information so exchanged shall be treated as secret and shall not be disclosed to any persons other than persons (including a Court or administrative body) concerned with the assessment or collection of, or prosecution in respect of, or the determination of appeals in relation to, the taxes which are the subject of the Convention.

(2) In no case shall the provisions of paragraph (1) of this Article be construed so as to impose on the competent authority of either Contracting State the obligation:

(*a*) to carry out administrative measures at variance with the laws or administrative practice prevailing in either Contracting State;

(*b*) to supply particulars which are not obtainable under the laws or in the normal course of the administration of that or the other Contracting State;

(*c*) to supply information which would disclose any business, trade, industrial, commercial or professional secret or trade process, or information, the disclosure of which would be contrary to public policy.

Article 27 Entry into force

Note: Article 27 provided for the entry into force of this Convention. It takes effect in the UK from the year of assessment 1981–82 (income tax and capital gains tax) and from the financial year beginning on 1 April 1981 (corporation tax).

Official languages: The Thai language text and the English language text of this Convention are equally authoritative.

TRINIDAD AND TOBAGO

Convention of 31 December 1982 (SI 1983 No 1903)

Article 1 Personal scope

This Convention shall apply to persons who are residents of one or both of the Contracting States.

Article 2 Taxes covered

(1) The taxes which are the subject of this Convention are:
  (*a*) in the United Kingdom:
      (i) the income tax; and
      (ii) the corporation tax;
      (hereinafter referred to as "United Kingdom tax");
  (*b*) in Trinidad and Tobago:
      (i) the income tax;
      (ii) the corporation tax;
      (iii) the unemployment levy; and
      (iv) the petroleum profits tax;
      (hereinafter referred to as "Trinidad and Tobago tax").

(2) This Convention shall also apply to any identical or substantially similar taxes which are imposed by either Contracting State after the date of signature of this Convention in addition to, or in place of, the existing taxes. The competent authorities of the Contracting States shall notify each other of any substantial changes which are made in their respective taxation laws.

Article 3 General definitions

(1) In this Convention, unless the context otherwise requires:
  (*a*) the term "United Kingdom" means Great Britain and Northern Ireland, including any area outside the territorial sea of the United Kingdom which in accordance with international law has been or may hereafter be designated, under the laws of the United Kingdom concerning the Continental Shelf, as an area within which the rights of the United Kingdom with respect to the sea-bed and sub-soil and their natural resources may be exercised;
  (*b*) the term "Trinidad and Tobago" means the islands of Trinidad and Tobago including any area adjacent to the territorial waters of Trinidad and Tobago which by Trinidad and Tobago legislation and in accordance with international law concerning the Continental Shelf has been or may hereafter be designated as an area within which the rights of Trinidad and Tobago with respect to the sea bed and the sub-soil and their natural resources may be exercised.
  (*c*) the term "national" means:
      (i) in relation to the United Kingdom, any individual who has under the law in the United Kingdom the status of United Kingdom national, provided he has the right of abode in the United Kingdom, and any legal person, partnership, association or other entity deriving its status as such from the law in force in the United Kingdom;
      (ii) in relation to Trinidad and Tobago, any individual who is a Trinidad and Tobago citizen and any legal person, partnership and association deriving its status as such from the law of Trinidad and Tobago.
  (*d*) the terms "a Contracting State" and "the other Contracting State" mean the United Kingdom or Trinidad and Tobago as the context requires;

305

(*e*) the term "person" comprises an individual, a company and any other body of persons;

(*f*) the term "company" means any body corporate or any entity which is treated as a body corporate for tax purposes;

(*g*) the terms "enterprise of a Contracting State" and "enterprise of the other Contracting State" mean respectively an enterprise carried on by a resident of a Contracting State and an enterprise carried on by a resident of the other Contracting State;

(*h*) the term "international traffic" means any transport by a ship or aircraft operated by an enterprise which has its place of effective management in a Contracting State, except when the ship or aircraft is operated solely between places in the other Contracting State;

(*i*) the term "competent authority" means, in the case of the United Kingdom, the Commissioners of Inland Revenue or their authorised representative, and in the case of Trinidad and Tobago, the Minister of Finance or his authorised representative.

(2) As regards the application of this Convention by a Contracting State any term not otherwise defined shall, unless the context otherwise requires, have the meaning which it has under the laws of that Contracting State relating to the taxes which are the subject of this Convention.

Article 4 Fiscal domicile

(1) For the purposes of this Convention, the term "resident of a Contracting State" means any person who, under the law of that State, is liable to tax therein by reason of his domicile, residence, place of management or any other criterion of a similar nature.

(2) Where by reason of the provisions of paragraph (1) of this Article an individual is a resident of both Contracting States, then his status shall be determined in accordance with the following rules:

(*a*) he shall be deemed to be a resident of the State in which he has a permanent home available to him; if he has a permanent home available to him in both States, he shall be deemed to be a resident of the State with which his personal and economic relations are closer (centre of vital interests);

(*b*) if the State in which he has his centre of vital interests cannot be determined, or if he has not a permanent home available to him in either State, he shall be deemed to be a resident of the State in which he has an habitual abode;

(*c*) if he has an habitual abode in both States or in neither of them, he shall be deemed to be a resident of the State of which he is a national;

(*d*) if he is a national of both States or of neither of them, the competent authorities of the Contracting States shall settle the question by mutual agreement.

(3) Where by reason of the provisions of paragraph (1) of this Article a person other than an individual is a resident of both Contracting States, then it shall be deemed to be a resident of the State in which its place of effective management is situated.

Article 6 Income from immovable property

(1) (Taxation of income from immovable property.)

(2) The term "immovable property" shall have the meaning which it has under the law of the Contracting State in which the property in question is situated. The term shall in any case include property accessory to immovable property, livestock and equipment used in agriculture and forestry, rights to which the provisions of general law respecting landed property apply, usufruct of immovable property and rights to variable or fixed payments as consideration for the working of, or the right to work, mineral deposits, sources and other natural resources; ships, boats and aircraft shall not be regarded as immovable property.

(3) . . .

(4) . . .

Article 8 Shipping and air transport

(1) Profits from the operation of ships or aircraft in international traffic shall be taxable only in the Contracting State in which the place of effective management of the enterprise is situated.

(2) If the place of effective management of a shipping enterprise is aboard a ship, then it shall be deemed to be situated in the Contracting State in which the home harbour of the ship is situated, or, if there is no such home harbour, in the Contracting State of which the operator of the ship is a resident.

(3) The provisions of this Article shall also apply to profits derived from participation in a pool, a joint business or an international operating agency.

Article 24 Non-discrimination

(1) Nationals of a Contracting State shall not be subjected in the other Contracting State to any taxation or any requirement connected therewith which is other or more burdensome than the taxation and connected requirements to which nationals of that other State in the same circumstances are or may be subjected.

(2) The taxation on a permanent establishment which an enterprise of a Contracting State has in the other Contracting State shall not be less favourably levied in that other State than the taxation levied on enterprises of that other State carrying on the same activities.

(3) Notwithstanding the provisions of paragraph (2) of this Article, where a company which is a resident of one of the Contracting States, having a permanent establishment in the other Contracting State, derives profits or income from that permanent establishment, any remittance of such profits by the permanent establishment to a resident of the first-mentioned Contracting State may be taxed (in addition to the tax which would be chargeable on those profits if they were the profits of a company which was a resident of that other Contracting State) in accordance with the law of the other Contracting State, but the rate of tax so imposed shall not exceed 10 per cent of the amount of these profits remitted or deemed to be remitted.

(4) Enterprises of a Contracting State, the capital of which is wholly or partly owned or controlled, directly or indirectly, by one or more residents of the other Contracting State, shall not be subjected in the first-mentioned State to any taxation or any requirement connected therewith which is other or more burdensome than the taxation and connected requirements to which other similar enterprises of that first-mentioned State are or may be subjected.

(5) Except where the provisions of Article 9, paragraph (7) of Article 11, paragraph (7) of Article 12, or paragraph (6) of Article 13 apply, interest, royalties, technical fees and other disbursements paid by an enterprise of a Contracting State to a resident of the other Contracting State shall, for the purpose of determining the taxable profits of such enterprise, be deductible under the same conditions as if they had been paid to a resident of the first-mentioned State.

(6) Nothing contained in this Article shall be construed as obliging either Contracting State to grant to individuals not resident in that State any of the personal allowances, reliefs and reductions for tax purposes which are granted to individuals so resident.

(7) In this Article the term "taxation" means taxes of every kind and description.

Article 25 Mutual agreement procedure

(1) Where a resident of a Contracting State considers that the actions of one or both of the Contracting States result or will result for him in taxation not in accordance with this Convention, he may, irrespective of the remedies provided by the domestic law of those States, present his case to the competent authority of the Contracting State of which he is a resident.

(2) The competent authority shall endeavour, if the objection appears to it to be justified and if it is not itself able to arrive at a satisfactory solution, to resolve the case by mutual agreement with the competent authority of the other Contracting State, with a view to the avoidance of taxation not in accordance with the Convention.

(3) The competent authorities of the Contracting States shall endeavour to resolve by

mutual agreement any difficulties or doubts arising as to the interpretation or application of the Convention.

(4) The competent authorities of the Contracting States may communicate with each other directly for the purpose of reaching an agreement in the sense of the preceding paragraphs.

Article 26 Exchange of information

(1) The competent authorities of the Contracting States shall exchange such information as is necessary for carrying out the provisions of this Convention or of the domestic laws of the Contracting States concerning taxes covered by the Convention insofar as the taxation thereunder is not contrary to the Convention. Any information received by a Contracting State shall be treated as secret and shall be disclosed only to persons or authorities (including courts and administrative bodies) involved in the assessment or collection of, the enforcement or prosecution in respect of, or the determination of appeals in relation to, the taxes covered by the Convention. Such persons or authorities shall use the information only for such purposes. They may disclose the information in public court proceedings or in judicial decisions.

(2) In no case shall the provisions of paragraph (1) of this Article be construed so as to impose on the competent authority of either Contracting State the obligation:

(a) to carry out administrative measures at variance with laws and administrative practice prevailing in either Contracting State;

(b) to supply information which is not obtainable under the laws or in the normal course of the administration of either Contracting State;

(c) to supply information which would disclose any trade, business, industrial, commercial or professional secret or trade process, or information the disclosure of which would be contrary to public policy.

Article 28 Entry into force

Note: Article 28 provided for the entry into force of this Convention. It takes effect in the UK from the year of assessment 1984–85 (income tax) and from the financial year beginning on 1 April 1984 (corporation tax).

Official language: English.

TUNISIA

Convention of 15 December 1982 (SI 1984 No 133)

Article 1 Personal scope

This Convention shall apply to persons who are residents of one or both of the Contracting States.

Article 2 Taxes covered

(1) This Convention shall apply to the existing taxes on income and capital gains which are imposed by either Contracting State, and also to any identical or substantially similar taxes which are imposed after the date of signature of this Convention in addition to, or in place of, the existing taxes.

(2) In this Article the term "the existing taxes" means:

(*a*) in relation to the United Kingdom of Great Britain and Northern Ireland:

(i) the income tax;

(ii) the corporation tax; and

(iii) the capital gains tax;

(hereinafter referred to as "United Kingdom tax");

(*b*) in relation to Tunisia:

(i) the trade tax (*l'impôt de la patente*);

(ii) the tax on the profits of non-commercial professions (*l'impôt sur les bénéfices des professions non-commerciales*);

(iii) the tax on salaries and wages (*l'impôt sur les traitements et salaires*);

(iv) the agricultural tax (*l'impôt agricole*);

(v) the tax on income from transferable securities (*l'impôt sur le revenu des valeurs mobilières*);

(vi) the tax on income from debts, deposits, sureties and current accounts (IRC) (*l'impôt sur le revenu des créances, dépôts, cautionnements et comptes courants (IRC)*);

(vii) the capital gains tax on immovable property (*l'impôt sur les plusvaleurs immobilières*);

(viii) the special solidarity levy (*la contribution exceptionelle de solidarité*); and

(ix) the State personal levy (*la contribution personnelle d'Etat*);

(hereinafter referred to as "Tunisian tax").

(3) The competent authorities of the Contracting States shall notify each other of any substantial changes which are made in their respective taxation laws.

Article 3 General definitions

(1) In this Convention, unless the context otherwise requires:

(*a*) the terms "a Contracting State" and "the other Contracting State" mean the United Kingdom or Tunisia, as the context requires;

(*b*) the term "person" comprises an individual, a company and any other body of persons;

(*c*) the term "company" means any body corporate or any entity which is treated as a body corporate for tax purposes;

(*d*) the terms "enterprise of a Contracting State" and "enterprise of the other Contracting State" mean respectively an enterprise carried on by a resident of a Contracting State and an enterprise carried on by a resident of the other Contracting State;

(*e*) the term "competent authority" means, in the case of the United Kingdom, the Commissioners of Inland Revenue or their authorised representative, and in the case of Tunisia, the Minister of Finance or his authorised representative;

(*f*) the term "international traffic" means any transport by a ship or aircraft operated by an enterprise which has its place of effective management in a Contracting State, except when the ship or aircraft is operated solely between places in the other Contracting State;

(*g*) the term "United Kingdom" means Great Britain and Northern Ireland, including any area outside the territorial sea of the United Kingdom which in accordance with international law has been or may hereafter be designated, under the laws of the United Kingdom concerning the Continental Shelf, as an area within which the rights of the United Kingdom with respect to the sea-bed and sub-soil and their natural resources may be exercised;

(*h*) the term "Tunisia" used in a geographical sense, means the territory of the Tunisian Republic, including any area lying beyond the territorial waters of Tunisia which, under the laws of Tunisia and in accordance with international law, is an area within which Tunisia may exercise rights in respect of the sea-bed and its subsoil and their natural resources;

(*i*) the term "national" means:

    (i) in relation to the United Kingdom, any individual who has under the law in the United Kingdom the status of United Kingdom national, provided he has the right of abode in the United Kingdom; and any legal person, partnership, association or other entity deriving its status as such from the law in force in the United Kingdom;

    (ii) in relation to Tunisia, any individual possessing Tunisian nationality and any legal person, partnership, association or other entity deriving its status from the law in force in Tunisia.

(2) As regards the application of this Convention by a Contracting State any term not otherwise defined shall, unless the context otherwise requires, have the meaning which it has under the laws of that Contracting State relating to the taxes which are the subject of this Convention.

Article 4 Fiscal domicile

(1) For the purposes of this Convention, the term "resident of a Contracting State" means any person who, under the laws of that State, is liable to tax therein by reason of his domicile, residence, place of management or any other criterion of a similar nature.

(2) Where by reason of the provisions of paragraph (1) of this Article an individual is a resident of both Contracting States, then his status shall be determined as follows:

(*a*) he shall be deemed to be a resident of the Contracting State in which he has a permanent home available to him. If he has a permanent home available to him in both Contracting States, he shall be deemed to be a resident of the Contracting State with which his personal and economic relations are closer (centre of vital interests);

(*b*) if the Contracting State in which he has his centre of vital interests cannot be determined, or if he has not a permanent home available to him in either Contracting State, he shall be deemed to be a resident of the Contracting State in which he has an habitual abode;

(*c*) if he has an habitual abode in both Contracting States or in neither of them, he shall be deemed to be a resident of the Contracting State of which he is a national;

(*d*) if he is a national of both Contracting States or of neither of them, the competent authorities of the Contracting States shall settle the question by mutual agreement.

(3) Where by reason of the provisions of paragraph (1) of this Article a person other than an individual is a resident of both Contracting States, then it shall be deemed to be a resident of the Contracting State in which its place of effective management is situated.

Article 6 Income from immovable property

(1) (Taxation of income from immovable property.)

(2) The term "immovable property" shall be defined in accordance with the law of the Contracting State in which the property is situated. The term shall in any case include property accessory to immovable property, livestock and equipment used in agriculture and forestry, rights to which the provisions of general law respecting landed property apply, usufruct of immovable property and rights to variable or fixed payments as consideration for the working of, or the right to work, mineral deposits, sources and other natural resources; ships, boats and aircraft shall not be regarded as immovable property.

(3) . . .

(4) . . .

Article 8 Shipping, inland waterways transport and air transport

(1) Profits from the operation of ships or aircraft in international traffic shall be taxable only in the Contracting State in which the place of effective management of the enterprise is situated.

(2) Profits from the operation of boats engaged in inland waterways transport shall be taxable only in the Contracting State in which the place of effective management of the enterprise is situated.

(3) If the place of effective management of a shipping enterprise or of an inland waterways transport enterprise is aboard a ship or boat, then it shall be deemed to be situated in the Contracting State in which the home harbour of the ship or boat is situated, or, if there is no such home harbour, in the Contracting State of which the operator of the ship or boat is a resident.

(4) The provisions of paragraph (1) of this Article shall also apply to profits from the participation in a pool, a joint business or an international operating agency.

Article 13 Capital gains

(1) . . .

(2) (Taxation of gains from alienation of movable business property.)

(3) Notwithstanding the provisions of paragraph (2) of this Article, capital gains derived by a resident of a Contracting State from the alienation of ships and aircraft operated in international traffic and movable property pertaining to the operation of such ships and aircraft shall be taxable only in that Contracting State.

(4) . . .

Article 23 Non-discrimination

(1) The nationals of a Contracting State shall not be subjected in the other Contracting State to any taxation or any requirement connected therewith which is other or more burdensome than the taxation and connected requirements to which nationals of that other State in the same circumstances are or may be subjected.

(2) The taxation on a permanent establishment which an enterprise of a Contracting State has in the other Contracting State shall not be less favourably levied in that other State than the taxation levied on enterprises of that other State carrying on the same activities.

(3) Enterprises of a Contracting State, the capital of which is wholly or partly owned or controlled, directly or indirectly, by one or more residents of the other Contracting State, shall not be subjected in the first-mentioned Contracting State to any taxation or any requirement connected therewith which is other or more burdensome than the taxation and connected requirements to which other similar enterprises of that first-mentioned State are or may be subjected.

(4) Nothing contained in this Article shall be construed as obliging either Contracting State to grant to individuals not resident in that State any of the personal allowances, reliefs and reductions for tax purposes which are granted to individuals so resident.

(5) In this Article the term "taxation" means taxes referred to in Article 2 of this Convention.

Article 24 Mutual agreement procedure

(1) Where a resident of a Contracting State considers that the actions of one or both of the Contracting States result or will result for him in taxation not in accordance with this Convention, he may, notwithstanding the remedies provided by the national laws of those States, present his case to the competent authority of the Contracting State of which he is a resident.

(2) The competent authority shall endeavour, if the objection appears to it to be justified and if it is not itself able to arrive at an appropriate solution, to resolve the case by mutual agreement with the competent authority of the other Contracting State, with a view to the avoidance of taxation not in accordance with the Convention.

(3) The competent authorities of the Contracting States shall endeavour to resolve by

mutual agreement any difficulties or doubts arising as to the interpretation or application of the Convention.

(4) The competent authorities of the Contracting States may communicate with each other directly for the purpose of reaching an agreement in the sense of the preceding paragraphs of this Article.

Article 25 Exchange of information

The competent authorities of the Contracting States shall exchange such information (being information which is at their disposal under their respective taxation laws in the normal course of administration) as is necessary for carrying out the provisions of this Convention or for the prevention of fraud or the administration of statutory provisions against legal avoidance in relation to the taxes which are the subject of this Convention. Any information so exchanged shall be treated as secret but may be disclosed to persons (including a court or administrative body) concerned with assessment, collection, enforcement or prosecution in respect of taxes which are the subject of this Convention. No information shall be exchanged which would disclose any trade, business, industrial or professional secret or any trade process.

Article 27 Entry into force

Note: Article 27 provided for the entry into force of this Convention. It takes effect in the UK from the year of assessment 1984–85 (income tax and corporation tax) and from the financial year beginning on 1 April 1984 (corporation tax).

Official languages: The French language, Arabic language and English language texts of this Convention are equally authoritative.

TURKEY

Agreement of 19 February 1986 (SI 1988/Draft)

Article 1 Personal scope

This Agreement shall apply to persons who are residents of one or both of the Contracting States.

Article 2 Taxes covered

(1) This agreement shall apply to taxes on income and on capital gains imposed by either Contracting State irrespective of the manner in which they are levied.

(2) There shall be regarded as taxes on income and on capital gains all taxes imposed on total income, on total capital gains, or on elements of income or of capital gains, including taxes on gains from the alienation of movable or immovable property, as well as taxes on capital appreciation.

(3) The existing taxes which are the subject of this Agreement are:

    (*a*) in the Republic of Turkey:

        (i) the income tax; and

        (ii) the corporation tax;

    (hereinafter referred to as "Turkish tax");

    (*b*) in the United Kingdom of Great Britain and Northern Ireland:

        (i) the income tax;

        (ii) the corporation tax; and

        (iii) the capital gains tax;

    (hereinafter referred to as "United Kingdom tax").

(4) This Agreement shall also apply to any identical or substantially similar taxes which are imposed by either Contracting State after the date of signature of this Agreement in addition to, or in place of, the existing taxes. The competent authorities of the Contracting States shall notify each other of changes which have been made in their respective taxation laws.

Article 3 General definitions

(1) For the purposes of this Agreement, unless the context otherwise requires:

    (*a*) the term "Turkey" means the territory of the Republic of Turkey, and any area in which the laws of Turkey are in force, as well as the Continental Shelf over which Turkey has, in accordance with international law, sovereign rights to explore and exploit its natural resources;

    (*b*) the term "United Kingdom" means Great Britain and Northern Ireland, including any area outside the territorial sea of the United Kingdom which in accordance with international law has been or may hereafter be designated, under the laws of the United Kingdom concerning the Continental Shelf, as an area within which the rights of the United Kingdom with respect to the sea-bed and sub-soil and their natural resources may be exercised;

    (*c*) the term "national" means:

        (i) in relation to Turkey, any individual possessing Turkish nationality in accordance with the Turkish Nationality Code; and any legal person, partnership or association deriving its status as such from the law in force in Turkey;

        (ii) in relation to the United Kingdom, any British citizen or any British subject not possessing the citizenship of any other Commonwealth country or territory, provided he has the right of abode in the United Kingdom; and any legal person, partnership, association or other entity deriving its status as such from the law in force in the United Kingdom;

    (*d*) the terms "a Contracting State" and "the other Contracting State" mean Turkey or the United Kingdom as the context requires;

    (*e*) the term "tax" means any tax covered by Article 2 of this Agreement;

    (*f*) the term "person" comprises an individual, a company and any other body of persons;

    (*g*) the term "company" means any body corporate or any entity which is treated as a body corporate for tax purposes;

    (*h*) the term "registered office" in relation to Turkey means the legal head office registered under the Turkish Code of Commerce;

    (*i*) the terms "enterprise of a Contracting State" and "enterprise of the other Contracting State" means respectively an enterprise carried on by a resident of a Contracting State and an enterprise carried on by a resident of the other Contracting State;

    (*j*) the term "international traffic" means any transport by a ship, an aircraft or a road vehicle operated by an enterprise of a Contracting State, except where the ship, aircraft or road vehicle is operated solely between places in the other Contracting State;

(k) the term "political subdivision" in relation to the United Kingdom, includes Northern Ireland;

(l) the term "competent authority" means, in the case of Turkey the Minister of Finance and Customs or his authorised representative, and in the case of the United Kingdom the Commissioners of Inland Revenue or their authorised representative.

(2) As regards the application of this Agreement by a Contracting State any term not otherwise defined shall, unless the context otherwise requires, have the meaning which it has under the laws of that Contracting State relating to the taxes which are the subject of this Agreement.

Article 4 Residence

(1) For the purposes of this Agreement, the term "resident of a Contracting State" means any person who, under the laws of that State, is liable to tax therein by reason of his domicile, residence, registered office, place of management or any other criterion of a similar nature.

(2) Where by reason of the provisions of paragraph (1) of this Article an individual is a resident of both Contracting States, then his status shall be determined as follows:

(a) he shall be deemed to be a resident of the Contracting State in which he has a permanent home available to him; if he has a permanent home available to him in both Contracting States, he shall be deemed to be a resident of the Contracting State with which his personal and economic relations are closer (centre of vital interest);

(b) if the Contracting State in which he has his centre of vital interests cannot be determined, or if he has not a permanent home available to him in either Contracting State, he shall be deemed to be a resident of the Contracting State in which he has an habitual abode;

(c) if he has an habitual abode in both Contracting States or in neither of them, he shall be deemed to be a resident of the Contracting State of which he is a national;

(d) if he is a national of both Contracting States or of neither of them, the competent authorities of the Contracting States shall settle the question by mutual agreement.

(3) Where by reason of the provisions of paragraph (1) of this Article a person other than an individual is a resident of both Contracting States, then it shall be deemed to be a resident of the Contracting State in which its place of effective management is situated. However, where such a person has the place of effective management of its business in one of the Contracting States and the place of its registered office in the other Contracting State, then the competent authorities of the Contracting States shall determine by mutual agreement the Contracting State of which the company shall be deemed to be a resident for the purposes of this Agreement.

Article 6 Income from immovable property

(1) (Taxation of income from immovable property.)

(2) The term "immovable property" shall have the meaning which it has under the law of the Contracting State in which the property in question is situated. The term shall in any case include property accessory to immovable property, livestock and equipment used in agriculture and forestry, fisheries, rights to which the provisions of general law respecting landed property apply, usufruct of immovable property and rights to variable or fixed payments as consideration for the working of, or the right to work, mineral deposits, sources and other natural resources; ships, boats and aircraft shall not be regarded as immovable property. The term shall not, however, include any property or rights income from which is a royalty as defined in paragraph (3) of Article 12 of this Agreement.

(3) . . .

(4) . . .

Article 8 International transport

(1) Profits derived by an enterprise of a Contracting State from the operation of ships, aircraft or road vehicles in international traffic shall be taxable only in that State.

(2) The provisions of paragraph (1) of this Article shall also apply to profits derived from the participation in a pool, a joint business or an international operating agency.

Article 13 Capital gains

(1) . . .

(2) . . .

(3) Gains derived by a resident of a Contracting State from the alienation of ships, aircraft and road vehicles operated in international traffic or movable property pertaining to the operation of such ships, aircraft and road vehicles shall be taxable only in that Contracting State.

(4) . . .

Article 24 Non-discrimination

(1) Nationals of a Contracting State shall not be subjected in the other Contracting State to any taxation or any requirement connected therewith which is other or more burdensome than the taxation and connected requirements to which nationals of that other State in the same circumstances are or may be subjected.

(2) Subject to the provisions of paragraph (4) of Article 10 of this Agreement, the taxation on a permanent establishment which an enterprise of a Contracting State has in the other Contracting State shall not be less favourably levied in that other State than the taxation levied on enterprises of that other State carrying on the same activities.

(3) Enterprises of a Contracting State, the capital of which is wholly or partly owned or controlled, directly or indirectly, by one or more residents of the other Contracting State, shall not be subjected in the first-mentioned State to any taxation or any requirement connected therewith which is other or more burdensome than the taxation and connected requirements to which other similar enterprises of the first-mentioned State are or may be subjected.

(4) Except where the provisions of Article 9, paragraph (7) of Article 11, or paragraph (6) of Article 12 of this Agreement apply, and subject to the provisions of paragraph (8) of Article 11 of this Agreement, interest, royalties and other disbursements paid by an enterprise of a Contracting State to a resident of the other Contracting State shall, for the purpose of determining the taxable profits of such enterprise, be deductible under the same conditions as if they had been paid to a resident of the first-mentioned State.

(5) Nothing contained in this Article shall be construed as obliging either Contracting State to grant to individuals not resident in that State any of the personal allowances, reliefs and reductions for tax purposes on account of civil status or family responsibilities which it grants to its own residents.

Article 25 Mutual agreement procedure

(1) Where a resident of a Contracting State considers that the actions of one or both of the Contracting States result or will result for him in taxation not in accordance with this Agreement, he may, irrespective of the remedies provided by the domestic laws of those States, present his case to the competent authority of the Contracting State of which he is a resident.

(2) The competent authority shall endeavour, if the objection appears to it to be justified and if it is not itself able to arrive at a satisfactory solution, to resolve the case by mutual agreement with the competent authority of the other Contracting State, with a view to the avoidance of taxation not in accordance with the Agreement.

(3) The competent authorities of the Contracting States shall endeavour to resolve by mutual agreement any difficulties or doubts arising as to the interpretation or application of the Agreement.

(4) The competent authorities of the Contracting States may communicate with each

other directly for the purpose of reaching an agreement in the sense of the preceding paragraphs.

Article 26 Exchange of information

(1) The competent authorities of the Contracting States shall exchange such information as is necessary for carrying out the provisions of this Agreement or of the domestic laws of the Contracting States concerning taxes covered by the Agreement insofar as the taxation thereunder is not contrary to the agreement. Any information received by a Contracting State shall be treated as secret and shall be disclosed only to persons or authorities (including courts and administrative bodies) involved in the assessment or collection of, the enforcement or prosecution in respect of, or the determination of appeals in relation to, the taxes covered by the Agreement. Such persons or authorities shall use the information only for such purposes. They may disclose the information in public court proceedings or in judicial decisions.

(2) In no case shall the provisions of paragraph (1) of this Article be construed so as to impose on a Contracting State the obligation:

> (a) to carry out administrative measures at variance with the law and the administrative practice of that or of the other Contracting State;
> (b) to supply information which is not obtainable under the law or in the normal course of the administration of that or of the other Contracting State;
> (c) to supply information which would disclose any trade, business, industrial, commercial or professional secret or trade process, or information, the disclosure of which would be contrary to public policy (*ordre public*).

Article 28 Entry into force

Each of the Contracting States shall notify to the other the completion of the procedures required by its law for the bringing into force of this Agreement. The agreement shall enter into force on the date of the later of these notifications and shall thereupon have effect:

> (a) in Turkey, in respect of income tax and corporation tax, for any fiscal year beginning on or after 1 January in the calendar year next following that in which the later of these notifications is given; and
> (b) in the United Kingdom:
>> (i) in respect of income tax and capital gains tax, for any year of assessment beginning on or after 6 April in the calendar year next following that in which the later of these notifications is given;
>> (ii) in respect of corporation tax, for any financial year beginning on or after 1 April in the calendar year next following that in which the later of these notifications is given.

Note: This Agreement had not entered into force on 6 April 1988.

Official languages: The Turkish language text and the English language text of this Agreement are equally authoritative.

TUVALU
(Kiribati and Tuvalu: formerly the Gilbert and Ellice Islands)

Arrangement of 10 May 1950 (SI 1950 No 750)

(The Arrangements of 4 March 1968 (SI 1968 No 309) and 25 July 1974 (SI 1974 No 1271) do not amend the paragraphs printed below.)

Paragraph 1 [Taxes covered]

(1) The taxes which are the subject of this Arrangement are—
   (*a*) In the United Kingdom:
      The income tax (including surtax) and the profits tax (hereinafter referred to as "United Kingdom tax").
   (*b*) In the Gilbert and Ellice Islands Colony:
      The normal tax and the surtax (hereinafter referred to as "Colonial tax").

(2) This Arrangement shall also apply to any other taxes of a substantially similar character imposed in the United Kingdom or the Gilbert and Ellice Islands Colony after this Arrangement has come into force.

Corporation tax: This Arrangement covers United Kingdom corporation tax, by virtue of ICTA 1988 s 789(1).

Paragraph 2 [General definitions]

(1) In this Arrangement, unless the context otherwise requires—
   (*a*) The term "United Kingdom" means Great Britain and Northern Ireland, excluding the Channel Islands and the Isle of Man.
   (*b*) The term "the Colony" means the Gilbert and Ellice Islands Colony.
   (*c*) The terms "one of the territories" and "the other territory" mean the United Kingdom or the Colony, as the context requires.
   (*d*) The term "tax" means United Kingdom tax or Colonial tax, as the context requires.
   (*e*) The term "person" includes any body of persons, corporate or not corporate.
   (*f*) The term "company" includes any body corporate.
   (*g*) The terms "resident of the United Kingdom" and "resident of the Colony" mean respectively any person who is resident in the United Kingdom for the purposes of United Kingdom tax and not resident in the Colony for the purposes of Colonial tax and any person who is resident in the Colony for the purposes of Colonial tax and not resident in the United Kingdom for the purposes of United Kingdom tax; and a company shall be regarded as resident in the United Kingdom if its business is managed and controlled in the United Kingdom and as resident in the Colony if its business is managed and controlled in the Colony.
   (*h*) The terms "resident of one of the territories" and "resident of the other territory" mean a person who is a resident of the United Kingdom or a person who is a resident of the Colony, as the context requires.
   (*i*)–(*k*) . . .

(2) Where under this Arrangement any income is exempt from tax in one of the territories if (with or without other conditions) it is subject to tax in the other territory, and that income is subject to tax in that other territory by reference to the amount thereof which is remitted to or received in that other territory, the exemption to be allowed under this Arrangement in the first-mentioned territory shall apply to the amount so remitted or received.

(3) In the application of the provisions of this Arrangement by the United Kingdom or the Colony, any term not otherwise defined shall, unless the context otherwise requires, have the meaning which it has under the laws of the United Kingdom, or, as the case may be, the Colony, relating to the taxes which are the subject of this Arrangement.

Paragraph 5 [Shipping and air transport]

Notwithstanding the provisions of paragraphs 3 and 4, profits which a resident of one of the territories derives from operating ships or aircraft shall be exempt from tax in the other territory.

Paragraph 3: Taxation of industrial or commercial profits.
Paragraph 4: Taxation of profits of associated enterprises.

Paragraph 14 [Exchange of information]

(1) The taxation authorities of the United Kingdom and the Colony shall exchange such information (being information available under their respective taxation laws) as is necessary for carrying out the provisions of this Arrangement or for the prevention of fraud or the administration of statutory provisions against legal avoidance in relation to the taxes which are the subject of this Arrangement. Any information so exchanged shall be treated as secret and shall not be disclosed to any persons other than those concerned with the assessment and collection of the taxes which are the subject of this Arrangement. No information shall be exchanged which would disclose any trade secret or trade process.

(2) As used in this paragraph, the term "taxation authorities" means the Commissioners of Inland Revenue or their authorised representative in the case of the United Kingdom and the Treasurer or his authorised representative in the case of the Colony.

Paragraph 15 [Entry into force]

Note: Paragraph 15 provided for the entry into force of this Arrangement. It takes effect in the UK from April 1949.

Official language: English.

UGANDA

Arrangement of 24 June 1952 (SI 1952 No 1213)

Paragraph 1 [Taxes covered]

(1) The taxes which are the subject of this Arrangement are—
    (a) In the United Kingdom:
        The income tax (including surtax) and the profits tax (hereinafter referred to as "United Kingdom tax");
    (b) In Uganda:
        The income tax (including surtax) and the non-native poll tax (hereinafter referred to as "Uganda tax").

(2) This Arrangement shall also apply to any other taxes of a substantially similar character imposed in the United Kingdom or Uganda after this Arrangement has come into force.

Corporation tax: This Arrangement covers United Kingdom corporation tax, by virtue of ICTA 1988 s 789(1).

Paragraph 2 [General definitions]

(1) In this Arrangement, unless the context otherwise requires:

    (a) the term "United Kingdom" means Great Britain and Northern Ireland, excluding the Channel Islands and the Isle of Man;

    (b) the term "Uganda" means the Protectorate of Uganda;

    (c) the terms "one of the territories" and "the other territory" mean the United Kingdom or Uganda, as the context requires;

    (d) the term "tax" means United Kingdom tax or Uganda tax, as the context requires;

    (e) the term "person" includes any body of persons, corporate or not corporate;

    (f) the term "company" includes any body corporate;

    (g) the terms "resident of the United Kingdom" and "resident of Uganda" mean respectively any person who is resident in the United Kingdom for the purposes of United Kingdom tax and not resident in Uganda for the purposes of Uganda tax and any person who is resident in Uganda for the purposes of Uganda tax and not resident in the United Kingdom for the purposes of United Kingdom tax; and a company shall be regarded as resident in the United Kingdom if its business is managed and controlled in the United Kingdom and as resident in Uganda if its business is managed and controlled in Uganda;

    (h) the terms "resident of one of the territories" and "resident of the other territory" mean a person who is a resident of the United Kingdom or a person who is a resident of Uganda, as the context requires;

(i)–(k) . . .

(2) The terms "United Kingdom tax" and "Uganda tax", as used in this Arrangement, do not include any tax payable in the United Kingdom or Uganda which is payable in respect of any default or omission in relation to the taxes which are the subject of this Arrangement or which represents a penalty imposed under the law of the United Kingdom or Uganda relating to those taxes.

(3) Where under this Arrangement any income is exempt from tax in one of the territories if (with or without other conditions) it is subject to tax in the other territory, and that income is subject to tax in that other territory by reference to the amount thereof which is remitted to or received in that other territory, the exemption to be allowed under this Arrangement in the first-mentioned territory shall be determined by reference to the amount so remitted or received.

(4) In the application of the provisions of this Arrangement by the United Kingdom or Uganda, any term not otherwise defined shall, unless the context otherwise requires, have the meaning which it has under the laws of the United Kingdom, or, as the case may be, Uganda, relating to the taxes which are the subject of this Arrangement.

Paragraph 5 [Shipping and air transport]

Notwithstanding the provisions of paragraphs 3 and 4, profits which a resident of one of the territories derives from operating ships or aircraft shall be exempt from tax in the other territory.

Paragraph 3: Taxation of industrial or commercial profits.
Paragraph 4: Taxation of profits of associated enterprises.

Paragraph 13 [Exchange of information]

(1) The taxation authorities of the United Kingdom and Uganda shall exchange such information (being information available under their respective taxation laws) as is necessary

for carrying out the provisions of this Arrangement or for the prevention of fraud or the administration of statutory provisions against legal avoidance in relation to the taxes which are the subject of this Arrangement. Any information so exchanged shall be treated as secret and shall not be disclosed to any persons other than persons (including a Court) concerned with the assessment and collection of, or the determination of appeals in relation to, the taxes which are the subject of this Arrangement. No information shall be exchanged which would disclose any trade secret or trade process.

(2) As used in this paragraph, the term "taxation authorities" means the Commissioners of Inland Revenue or their authorised representative in the case of the United Kingdom and the Commissioner of Income Tax or his authorised representative in the case of Uganda.

Paragraph 14 [Entry into force]

Note: Paragraph 14 provides for the entry into force of this Arrangement. It takes effect from the year 1950–51.

Official language: English.

UNION OF SOVIET SOCIALIST REPUBLICS

Convention of 31 July 1985 (SI 1986 No 224)

Article 1 Scope of the Convention

(1) This Convention shall apply to persons who are considered to be residents for tax purposes of one or both of the Contracting States.

(2) This Convention extends to the territory of each Contracting State and to those areas of the Continental Shelf adjacent to the outer limit of the territorial sea of each State over which it exercises, in accordance with international law, sovereign rights for the purpose of exploration and exploitation of the natural resources of such areas.

(3) In this Convention references to either of the Contracting States shall be treated as including references both to the territory of the State concerned and to those areas of the Continental Shelf adjacent to the outer limit of the territorial sea of that State which are mentioned in paragraph (2) of this Article.

Article 2 Taxes covered

(1) This Convention shall apply to the following taxes:
    (a) in the United Kingdom of Great Britain and Northern Ireland:

(i) the income tax;

(ii) the corporation tax; and

(iii) the capital gains tax;

(b) in the Union of Soviet Socialist Republics:

(i) the income tax on foreign legal persons; and

(ii) the income tax on the population.

(2) This Convention shall also apply to any identical or substantially similar taxes which are imposed by either Contracting State after the date of signature of this Convention in addition to, or in place of, the existing taxes mentioned in paragraph (1) of this Article.

Article 3 General definitions

(1) In this Convention:

(a) the term "United Kingdom" means the territory of Great Britain and Northern Ireland;

(b) the terms "Union of Soviet Socialist Republics" and "USSR" mean the territories of all the Union Republics;

(c) the term "Contracting State" means the United Kingdom or the USSR, as the context requires;

(d) the term "person" means an individual and:

(i) in relation to the United Kingdom, also a company or any body corporate or any other entity which is treated as a body corporate for the purposes of taxation in the United Kingdom;

(ii) in relation to the USSR, also any legal person or other organisation created under the laws of the USSR or any Union Republic and treated as a legal person for the purposes of taxation in the USSR;

(e) the term "resident of a Contracting State" means any person who, under the laws of that State, is liable to tax therein by reason of his domicile, residence, place of management or any other criterion of a similar nature. This term does not include any person who is liable to tax in that Contracting State only if he derives income from sources therein;

(f) the term "international traffic" means any transport by ship, aircraft, motor vehicle or railway operated by a resident of a Contracting State except when the transport is operated solely between places in the other Contracting State;

(g) the term "technical specialists" means individuals employed in the provision of expert services of any kind and includes physicians, scientists, lawyers, accountants, architects, engineers and personnel performing training and supervisory activities;

(h) the term "competent authority" means:

(i) in the case of the United Kingdom, the Board of Inland Revenue or their authorised representative;

(ii) in the case of the USSR, the Ministry of Finance of the USSR or their authorised representative.

(2) As regards the application of this Convention by the Contracting States any term not defined therein shall, unless the context otherwise requires, have the meaning which it has under the laws of the Contracting State levying the taxes which are covered by this Convention.

Article 4 Residence for tax purposes

(1) Where by reason of the provisions of sub-paragraph (e) of paragraph (1) of Article 3 an individual is deemed to be a resident of both Contracting States, then his status shall be determined in accordance with the following rules:

(a) he shall be deemed to be a resident of the Contracting State in which he has a permanent home available to him; if he has a permanent home available to him in both Contracting States, he shall be deemed to be a resident of the Contracting

State with which his personal and economic relations are closer (centre of vital interests);

(b) if the Contracting State in which he has his centre of vital interests cannot be determined, or if he has no permanent home available to him in either Contracting State, he shall be deemed to be a resident of the Contracting State in which he has an habitual abode;

(c) if he has an habitual abode in both Contracting States, or in neither of them, he shall be deemed to be a resident of the Contracting State of which he is a national;

(d) if each Contracting State regards him as a national of that State or if he is a national of neither of them, the competent authorities of the Contracting States shall settle the question by mutual agreement.

(2) Where by reason of the provisions of sub-paragraph (e) of paragraph (1) of Article 3 a person other than an individual is deemed to be a resident of both Contracting States, then it shall be deemed to be a resident of the Contracting State in which its place of effective management is situated.

Article 7 Profits from international traffic

(1) Profits derived by a resident of a Contracting State from international traffic shall be taxable only in that State.

(2) The provisions of paragraph (1) of this Article shall also apply to profits from the participation in a pool, a joint business or an international transport operating agency.

Article 12 Capital gains

(1) . . .

(2) (Taxation of gains from alienation of movable property.)

(3) Notwithstanding the provisions of paragraph (2) of this Article, gains from the alienation of ships, aircraft, railway and road vehicles operated in international traffic and movable property pertaining to the operation of such ships, aircraft, railway and road vehicles shall be taxable only in the Contracting State in which, under the provisions of Article 7, profits from such activities are taxable.

(4) . . .

Article 21 Non-discrimination

(1) Nationals of a Contracting State shall not be subjected in the other Contracting State to any taxation which is other or more burdensome than the taxation to which nationals of that other State in the same circumstances are or may be subjected.

(2) The taxation of the income or profits which a resident of a Contracting State derives through a permanent establishment in the other Contracting State shall not be less favourably levied in that other State than the taxation levied on the income or profits derived through a permanent establishment in that State by residents of third States carrying on similar activities in the same circumstances.

(3) Nothing contained in this Article shall be construed as obliging either Contracting State to grant to individuals not resident in that State any of the allowances, reliefs and reductions for tax purposes, which are granted to individuals who are resident in that State.

Article 22 Mutual agreement procedure for settling disputes

(1) Where a person to whom this Convention applies considers that the actions of one or both of the Contracting States result or will result for him in taxation not in accordance with the provisions of this Convention he may, notwithstanding the remedies provided by the national laws of those States, present his case to the competent authority of the Contracting State of which he is a resident.

(2) The competent authority to whom the case is presented will endeavour, if the case

appears to it to be justified and if it is not itself able to arrive at a satisfactory solution, to resolve the matter by mutual agreement with the competent authority of the other Contracting State, with a view to the avoidance of taxation not in accordance with the provisions of this Convention.

(3) The competent authorities of the Contracting States will endeavour to resolve by mutual agreement any difficulties or doubts arising as to the interpretation or application of this Convention.

Article 23 Exchange of information

(1) The competent authorities of the Contracting States shall, to the extent permitted by their respective laws, exchange such information as is necessary for the carrying out of this Convention and of the domestic laws of the Contracting States concerning taxes covered by this Convention insofar as the taxation thereunder is in accordance with this Convention.

(2) In no case shall the provisions of paragraph (1) of this Article be regarded as imposing on the competent authority of either Contracting State the obligation:

(a) to carry out administrative measures at variance with the laws or administrative practice prevailing in either Contracting State;

(b) to supply information which is not obtainable under the laws or in the normal course of the administration of either Contracting State;

(c) to supply information which would disclose any industrial, commercial or professional secret or process, or information, the disclosure of which would be contrary to public policy.

(3) The competent authorities of the Contracting States shall supply to each other details of any substantial changes which are made in their respective taxation laws.

(4) Any information exchanged under the provisions of this Article shall be treated as secret and shall not be disclosed to any persons other than persons concerned with the implementation of the laws relating to the taxes covered by this Convention.

Article 26 Entry into force of the Convention

Note: Article 26 provided for the entry into force of this Convention. It takes effect in the UK from the year of assessment 1986–87 (income tax and capital gains tax) and from the financial year beginning on 1 April 1986 (corporation tax).

Official languages: The Russian language text and the English language text of this Convention are equally authoritative.

UNITED STATES OF AMERICA

Convention of 31 December 1975 (SI 1980 No 568)

Printed as amended by the Exchange of Notes of 13 April 1976 and the Protocols of 26 August 1976, 31 March 1977 and 15 March 1979 (all of which are published in SI 1980 No 568).

UNITED STATES OF AMERICA

Article 1 Personal scope

(1) Except as specifically provided herein, this Convention is applicable to persons who are residents of one or both of the Contracting States.

(2) A corporation which is both a resident of the United Kingdom within the meaning of paragraph (1)(*a*)(ii) of Article 4 (Fiscal residence), and a resident of the United States within the meaning of paragraph (2) of Article 8 (Shipping and air transport), of Article 23 (Elimination of double taxation) with respect to paragraph (1)(*c*) thereof and the petroleum revenue tax referred to in paragraph (2)(*b*) of Article 2 (Taxes covered), of Article 24 (Non-discrimination) and of Article 28 (Entry into force) and the provisions of paragraph (7) of Article 11 (Interest) shall apply to it.

(3) Notwithstanding any provision of this Convention except paragraph (4) of this Article, a Contracting State may tax its residents (as determined under Article 4 (Fiscal residence)) and its nationals as if this Convention had not come into effect.

(4) Nothing in paragraph (3) of this Article shall affect the application by a Contracting State of:

    (*a*) paragraph (4) of Article 4 (Fiscal residence), paragraph (2) of Article 8 (Shipping and air transport), and Articles 9 (Associated enterprises), 23 (Elimination of double taxation), 24 (Non-discrimination), and 25 (Mutual agreement procedure); and

    (*b*) Articles 19 (Government service), 20 (Teachers), 21 (Students and trainees) and 27 (Effect on diplomatic and consular officials and domestic laws), with respect to individuals who are neither nationals of, nor have immigrant status in, that State.

Article 2 Taxes covered

(1) This Convention shall apply to taxes on income imposed by each Contracting State and as hereinafter provided to taxes imposed by its political subdivisions or local authorities.

(2) The existing taxes to which this Convention shall apply are:

    (*a*) in the case of the United States, the Federal income taxes imposed by the Internal Revenue Code and the tax on insurance premiums paid to foreign insurers; but (except as provided in paragraph (6) of Article 10 (Dividends)) excluding the accumulated earnings tax and the personal holding company tax. The foregoing taxes covered are hereinafter referred to as "United States tax";

    (*b*) in the case of the United Kingdom, the income tax, the capital gains tax, the corporation tax and the petroleum revenue tax. The foregoing taxes covered are hereinafter referred to as "United Kingdom tax"; . . .

    (*c*) . . .

(3) This Convention shall also apply to any identical or substantially similar taxes which are imposed by a Contracting State . . . after the date of signature of this Convention in addition to, or in place of, the existing taxes. The competent authorities of the Contracting States shall notify each other of any changes which have been made in their respective taxation laws.

(4) For the purpose of Article 24 (Non-discrimination), this Convention shall also apply

to taxes of every kind and description imposed by each Contracting State, or by its political subdivisions or local authorities.

Article 3 General definitions

(1) In this Convention, unless the context otherwise requires:

    (a) the term "corporation" means a United States corporation, a United Kingdom corporation, or any body corporate or other entity of a third State which is treated as a body corporate for tax purposes by both Contracting States;

    (b) (i) the term "United States corporation" means a corporation (or any unincorporated entity treated as a corporation for United States tax purposes) which is created or organised under the laws of the United States or any State thereof or the District of Columbia; and

        (ii) the term "United Kingdom corporation" means any body corporate or unincorporated association created or organised under the laws of the United Kingdom, but does not include a partnership, a local authority, or a local authority association;

    (c) the term "person" includes an individual, a corporation, a partnership, an estate, a trust and any other body of persons;

    (d) the term "enterprise of a Contracting State" means an industrial or commercial undertaking carried on by a resident of a Contracting State;

    (e) the term "international traffic" means any transport by a ship or aircraft operated by an enterprise of a Contracting State, except when the ship or aircraft is operated solely between places in the other Contracting State;

    (f) the term "competent authority" means:

        (i) in the case of the United States, the Secretary of the Treasury or his delegate, and

        (ii) in the case of the United Kingdom, the Commissioners of Inland Revenue or their authorised representative;

    (g) (i) the term "United States" means the United States of America; and

        (ii) when used in a geographical sense, the States thereof and the District of Columbia.

        Such term also includes:

        (aa) the territorial sea thereof, and

        (bb) the sea-bed and sub-soil of the submarine areas adjacent to the coast thereof, but beyond the territorial sea, over which the United States exercises sovereign rights, in accordance with international law, for the purpose of exploration for and exploitation of the natural resources of such areas, but only to the extent that the person, property, or activity to which the Convention is being applied is connected with such exploration or exploitation;

    (h) the term "United Kingdom" means Great Britain and Northern Ireland, including any area outside the territorial sea of the United Kingdom which in accordance with international law has been or may hereafter be designated, under the laws of the United Kingdom concerning the Continental Shelf, as an area within which the rights of the United Kingdom with respect to the sea-bed and sub-soil and their natural resources may be exercised;

    (i) the term "Contracting State" means the United States or the United Kingdom, as the context requires;

    (j) the term "third State" means any State or territory other than the United States or the United Kingdom and the term "enterprise of a third State" shall be construed accordingly;

    (k) the term "nationals" means:

        (i) in relation to the United Kingdom, all citizens of the United Kingdom and Colonies, British subjects under sections 2, 13(1) or 16 of the British Nationality Act 1948, and British subjects by virtue of section 1 of the British

Nationality Act 1965, provided they are patrial within the meaning of the Immigration Act 1971, so far as these provisions are in force on the date of entry into force of this Convention or have been modified only in minor respects so as not to affect their general character;

    (ii) in relation to the United States, United States citizens.

(2) As regards the application of this Convention by a Contracting State any term not otherwise defined shall, unless the context otherwise requires and subject to the provisions of Article 25 (Mutual agreement procedure), have the meaning which it has under the laws of that Contracting State relating to the taxes which are the subject of this Convention.

Article 4 Fiscal residence

(1) For the purpose of this Convention:

    (a) the term "resident of the United Kingdom" means:

        (i) any person, other than a corporation, resident in the United Kingdom for the purposes of United Kingdom tax; but in the case of a partnership, estate, or trust, only to the extent that the income derived by such partnership, estate, or trust is subject to United Kingdom tax as the income of a resident, either in its hands or in the hands of its partners or beneficiaries; and

        (ii) a corporation whose business is managed and controlled in the United Kingdom;

    (b) the term "resident of the United States" means:

        (i) any person, other than a corporation, resident in the United States for the purposes of United States tax; but in the case of a partnership, estate, or trust, only to the extent that the income derived by such partnership, estate, or trust is subject to United States tax as the income of a resident, either in its hands or in the hands of its partners or beneficiaries; and

        (ii) a United States corporation.

(2) Where by reason of the provisions of paragraph (1) an individual is a resident of both Contracting States, then the individual's tax status shall be determined as follows:

    (a) the individual shall be deemed to be a resident of the Contracting State in which he has a permanent home available to him. If the individual has a permanent home available to him in both Contracting States or in neither of the Contracting States, he shall be deemed to be a resident of the Contracting State with which his personal and economic relations are closest (centre of vital interests);

    (b) if the Contracting State in which the individual's centre of vital interests is located cannot be determined, he shall be deemed to be a resident of that Contracting State in which he has an habitual abode;

    (c) if the individual has an habitual abode in both Contracting States or in neither of them, he shall be deemed to be a resident of the Contracting State of which he is a national; and

    (d) if the individual is a national of both Contracting States or of neither of them, the competent authorities of the Contracting States shall settle the question by mutual agreement.

(3) Where by reason of the provisions of paragraph (1) an estate or trust may be a resident of both Contracting States, the competent authorities of the Contracting States may settle the question of residence by mutual agreement.

(4) A marriage before 1 January 1974 between a woman who is a United States national and a man domiciled within the United Kingdom shall be deemed to have taken place on 1 January 1974 for the purpose of determining her domicile on or after 6 April 1976 for United Kingdom tax purposes.

(5) Where under any provision of this Convention income arising in one of the Contracting States is relieved from tax in that Contracting State and, under the law in force in the other Contracting State a person, in respect of the said income, is subject to tax by reference to the amount thereof which is remitted to or received in that other Contracting State and not by reference to the full amount thereof, then the relief to be allowed under this Convention in the

first-mentioned Contracting State shall apply only to so much of the income as is remitted to or received in the other Contracting State.

Article 6 Income from immovable property (real property)

(1) (Taxation of income from immovable property.)

(2) The term "immovable property" shall be defined in accordance with the law of the Contracting State in which the property in question is situated. The term shall in any case include usufruct of immovable property and rights to variable or fixed payments as consideration for the working of, or the right to work, mineral deposits, sources and other natural resources; ships, boats and aircraft shall not be regarded as immovable property.

(3) . . .

Article 8 Shipping and air transport

(1) Profits derived by an enterprise of a Contracting State from the operation of ships or aircraft in international traffic shall be taxable only in that State.

(2) Notwithstanding any other provision of this Convention, profits which a national of the United States not resident in the United Kingdom or a United States corporation derives from operating ships documented or aircraft registered under the laws of the United States shall be exempt from United Kingdom tax.

(3) For the purposes of this Article, profits from the operation of ships or aircraft . . . include profits derived from the rental on a bareboat basis of ships or aircraft . . . if such rental income is incidental to other income described in paragraph (1) of this Article.

(4) Notwithstanding the provisions of Article 7 (Business profits), profits of an enterprise of a Contracting State from the use, maintenance or rental of containers (including trailers and related equipment for the transport of containers) used for the transport of goods or merchandise shall be taxable only in that State, except where such containers are used for the transport of goods or merchandise solely between places within the other Contracting State.

(5) The provisions of this Article shall apply also to profits derived by an enterprise of a Contracting State from participation in a pool, a joint business or an international operating agency.

(6) Gains derived by an enterprise of a Contracting State from the alienation of ships, aircraft or containers owned and operated by the enterprise, the income from which is taxable only in that State, shall be taxable only in that State.

Offshore activities: See Article 27A(3) in relation to offshore activities.

Article 13 Capital gains

Except as provided in Article 8 (Shipping and air transport) of this Convention each Contracting State may tax capital gains in accordance with the provision of its domestic law.

Article 24 Non-discrimination

(1) Individuals who are nationals of a Contracting State and who are residents of the other Contracting State shall not be subjected in that other State to any taxation or any requirement connected therewith which is other or more burdensome than the taxation and connected requirements to which nationals of that other State in the same circumstances are or may be subjected.

(2) The taxation on a permanent establishment which an enterprise of a Contracting State has in the other Contracting State shall not be less favourably levied in that other State than the taxation levied on enterprises of that other State carrying on the same activities.

(3) Subject to the provisions of paragraph (4) of this Article, interest, royalties and other disbursements paid by an enterprise of a Contracting State to a resident of the other Contract-

ing State shall, if reasonable in amount, be deductible for the purpose of determining the taxable profits of such enterprise under the same conditions as if they had been paid to a resident of the first-mentioned State. For the purposes of this paragraph, the term "other disbursements" shall include charges for amounts expended by such residents for the purposes of such enterprise, including a reasonable allocation of executive and general administrative expenses (except to the extent representing the expenses of a type of activity which is not for the benefit of such enterprise, but constitutes "stewardship" or "over-seeing" functions undertaken for such resident's own benefit as an investor in the enterprise), research and development in respect of which such enterprise has the benefits under a cost and risk sharing agreement and other expenses incurred by such resident for the benefit of a group of related enterprises including such enterprise.

(4) Paragraph (3) shall not apply to any interest, royalties, or other disbursements to which the provisions of Article 9 (Associated enterprises), paragraphs (5) and (7) or Article 11 (Interests) or paragraph (5) of Article 12 (Royalties) apply.

(5) Enterprises of a Contracting State, the capital of which is wholly or partly owned or controlled, directly or indirectly, by one or more residents of the other Contracting State, shall not be subjected in the first-mentioned Contracting State to any taxation or any requirement connected therewith which is other or more burdensome than the taxation and connected requirements to which other similar enterprises of the first-mentioned State are or may be subjected.

(6) Nothing contained in this Article shall be construed as obliging either Contracting State to grant to individuals not resident in that State any of the personal allowances and reliefs which are granted to individuals so resident.

Article 25 Mutual agreement procedure

(1) Where a resident or national of a Contracting State considers that the actions of one or both of the Contracting States result or will result in taxation not in accordance with this Convention, he may, notwithstanding the remedies provided by the national laws of those States, present his case to the competent authority of the Contracting State of which he is a resident or national.

(2) The competent authority shall endeavour, if the objection appears to it to be justified and if it is not itself able to arrive at an appropriate solution, to resolve the case by mutual agreement with the competent authority of the other Contracting State, with a view to the avoidance of taxation not in accordance with the Convention. Where an agreement has been reached, a refund as appropriate shall be made to give effect to the agreement.

(3) The competent authorities of the Contracting States shall endeavour to resolve by mutual agreement any difficulties or doubts arising as to the interpretation or application of the Convention. In particular the competent authorities of the Contracting States may reach agreement on:

> (a) the attribution of income, deductions, credits, or allowances of an enterprise of a Contracting State to its permanent establishment situated in the other Contracting State;
> (b) the allocation of income, deductions, credits, or allowances between persons;
> (c) the nature of particular items of income;
> (d) the meaning of terms not otherwise defined in this Convention;
> (e) the place where a particular item of income has its source;
> (f) the elimination of double taxation in respect of income paid out of trusts.

(4) The competent authorities of the Contracting States may communicate with each other directly for the purpose of reaching agreement as contemplated by this Convention.

Article 26 Exchange of information and administrative assistance

(1) The competent authorities of the Contracting States shall exchange such information (being information available under the respective taxation laws of the Contracting States) as is necessary for carrying out the provisions of this Convention or for the prevention of fraud or

the administration of statutory provisions against legal avoidance in relation to the taxes which are the subject of this Convention. Any information so exchanged shall be treated as secret but may be disclosed to persons (including a court or administrative body) concerned with the assessment, collection, enforcement or prosecution in respect of taxes which are the subject of this Convention. No information shall be exchanged which would disclose any trade, business, industrial or professional secret or any trade process.

(2) Each of the Contracting States will endeavour to collect on behalf of the other Contracting State such amounts as may be necessary to ensure that relief granted by this Convention from taxation imposed by such other Contracting State does not enure to the benefit of persons not entitled thereto. The United Kingdom will be regarded as fulfilling this obligation by the continuation of its existing arrangements for ensuring that relief from taxation imposed by the laws of the United States does not enure to the benefits of persons not entitled thereto.

(3) Paragraph (2) of this Article shall not impose upon either of the Contracting States the obligation to carry out administrative measures which are of a different nature from those used in the collection of its own tax, or which would be contrary to its sovereignty, security or public policy. In determining the administrative measures to be carried out, each Contracting State may take into account the administrative measures and practices of the other Contracting State in recovering taxes on behalf of the first-mentioned Contracting State.

(4) The competent authorities of the Contracting States shall consult with each other for the purpose of co-operating and advising in respect of any action to be taken in implementing this Article.

Article 27A Offshore activities

(1) Notwithstanding the provisions of Article 5 (Permanent establishment) and Article 14 (Independent personal services), a person who is a resident of a Contracting State and carries on activities in the other Contracting State in connection with the exploration or exploitation of the sea-bed and sub-soil and their natural resources situated in that other Contracting State shall be deemed to be carrying on in respect of those activities a business in that other Contracting State through a permanent establishment or fixed base situated therein.

(2) The provisions of paragraph (1) shall not apply where the activities are carried on for a period not exceeeding 30 days in aggregate in any 12 month period. However, for the purpose of this paragraph, activities carried on by an enterprise related to another enterprise shall be regarded as carried on by the enterprise to which it is related if the activities in question are substantially the same as those carried on by the last-mentioned enterprise.

(3) The provisions of Article 8 (Shipping and air transport) shall not apply to a drilling rig or any vessel the principal function of which is the performance of activities other than the transportation of goods or passengers.

Article 28 Entry into force

Note: Article 28 provided for the entry into force of the 1975 Convention (which was amended by the Protocols of 1976, 1977 and 1979 before it entered into force). It takes effect in the UK from the year of assessment, financial year or chargeable period (as appropriate) beginning in 1975.

Official language: English.

Capital taxes

Convention of 19 October 1978 (SI 1979 No 1454)

Article 1 Scope

This Convention shall apply to any person who is within the scope of a tax which is the subject of this Convention.

Article 2 Taxes covered

(1) The existing taxes to which this Convention shall apply are:
> (a) in the United States: the Federal gift tax and the Federal estate tax, including the tax on generation-skipping transfers; and
> (b) in the United Kingdom: the capital transfer tax.

(2) This Convention shall also apply to any identical or substantially similar taxes which are imposed by a Contracting State after the date of signature of the Convention in addition to, or in place of, the existing taxes. The competent authorities of the Contracting States shall notify each other of any changes which have been made in their respective taxation laws.

Inheritance tax: United Kingdom capital transfer tax is known as inheritance tax by virtue of FA 1986, s 100.

Article 3 General definitions

(1) In this Convention:
> (a) the term "United States" means the United States of America, but does not include Puerto Rico, the Virgin Islands, Guam or any other United States possession or territory;
> (b) the term "United Kingdom" means Great Britain and Northern Ircland;
> (c) the term "enterprise" means an industrial or commercial undertaking;
> (d) the term "competent authority" means:
>> (i) in the United States: the Secretary of the Treasury or his delegate, and
>> (ii) in the United Kingdom: the Commissioners of Inland Revenue or their authorised representative;
> (e) the term "nationals" means:
>> (i) in relation to the United States, United States citizens, and

      (ii) in relation to the United Kingdom, any citizen of the United Kingdom and Colonies, or any British subject not possessing that citizenship or the citizenship of any other Commonwealth country or territory, provided in either case he had the right of abode in the United Kingdom at the time of the death or transfer;

  (f) the term "tax" means:

      (i) the Federal gift tax or the Federal estate tax, including the tax on generation-skipping transfers, imposed in the United States, or

      (ii) the capital transfer tax imposed in the United Kingdom, or

      (iii) any other tax imposed by a Contracting State to which this Convention applies by virtue of the provisions of paragraph (2) of Article 2;

    as the context requires; and

  (g) the term "Contracting State" means the United Kingdom or the United States as the context requires.

(2) As regards the application of the Convention by a Contracting State, any term not otherwise defined shall, unless the context otherwise requires and subject to the provisions of Article 11 (Mutual Agreement Procedure), have the meaning which it has under the laws of that Contracting State relating to the taxes which are the subject of the Convention.

Article 4 Fiscal domicile

(1) For the purposes of this Convention an individual was domiciled:

  (a) in the United States: if he was a resident (domiciliary) thereof or if he was a national thereof and had been a resident (domiciliary) thereof at any time during the preceding three years; and

  (b) in the United Kingdom: if he was domiciled in the United Kingdom in accordance with the law of the United Kingdom or is treated as so domiciled for the purposes of a tax which is the subject of this Convention.

(2) Where by reason of the provisions of paragraph (1) an individual was at any time domiciled in both Contracting States, and

  (a) was a national of the United Kingdom but not of the United States, and

  (b) had not been resident in the United States for Federal income tax purposes in seven or more of the ten taxable years ending with the year in which that time falls,

he shall be deemed to be domiciled in the United Kingdom at that time.

(3) Where by reason of the provisions of paragraph (1) an individual was at any time domiciled in both Contracting States, and

  (a) was a national of the United States but not of the United Kingdom, and

  (b) had not been resident in the United Kingdom in seven or more of the ten income tax years of assessment ending with the year in which that time falls,

he shall be deemed to be domiciled in the United States at that time. For the purposes of this paragraph, the question of whether a person was so resident shall be determined as for income tax purposes but without regard to any dwelling-house available to him in the United Kingdom for his use.

(4) Where by reason of the provisions of paragraph (1) an individual was domiciled in both Contracting States, then, subject to the provisions of paragraphs (2) and (3), his status shall be determined as follows:

  (a) the individual shall be deemed to be domiciled in the Contracting State in which he had a permanent home available to him. If he had a permanent home available to him in both Contracting States, or in neither Contracting State, he shall be deemed to be domiciled in the Contracting State with which his personal and economic relations were closest (centre of vital interests);

  (b) if the Contracting State in which the individual's centre of vital interests was located cannot be determined, he shall be deemed to be domiciled in the Contracting State in which he had an habitual abode;

  (c) if the individual had an habitual abode in both Contracting States or in neither of them, he shall be deemed to be domiciled in the Contracting State of which he was a national; and

(*d*) if the individual was a national of both Contracting States or of neither of them, the competent authorities of the Contracting States shall settle the question by mutual agreement.

(5) An individual who was a resident (domiciliary) of a possession of the United States and who became a citizen of the United States solely by reason of his

(*a*) being a citizen of such possession, or

(*b*) birth or residence within such possession,

shall be considered as neither domiciled in nor a national of the United States for the purposes of this Convention.

Article 5 Taxing rights

(1) (*a*) Subject to the provisions of Articles 6 (Immovable Property (Real Property)) and 7 (Business Property of a Permanent Establishment and Assets Pertaining to a Fixed Base Used for the Performance of Independent Personal Services) and the following paragraphs of this Article, if the decedent or transferor was domiciled in one of the Contracting States at the time of the death or transfer, property shall not be taxable in the other State.

(*b*) Sub-paragraph (*a*) shall not apply if at the time of the death or transfer the decedent or transferor was a national of that other State.

(2) Subject to the provisions of the said Articles 6 and 7, if at the time of the death or transfer the decedent or transferor was domiciled in neither Contracting State and was a national of one Contracting State (but not of both), property which is taxable in the Contracting State of which he was a national shall not be taxable in the other Contracting State.

(3) Paragraphs (1) and (2) shall not apply in the United States to property held in a generation-skipping trust or trust equivalent on the occasion of a generation-skipping transfer; but, subject to the provisions of the said Articles 6 and 7, tax shall not be imposed in the United States on such property if at the time when the transfer was made the deemed transferor was domiciled in the United Kingdom and was not a national of the United States.

(4) Paragraphs (1) and (2) shall not apply in the United Kingdom to property comprised in a settlement; but, subject to the provisions of the said Articles 6 and 7, tax shall not be imposed in the United Kingdom on such property if at the time when the settlement was made the settlor was domiciled in the United States and was not a national of the United Kingdom.

(5) If by reason of the preceding paragraphs of this Article any property would be taxable only in one Contracting State and tax, though chargeable is not paid (otherwise than as a result of a specific exemption, deduction, exclusion, credit or allowance) in that State, tax may be imposed by reference to that property in the Contracting State notwithstanding those paragraphs.

(6) If at the time of the death or transfer the decedent or transferor was domiciled in neither Contracting State and each State would regard any property as situated in its territory and in consequence tax would be imposed in both States, the competent authorities of the Contracting States shall determine the situs of the property by mutual agreement.

Article 6 Immovable property (real property)

(1) (Taxation of immovable property.)

(2) The term "immovable property" shall be defined in accordance with the law of the Contracting State in which the property in question is situated, provided always that debts secured by mortgage or otherwise shall not be regarded as immovable property. The term shall in any case include property accessory to immovable property, livestock and equipment used in agriculture and forestry, rights to which the provisions of general law respecting landed property apply, usufruct of immovable property and rights to variable or fixed payments as consideration for the working of, or the right to work, mineral deposits, sources and

other natural resources; ships, boats, and aircraft shall not be regarded as immovable property.

(3) . . .

Article 8 Deductions, exemptions etc

(1) In determining the amount on which tax is to be computed, permitted deductions shall be allowed in accordance with the law in force in the Contracting State in which tax is imposed.

(2) Property which passes to the spouse from a decedent or transferor who was domiciled in or a national of the United Kingdom and which may be taxed in the United States shall qualify for a marital deduction there to the extent that a marital deduction would have been allowable if the decedent or transferor had been domiciled in the United States and if the gross estate of the decedent had been limited to property which may be taxed in the United States or the transfers of the transferor had been limited to transfers of property which may be so taxed.

(3) Property which passes to the spouse from the decedent or transferor who was domiciled in or a national of the United States and which may be taxed in the United Kingdom shall, where

    (a) the transferor's spouse was not domiciled in the United Kingdom but the transfer would have been wholly exempt had the spouse been so domiciled, and

    (b) a greater exemption for transfers between spouses would not have been given under the law of the United Kingdom apart from this Convention,

be exempt from tax in the United Kingdom to the extent of 50 per cent of the value transferred, calculated as a value on which no tax is payable and after taking account of all exemptions except those for transfers between spouses.

    (4) (a) Property which on the death of a decedent domiciled in the United Kingdom became comprised in a settlement shall, if the personal representatives and the trustees of every settlement in which the decedent had an interest in possession immediately before death so elect and subject to sub-paragraph (b), be exempt from tax in the United Kingdom to the extent of 50 per cent of the value transferred (calculated as in paragraph (3)) on the death of the decedent if:

        (i) under the settlement the spouse of the decedent was entitled to an immediate interest in possession,

        (ii) the spouse was domiciled in or a national of the United States,

        (iii) the transfer would have been wholly exempt had the spouse been domiciled in the United Kingdom, and

        (iv) a greater exemption for transfers between spouses would not have been given under the law of the United Kingdom apart from this Convention.

    (b) Where the spouse of the decedent becomes absolutely and indefeasibly entitled to any of the settled property at any time after the decedent's death, the election shall, as regards that property, be deemed never to have been made and tax shall be payable as if on the death such property had been given to the spouse absolutely and indefeasibly.

(5) Where property may be taxed in the United States on the death of a United Kingdom national who was neither domiciled in nor a national of the United States and a claim is made under this paragraph, the tax imposed in the United States shall be limited to the amount of tax which would have been imposed had the decedent become domiciled in the United States immediately before his death, on the property which would in that event have been taxable.

Article 9 Credits

(1) Where under this Convention the United States may impose tax with respect to any property other than property which the United States is entitled to tax in accordance with Article 6 (Immovable Property (Real Property)) or 7 (Business Property of a Permanent Establishment and Assets Pertaining to a Fixed Base Used for the Performance of Independent Personal Services) (that is, where the decedent or transferor was domiciled in or a

national of the United States), then, except in cases to which paragraph (3) applies, double taxation shall be avoided in the following manner:

    (*a*) Where the United Kingdom imposes tax with respect to property in accordance with the said Article 6 or 7, the United States shall credit against the tax calculated according to its law with respect to that property an amount equal to the tax paid in the United Kingdom with respect to that property.

    (*b*) Where the United Kingdom imposes tax with respect to property not referred to in sub-paragraph (*a*) and the decedent or transferor was a national of the United States and was domiciled in the United Kingdom at the time of the death or transfer, the United States shall credit against tax calculated according to its law with respect to that property an amount equal to the tax paid in the United Kingdom with respect to that property.

(2) Where under this Convention the United Kingdom may impose tax with respect to any property other than property which the United Kingdom is entitled to tax in accordance with the said Article 6 or 7 (that is, where the decedent or transferor was domiciled in or a national of the United Kingdom), then, except in the cases to which paragraph (3) applies, double taxation shall be avoided in the following manner:

    (*a*) Where the United States imposes tax with respect to property in accordance with the said Article 6 or 7, the United Kingdom shall credit against the tax calculated according to its law with respect to that property an amount equal to the tax paid in the United States with respect to that property.

    (*b*) Where the United States imposes tax with respect to property not referred to in sub-paragraph (*a*) and the decedent or transferor was a national of the United Kingdom and was domiciled in the United States at the time of the death or transfer, the United Kingdom shall credit against the tax calculated according to its law with respect to that property an amount equal to the tax paid in the United States with respect to that property.

(3) Where both Contracting States impose tax on the same event with respect to property which under the law of the United States would be regarded as property held in a trust or trust equivalent and under the law of the United Kingdom would be regarded as property comprised in a settlement, double taxation shall be avoided in the following manner:

    (*a*) Where a Contracting State imposes tax with respect to property in accordance with the said Article 6 or 7, the other Contracting State shall credit against the tax calculated according to its law with respect to that property an amount equal to the tax paid in the first-mentioned Contracting State with respect to that property.

    (*b*) Where the United States imposes tax with respect to property which is not taxable in accordance with the said Article 6 or 7 then

        (i) where the event giving rise to a liability to tax was a generation-skipping transfer and the deemed transferor was domiciled in the United States at the time of that event,

        (ii) where the event giving rise to a liability to tax was the exercise or lapse of a power of appointment and the holder of the power was domiciled in the United States at the time of that event, or

        (iii) where (i) or (ii) does not apply and the settlor or grantor was domiciled in the United States at the time when the tax is imposed, the United Kingdom shall credit against the tax calculated according to its law with respect to that property an amount equal to the tax paid in the United States with respect to that property.

    (*c*) Where the United States imposes tax with respect to property which is not taxable in accordance with the said Article 6 or 7 and sub-paragraph (*b*) does not apply, the United States shall credit against the tax calculated according to its law with respect to that property an amount equal to the tax paid in the United Kingdom with respect to that property.

(4) The credits allowed by a Contracting State according to the provisions of paragraphs (1), (2) and (3) shall not take into account amounts of such taxes not levied by reason of a credit otherwise allowed by the other Contracting State. No credit shall be finally allowed

under those paragraphs until the tax (reduced by any credit allowable with respect thereto) for which the credit is allowable has been paid. Any credit allowed under those paragraphs shall not, however, exceed the part of the tax paid in a Contracting State (as computed before the credit is given but reduced by any credit for other tax) which is attributable to the property with respect to which the credit is given.

(5) Any claim for a credit or for a refund of tax founded on the provisions of the present Convention shall be made within six years from the date of the event giving rise to a liability to tax or, where later, within one year from the last date on which tax for which credit is given is due. The competent authority may, in appropriate circumstances, extend this time limit where the final determination of the taxes which are the subject of the claim for credit is delayed.

Article 10 Non-discrimination

(1) (*a*) Subject to the provisions of sub-paragraph (*b*), nationals of a Contracting State shall not be subjected in the other State to any taxation or any requirement connected therewith which is other or more burdensome than the taxation and connected requirements to which nationals of that other State in the same circumstances are or may be subjected.

(*b*) Sub-paragraph (*a*) shall not prevent the United States from taxing a national of the United Kingdom, who is not domiciled in the United States, as a non-resident alien under its law, subject to the provisions of paragraph (5) of Article 8 (Deductions, exemptions etc).

(2) The taxation on a permanent establishment which an enterprise of a Contracting State has in the other Contracting State shall not be less favourably levied in that other State than the taxation levied on enterprises of that other State carrying on the same activities.

(3) Nothing contained in this Article shall be construed as obliging either Contracting State to grant to individuals not domiciled in that Contracting State any personal allowances, reliefs and reductions for taxation purposes which are granted to individuals so domiciled.

(4) Enterprises of a Contracting State, the capital of which is wholly or partly owned or controlled, directly or indirectly, by one or more residents of the other Contracting State, shall not be subjected in the first-mentioned Contracting State to any taxation or any requirement connected therewith which is other or more burdensome than the taxation and connected requirements to which other similar enterprises of the first-mentioned State are or may be subjected.

(5) The provisions of this Article shall apply to taxes which are the subject of this Convention.

Article 11 Mutual agreement procedure

(1) Where a person considers that the actions of one or both of the Contracting States result or will result in taxation not in accordance with the provisions of this Convention, he may, irrespective of the remedies provided by the domestic laws of those States, present his case to the competent authority of either Contracting State.

(2) The competent authority shall endeavour, if the objection appears to it to be justified and it is not itself able to arrive at an appropriate solution, to resolve the case by mutual agreement with the competent authority of the other Contracting State, with a view to the avoidance of taxation not in accordance with the Convention. Where an agreement has been reached, a refund as appropriate shall be made to give effect to the agreement.

(3) The competent authorities of the Contracting States shall endeavour to resolve by mutual agreement any difficulties or doubts arising as to the interpretation or application of the Convention. In particular the competent authorities of the Contracting States may reach agreement on the meaning of the terms not otherwise defined in this Convention.

(4) The competent authorities of the Contracting States may communicate with each other directly for the purpose of reaching an agreement as contemplated by this Convention.

UNITED STATES OF AMERICA

Article 12 Exchange of information

The competent authorities of the Contracting States shall exchange such information (being information available under the respective taxation laws of the Contracting States) as is necessary for the carrying out of the provisions of this Convention or for the prevention of fraud or the administration of statutory provisions against legal avoidance in relation to the taxes which are the subject of this Convention. Any information so exchanged shall be treated as secret and shall not be disclosed to any persons other than persons (including a court or administrative body) concerned with the assessment, enforcement, collection, or prosecution in respect of the taxes which are the subject of the Convention. No information shall be exchanged which would disclose any trade, business, industrial or professional secret or any trade process.

Article 14 Entry into force

Note: This Convention applies in the UK in respect of property by reference to which there is a charge to tax which arises after 11 November 1979 (subject to transitional relief where, in respect of deaths before 27 March 1981, the 1945 Convention would have afforded greater relief).

Official language: English.

VENEZUELA

Agreement of 8 March 1978 (SI 1979 No 301)

The Protocol of 23 November 1987 (SI 1988/Draft), which amends Articles 1, 2 and 4 below, had not entered into force on 6 April 1988. It takes effect as regards profits, income or capital gains arising after 31 December 1987.

Article 1 [Exemption from tax]

(1) Subject to Article 2 of this Agreement all profits, income and capital gains derived by an undertaking of one of the Contracting States from the business of shipping and air transport shall be exempt in the other Contracting State from all the taxes of that other Contracting State (other than municipal taxes) which are, or may become, chargeable on profits, income and capital gains.

(2) The provisions of this Article shall also apply to profits from the participation in a pool, a joint business or an international operating agency.

Article 1(1): The Protocol of 23 November 1987 (SI 1988/Draft) substitutes the words "any undertaking" for the words "an undertaking".

Article 2 [Application]

(1) The exemption provided under Article 1 shall apply to an undertaking of one of the Contracting States which, at the date of signature of the Agreement, regularly serves a port or airport situated in the territory of the other Contracting State.

(2) This exemption shall also apply, subject to mutual agreement between the competent authorities of the Contracting States, to an undertaking of either Contracting State which may subsequently operate a regular service to a port or airport situated in the territory of the other Contracting State, or which may be designated under agreements between the Contracting States.

(3) All undertakings of each of the Contracting States which are exempt from tax in accordance with the provisions of this Agreement shall present to the competent authority of the other Contracting State, for statistical purposes only, an annual statement of the financial results of those enterprises from the business of shipping or air transport (and of any connected operations) carried out by them in the other Contracting State.

Article 2: The Protocol of 23 November 1987 (SI 1988/Draft) substitutes the following words for Article 2: "The exemption provided under Article 1 shall apply to any undertaking of one of the Contracting States which serves any port or airport situated in the territory of the other Contracting State."

Article 3 [Mutual agreement procedure]

The competent authorities of the Contracting States shall endeavour to resolve by mutual agreement any difficulty or doubt arising out of the application of this Agreement. The competent authorities may communicate with each other for this purpose. Where it seems advisable for this purpose to have direct consultations, these shall take place within a reasonable time of a request for such consultations being made by the competent authority of either Contracting State to the competent authority of the other Contracting State.

Article 4 [General definitions]

For the purposes of this Agreement:
  (a) The expressions "one of the Contracting States" and "the other Contracting State" mean the Republic of Venezuela or the United Kingdom of Great Britain and Northern Ireland as the context requires.
  (b) The expression "undertaking of one of the Contracting States" means the Government of that Contracting State, a physical person resident in that Contracting State and not resident in the other Contracting State and a company or partnership constituted under the laws in force and managed and controlled in that Contracting State.
  (c) The expression "the business of shipping and air transport" means the business of transporting persons, animals, goods and mail carried on by the owner or charterer of ships or aircraft.
  (d) The expression "competent authority" means, in the case of Venezuela, the Dirección General de Rentas or its authorised representative, and in the case of the United Kingdom, the Commissioners of Inland Revenue or their authorised representative.

Article 4 (c) and (d): The Protocol of 23 November 1987 (SI 1988/Draft) substitutes the following for paragraphs (c) and (d):
  "(c) The expression 'the business of shipping and air transport' means the business of transporting persons, animals, goods (excluding hydrocarbons) and mail carried on by the owner or charterer of ships or aircraft. The term 'hydrocarbons' means natural gas, liquefied natural gas, crude petroleum and the products derived exclusively from the first phase of the refining of crude petroleum.
  (d) The expression 'competent authority' means, in the case of Venezuela, the Dirección

337

General Sectorial de Rentas, and in the case of the United Kingdom, the Commissioners of Inland Revenue or their authorised representative."

Article 5 [Entry into force]

Note: Article 5 provided for the entry into force of this Agreement. It takes effect as regards profits, income or capital gains arising after 31 December 1976.

Official languages: The Spanish language text and the English language text of this Agreement are equally authoritative.

YUGOSLAVIA

Convention of 6 November 1981 (SI 1981 No 1815)

Article 1 Personal scope

This Convention shall apply to persons who are residents of one or both of the Contracting States.

Article 2 Taxes covered

(1) The taxes which are the subject of this Convention are, subject to the provisions of Article 3(1)(*d*) of this Convention:

    (*a*) in the United Kingdom:

        (i) the income tax;

        (ii) the capital gains tax; and

        (iii) the corporation tax;

    (*b*) in Yugoslavia:

        (i) the tax and contributions on income of organisations of associated labour (*porez i doprinosi iz dohotka organizacija udruženog rada*);

        (ii) the tax and contributions on personal income derived from dependent personal services (*porez i doprinosi iz ličnog dohotka iz radnog odnosa*);

        (iii) the tax and contributions on personal income derived from agricultural activities (*porez i doprinosi iz ličnog dohotka od poljoprivredne delatnosti*);

        (iv) the tax and contributions on personal income derived from independent economic and non-economic activities (*porez i doprinosi iz ličnog dohotka od samostalnog obavljanja privrednih i neprivrednih delatnosti*);

       (v) the tax on personal income derived from copyrights, patents and technical improvements (*porez iz ličnog dohotka od autorskih prava, patenata i tehničkih unapredjenja*);

  (vi) the tax on income from capital and capital rights (*porez na prihod od imovine i imovinskih prava*);
  (vii) the tax on total income of citizens (*porez iz ukupnog prihoda gradjana*);
  (viii) the tax on profits of foreign persons derived from investments in a domestic organisation of associated labour for the purposes of joint business operations (*porez na dobit stranih lica ostvarenu ulaganjem u domaců organizaciju udruženog rada za svrhe zajedničkog poslovanja*);
  (ix) the tax on profits of foreign persons derived from investment projects (*porez na dobit stranih lica ostvarenu izvodjenjem investicionih radova*); and
  (x) the tax on income of foreign persons derived from passenger and cargo transport (*porez na prihod stranih lica ostvaren od prevoza putnika i robe*).

(2) This Convention shall also apply to any identical or substantially similar taxes which are imposed by either Contracting State after the date of signature of this Convention in addition to, or in place of, the existing taxes. The competent authorities of the Contracting States shall notify to each other any substantial changes which have been made in their respective taxation laws.

Article 3 General definitions

(1) For the purposes of this Convention:
  (*a*) the term "United Kingdom" means Great Britain and Northern Ireland, including any area outside the territorial sea of the United Kingdom which in accordance with international law has been or may hereafter be designated, under the laws of the United Kingdom concerning the Continental Shelf, as an area within which the rights of the United Kingdom with respect to the sea-bed and sub-soil and their natural resources may be exercised;
  (*b*) the term "Yugoslavia" means the territory of the Socialist Federal Republic of Yugoslavia including also any area outside the territorial sea of Yugoslavia which has been or may hereafter be designated under the laws of Yugoslavia and in accordance with international law, as an area within which the rights of Yugoslavia to the sea-bed and sub-soil and their natural resources may be exercised;
  (*c*) the term "national" means:
    (i) in relation to the United Kingdom, any citizen of the United Kingdom and Colonies who derives his status as such from his connection with the United Kingdom;
    (ii) in relation to Yugoslavia, a Yugoslav citizen and any other individual who derives his status as such from the law in force in Yugoslavia;
  (*d*) the term "United Kingdom tax" means tax imposed by the United Kingdom being tax to which this Convention applies by virtue of the provisions of Article 2; the term "Yugoslav tax" means taxes and contributions, with the exception of the contribution for social security, imposed in Yugoslavia being tax to which this Convention applies by virtue of the provisions of Article 2;
  (*e*) the term "tax" means United Kingdom tax or Yugoslav tax, as the context requires;
  (*f*) the terms "a Contracting State" and "the other Contracting State" mean the United Kingdom or Yugoslavia, as the context requires;
  (*g*) the term "person" means, in the case of the United Kingdom, an individual, a company and any other body of persons, and in the case of Yugoslavia, an individual and any legal person;
  (*h*) the term "company" means, in the case of the United Kingdom, any body corporate or any entity which is treated as a body corporate for tax purposes, and in the case of Yugoslavia, an organisation of associated labour and any other legal person subject to tax;
  (*i*) the terms "enterprise of a Contracting State" and "enterprise of the other Contracting State" mean, as the context requires, in the case of the United Kingdom, an enterprise carried on by a resident of the United Kingdom and, in the case of

Yugoslavia, an organisation of associated labour, a self-managed organisation or community, working people who individually perform activities independently and an enterprise established in accordance with the laws of Yugoslavia carried on by a resident of Yugoslavia;

(j) the term "competent authority" means, in the case of the United Kingdom the Board of Inland Revenue or its authorised representative, and in the case of Yugoslavia the Federal Secretariat for Finance or its authorised representative;

(k) the term "international traffic" means any transport by a ship or aircraft operated by an enterprise which has its place of effective management in a Contracting State, except when the ship or aircraft is operated solely between places in the other Contracting State.

(2) As regards the application of this Convention by a Contracting State, any term not defined therein shall have the meaning which it has under the laws of that State concerning the taxes to which the Convention applies.

Article 4 Fiscal domicile

(1) For the purposes of this Convention, the term "resident of a Contracting State" means, subject to the provisions of paragraphs (2) and (3) of this Article, any person who, under the law of that State, is liable to taxation therein by reason of his domicile, residence, place of management or any other criterion of a similar nature. The terms "resident of the United Kingdom" and "resident of Yugoslavia" shall be construed accordingly.

(2) Where by reason of the provisions of paragraph (1) of this Article an individual is a resident of both Contracting States, then his status shall be determined in accordance with the following rules:

(a) he shall be deemed to be a resident of the Contracting State in which he has a permanent home available to him. If he has a permanent home available to him in both Contracting States, he shall be deemed to be a resident of the Contracting State with which his personal and economic relations are closer (centre of vital interests);

(b) if the Contracting State in which he has his centre of vital interests cannot be determined, or if he has not a permanent home available to him in either Contracting State, he shall be deemed to be a resident of the Contracting State in which he has an habitual abode;

(c) if he has an habitual abode in both Contracting States or if he has not an habitual abode in either Contracting State, he shall be deemed to be a resident of the Contracting State of which he is a national;

(d) if he is a national of both Contracting States or of neither of them, the competent authorities of the Contracting States shall settle the question by mutual agreement.

(3) Where by reason of the provisions of paragraph (1) of this Article a person other than an individual is a resident of both Contracting States, then it shall be deemed to be a resident of the Contracting State in which its place of effective management is situated.

Article 6 Income from immovable property

(1) (Taxation of income from immovable property.)

(2) The term "immovable property" shall have the meaning which it has under the law of the Contracting State in which the property in question is situated. Ships, boats and aircraft shall not be regarded as immovable property.

(3) . . .

(4) . . .

Article 8 Shipping and air transport

(1) Profits from the operation of ships or aircraft in international traffic shall be taxable only in the Contracting State in which the place of effective management of the enterprise is situated.

(2) If the place of effective management of a shipping enterprise is aboard a ship, then it shall be deemed to be situated in the Contracting State in which the home harbour of the ship is situated, or, if there is no such home harbour, in the Contracting State of which the operator of the ship is a resident.

(3) The provisions of this Article shall also apply to profits derived from the participation in a pool, a joint business or in an international operating agency.

Article 13 Capital gains

(1) . . .

(2) (Taxation of gains from alienation of movable business property.)

(3) Notwithstanding the provisions of paragraph (2) of this Article, capital gains derived from the alienation of ships and aircraft operated in international traffic and movable property pertaining to the operation of such ships and aircraft shall be taxable only in the Contracting State in which the place of effective management of the enterprise is situated.

(4) . . .

Article 23 Non-discrimination

(1) Nationals and legal persons, deriving their status as such from the law in force in a Contracting State, shall not be subjected in the other Contracting State to any taxation or any requirement connected therewith which is other or more burdensome than the taxation and connected requirements to which nationals and legal persons, deriving their status as such from the law in force in that other State, in the same circumstances are or may be subjected.

(2) The taxation on a permanent establishment which an enterprise of a Contracting State has in the other Contracting State shall not be less favourably levied in that other State than the taxation levied on enterprises of that other State carrying on the same activities.

(3) Enterprises of a Contracting State, the capital of which is wholly or partly owned or controlled, directly or indirectly, by one or more residents of the other Contracting State, shall not be subjected in the first-mentioned Contracting State to any taxation or any requirement connected therewith which is other or more burdensome than the taxation and connected requirements to which other similar enterprises of that first-mentioned State are or may be subjected.

(4) Nothing contained in this Article shall be construed as obliging either Contracting State to grant to persons who are not resident in that State any of the personal allowances, reliefs and reductions for tax purposes which are granted to persons who are resident in that State.

(5) In this Article the term "taxation" means taxes of every kind and description.

Article 24 Mutual agreement procedure

(1) Where a resident of a Contracting State considers that the actions of one or both of the Contracting States result or will result for him in taxation not in accordance with this Convention, he may, notwithstanding the remedies provided by the national laws of those States, present his case to the competent authority of the Contracting State of which he is a resident.

(2) The competent authority shall endeavour, if the objection appears to it to be justified and if it is not itself able to arrive at an appropriate solution, to resolve the case by mutual agreement with the competent authority of the other Contracting State, with a view to the avoidance of taxation not in accordance with the Convention.

(3) The competent authorities of the Contracting States shall endeavour to resolve by mutual agreement any difficulties or doubts arising as to the interpretation or application of the Convention.

(4) The competent authorities of the Contracting States may communicate with each other directly for the purpose of reaching an agreement in the sense of the preceding paragraphs.

Article 25 Exchange of information

(1) The competent authorities of the Contracting States shall exchange such information as is necessary for the carrying out of this Convention and of the domestic laws of the Contracting States concerning taxes covered by this Convention insofar as the taxation thereunder is in accordance with this Convention. Any information so exchanged shall be treated as secret and shall not be disclosed to any persons other than persons (including a Court or administrative body) concerned with the assessment or collection of, or prosecution in respect of, or the determination of appeals in relation to, the taxes which are the subject of the Convention.

(2) In no case shall the provisions of paragraph (1) of this Article be construed so as to impose on the competent authority of either Contracting State the obligation:

(*a*) to carry out administrative measures at variance with the laws or administrative practice prevailing in either Contracting State;

(*b*) to supply particulars which are not obtainable under the laws or in the normal course of the administration of that or the other Contracting State;

(*c*) to supply information which would disclose any business or official secret or trade process, or information, the disclosure of which would be contrary to public policy (*ordre public*) or, in the case of the United Kingdom, the obligation to supply information which would disclose any trade, industrial, commercial or professional secret.

Article 27 Entry into force

Note: Article 27 provided for the entry into force of this Convention. It takes effect in the UK from the year of assessment 1983–84 (income tax and capital gains tax) and from the financial year beginning on 1 April 1983 (corporation tax).

Official languages: The Serbocroatian language text and the English language text of this Convention are equally authoritative.

ZAIRE

Agreement of 11 October 1976 (SI 1977 No 1298)

Article 1 [General definitions]

(1) The terms "one of the Contracting States" and "the other Contracting State" mean the United Kingdom of Great Britain and Northern Ireland or the Republic of Zaire, as the context requires.

(2) The term "the business of shipping or air transport" means the business of transporting by air and/or sea persons, animals, goods or mail including the sale of travel tickets connected with such transport by sea and/or air transport undertakings.

(3) The term "international traffic" means any transport by a ship or aircraft operated by an undertaking of one of the Contracting States, except when the ship or aircraft is operated solely between places in the other Contracting State.

(4) The term "United Kingdom undertakings" means public, semi-public or private sea

and/or air transport undertakings constituted under the laws in force in the United Kingdom and managed and controlled in the United Kingdom.

(5) The term "Zairian undertakings" means public, semi-public or private sea and/or air transport undertakings constituted under the laws in force in the Republic of Zaire and managed and controlled in the Republic of Zaire.

Article 2 [Application]

(1) The United Kingdom undertakes to exempt Zairian undertakings from all taxes on income, profits or capital gains arising from the business of shipping and/or air transport in international traffic carried on in the United Kingdom and taxable in the Republic of Zaire.

(2) The Republic of Zaire undertakes to exempt United Kingdom undertakings from all taxes on income, profits or capital gains arising from the business of shipping and/or air transport in international traffic carried on in the Republic of Zaire and taxable in the United Kingdom.

(3) The provisions of this Article shall likewise apply to income, profits or capital gains derived by such an undertaking from the participation in a pool, a joint business or an international operating agency.

Article 4 [Entry into force]

Note: Article 4 provided for the entry into force of this Agreement. It applies to income, profits and capital gains arising after 10 October 1976.

Official languages: The French language text and the English language text of this Agreement are equally authoritative.

ZAMBIA

Convention of 22 March 1972 (SI 1972 No 1721)

(The Protocol of 30 April 1981 (SI 1981 No 1816) does not amend the Articles printed below.)

Article 1 Personal scope

This Convention shall apply to persons who are residents of one or both of the Contracting States.

Article 2 Taxes covered

(1) The taxes which are the subject of this Convention are—
    (*a*) in the United Kingdom of Great Britain and Northern Ireland:

      (i) the income tax (including surtax);

      (ii) the corporation tax; and

      (iii) the capital gains tax;

   (b) in Zambia:

      (i) the income tax;

      (ii) the mineral tax; and

      (iii) the personal levy.

(2) This Convention shall also apply to any identical or substantially similar taxes which are imposed by either Contracting State after the date of signature of this Convention in addition to, or in place of, the existing taxes.

(3) The competent authorities of the Contracting States shall notify to each other any changes which are made in their respective taxation laws.

Article 3 General definitions

(1) In this Convention, unless the context otherwise requires—

   (a) the term "United Kingdom" means Great Britain and Northern Ireland, including any area outside the territorial sea of the United Kingdom which in accordance with international law has been or may hereafter be designated, under the laws of the United Kingdom concerning the Continental Shelf, as an area within which the rights of the United Kingdom with respect to the sea-bed and sub-soil and their natural resources may be exercised;

   (b) the term "Zambia" means the Republic of Zambia;

   (c) the term "nationals" means—

      (i) in relation to the United Kingdom, all citizens of the United Kingdom and Colonies who derive their status as such from their connection with the United Kingdom and all legal persons, partnerships and associations deriving their status as such from the law in force in the United Kingdom;

      (ii) in relation to Zambia, all citizens of Zambia and all legal persons, partnerships and associations deriving their status as such from the law in force in Zambia;

   (d) the term "United Kingdom" means tax imposed by the United Kingdom being tax to which this Convention applies by virtue of the provisions of Article 2; the term "Zambia tax" means tax imposed by Zambia being tax to which this Convention applies by virtue of the provisions of Article 2;

   (e) the term "tax" means United Kingdom tax or Zambia tax, as the context requires;

   (f) the terms "a Contracting State" and "the other Contracting State" mean the United Kingdom or Zambia, as the context requires;

   (g) the term "persons" comprises an individual, a company and any other body of persons;

   (h) the term "company" means any body corporate or any entity which is treated as a body corporate for tax purposes;

   (i) the terms "enterprise of a Contracting State" and "enterprise of the other Contracting State" mean respectively an enterprise carried on by a resident of a Contracting State and an enterprise carried on by a resident of the other Contracting State;

   (j) the term "competent authority" means, in the case of the United Kingdom the Commissioners of Inland Revenue or their authorised representative, and in the case of Zambia, the Commissioner of Taxes or his authorised representative.

(2) As regards the application of this Convention by a Contracting State any term not otherwise defined shall, unless the context otherwise requires, have the meaning which it has under the laws of that Contracting State relating to the taxes which are the subject of this Convention.

Article 4 Fiscal domicile

(1) For the purposes of this Convention, the term "resident of a Contracting State" means, subject to the provisions of paragraphs (2) and (3) of this Article, any person who,

under the law of that State, is liable to taxation therein by reason of his domicile, residence, place of management or any other criterion of a similar nature. The terms "resident of the United Kingdom" and "resident of Zambia" shall be construed accordingly.

(2) Where by reason of the provisions of paragraph (1) of this Article an individual is a resident of both Contracting States, then his status shall be determined in accordance with the following rules:

(a) he shall be deemed to be a resident of the Contracting State in which he has a permanent home available to him. If he has a permanent home available to him in both Contracting States, he shall be deemed to be a resident of the Contracting State with which his personal and economic relations are closest (centre of vital interests);

(b) if the Contracting State in which he has his centre of vital interests cannot be determined, or if he has not a permanent home available to him in either Contracting State, he shall be deemed to be a resident of the Contracting State in which he has an habitual abode;

(c) if he has an habitual abode in both Contracting States or in neither of them, he shall be deemed to be a resident of the Contracting State of which he is a national;

(d) if he is a national of both Contracting States or of neither of them, the competent authorities of the Contracting States shall settle the question by mutual agreement.

(3) Where by reason of the provisions of paragraph (1) of this Article a person other than an individual is a resident of both Contracting States, then it shall be deemed to be a resident of the Contracting State in which its place of effective management is situated.

Article 7 Income from immovable property

(1) (Taxation of income immovable property.)

(2) (a) The term "immovable property" shall, subject to the provisions of sub-paragraph (b) below, be defined in accordance with the law of the Contracting State in which the property in question is situated.

(b) The term "immovable property" shall in any case include property accessory to immovable property, livestock and equipment used in agriculture and forestry, rights to which the provisions of general law respecting landed property apply, usufruct of immovable property and rights to variable or fixed payments as consideration for the working of, or the right to work, mineral deposits, sources and other natural resources; ships, boats and aircraft shall not be regarded as immovable property.

(3)–(5) . . .

Article 9 Shipping and air transport

Profits derived from the operation of ships or aircraft in international traffic by an enterprise of a Contracting State shall be exempt from tax in the other Contracting State.

Article 14 Capital gains

(1) (Taxation of gains from alienation of movable business property.)

(2) Notwithstanding the provisions of paragraph (1) of this Article, capital gains derived by a resident of a Contracting State from the alienation of ships and aircraft operated in international traffic and movable property pertaining to the operation of such ships and aircraft shall be taxable only in that Contracting State.

(3) . . .

(4) . . .

Article 25 Non-discrimination

(1) The nationals of a Contracting State shall not be subjected in the other Contracting State to any taxation or any requirement connected therewith which is other or more burden-

some than the taxation and connected requirements to which nationals of that other State in the same circumstances are or may be subjected.

(2) The taxation on a permanent establishment which an enterprise of a Contracting State has in the other Contracting State shall not be less favourably levied in that other State than the taxation levied on enterprises of that other State carrying on the same activities.

(3) Enterprises of a Contracting State, the capital of which is wholly or partly owned or controlled, directly or indirectly, by one or more residents of the other Contracting State, shall not be subjected in the first-mentioned Contracting State to any taxation or any requirement connected therewith which is other or more burdensome than the taxation and connected requirements to which other similar enterprises of that first-mentioned State are or may be subjected.

(4) Nothing contained in this Article shall be construed as obliging either Contracting State to grant to individuals not resident in that State any of the personal allowances, reliefs and reductions for tax purposes which are granted to individuals so resident, nor as obliging Zambia to grant to non-nationals the relief available to Zambian nationals under section 42C of the Zambian Income Tax Act, 1966, nor as conferring any exemption from tax in a Contracting State in respect of dividends paid to a company which is a resident of the other Contracting State.

(5) In this Article the term "taxation" means taxes of every kind and description.

Article 26 Mutual agreement procedure

(1) Where a resident of a Contracting State considers that the actions of one or both of the Contracting States result or will result for him in taxation not in accordance with this Convention, he may, notwithstanding the remedies provided by the national laws of those States, present his case to the competent authority of the Contracting State of which he is a resident.

(2) The competent authority shall endeavour, if the objection appears to it to be justified and if it is not itself able to arrive at an appropriate solution, to resolve the case by mutual agreement with the competent authority of the other Contracting State, with a view to the avoidance of taxation not in accordance with the Convention.

(3) The competent authorities of the Contracting States shall endeavour to resolve by mutual agreement any difficulties or doubts arising as to the interpretation or application of the Convention.

(4) The competent authorities of the Contracting States may communicate with each other directly for the purpose of reaching an agreement in the sense of the preceding paragraphs.

Article 27 Exchange of information

The competent authorities of the Contracting States shall exchange such information (being information which is at their disposal under their respective taxation laws in the normal course of administration) as is necessary for carrying out the provisions of this Convention or for the prevention of fraud or the administration of statutory provisions against legal avoidance in relation to the taxes which are the subject of this Convention. Any information so exchanged shall be treated as secret but may be disclosed to persons (including a court or administrative body) concerned with assessment, collection, enforcement or prosecution in respect of taxes which are the subject of this Convention. No information shall be exchanged which would disclose any trade, business, industrial or professional secret or any trade process.

Article 29 Entry into force

Note: Article 29 provided for the entry into force of this Convention. It takes effect in the UK from the year of assessment 1972–73 (income tax and capital gains tax) and from the financial year beginning on 1 April 1972 (corporation tax).

Official language: English.

ZIMBABWE

Convention of 19 October 1982 (SI 1982 No 1842)

Article 1 Personal scope

This Convention shall apply to persons who are residents of one or both of the Contracting States.

Article 2 Taxes covered

(1) The taxes which are the subject of this Convention are:
- (a) in the United Kingdom:
  - (i) the income tax;
  - (ii) the corporation tax; and
  - (iii) the capital gains tax;
  - (hereinafter referred to as "United Kingdom tax");
- (b) in Zimbabwe:
  - (i) the income tax;
  - (ii) the branch profits tax;
  - (iii) the non-resident shareholders' tax;
  - (iv) the non-residents' tax on interest;
  - (v) the capital gains tax;
  - (hereinafter referred to as "Zimbabwean tax").

(2) This Convention shall apply also to any identical or substantially similar taxes which are imposed by either Contracting State after the date of signature of this Convention in addition to, or in place of, the existing taxes. The competent authorities of the Contracting States shall notify each other of any substantial changes which are made in their respective taxation laws.

Article 3 General definitions

(1) In this Convention, unless the context otherwise requires:
- (a) the term "United Kingdom" means Great Britain and Northern Ireland, including any area outside the territorial sea of the United Kingdom which in accordance with international law has been or may hereafter be designated, under the laws of the United Kingdom concerning the Continental Shelf, as an area within which the rights of the United Kingdom with respect to the sea-bed and sub-soil and their natural resources may be exercised;
- (b) the term "Zimbabwe" means the Republic of Zimbabwe;
- (c) the term "national" means:
  - (i) in relation to the United Kingdom, any individual who has under the law in the United Kingdom the status of United Kingdom national provided he has

347

the right of abode in the United Kingdom; and any legal person, partnership, association or other entity deriving its status as such from the law in force in the United Kingdom;

    (ii) in relation to Zimbabwe, any citizen of Zimbabwe and any legal person, partnership, association or other entity deriving its status as such from the law in force in Zimbabwe;

(d) the terms "a Contracting State" and "the other Contracting State" mean the United Kingdom or Zimbabwe as the context requires;

(e) the term "person" includes an individual, a company, an estate, a trust and any other body of persons;

(f) the term "company" means any body corporate or any entity which is treated as a body corporate for tax purposes;

(g) the terms "enterprise of a Contracting State" and "enterprise of the other Contracting State" mean respectively an enterprise carried on by a resident of a Contracting State and an enterprise carried on by a resident of the other Contracting State;

(h) the term "international traffic" means any transport by a ship or aircraft, including transport by container, operated by an enterprise which has its place of effective management in a Contracting State, except when the ship or aircraft is operated solely between places in the other Contracting State;

(i) the term "competent authority" means, in the case of the United Kingdom the Commissioners of Inland Revenue or their authorised representative, and in the case of Zimbabwe the Commissioner of Taxes or his authorised representative.

(2) As regards the application of this Convention by a Contracting State any term not otherwise defined shall, unless the context otherwise requires, have the meaning which it has under the laws of that Contracting State relating to the taxes which are the subject of this Convention.

Article 4 Fiscal domicile

(1) For the purposes of this Convention, the term "resident of a Contracting State" means any person who, under the law of that State, is liable to tax therein by reason of his domicile, residence, place of management or any other criterion.

(2) Where by reason of the provisions of paragraph (1) of this Article an individual is a resident of both Contracting States, then his status shall be determined in accordance with the following rules:

(a) he shall be deemed to be a resident of the State in which he has a permanent home available to him; if he has a permanent home available to him in both States, he shall be deemed to be a resident of the State with which his personal and economic relations are closer (centre of vital interests);

(b) if the State in which he has his centre of vital interests cannot be determined, or if he has not a permanent home available to him in either State, he shall be deemed to be a resident of the State in which he has an habitual abode;

(c) if he has an habitual abode in both States or in neither of them, he shall be deemed to be a resident of the State of which he is a national;

(d) if he is a national of both States or of neither of them, the competent authorities of the Contracting States shall settle the question by mutual agreement.

(3) Where by reason of the provision of paragraph (1) of this Article a person other than an individual is a resident of both Contracting States, then it shall be deemed to be a resident of the State in which its place of effective management is situated.

Article 6 Income from immovable property

(1) (Taxation of income from immovable property.)

(2) The term "immovable property" shall have the meaning which it has under the law of the Contracting State in which the property in question is situated. The term shall in any case

include property accessory to immovable property, livestock and equipment used in agriculture and forestry, rights to which the provisions of general law respecting landed property apply, usufruct of immovable property and rights to variable or fixed payments as consideration for the working of, or the right to work, mineral deposits, sources and other natural resources; ships, boats and aircraft shall not be regarded as immovable property.

(3) . . .

(4) . . .

Article 8 International traffic

(1) Profits from international traffic shall be taxable only in the Contracting State in which the place of effective management of the enterprise is situated.

(2) If the place of effective management of a shipping enterprise is aboard a ship, then it shall be deemed to be situated in the Contracting State in which the home harbour of the ship is situated, or, if there is no such home harbour, in the Contracting State of which the operator of the ship is a resident.

(3) The provisions of paragraph (1) of this Article shall apply also to profits from participation in a pool, a joint business or an international operating agency.

Article 14 Capital gains

(1) . . .

(2) . . .

(3) Gains from the alienation of ships or aircraft operated in international traffic or movable property pertaining to the operation of such ships or aircraft shall be taxable only in the Contracting State in which the place of effective management of the enterprise is situated.

(4) . . .

Article 24 Non-discrimination

(1) Nationals of a Contracting State shall not be subjected in the other Contracting State to any taxation or any requirement connected therewith which is other or more burdensome than the taxation and connected requirements to which nationals of that other State in the same circumstances are or may be subjected.

(2) The taxation on a permanent establishment which an enterprise of a Contracting State has in the other Contracting State shall not be less favourably levied in that other State than the taxation levied on enterprises of that other State carrying on the same activities. Provided that this paragraph shall not prevent a Contracting State from imposing on the profits attributable to a permanent establishment in that Contracting State of a company which is a resident of the other Contracting State a tax not exceeding $2\frac{1}{2}$ per cent of those profits in addition to the tax which would be chargeable on those profits if they were profits of a company which was a resident of the first-mentioned State.

(3) Enterprises of a Contracting State, the capital of which is wholly or partly owned or controlled, directly or indirectly, by one or more residents of the other Contracting State, shall not be subjected in the first-mentioned State to any taxation or any requirement connected therewith which is other or more burdensome than the taxation and connected requirements to which other similar enterprises of that first-mentioned State are or may be subjected.

(4) Except where the provisions of paragraph (1) of Article 9, paragraph (8) of Article 11, paragraph (6) of Article 12, or paragraph (6) of Article 13 apply, interest, royalties, technical fees and other disbursements paid by an enterprise of a Contracting State to a resident of the other Contracting State shall, for the purpose of determining the taxable profits of such enterprise, be deductible under the same conditions as if they had been paid to a resident of the first-mentioned State.

(5) Nothing contained in this Article shall be construed as obliging either Contracting State to grant to individuals not resident in that State any of the personal allowances, reliefs and reductions for tax purposes which are granted to individuals so resident.

(6) In this Article the term "taxation" means taxes of every kind and description.

Article 25 Mutual agreement procedure

(1) Where a resident of a Contracting State considers that the actions of one or both of the Contracting States result or will result for him in taxation not in accordance with this Convention, he may, irrespective of the remedies provided by the domestic law of those States, present his case to the competent authority of the Contracting State of which he is a resident.

(2) The competent authority shall endeavour, if the objection appears to it to be justified and if it is not itself able to arrive at a satisfactory solution, to resolve the case by mutual agreement with the competent authority of the other Contracting State, with a view to the avoidance of taxation not in accordance with the Convention.

(3) The competent authorities of the Contracting States shall endeavour to resolve by mutual agreement any difficulties or doubts arising as to the interpretation or application of the Convention.

(4) The competent authorities of the Contracting States may communicate with each other directly for the purpose of reaching an agreement in the sense of the preceding paragraphs.

Article 26 Exchange of information

The competent authorities of the Contracting States shall exchange such information (being information which is at their disposal under their respective taxation laws in the normal course of administration) as is necessary for carrying out the provisions of this Convention or for the prevention of fraud or the administration of statutory provisions against legal avoidance in relation to the taxes which are the subject of this Convention. Any information so exchanged shall be treated as secret but may be disclosed to persons (including a court or administrative body) concerned with assessment, collection, enforcement or prosecution in respect of taxes which are the subject of this Convention. No information shall be exchanged which would disclose any trade, business, industrial or professional secret or any trade process.

Article 28 Entry into force

Note: Article 28 provided for the entry into force of this Convention. It takes effect in the UK from the year of assessment 1981–82 (income tax and capital gains tax) and from the financial year beginning on 1 April 1981 (corporation tax).

Official language: English.

APPENDIX I

USEFUL ADDRESSES

British Maritime Law Association
33–35 St Mary Axe
London EC3A 8AA
Telephone: (01) 626 5392

British Shippers' Council
Hermes House
St John's Road
Tunbridge Wells
Kent TN4 9UZ
Telephone: (0892) 26171

General Council of British Shipping
30–32 St Mary Axe
London EC3A 8ET
Telephone: (01) 283 2922
626 8131

Inland Revenue
General:
Somerset House
London WC2R 1LB
Telephone: (01) 438 6622

Foreign Claims Branch:
St John's House
Merton Road
Stanley Precinct
Bootle
Merseyside L69 4EJ
Telephone: (051) 922 6363

Inspector of Foreign Dividends:
Hinchley Wood
Lynwood Road
Thames Ditton
Surrey KT7 0DP
Telephone: (01) 398 4242

Continued on next page

USEFUL ADDRESSES

**Organisation for Economic Cooperation
& Development (OECD)**
2 Rue André Pascal
F–75775 Paris Cedex 16
France
Telephone: (010 33) (1) 45248200

APPENDIX II

OFFICIAL LANGUAGES

Antigua and Barbuda: Arrangement of 19 December 1947—English
Argentina: Agreement of 28 July 1949—English
Aruba: Convention of 31 October 1967—English; Dutch
Australia: Agreement of 7 December 1967—English
Austria: Convention of 30 April 1969—English; German
Bangladesh: Convention of 8 August 1979—English
Barbados: Agreement of 26 March 1970—English
Belgium: Convention of 1 June 1987—English; French; Dutch
              Convention of 29 August 1967 (superseded)—English; French; Dutch
Belize: Arrangement of 19 December 1947—English
Botswana: Agreement of 5 October 1977—English
Brazil: Agreement of 29 December 1967—English
Brunei: Arrangement of 8 December 1950—English
Bulgaria: Convention of 16 September 1987—English; Bulgarian
Burma: Agreement of 13 March 1950—English
Canada: Convention of 8 September 1978—English; French
China: Agreement of 26 July 1984—English; Chinese
Cyprus: Convention of 20 June 1974—English
Denmark: Convention of 11 November 1980—English; Danish
Egypt: Convention of 25 April 1977—English
Falkland Islands: Arrangement of 14 March 1984—English
Faroe Islands: Convention of 27 March 1950—English; Danish
Fiji: Convention of 21 November 1975—English
Finland: Convention of 17 July 1969—English; Finnish
France: Convention of 22 May 1968—English; French
             (Capital taxes) Convention of 21 June 1963—English; French
Gambia: Convention of 20 May 1980—English
German Federal Republic: Convention of 26 November 1964—English; German
Ghana: Convention of 29 November 1977—English
Greece: Convention of 25 June 1953—English; Greek
Grenada: Arrangement of 4 March 1949—English
Guernsey: Arrangement of 24 June 1952—English
Hungary: Convention of 28 November 1977—English; Hungarian
Iceland: Agreement of 27 April 1928—English
India: Convention of 16 April 1981—English; Hindi
            (Capital taxes) 3 April 1956—English
Indonesia: Agreement of 13 March 1974—English
Irish Republic: Convention of 2 June 1976—English
                     (Capital taxes) Convention of 7 December 1977—English
Isle of Man: Arrangement of 29 July 1955—English
Israel: Convention of 26 September 1962—English; Hebrew
Italy: Convention of 4 July 1960—English; Italian
            (Capital taxes) Convention of 15 February 1966—English; Italian
Ivory Coast: Convention of 28 June 1985—English; French
Jamaica: Agreement of 16 March 1973—English

353

OFFICIAL LANGUAGES

Japan: Convention of 10 February 1969—English; Japanese
Jersey: Arrangement of 24 June 1952—English
Jordan: Agreement of 6 March 1978—English
Kenya: Agreement of 31 July 1973—English
Kiribati: Arrangement of 10 May 1950—English
Korea: Convention of 21 April 1977—English; Korean
Lebanon: Agreement of 26 February 1964—English
Lesotho: Arrangement of 25 November 1949—English
Luxembourg: Convention of 24 May 1967—English; French
Malawi: Agreement of 25 November 1955—English
Malaysia: Agreement of 30 March 1973—English
Malta: Arrangement of 28 March 1962—English
Mauritius: Convention of 11 February 1981—English
Montserrat: Arrangement of 19 December 1947—English
Namibia: Convention of 28 May 1962—English; Afrikaans
Netherlands: Convention of 7 November 1980—English; Dutch
                  (Capital taxes) Convention of 11 December 1979—English; Dutch
Netherlands Antilles: Convention of 31 October 1979—English; Dutch
New Zealand: Convention of 4 August 1967—English
Nigeria: Agreement of 9 June 1987—English
Norway: Convention of 3 October 1985—English; Norwegian
Pakistan: Convention of 24 November 1986—English
               (Capital taxes) Agreement of 8 June 1957—English
Philippines: Convention of 10 June 1976—English
Poland: Convention of 16 December 1979—English; Polish
Portugal: Convention of 27 March 1968—English; Portuguese
Romania: Convention of 18 September 1975—English; Romanian
St Christopher (St Kitts) and Nevis: Arrangement of 19 December 1947—English
Sierra Leone: Arrangement of 19 December 1947—English
Singapore: Agreement of 1 December 1966—English
Solomon Islands: Arrangement of 10 May 1950—English
South Africa: Convention of 21 November 1968—English; Afrikaans
                   (Capital taxes) Convention of 31 July 1978—English; Afrikaans
Spain: Convention of 21 October 1975—English; Spanish
Sri Lanka: Convention of 21 June 1979—English; Sinhala
Sudan: Convention of 8 March 1975—English
Swaziland: Agreement of 26 November 1968—English
Sweden: Convention of 30 August 1983—English; Swedish
             (Capital taxes) Convention of 8 October 1980—English; Swedish
Switzerland: Convention of 8 December 1977—English; French
                  (Capital taxes) Convention of 12 June 1956—English; French
Thailand: Convention of 18 February 1981—English; Thai
Trinidad and Tobago: Convention of 31 December 1982—English
Tunisia: Convention of 15 December 1982—English; French; Arabic
Turkey: Agreement of 19 February 1986—English; Turkish
Tuvalu: Agreement of 10 May 1950—English
Uganda: Arrangement of 24 June 1952—English
Union of Soviet Socialist Republics: Convention of 31 July 1985—English; Russian
United States of America: Convention of 31 December 1975—English
                               (Capital taxes) Convention of 19 October 1978—English
Venezuela: Agreement of 8 March 1978—English; Spanish
Yugoslavia: Convention of 6 November 1981—English; Serbo-Croatian
Zaire: Agreement of 11 October 1976—English; French
Zambia: Convention of 22 March 1972—English
Zimbabwe: Convention of 19 October 1982—English